INTRODUCTORY GRANTOLOGY

This book addresses the lack of systematic training in journal publication and grant pursuit for new scholars, two key skills in today's academic landscape. It introduces "grantology," the science of pursuing grants, and provides evidence-based practical strategies. Structured like a graduate course, each chapter follows a five-step cognitive sequence based on Daniel Kahneman's intuitive judgment theory. The book explores over fifty real-life cases, draws from nearly 200 research articles, and compares grantology with journalology. With scientific insights and actionable advice, this guide supports junior researchers, graduate students, and new grant writers in developing the skills needed to pursue competitive grants and advance their careers.

ZHENG YAN received his EdD in Human Development and Psychology from Harvard University and is Professor of Developmental and Educational Psychology at University at Albany. His recent books include *Mobile Phone Behavior* (2018), *Publishing Journal Articles* (2020), and *Cambridge Handbook of Cyber Behavior* (2024).

INTRODUCTORY GRANTOLOGY
A Guide for Pursuing Competitive Grants

ZHENG YAN
University at Albany

Shaftesbury Road, Cambridge CB2 8EA, United Kingdom

One Liberty Plaza, 20th Floor, New York, NY 10006, USA

477 Williamstown Road, Port Melbourne, VIC 3207, Australia

314–321, 3rd Floor, Plot 3, Splendor Forum, Jasola District Centre, New Delhi – 110025, India

103 Penang Road, #05–06/07, Visioncrest Commercial, Singapore 238467

Cambridge University Press is part of Cambridge University Press & Assessment, a department of the University of Cambridge.

We share the University's mission to contribute to society through the pursuit of education, learning and research at the highest international levels of excellence.

www.cambridge.org
Information on this title: www.cambridge.org/9781009381321

DOI: 10.1017/9781009381338

© Zheng Yan 2025

This publication is in copyright. Subject to statutory exception and to the provisions of relevant collective licensing agreements, no reproduction of any part may take place without the written permission of Cambridge University Press & Assessment.

When citing this work, please include a reference to the DOI 10.1017/9781009381338

First published 2025

Cover image: krisanapong detraphiphat/Getty Images

A catalogue record for this publication is available from the British Library

Library of Congress Cataloging-in-Publication Data
NAMES: Yan, Zheng, 1958– author
TITLE: Introductory grantology : a guide for pursuing competitive grants / Zheng Yan, University at Albany.
DESCRIPTION: Cambridge, United Kingdom ; New York, NY, USA : Cambridge University Press, [2025] | Includes bibliographical references and index.
IDENTIFIERS: LCCN 2025010087 | ISBN 9781009381376 hardback | ISBN 9781009381338 ebook
SUBJECTS: LCSH: Proposal writing for grants | Research grants
CLASSIFICATION: LCC HG177 .Y36 2025 | DDC 658.15/224–dc23/eng/20250529
LC record available at https://lccn.loc.gov/2025010087

ISBN 978-1-009-38137-6 Hardback
ISBN 978-1-009-38132-1 Paperback

Cambridge University Press & Assessment has no responsibility for the persistence or accuracy of URLs for external or third-party internet websites referred to in this publication and does not guarantee that any content on such websites is, or will remain, accurate or appropriate.

*To Martin (Marty) Cooper, the Father of the cellphone,
who is passionate about staying mobile, staying healthy,
and serving the positive needs of all humanity at 95.*

*To Catherine Snow, John H. and Elisabeth A. Hobbs
Professor of Cognition and Education at Harvard University,
who has been hosting the wonderful research group meeting
with various "snowcats" every other week year round.*

Contents

List of Figures	*page* viii
List of Tables	ix
Preface	xi

PART I FOUNDATION

1	Grants	3
2	Grantology	38

PART II GRANT PURSUIT

3	Grant Writers	81
4	Grant Agencies	121
5	Grant Writing	157
6	Grant Review	190
7	Grant Decisions	229
8	Grant Management	267
9	Grant Impacts	293

PART III CONCLUSION

10	Pursuing Grants in the Future	327

Appendix: The Science of Research Grants: A Scoping Review of Journal Articles in Grantology Published in 1970–2020	355
Index	405

Figures

0.1	The basic dynamic model of the grant process	*page* xvi
1.1	A new typology of grants primarily based on the four basic elements of a grant	19
2.1	A multi-step linear forward workflow of how to manage grants	64
2.2	A multi-step linear forward streamline of how to pursue grants for grantees	65
2.3	A comprehensive linear forward process model of the grant lifecycle	66
2.4	The basic dynamic model of the grant process	70
7.1	The importance of grant decisions in the grant process	232
A.1	Growth of the number of journal articles on research grants published in 1946–2019	358
A.2	The flowchart of the literature search process	361
A.3	Conceptual framework of seeking research grants as a scientific research process	362
A.4	Well-studied areas and much-needed areas in grantology as the science of research grants	383

Tables

A.1 An overview of existing studies on
    grant writers (N = 36)   *page* 364
A.2 An overview of existing research on grant writing (N = 60)   368
A.3 An overview of literature on grant agencies (N = 36)   371
A.4 An overview of existing studies on grant review (N = 54)   374
A.5 An overview of studies on grant projects (N = 47)   377
A.6 An overview of existing studies on grant impacts (N = 49)   380

Preface

It is always a pleasure to write the preface after completing a book. This preface starts with a brief introduction of three basic messages of the book, then reflects on a special eight-year intellectual journey of the Big Two Project, presents major motivations for writing the book, specifies both major features and the main structure of the book, outlines grantology as a field, introduces other good books on grant writing, and concludes with a typical but important acknowledgment.

Three Basic Messages

This book is titled *Introductory Grantology: A Guide for Pursuing Competitive Grants*, which delivers three basic messages. (1) It introduces *grantology*, the science of the grant process, as a branch in metascience for the first time rather than focusing merely on offering a collection of practical tips of grantsmanship. The goal is to synthesize the scientific knowledge in grantology and guide the practice of pursuing grants. (2) It offers *a guide* for *pursuing competitive grants* that is inherently research-based rather than experience-based only. Practical experiences are often useful but largely intuitive; research-based knowledge makes grant pursuit efforts more effective and efficient. (3) It is designed and written as an *Introductory* text for new grant writers as the target readers rather than established grant writers. This is because new grant writers need scientific knowledge most to continue their grant pursuit efforts, especially with almost unavoidable failures, before they become established grant writers. The target readers also include those who (1) run workshops and courses to train new grant writers, (2) design special funding programs for early-stage investigators and young scholars, and (3) study grantology as an emerging field. For new grant writers, my simplest message is to team up with established grant writers to pursue the first competitive grant rather than work alone.

The Eight-Year Journey

In 2016, I had a fabulous sabbatical leave, working with Catherine Snow as the faculty sponsor at Harvard Graduate School of Education. Through stimulating discussions, Catherine and I developed a basic judgment: Journal publication and grant writing are two core intellectual skills for young scholars today; however, systematic training in these two core skills is not typically offered in graduate programs around the world, nor are they dealt with more than incidentally in coursework; without deliberated and effective efforts, the dissertation-centered tradition, the underestimation of the rich content in journalology and grantology, and the trial-and-error method will continue to dominate graduate training and professional development. This judgment became the beginning of the Big Two Project as initial efforts to address challenges in systematic training in journal publication and grant application.

After five years, with the support of Catherine and the wonderful members of the Snowcat Research Group, I completed the first book, *Publishing Journal Articles* in 2021, using the scientific knowledge of journalology to develop actionable guides for publishing articles. In 2023, I was lucky enough to have another fabulous sabbatical leave, working with Catherine again as the faculty sponsor. After nearly three years of work since 2021, again with the support of Catherine and wonderful members of the Snowcat Research Group, this second book, *Introductory Grantology: A Guide for Pursuing Competitive Grants*, is completed, using the scientific knowledge of grantology to develop actionable guides for pursuing grants. It marks the end of the eight-year intellectual journey of the Big Two Project and the beginning of a new journey to study and promote journalology and grantology in the real world.

Three Major Motivations

The first motivation for writing the book is to **develop the Big Two competencies**. Journal publication and research grant application are two core professional competencies, or the Big Two, for young scholars across the world today. However, systematic training in these two core competencies is not typically offered in graduate programs around the world. Furthermore, graduate programs, especially doctoral programs, historically have a dissertation-centered tradition. While dissertation-centered training is in some way associated with journal article publication, research grant applications are clearly the weakest link among graduate students and young researchers. They do have various experiences in applying for admissions, scholarships, fellowships, internships, postdocs, seed grants, and jobs. However, their hands-on practical experiences might not be sufficiently useful for them to win much more competitive and sophisticated research grants. Thus, systematic training on pursuing grants is particularly needed to change this problematic circumstance.

The second motivation is to **synthesize grantology research**. It is often assumed that the topic of pursuing grants involves limited practical knowledge and thus would not support a formal course or a strong curriculum for scientific training. However, our literature search indicates that approximately 1,000 journal articles, twenty literature reviews, and eighty books on grant writing have been published, making significant theoretical, methodological, empirical, and practical contributions in multiple areas, such as grant agency, grant writers, grant writing, grant review, and grant impacts. The science of pursuing grants or *grantology* has emerged as an interdisciplinary field relevant to sociology, economics, biomedicine, public health, politics, business, linguistics, psychology, education, communication, bibliometrics, and other areas. Thus, grantology needs to be introduced in a timely, effective, and efficient manner.

The third motivation is to **correct existing misconceptions**. Pursuing research grants has often been approached simply as a skill acquired through practice, namely, essentially a matter of trial and error. However, empirical research and everyday observation suggest that graduate students and junior grant writers hold multiple intuition-based folk theories about the grant process. These folk theories lead to robust cognitive biases that block success in pursuing research grants. For instance, some students may be ignorant of why, where, and how to find and pursue grant opportunities during their doctoral program. As a result, among them, pursuing or receiving research grants is perceived as an exception rather than the norm when receiving a PhD degree. Similarly, some junior researchers lack basic knowledge about the importance of resubmitting grant proposals that are initially rejected as a key step in the grant cycle, one of the most critical and challenging tasks for success in the grant-writing enterprise. In contrast, experienced grant writers know when and how to revise and resubmit a rejected grant proposal so that eventually it will be funded successfully. Thus, bias-related intuitive knowledge that widely exists among new researchers needs to be corrected and updated to research-based scientific knowledge with best practices.

These three motivations make it important to develop a thoughtful introductory book on research grant writing and provide a knowledge base for systematic training of the next generation of scholars, especially those who are in scientific communities with a shorter history of grant writing and facing increasing pressures to secure research grants in professional settings. Otherwise, without deliberated efforts, the dissertation-centered tradition, the trial-and-error practice, and the popular misconceptions will continue to dominate graduate training and professional development.

Six Features of the Book

First, the book is **grantology-based**. The book is based on the science of pursuing grants, or *grantology*. It synthesizes major advances in *grantology* and uses them to offer evidence-based suggestions, while simultaneously integrating existing rich practical knowledge. It is the right time now to publish a grantology-based book to inform best practices in pursuing grants, given many practice-based books already exist on the market. The main goal is to provide not only hands on (how), but most importantly minds-on (why) experience of pursuing grants.

Second, the book is **theory-guided**. To avoid the trial-and-error method, Daniel Kahneman's System-1-vs.-System-2 theory is used as the epistemological underpinning to help readers move from intuitive thinking to rational thinking. Each chapter starts with readers' common biased intuitive thinking about grants and ends with science-based rational thinking.

Third, the book is **case-oriented**. Each chapter will offer real-life cases that I as a grant writer and a grant reviewer have encountered directly or observed indirectly over the past twenty years. Approximately fifty concrete authentic cases will illustrate the most important, challenging, and common issues often encountered by new grant writers.

Fourth, the book is **research-centered**. Research evidence from around 100 research articles in grantology is used to discuss core concepts involved in a competitive grant application, such as grant writer development, grant review biases, funding priorities, program officers' roles, grant management, grant impacts, and grant cycles. These articles not only analyze successful examples, but also examine unsuccessful examples. Failure is the mother of success. The literature indicates that this is especially true and critical to secure the very first successful grant after initial rejections.

Fifth, the book is **comparison-minded**. It will compare research grant application with journal article publication, the two core professional skills for young scientists throughout the world today. Similarities and differences between these two skills will be compared and discussed in each chapter of the book in order to help young scientists to integrate their development of the two core professional skills effectively and efficiently.

Sixth, the book is **action-targeted**. Each chapter will end with actionable suggestions, such as searching existing grants, studying articles on grantology, identifying a profile as a grant writer, developing a grant portfolio, drafting a proposal, and outlining your futures as grant writers, grant professionals, and/or grant scholars.

With these six features, I hope to offer a unique contemporary science-based book that both surveys the science of grant application based on the existing literature and integrates practical wisdom based on real-world experiences.

The Structure of the Book

The grant process is complex and dynamic, which can be presented via a basic model as shown in Figure 0.1 (see Chapter 2 for details). The model features: (1) four basic elements (grant writer, grant agency, grant decision, and grant impact) that are connected with four basic steps (grant writing, grant developing, grant reviewing, and grant managing); (2) two basic channels (grantor and grantee); and (3) three basic cycles generated by three feedback loops, namely, the grantor management cycle, the grantee revision cycle, and the grantee new submission cycle.

The book uses this basic dynamic model to organize the presentation of core contents. Its ten chapters consist of three major parts. The first two chapters are an overview of two fundamental concepts, grant and grantology, and lay a conceptual foundation for the book. The following seven chapters examine seven major components of the grant process: grant writer, grant agency, grant writing, grant review, grant decision, grant management, and grant impacts, as shown in the basic dynamic model of the grant process. The final chapter is the conclusion of the book, discussing the future of grant writers, grant professionals, and grant scholars.

Each chapter follows a five-step sequence: starting with people's intuitive knowledge, followed by real-life cases, scientific knowledge of core concepts, a comparison between grantology and journalology, and ending with a summary and action suggestions for new grant writers to develop scientific knowledge and pursue competitive grants.

With that said, readers might choose different sequences and strategies to read and use the book. For instance, a reader who is writing their first grant proposal might start with the chapter on the future of grant writers,

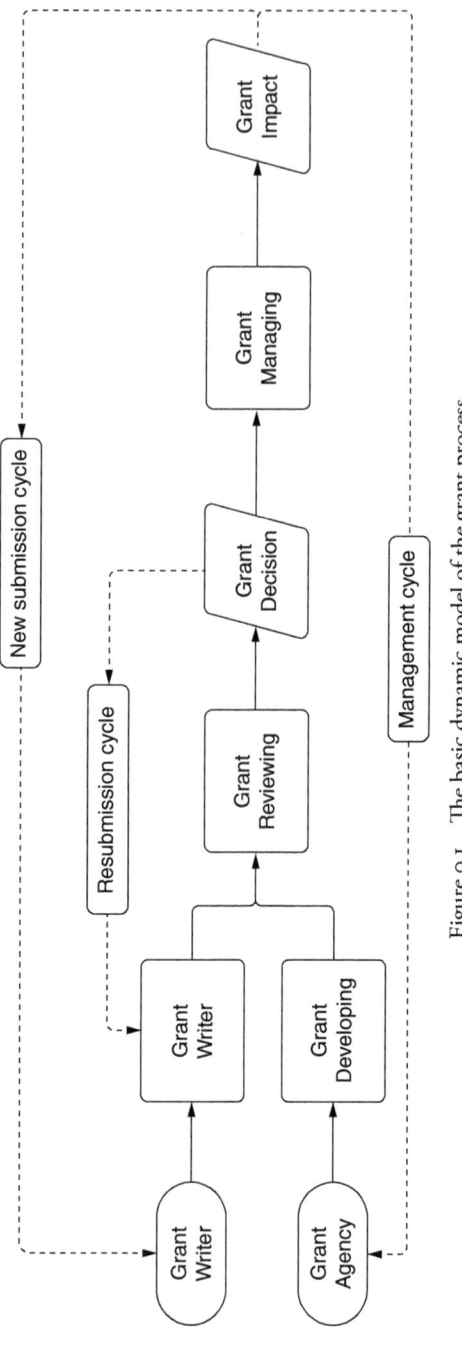

Figure 0.1 The basic dynamic model of the grant process

Preface   xvii

grant professionals, and grant scholars, as suggested thoughtfully by one of the external reviewers of the book proposal, then read the middle seven chapters on the seven major components of the grant process, before reading the first two chapters on theoretical discussions; an instructor working on a sixteen-week graduate course might cover the first two chapters in the first week as the introduction, teach each of the next seven chapters, two weeks per chapter, to training seven specific grant pursuit skills, and study the final chapter in the final week as the conclusion.

Grantology as a Discipline

As discussed in Chapter 2 in detail, grantology focuses on the grant process that is both complex and dynamic. It is a research field that is emerging, interdisciplinary, applied, and a sub-field of metascience.

Grantology has multiple excellent research centers in the world. These centers include but are not limited to the NBER's Science of Science Funding Initiative, the Technological Innovation, Entrepreneurship, and Strategic Management Group at MIT, the Center for Science of Science and Innovation at Northwestern University, the Danish Centre for Studies in Research and Research Policy at Aarhus University, the Science and Technology Policy Unit at the University of Sussex, the National Science Foundation's National Center for Science and Engineering Statistics, and the National Institutes of Health's Office of Extramural Research.

Grantology also has a relatively long list of distinguished scholars worldwide. These scholars include but are not limited to Pierre Azoulay at MIT, Danielle Li at MIT, Robert May at Cambridge University, David King at Cambridge University, Cassius James Van Slyke at the NIH, Robert Merton at Columbia University, Arnout van de Rijt at European University Institute, Grit Laudel at Berlin University of Technology, Kristine Kulage at Columbia University, Dashun Wang at Northwestern University, Yang Wang at Xi'an Jiaotong University, Donna Ginther at the University of Kansas, Walter Schaffer at the NIH, Paula Stephon at Georgia State University, Ernest Mason Allen at the NIH, David Markowitz at Michigan State University, Hillary Shulman at Ohio State University, Ulla Connor at Indiana University Indianapolis, Anne Marie Weber-Main at the University of Minnesota, Stephen Cole at State University of New York Stony Brook, Jonathan Cole at Columbia University, Sven Hug at the University of Zurich, Robyn Tamblyn at McGill University, Michael Lauer at the NIH, Brian Jacob at the University of Michigan, Bruce Weinberg at Ohio State University, Carter Bloch at Aarhus University,

A. Abigail Payne at the University of Melbourne, Ammon Salter at the University of Warwick, Ben Martin at the University of Sussex, and Lutz Bornmann at the Max Planck Society.

These excellent centers and distinguished scholars have provided endless inspirations and beautiful exemplars for grantology research.

Other Books on Grant Writing

There are approximately eighty books on grant writing on the market. These existing books can be grouped into two major types: how to pursue grants in general and how to pursue specific grants in particular. Below are good examples of these two types of books.

Good examples of books that focus on how to pursue grants in general are:

- Bauer, D. G. (2015). *The "How to" Grants Manual: Successful Grantseeking Techniques for Obtaining Public and Private Grants.* Rowman & Littlefield.
- Browning, B. A. (2014). *Grant Writing for Dummies.* John Wiley & Sons.
- Friedland, A. J., Folt, C. L., & Mercer, J. L. (2018). *Writing Successful Science Proposals.* Yale University Press.
- Karsh, E., & Fox, A. S. (2019). *The Only Grant-Writing Book You'll Ever Need.* Basic Books.
- Miner, J. T., & Ball-Stahl, K. C. (2019). *Proposal Planning & Writing.* Bloomsbury Publishing.
- Smith, N. B., & Works, E. G. (2006). *The Complete Book of Grant Writing.* Sourcebooks.
- Sternberg, R. J. (ed.). (2013). *Writing Successful Grant Proposals from the Top Down and Bottom Up.* Sage Publications.

Good examples of books that focus on how to pursue specific grants are:

- Davis, M. S. (1999). *Grantsmanship for Criminal Justice and Criminology.* Sage Publications.
- Gajda, R., & Tulikangas, R. (2005). *Getting the Grant: How Educators Can Write Winning Proposals and Manage Successful Projects.* Association for Supervision and Curriculum Development.
- Holtzclaw, B., Kenner, C., & Walden, M. (2018). *Grant Writing Handbook for Nurses and Health Professionals.* Springer Publishing.
- Li, P., & Marrongelle, K. (2012). *Having Success with NSF: A Practical Guide.* John Wiley & Sons.

- Russell, S. W., & Morrison, D. C. (2023). *The Grant Application Writer's Workbook* (the NIH version, the NSF version, the USDA-NIFA version, the other agency version). Grant Writers' Seminars and Workshops, LLC.
- Scheier, L. M., & Dewey, W. L. (2008). *The Complete Writing Guide to NIH Behavioral Science Grants*. Oxford University Press.

The books listed above as well as other books on the market have significantly contributed to the practical knowledge of how to pursue various grants by using authors' real-world experiences and providing useful guidelines. What contribution will this eighty-first book add to the existing literature? Well, the key to a book with a novelty is not how many books of this type have been published already, but rather what unique feature a new book will have. This book will be the first to use grantology as its framework so that it becomes a hybrid of science and art of pursuing research grants, in addition to the other four features specified in the previous section. Thus, while new grant writers can use the present book as scientific guidelines based on grantology, they should also choose and consult other good books when seeking practical guides.

Heartfelt Thanks

I am extremely grateful to those who have made this book possible, while many of them might not have been acknowledged here. My heartfelt thanks go to:

Marty Cooper for being my best model of life.
Catherine Snow for her extraordinary wisdom.
Victor and Heng, the two outstanding NSF program officers, who taught me about the NSF's funding processes.
Robert Steinburg at Cornell University, who taught me the concept of grant success rate for the first time.
Paula Stephan at Georgia State University, who has responded to my many inquiries promptly and attentively.
Dave Repetto, Executive Publisher at Cambridge University Press, for his vision, support, and enthusiasm.
The four external reviewers who have provided particularly insightful and constructive reviews of the book proposal.
Scholars who spent their precious time thoughtfully and patiently answering my questions regarding their research: Jeremy Berg

at the NIH and University of Pittsburgh School of Medicine, Carter Walter Bloch at Aarhus University, Priscilla Cushman at the University of Minnesota, Jamie Doyle at the NIH, Brion Duffy at Zurich University of Applied Sciences, Santo Fortunato at Indiana University, George Hazelrigg at the NSF and George Mason University, Brian Jacob at the University of Michigan, Sorin Krammer at the University of Surrey, Xiufeng Liu at the University at Buffalo, Jeff Martin at Wayne State University, Marcus Munafò at University of Bristol, Kendall Powell at *Nature*, Nicholson Price II at the University of Michigan, Marco Ottaviani at Università Bocconi, Fabio Rezzonico at Zurich University of Applied Sciences, Mike Thelwall at the University of Sheffield, Jeff Trinkle at the NSF and Lehigh University, Ted von Hippel at Embry-Riddle Aeronautical University, and Sir Simon Wessely at King's College London.

The Snowcat Research Group members for their encouragement and useful feedback on my grantology presentations.

Panpan Yang, Qingyang Liu, and Joan Erickson for writing a review paper together on grantology in 2020, which significantly developed my knowledge of grantology and is now included in an appendix as a historical record at the end of the book.

All the new grant writers who shared with me their intuitive knowledge of grantology, especially JE, LZ, NE, SP, SQ, YK, and YS.

Three computer tools: OneDrive, which saves my writing instantly and prevents me from losing multiple weeks of writing again after my laptop hard drive completely failed and Windows often crashed with the famous Blue Screen of Death; Grammarly, which detects even the most minor typos; and the read aloud feature in MS Word that saves my eyesight.

And, last, the YMCA swimming pools, the BC Pond, and Blue Hills where I have swum, walked, or hiked regularly to maintain my health and rest my mind over the past several years.

An African proverb says that it takes a village to raise a child. Indeed, it takes a large community, even including the YMCA pools, the BC Pond, and Blue Hills, to complete this book project as an intellectual child of grantology!

PART I

Foundation

CHAPTER I

Grants

Outline

1	Intuitive Knowledge: What Is a Grant?	4
	1.1 Responses from New Grant Writers	4
	1.2 Understanding Basic Elements and a Wide Diversity of Grants	5
2	Real-Life Cases: From Local Non-Profits to ERC Research Grants	6
	2.1 A Non-Profit Grant from the Rhode Island Foundation	6
	2.2 The Esther Katz Rosen Fund Grant from the APF	7
	2.3 The STEM Research Grants from the Society for Science	9
	2.4 The Largest Grant from the Bill and Melinda Gates Foundation	10
	2.5 A Federal Grant on Cyber Privacy from the NSF	11
	2.6 A Large, Complex Federal Grant from the NIH	12
	2.7 A Research Network Grant from the IES	14
	2.8 A Comprehensive Research Grant from the MRC	15
	2.9 A Young Scientist Grant from the NSFC	16
	2.10 A Grant to a Noble Prize Winner from the ERC	17
	2.11 A Typology of Grants	18
3	Scientific Knowledge: Three Theoretical Articles on Grants	21
	3.1 Azoulay & Li (2020): Grants as a Science Policy Tool for Innovation	22
	3.2 Price (2019): Grants as Effective Innovation Levels	27
	3.3 May (1998): Grants as Scientific Investments	30
4	Grantology vs. Journalology: Grant and Article	32
	4.1 Grant	32
	4.2 Article	34
5	Action Suggestions: Searching and Analyzing Two Existing Grants	36
	5.1 Understanding Basic Elements and a Wide Diversity of Grants	36
	5.2 Locating and Analyzing Public and Private Grants	37

1 Grants

1 Intuitive Knowledge: What Is a Grant?

1.1 Responses from New Grant Writers

"Happy 2023, everyone!" I sent my first email at the beginning of 2023 to several talented and hardworking graduate students. I then wrote: "I need help in answering short questions for my book on grants. Today, could you answer the following question quickly and briefly? What is a grant? There are no right or wrong answers, but your answers will be very helpful for me to think about how to write a book for readers like you. No identifiable information will appear in the book." Below are some of the answers I have received from some of them.

- Response 1: From my understanding, a grant is financial support from the government and industry that aims to explore and validate original and innovative research.
- Response 2: A grant is a fund that is offered to people for basic and applied research purposes. It provides the monetary basis for research, but it also represents a recognition within certain fields of the potential contribution of a research proposal as well as the research and management skills of the researchers. For me, the term grant means recognition more than money. I see a grant as an important "brick" of my career development.
- Response 3: I think a grant is funding from the university, government, organization, or even individuals to support researchers' projects that have strong potential. A grant can support a lot on my research. First, receiving a grant means that I can have good equipment, an adequate budget, and more participants in my research. Furthermore, receiving a grant allows me to be more competitive in the job market. Last, I would have the opportunity to show my proposal to the public. This is a good approval before the project completes. I would be more confident in my research.
- Response 4: First, a grant is an opportunity from a personal point of view. Each grant has a clear goal and name, which means that recipients of the grant should use it with appropriate goals. Therefore, receiving a grant means that students or researchers who have the ability and willingness to realize the goals of the grant will be given the opportunity to overcome financial barriers and realize their growth. Second, from a social point of view, a grant is a steppingstone to growth. Grant is money that doesn't have to be returned, and may not get immediate results or desired results.

However, with the accumulation of these studies in the future, academia can develop gradually, and this development can eventually lead to positive social growth.

1.2 Understanding Basic Elements and a Wide Diversity of Grants

These graduate students' responses presented above are particularly interesting for four specific reasons. First, these responses are **authentic**, vividly representing their current genuine knowledge as novice grant writers who do not yet have much experience with grants. Second, these responses are **thoughtful**, showing some good understanding of grants. For example, they all know that grants are money "from the university, government, organization, or even individuals". Third, these responses are **limited**, revealing their limited knowledge about grants. Grants can serve a wide variety of purposes, including but not limited to scientific research (e.g. there are various grants for social development). Even for scientific research grants, some of them could involve research training (e.g. undergraduate fellowship grants, predoctoral training grants, or postdoc training grants). Last, these responses are extremely **useful** to be used as baseline knowledge so that the first chapter of this book can be designed and written based on this baseline knowledge as the starting point to further develop a better understanding of grants.

Building on these intuitive responses as the baseline knowledge, this chapter aims to achieve two goals: to understand the **basic elements** of grants; and to understand **the wide diversity** of grants. Going deep, understanding the basic elements of grants can help us learn the fundamental features of a grant. Going broad, understanding the wide diversity of grants can help us see the complexity of a wide variety of grants in the real world. For new grant writers, completing the intellectual journey offered in this chapter will develop a good conceptual understanding of grants and help them pursue competitive grants effectively and efficiently.

To achieve our two learning goals, we will first look at multiple real-life examples of grants to analyze the basic elements and diversity features of each grant, then discuss the scientific knowledge on grants in detail to further develop a theoretical understanding of grants, then compare two basic concepts (i.e. article and grant) to see more clearly what a grant is in comparison to an article, and end the chapter with action suggestions. A five-step sequence will be followed in each chapter of the book, from intuitive ideas, to real-life examples, research summary, concept comparison, and action suggestions. Based on Nobel Prize winner Daniel

Kahneman's intuitive judgment theory,[1,2] we hope to go through this five-step sequence to start with common intuitive thinking (System 1) that is based on our daily experience, then build rational thinking (System 2) that is based on scientific knowledge, and eventually foster intuitive rational thinking (System 3) that is based on deliberate and persistent training and practice using scientific knowledge.

2 Real-Life Cases: From Local Non-Profits to ERC Research Grants

It is theoretically challenging to define a grant in a way everyone would agree and accept, due to the complexity of various grants involved in the real-life world. However, it is methodologically feasible and practically useful to identify at least four basic elements that a grant must involve: (1) **amount** (e.g. a large grant vs. a small grant); (2) **grantor** (e.g. a public funder vs. a private funder); (3) **grantee** (e.g. an individual grantee vs. an institutional grantee); and (4) **purpose** (e.g. a basic research grant vs. a social development grant). While there could be other elements involved (e.g. a competitive grant vs. a non-competitive grant; a new grant vs. a continuous grant), the above four elements are essential and fundamental for any grant. While these elements are basic and fundamental, each of them has a particularly wide variety (e.g. there are different kinds of grantors and grantees in the world) and thus we need to understand the diversity of grants. Now, we will use ten real-life grant examples to understand the basic elements and wide diversity of grants.

2.1 *A Non-Profit Grant from the Rhode Island Foundation*

In 2022, when COVID-19 was fading and normal life started to resume, my family went to Rhode Island to attend my daughter's high school

---

[1] Kahneman, D. (2011). *Thinking, Fast and Slow*. Macmillan. Gs52164.
[2] Note that there exist various bibliometric databases (e.g. Google Scholar, Scopus, Web of Science, Microsoft Academic, and Dimensions). Extensive literature has compared these databases for their strengths and challenges. This book uses Google Scholar as the main database for article citation and author h-index. Typically, a citation from Google Scholar as of 2023 will be added at the end of a cited reference, for example, in the reference of "Kahneman, D. (2011). *Thinking, Fast and Slow*. Macmillan. Gs52164," "Gs52164" means this reference has been cited 52,164 times. This is because: (1) it is easily accessible by new grant writers across the world without institutional and individual subscriptions and (2) it is used as a relative proxy rather than an absolute statistic for within-database references (e.g. within Google Scholar, 100 citations of an article is higher than ninety citations of another article) rather than across-database comparisons (e.g. 100 citations in Google Scholar is not always higher than ninety citations in Web of Science).

2 Real-Life Cases

basketball holiday tournament. At a cafeteria, I picked up a local newspaper, *Newport This Week*, published on December 15, 2022. On page 9, I saw an article on grants,[3] titled "Grants awarded for housing, hunger, and mental health." It says that over $8 million from Rhode Island Foundation grants have been awarded to various local non-profits to address hunger, housing insecurity, and behavioral health across Aquidneck Island for recovering from COVID. The foundation encourages organizations to apply for the remaining $11.7 million, with the maximum grant being $150,000.

This grant has four basic elements: (1) the total amount of the grant program is about $20 million and the maximum amount for one project will be $150,000; (2) the grantor is Rhode Island Foundation, 1 of 800 community foundations in the United States and the largest funder of its non-profit organizations of Rhode Island; (3) the grantee will be local non-profits rather than research institutions; and (4) the purpose is to address urgent community needs rather than scientific research projects.

This grant also has a few unique features, showing three aspects of grant diversity: (1) it is a community grant or a social **development** grant rather than a science grant or a research grant; (2) it funds proposals through **internal** selection by program officers rather than through open competition via external reviewers or review panels; and (3) it is a **time-sensitive**, one-time grant responding to COVID related to the American Rescue Plan Act[4] rather than a regular or permanent grant.

2.2   The Esther Katz Rosen Fund Grant from the APF

In February 2023, I received an email regarding a grant opportunity. It was from Jolie Chaleff, Program Coordinator of the American Psychological Foundation. Her email states:

> I am reaching out on behalf of the American Psychological Foundation (APF) to share info about our Rosen Grant. This grant is open to graduate students, psychologists, or doctoral-level researchers in a closely related field. It would be great if this could be shared with members of Division 7 who are looking for research funding. Let me know if there is anyone else who would be a better point of contact to share this with!

---

[3] Grants awarded for housing, hunger, and mental health, *Rhode Island Foundation*, available at: https://rifoundation.org/grant/strategic-initiative-grants.
[4] Rhode Island Foundation, available at: https://rifoundation.org/community-investments/covid-19-response.

Regularly or casually, I have often received similar types of grant announcements, externally from funding agencies such as the National Institutes of Health (NIH), the National Science Foundation (NSF), and MacArthur Foundation, or internally from grant offices of my School of Education, the University at Albany, and the State University of New York.

This grant opportunity has four basic elements. First, the amount of this grant is up to $50,000. Second, the grantor is the APF. Located in Boston, the APF is affiliated with the American Psychological Association (APA). It is a grant-making foundation to fund early career psychologists and graduate students using psychology to solve important problems and improve people's lives. Third, the eligible grantees are either early career psychologists or graduate students in psychology. The Rosen Grant or the Esther Katz Rosen Fund Grant[5] is one of the various APF grant programs. Fourth, established in 1974, the Rosen Grant has a specific purpose, supporting activities related to the advancement and application of psychological knowledge about gifted children. One actual example is that Dr. Tzu-Jung Lin at Ohio State University received the Rosen Grant for his study on "The Impact of the COVID-19 Pandemic on Gifted Students' Academic Competence and Socioemotional Well-Being during the Middle School Transition."

This grant also has several specific features. First, while generally it is a science research grant, it is a **training** grant rather than a research grant. This is a major type of research grant – for example, the NIH and NSF have two general goals, to advance science and to develop future scientists, and have various training grants to develop young researchers. Interestingly enough, recently, we had a scholar coming to our university for a campus interview. In her job talk, she presented her major study funded by the Rosen Grant. Second, it is a **small** research grant compared to average research grants by the NIH or NSF, but it is one of the largest offered by the APF.[6] Third, the APF is a **private** grant agency rather than a public one, with a specialized goal of training young researchers and an even more specialized goal of studying gifted children for the Rosen Grant. These specific features help us understand the wide diversity of grants.

Note that people often use the word "grant" in two ways, as the following two examples demonstrate: "NIH announced a new grant" and "Dr. Smith

---

[5] Esther Katz Rosen Fund Grants, *American Psychological Association*, available at: www.apa.org/apf/funding/rosen/.
[6] Search scholarships, grants and awards, *American Psychological Association*, available at: www.apa.org/about/awards/search?query=&fq=(AwardSponsorTypeFilt%3A%22APF%22).

received a large grant." In the first example, "grant" refers to a **grant program** or a funding opportunity where a grantor plans to give the grant money to a grantee. In contrast, in the second example, "grant" refers to a **grant project** or a funded project in which a grantor has given the grant money to a grantee. Thus, the Esther Katz Rosen Fund Grant is a grant program or a funding opportunity **before** application submission, grant review, and funding decision, whereas Dr. Tzu-Jung Lin's received grant is a grant project or funded project **after** application submission, grant review, and funding decision. It is important to distinguish these two different meanings of grants used in daily conversion or scientific writing.

2.3 The STEM Research Grants from the Society for Science

In 2022, I saw a news headline that Alan Grinsteinner, a middle- and high school science teacher in Bison School District 52–1 of South Dakota, was among the 100 recipients of the US 2020–21 STEM Research Grant.[7] Using this grant, Alan Grinsteinner will buy new science lab equipment and motivate his students to seek science beyond high school. Here, the grant program is the US 2020–21 STEM Research Grant, and the grant project is Alan Grinsteinner's new science lab project.

This grant has three basic elements of a grant. First, for the STEM Research Grants, the amount of each grant recipient is up to **$5,000**. Second, the grantor is the Society for Science. Third, the grantees are middle- and high-school **educators**. Fourth, the grant has a purpose to support middle- and high-school teachers in their science education to engage their students in authentic scientific research.

This grant also has several unique features. First, over six years, $775,000 has been awarded to 367 teachers. Teachers can apply for up to $5,000 to purchase specialized equipment or $1,000 in preselected equipment, including Arduino starter kits, camera traps, and PocketLab sensors.[8] Second, founded in 1921, the Society is a **non-profit** organization dedicated to the promotion of science through its science competition programs (e.g. International Science and Engineering Fair, the Regeneron Science Talent Search), publication programs (e.g. *Science*

---

[7] Bringing a world of opportunity to rural classrooms, *Sanford Underground Research Facility*, available at: https://sanfordlab.org/article/bringing-world-opportunity-rural-classrooms; 2020–2021 STEM research grant recipients, *Society for Science*, available at: www.societyforscience.org/outreach-and-equity/stem-research-grants/recipients/2020-2021/.

[8] STEM research grants, *Society for Science*, available at: www.societyforscience.org/stem-outreach-programs/stem-research-grants/.

News, Science News Explores), and outreach programs (e.g. Middle School Research Teacher Conference, STEM Research Grants). Third, the eligible teachers come from twenty-nine states, the District of Columbia, the US territories of American Samoa, Guam, and Puerto Rico, as well as Mexico, Uruguay, and Peru. **Priority** consideration is given to teachers at schools that support students from low-income communities and demographics traditionally underrepresented in STEM fields. Alan Grinsteinner is one of these teachers. Fourth, the grant supports teachers to work with **students** on independent projects involving experimentation to answer one scientific question outside of regular classwork. These projects are frequently entered into the Society's science fairs and science competition programs.

2.4 The Largest Grant from the Bill and Melinda Gates Foundation

The Bill and Melinda Gates Foundation (BMGF) is one of the largest private foundations in the world. It has given out $72 billion since 2000. If we go to its funded grant page,[9] we can access its grant database. Among all the committed grants, one will stand out: In 2021, BMGF awarded GAVI Alliance $1.6 billion to save lives and protect people's health by increasing the equitable and sustainable use of vaccines.[10]

This grant or funded project has all four basic elements. First, the amount committed is $1.6 billion, its grant ID is INV-015714, the time committed is 2021, and the duration is 53 months. Second, the grantor is BMGF's Global Development Division, one of its six divisions. Third, the grantee is the GAVI Alliance, a Geneva-based global health organization aiming to increase access to immunization in poor countries.[11] Fourth, its purpose is to save lives and protect people's health by increasing the equitable and sustainable use of vaccines.

The grant also has several unique elements that show grant diversity. First, this is a very large grant. In fact, it is one of the largest grants in the history of the BMGF. Second, the grantor BMGF is private rather than public. Specifically, it is a section 501(c)(3) organization or a charitable organization, one of twenty-nine types of non-profit organizations based on the tax-exempt definition by the Internal Revenue Service of the

---

[9] Committed grants, *Gates Foundation*, available at: www.gatesfoundation.org/about/committed-grants.
[10] Annual report 2021, *Gates Foundation*, available at: www.gatesfoundation.org/about/financials/annual-reports/annual-report-2021.
[11] Gavi website, available at: www.gavi.org.

United States. It focuses on healthcare, education, and poverty reduction. Third, the grantee GAVI was founded in the same year as the BMGF and is among the top two grantees of the BMGF. As of 2015, GAVI has received $3.1 billion in funding, whereas the World Health Organization has received only $1.5 billion. Fourth, it is not a science grant or a research grant, but a development grant. Its purpose is to deliver vaccines rather than conduct basic or applied research.

2.5 A Federal Grant on Cyber Privacy from the NSF

If we go to the National Science Foundation (NSF) website,[12] we can find all the active or expired awards. Then we can search titles, abstracts, names, institutions, programs, and other information associated with an award from October 1959 to September 2023 (note that the NSF fiscal year is from October 1 to September 30). We can see one such funded project, "SaTC: CORE: Medium: Situation-Aware Identification and Rectification of Regrettable Privacy Decisions."

This grant has the following four basic elements, which can be extracted straightforwardly from the database. First, as a multi-year grant, its total awarded amount between 2018 and 2021 is $904,133. Second, the grantor is the NSF. More specifically, it is awarded by the NSF's program of Secure &Trustworthy Cyberspace (SaTC), Division of Computer and Network Systems (CNS), Directorate for Computer & Information Science and Engineering (CSE). The program manager is Dr. Kiesler. Third, the grantees are Xu, the principal investigator (PI) from American University, and Nan Zhang, the Co-PI from the same university. Fourth, the grant purpose focuses on cyber privacy, helping mobile phone users revisit and rectify past privacy decisions that they may regret, and developing a theory on how cognitive appraisal, affective states, and environmental cues lead to regrettable privacy decisions.

This grant also has several unique features. First, it is a "Continuing Grant" awarded in 2021. The grant was awarded for multiple years, starting in 2018, and will continue through 2021. Second, it is a grant under the designation of CORE. The program of SaTC has three designations: CORE, the focus of the multidisciplinary SaTC research program, EDU, focusing on cybersecurity and privacy education and training, and TTP, focusing on the Transition to Practice. Third, it is a grant of medium size. The program of SaTC has two classes of grant size: small projects – up to $600,000 for

---

[12] Awards simple search, *US National Science Foundation*, available at: www.nsf.gov/awardsearch/.

up to three years; and medium projects – $600,001–1,200,000 for up to four years. Note that the average annualized award size for the NSF in 2022 was $237,600.[13]

2.6 A Large, Complex Federal Grant from the NIH

NIH is one of the largest public funding agents in the world. If we go to its grant database website called RePORT (Research Portfolio Online Reporting Tools), we can access a variety of tools, reports, data, and analyses of NIH research activities. One of the tools available on RePORT is the RePORTER (RePORT Expenditures and Results), which is an electronic tool that allows users to search a repository of both intramural and extramural NIH-funded research projects from the past twenty-five years and access publications since 1980, and patents resulting from NIH funding. After the close of each fiscal year on October 31, NIH will begin to update all data reported on an annual basis. Updated reports with the prior fiscal year's data are typically posted to RePORT by the end of December. In general, the RePORTER database is updated weekly. Each update includes not only the addition of newly funded projects, but also revisions to prior awards (e.g. changing grantee institution or revising award amounts). Note that one can submit a written Freedom of Information Act (FOIA) application to request a copy of a specific grant.

Now using Reporter, we can locate a grant titled "RADx-UP CDCC, with Project Number: 5U24MD016258-03."[14] It is one of the largest NIH grants in 2023. RADx-UP stands for Rapid Acceleration of Diagnostics-Underserved Populations. CDCC stands for Coordination and Data Collection Center. RADx-UP and CDCC are two key components of this major project. Specifically: (1) RADx-UP consortium is a multidisciplinary program, including three cores involved in management, test, exchange, and data analysis. The three cores are as follows: the COVID-19 Testing Core will advise and guide COVID-19 testing protocols; the Community and Health System Engagement Core provides support in exchanging best practices across communities on recruitment, engagement, and retention of study participants; the Data Science and Biostatistics Core will manage data collection, integration, and sharing. (2) The three units, Duke

---

[13] NSF funding profile, *US National Science Foundation*, available at: https://nsf-gov-resources.nsf.gov/about/budget/fy2022/tables/st_02.xlsx.
[14] RePORTER, *NIH*, available at: https://reporter.nih.gov/search/AceIYcWK3kGCfMFrT5-F1Q/project-details/10439479.

Clinical Research Institute, the UNC Center for Health Equity Research, and Community-Campus Partnerships for Health, serve as the CDCC to provide management, direction, and overall coordination of the RADx-UP consortium.

Note that NIH has provided other useful information. (1) Program Official (PO) is Dorothy Castille. It is always useful to know the PO. (2) The grant proposal responded to NIH's Funding Opportunity Announcement (FOA) and Request for Applications (RFA),[15] specifically to an RFA, "Emergency Awards: RADx-UP Coordination and Data Collection Center (CDCC) (U24 Clinical Trial Optional)."[16] (3) The Study Section for this grant is a Special Emphasis Panel. It is very important to know it for peer review and fund recommendation. NIH has four groups of Study Sections, namely, All Study Sections, Standing Study Sections, Integrated Review Groups, and Special Emphasis Panels.[17]

This grant has four basic elements. First, this project has funding for over $32 million in 2023, with direct costs of over $24 million and indirect costs of over $7 million. Second, the grantor is NIH, with its administering institute of the National Institute on Minority Health and Health Disparities, one of NIH's thirteen institutes. Third, the grantee is Duke University. The contact PI/project leader (PL) is Michael Cohen-Wolkowiez at Duke University, along with two other PIs, Gaurav Dave at UNC and Warren Kibbe at Duke, and thirteen Co-PIs at Duke, all of whom are professors at Schools of Medicine. Fourth, the grant purpose is to respond to the declared public health emergency issued by the Secretary of Health and Human Services for COVID-19 through NIH's expedited funding mechanism. It funded a single CDCC as an integral part of the consortium, the RADx-UP initiative, and a consortium of community-engaged research projects to understand factors that have led to a disproportionate burden of the pandemic on the underserved and/or vulnerable populations so that interventions can be implemented to decrease these disparities.

---

[15] In general, the grant-making process could include the following steps: (1) FOA: The federal agency announces its intent to award grants or cooperative agreements. (2) Program announcement (PA): The agency discloses priorities and areas of emphasis, and sets the timing guidelines for the opportunity. (3) RFA: The agency solicits grant or cooperative agreement applications. (4) Request for proposals (RFP): The agency solicits contract proposals. (5) Notice (NOT): The agency announces policies and procedures, amendments to the RFA or PA announcements, and other informational items.

[16] Available at the NIH website: www.nimhd.nih.gov/programs/extramural/investigator-initiated-research/emergency-awards-RADx-UP.html.

[17] Study sections, *NIH*, available at: https://public.csr.nih.gov/StudySections.

This grant also has several unique features. First, this $32 million grant is one of the largest by NIH, while the average size of research project grants in 2022 is around $600,000.[18] Second, the grantor used this as an emergency grant. Third, grantees are three PIs and Leaders as well as Co-PIs. NIH has various types of grantees as leaders, including PI, PL, and project manager (PM). Based on MIH, the Project Lead must devote a minimum of 20 percent effort (i.e. 20 percent of their total working time) to the Project. If the Project Lead is also a PD/PI for the Overall Program, they must devote a minimum of 5 percent effort to one other component (e.g. another Project or a Core) for a total minimum of 3.0 calendar months (25 percent effort). Fourth, the purpose is to fund comprehensive research rather than clinical research. This project is not a typical clinic research project. It is to build a CDCC for RADx-UP to transform COVID-19 research to eliminate health disparities accentuated by the pandemic. It is a science grant, but not a pure research grant. It could be considered as a mixed, large development grant.

2.7 A Research Network Grant from the IES

The Institution of Education Sciences (IES) is one of the federal research funding agencies under the US Department of Education (DoE). Through the IES's website,[19] we can find a sample funded project called "MATHia: A Digital Learning Platform Supporting Core and Supplemental Instruction in Middle and High School Mathematics."[20]

This grant has four basic features. First, the award amount is $1,999,459 for five years between 2021 and 2026. Second, the grantor is IES, more specifically, the National Center for Education Research (NCER), one of the four major research centers of IES. It is from the grant program of Digital Learning Platforms to Enable Efficient Education Research Network, with Dr. Erin Higgins as the program officer. Third, the grantee is Carnegie Learning, a Pittsburgh-based K-12 education services company for math, literacy, English Language Arts, world languages, and applied sciences. The PI is Dr. Steven Ritter, one of the four co-founders and chief scientist of Carnegie Learning. Fourth, the grant purpose is, as a special type of grant on Methodological Innovation of IES, to meet an urgent need

---

[18] Research project grants: Average size, *NIH*, available at: https://report.nih.gov/nihdatabook/report/155.
[19] IES website, available at: https://ies.ed.gov.
[20] Available at: https://ies.ed.gov/funding/grantsearch/details.asp?ID=4705.

2 Real-Life Cases

to improve mathematics outcomes in the United States. This project is to integrate MATHia, an established adaptive one-on-one math learning platform for grades 6–12 that mirrors a human coach, with UpGrade, a new open-source platform that supports fair and rigorous randomized field trials that compare innovative practices with various approaches.

This grant also has several unique features. First, it is a **large** grant in the field of education and learning. Second, the grantor is not the NSF or NIH, the two most common federal funding agencies in the United States. It is the DoE as one of twenty-six federal funding **agencies**.[21] Third, the grantee is a research **firm** rather than a research university. Fourth, it is like a research and development (R&D) type of grant, integrating two computer programs for real-life educational practices, rather than a basic research grant. Fourth, this project is also not a stand-alone program. It is part of the Digital Learning Platforms Network, more specifically, the Digital Learning **Platforms** to Enable Efficient Education Research Network. It currently includes a network lead team, five platform teams, and a research team.

2.8 A Comprehensive Research Grant from the MRC

The Medical Research Council (MRC) is the largest governmental funding agency for medical research in the United Kingdom. Through its grant database,[22] we can find a sample grant titled "Adolescent Mental Health and Development in the Digital World" (#MR/W002450/1).[23]

The grant has only four elements. First, the grant amount is £3.9 million (about $4.8 million) for the funded period 2021–25. Second, the grantor is the MRC, under the Strategic Priorities Fund, which focuses on high-quality interdisciplinary research and innovative research that link up effectively with government departments' research priorities and opportunities, under the category of Research Grant, one of about thirty categories (e.g. Training Grant, Grant of research and development, Large Project). Third, the grantee is the University of Nottingham as the lead research organization. The PI is Chris Hollis in the School of Medicine at the University of Nottingham, with ten Co-PIs. It involved around twenty collaborative organizations, such as the London School of

---

[21] Grant-making agencies, *Grants.gov*, available at: www.grants.gov/learn-grants/grant-making-agencies.html.
[22] UKRI gateway, available at: https://gtr.ukri.org/.
[23] Adolescent mental health and development in the digital world, *UKRI*, available at: https://gtr.ukri.org/projects?ref=MR%2FW002450%2F1.

Economics and Political Science and the National Institute for Health and Care Excellence. Fourth, the grant purpose is to address two key research challenges: (1) using digital technologies to identify young people at risk of mental health problems and developing personalized digital interventions and (2) understanding how the digital environment influences adolescent mental health problems and their brain and cognitive development.

This grant has several unique features. First, it is a **large** grant, especially for mental health research. Second, the grantor is **MRC**. MRC is responsible for coordinating and funding medical research in the United Kingdom. It is part of UK Research and Innovation, the governmental funding agency that directs research and innovation funding in the United Kingdom and brings together its seven research councils, including the MRC.[24] Third, the grantees are a large research **team** with diverse interdisciplinary researchers to address how the new "digital environment" affects young people's mental health. Fourth, the grant is a **comprehensive** one, including basic and applied research.

2.9 A Young Scientist Grant from the NSFC

The National Natural Science Foundation of China (NSFC) was founded in 1986 and is the key governmental foundation in China, like the NSF in the United States. From its grant database,[25] I was able to find a sample grant titled "社交媒体中的品牌竞争扩散机理分析及影响因素研究" (Analysis of band competitive diffusions and influencing factors of social media) (#71702103).

This grant has four basic elements. First, its grant amount is ¥170,000 (about $23,630) between 2018 and 2020. Second, the grantor is the NSFC under the Young Scientist Grant Program, one of the NSFC's three major funding programs, namely, research advances, talent development, and infrastructure construction for basic research. Third, the grantee is the Information Science Institute of Shanghai Academy of Social Science. The PI is Jie Gu, with three Co-PIs. Fourth, the grant purpose is to conduct a quantitative study on competitive mechanisms of commercial brands in social media.

This grant also has its uniqueness. First, it is a grant in social sciences from China. Second, it is a small research grant for promising young

---

[24] Research councils UK, *Wikipedia*, available at: https://en.wikipedia.org/wiki/Research_Councils_UK.
[25] NSFC grant database, available at: https://kd.nsfc.gov.cn/resultInit.

scientists, slightly similar to the NSF's Faculty Early Career Development Program (CAREER).

2.10 A Grant to a Noble Prize Winner from the ERC

In 2023, Pierre Agostini, Ferenc Krausz, and Anne L'Huillier won the Nobel Prize in Physics "for experimental methods that generate attosecond pulses of light for the study of electron dynamics in the matter."[26] As various major research foundations often do after the Prize announcement, the European Research Council (ERC), the flagship funding agency in the European Union, immediately congratulated these Noble Prize laureates and stated that it has been funding Ferenc Krausz and Anne L'Huillier for their multiple research projects over the past two decades.[27] Through the ERC's grant database, we can locate one of the grants to Ferenc Krausz titled "Towards 4D Imaging of Fundamental Processes on the Atomic and Sub-Atomic Scale" (Grant agreement ID: 246799).[28]

This grant has all the four basic elements. First, the grant amount is €2.5 million (around $2.7 million) for the grant period 2010–15. Second, the grantor is the ERC, under the grant program of the Specific Programme that funds "ideas" for implementing the Seventh Framework Programme of the European Community for research, technological development, and demonstration activities. Third, the grantee is Universität München, Germany. The PI is Ferenc Krausz, a physicist at the Max Planck Institute of Quantum Optics and the Ludwig Maximilian University of Munich, Germany. Fourth, the grant purpose is to fund a project that will develop a 4D-imaging technique to directly observe atoms and electrons in their natural state in motion within the topic area of fundamental constituents of matter.

This grant also has a few unique features that help us understand further grant diversity. First, the ERC is a public research foundation across various countries within the European Union. In the United Nations system, there are various international organizations with funding functions, such as UNICEF and UNESCO. Perhaps the ERC is the only **region** foundation of this kind in the world. Second, the grant is an **Advanced** Grant, one of the ERC's three primary funding schemes to support researchers

---

[26] Nobel Prizes 2023, *The Nobel Prize*, available at: www.nobelprize.org/all-nobel-prizes-2023/.
[27] ERC grantees win 2023 Nobel Prize in Physics, *European Research Council*, available at: https://erc.europa.eu/news-events/news/2023-Nobel-physics-prize.
[28] Towards 4D Imaging of Fundamental Processes on the Atomic and Sub-Atomic Scale, *European Commission*, available at: https://cordis.europa.eu/project/id/246799.

who have already established themselves as independent research leaders with excellent scientific track records. The other two primary schemes are: (1) Starting Grants to those who have completed a PhD within two to seven years and are showing promising talents to conduct early scientific independent research and (2) Consolidator Grants to those who have completed a PhD within seven to twelve years and are consolidating their own independent research.

2.11 A Typology of Grants

Novice grant writers or even often experienced grant writers could feel overwhelmed to find the right grant programs. Thus, it is particularly useful to develop a good typology of grants and then check a variety of funding sources and grant programs, for example, finding grant programs by public funders[29] or private funders.[30]

The grantology literature shows several existing typologies of grants. For instance, there is a popular typology of four types of federal grant funding: (1) Competitive Grants that are based on the merit of a proposed project; (2) Formula Grants that use predetermined formulas rather than application processes to distribute federal funding; (3) Continuation Grants as renewal of an existing grant; and (4) Pass-Through Grants, where a federal agency issues funding to a state agency or institution that is then transferred to other state agencies, local governments, or eligible groups.[31] The NIH's well-known award mechanisms are another example of grant typology of biomedical funding: (1) Research training and career development (e.g. F series and K series); (2) Loan repayment programs (L series); (3) Program project grants (P series); (4) Research grants (e.g. R series); and (5) cooperative agreement grants (U series).[32]

Figure 1.1 presents a new typology of grants that is based on the concepts of grantology and will be used in this book for new grant writers.

Specifically, Figure 1.1 shows six basic features of the typology. First, the typology starts with **grant-related activities**. There are many activities, including some scientific research activities, that can be implemented successfully even without grants, but that is beyond the scope of the book. Second, the typology focuses on **competitive grants**. Various

---

[29] Sam.gov website, available at: https://sam.gov/content/home.
[30] Community Foundation Locator, *Council on Foundations*, available at: https://cof.org/page/community-foundation-locator.
[31] Grant terminology, *Grants.gov*, available at: www.grants.gov/learn-grants/grant-terminology.html.
[32] Mechanisms and guidelines, *NIH*, available at: www.niehs.nih.gov/funding/grants/mechanisms.

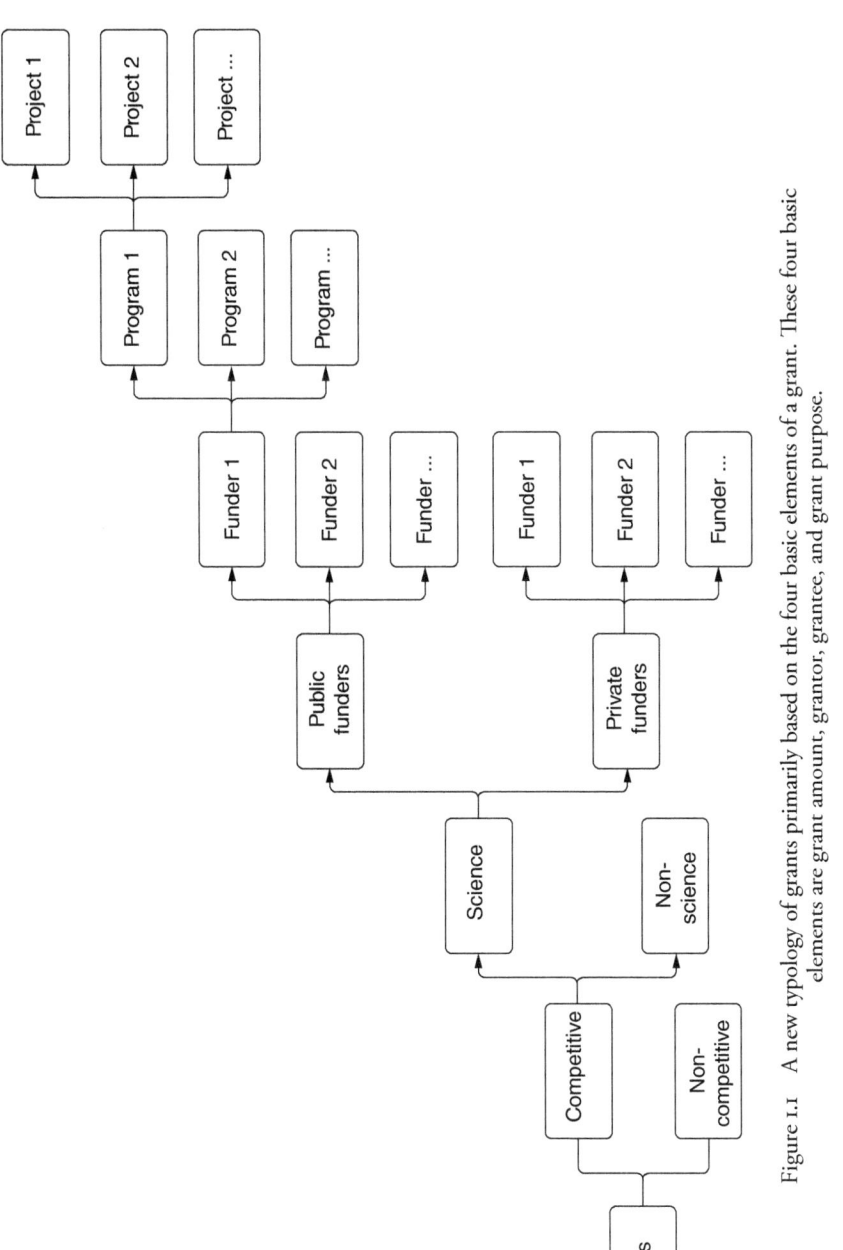

Figure 1.1 A new typology of grants primarily based on the four basic elements of a grant. These four basic elements are grant amount, grantor, grantee, and grant purpose.

grants (e.g. Formula Grants and Pass-Through Grants) do not go through competitive application and selection. Again, the book will not discuss them. Note that even within competitive grants, some are highly competitive (e.g. NIH's G01 grants), and others are much less competitive. Third, from the perspective of grant purposes, this typology distinguishes between **scientific grants** and **non-scientific grants**. While many grants support scientific investments (e.g. natural, social, and behavioral sciences; math, engineering, or biology), there exist various social grants, developmental grants, and other grants (e.g. vaccine distribution, social welfare provision, community development, and emergency responses) that serve societal purposes rather than support scientific investments. The book mainly focuses on scientific grants. Readers who are interested in social developmental grants might read extensive books on non-profit grants. Fourth, from the perspective of grantors, this typology distinguishes between **public** and **private funders**. In addition, other grantor-level elements could be related to whether a funder is national, regional, or international and whether a funder is disciplinary or multidisciplinary. Fifth, from the perspective of grantors, the typology covers different grant programs offered by a funder. For instance, a science-based funder may have **research** (e.g. basic, applied, and pilot research) vs. **non-research** grant programs (e.g. funding to support career development, equipment purchase, and infrastructure building). Additional elements at the grant program level include the grant amount (e.g. large, medium, and small grants) and the grant duration (e.g. short- and long-term grants). Last, from the perspective of grantees, the typology covers different grant projects under different grant programs. Note that **grant projects** differ from **grant programs**. The grant projects are related to the Post-Award phase and are funded grant projects where a grantor makes a monetary commitment to a grantee who will use this grant to complete a proposed project after the process of external review and funding decision, whereas grant programs are related to the Pre-Award phase and are grant opportunities developed by a funder to call for proposals. Additional elements at the grant project level could include the actual grant amount, actual grant length, and specific grant purposes. Note that here we do not discuss submitted but unfunded grants, a topic that will be discussed in more detail in Chapters 6 and 7.

Using this typology, we can analyze the basic important features of the ten grants we have discussed above. (1) The first grant, a *non-profit grant from the Rhode Island Foundation*, is a non-competitive, non-science, and non-research grant program from a private grantor. (2) *The Esther*

Katz Rosen Fund Grant from the APF is a competitive, science-based, non-research (i.e. training) grant program from a private grantor. (3) The third grant, the *STEM Research Grant from the Society for Science*, is a competitive, science-based, non-research grant program from a private grantor. (4) *The largest grant from the Bill and Melinda Gates Foundation* is a non-competitive, non-science (delivering vaccine) funded grant project from a private grantor. (5) *A federal grant on cyber privacy from the NSF* is a competitive, science-based, and research-based funded grant project from a public grantor. (6) *A large, complex federal grant from the NIH* is a competitive, science-based, multi-purposed funded grant project from a public grantor. (7) *A research network grant from the IES* is a competitive, science-based, multi-purposed funded grant project from a public grantor. (8) *A comprehensive research grant from the MRC* is a competitive, science-based, multi-purposed funded grant project from a public grantor in the United Kingdom. (9) *A young scientist grant from the NSFC*, is a competitive, science-based, non-research (i.e. training) funded grant project from a public grantor in China. (10) *A grant to a Nobel Prize winner from the ERC* is a highly competitive, science-based, research-based funded grant project from a public grantor in the European Union.

The above analysis of the ten grants shows that the new typology can capture the fundaments and complexity of grants in the real world, help us understand the four basic elements of grants and the wide diversity of grants, and be used as a practice-oriented typology of grants for new grant writers to understand and pursue grants (e.g. learning what a competitive grant is, understanding the existence of non-science grants, knowing various public and private funders, and studying different grant programs and grant projects). The key message here is that we should broaden our views on grants and be open-minded in searching for a grant program, writing a grant proposal, and conducting a grant project.

3   Scientific Knowledge: Three Theoretical Articles on Grants

Generally speaking, very little literature exists examining the nature of grants theoretically and developing a fundamental understanding of grants as a basic concept, while the existing extensive literature addresses various specific topics in pursuing grants (e.g. how to find a grant and how to write a proposal). Here, we will discuss three interesting and valuable articles to further our theoretical understanding of the concept of grants. Let us study the first theoretical article.

3.1 Azoulay & Li (2020): Grants as a Science Policy Tool for Innovation

Overview

This article[33] is titled "Scientific grant funding." Clearly, it focuses on science grants rather than non-science grants. This article is one of the most clearly articulated, thoughtful theoretical reviews. As of October 2023, it has been cited fifty-nine times based on Google Scholar. While the citation is not high as of now, this paper should become a classic, worthy of reading many times to gain various inspirations. It is well-written and extremely helpful for us to understand grants.

The first author, Pierre Azoulay, is the International Programs Professor of Management at the MIT Sloan School of Management and a *research associate* of the National Bureau of Economic Research (NBER). His research areas are the **economics of science**, innovation, and technical change. His h-index is 34. He has published a series of influential articles on grant funding and is one of the leading scholars in grantology. The second author, Danielle Li, is the Class of 1922 Career Development Professor and an associate professor at the MIT Sloan School of Management. She is also a *faculty research fellow* of the NBER. Her research areas are the economics of innovation, productivity, organizational economics, and applied microeconomics. Her h-index is 15. Often co-authored with Pierre Azoulay, she has also published multiple widely cited articles on R&D investment and NIH peer review. She is an emerging leading scholar in the field.

In the Author Note section, they acknowledge four scholars: Ben Jones at Northeastern University, Bhaven Sampat at Columbia University, Georg von Graevenitz at Queen Mary University of London, and Austan Goolsbee at the University of Chicago.[34] Mindful graduate students in grantology should pay attention to these acknowledged scholars, besides Pierre Azoulay and Danielle Li.

Here are two brief notes on the **NBER and its Working Papers**. First, the NBER – founded in 1920 and located in Cambridge, Massachusetts, near the Harvard campus – is a world-class research organization

---

[33] Azoulay, P., & Li, D. (2020). Scientific grant funding. Working Paper 26889. Cambridge, MA: National Bureau of Economic Research. G559.

[34] Benjamin F. Jones, *Northwestern Kellogg*, available at: www.kellogg.northwestern.edu/faculty/directory/jones_benjamin_f.aspx; Bhaven N. Sampat, *Columbia University Irving Medical Center*, available at: www.columbia.edu/~bns3/; Georg von Graevenitz, *University of Oxford, Law*, available at: www.law.ox.ac.uk/people/georg-von-graevenitz; Austan D. Goolsbee, *Chicago Booth*, available at: www.chicagobooth.edu/faculty/directory/g/austan-d-goolsbee.

conducting and disseminating non-partisan economic research. In a 2010 report by the University of Pennsylvania, the NBER was ranked as the second most influential domestic economic policy think tank after the Brookings Institution. The NBER includes more than 1,700 affiliated scholars based primarily at North American colleges and universities. NBER affiliates are selected through a rigorous and competitive process that begins with a call for nominations each February. Program directors, with the assistance of leading scholars in each field, review these nominations and recommend researchers for new affiliates. Among the NBER's affiliates, 80 percent are Research Associates who have tenure at their home institutions; untenured scholars are appointed as Faculty Research Fellows. Thirty-nine affiliated scholars are the winners of the Nobel Memorial Prize in Economic Sciences, including the most recent one, Claudia Goldin at Harvard University. The NBER's research activities are mostly identified by twenty research programs on different subjects (e.g. Economics of Aging, Productivity, Innovation, and Entrepreneurship) and fourteen working groups (e.g. Insurance and Urban Economics, Innovation Policy).

Second, this paper was initially published as an NBER Working Paper and later as a chapter of a book titled *Innovation and Public Policy*. Note that Working Papers are the NBER's major presentation format to share the latest findings that are written by NBER affiliates, and these are circulated for discussion and comment. The NBER distributes more than 1,200 Working Papers each year. These papers have not been peer-reviewed. In addition to Working Papers, the NBER disseminates affiliates' latest findings through a range of free periodicals (e.g. the *NBER Reporter*, the *NBER Digest*, the *Bulletin on Retirement and Disability*, the *Bulletin on Health*, and the *Bulletin on Entrepreneurship*), as well as online conference reports, video lectures, and interviews.

Highlights
While it is intended for the audience of science policymakers on scientific funding, this article provides an overview of grant funding as an innovation policy tool aimed at both practitioners and science policy scholars. It has five major sections, with a brief introduction containing two examples: (1) Why fund scientific research through grants (distinguishing grants from another four types of financial assistance, presenting five challenges, and discussing major functions); (2) A brief history of the scientific grant; (3) A guide to design grant programs; (4) Toward a science of scientific funding (using better methods); and (5) Conclusion.

Relevant to a basic understanding of basic elements or defining features of a grant, this article provides a series of important insights that are highlighted below.

First, its unusually short three-word title starts with an adjective, "**scientific**." It is an important adjective because it specifies the focus of this article on scientific grants rather than non-scientific grants. This is a thoughtful classification. Grants are extremely diverse; many grants focus on scientific projects (e.g. exploring a potential treatment of a disease), yet many other grants focus on social or societal projects (e.g. providing free meals to the homeless during the pandemic by a non-profit), as showing in the new typology of grants mentioned earlier in this chapter. The phrase "**grant funding**" used in the title is also useful. The three terms, grant, funding, and grant funding are often used interchangeably in the literature,[35] including in this paper itself. Yet there are subtle differences among them where grant funding might have the broadest and safest coverage comparing grant and funding. We will discuss further the defining features of grants in this chapter.

Second, the abstract states, "the paper first discusses how grants relate to other contractual mechanisms such as **patents**, **prizes**, or procurement **contracts**, and argue that, among these, grants are likely to be the most effective way of supporting early-stage, exploratory science." Here, the two authors used an effective strategy to define the key term **grant** by comparing a set of similar terms and real-life examples. After reading the paper, we will learn what is *not* a grant first and then we will understand what *is* a grant. The abstract also states: "We argue that, in making these choices, policy-makers might consider adopting a **portfolio**-based mindset that seeks a diversity of approaches, while accepting that high **failure rates** for individual projects are in fact part of an effective grant-making program act." This statement concerns two critical points: portfolio and failure rates. Developing a diverse grant portfolio is extremely helpful not only for grantors, but also for grantees – a topic that will be discussed further in Chapter 3 on grant writers for their grant portfolio. It is widely considered that a high failure rate or a low success rate for grant applications is a sign of the effectiveness of a grant program, although this is still a debatable topic, as we will discuss further in Chapter 7 on grant decisions.

---

[35] Price, W. N. (2019). Grants. *Berkeley Technology Law Journal*, 34(1), 1–66; Bunting, I. (2002). Funding. In *Transformation in Higher Education: Global Pressures and Local Realities*. Springer Netherlands, pp. 73–94; Fong, E. A., & Wilhite, A. W. (2021). The impact of false investigators on grant funding. *Research Policy*, 50(10), article 104366.

Third, the authors pointed out three key features of **innovations as a core concept**: (1) innovation projects are initially funded by public funders; (2) these projects were funded to conduct general inquiries rather than to generate immediate usefulness; and (3) while some innovation projects eventually successfully lead to tremendous societal gains, many other innovation projects might fail or generate only incremental benefits. These discussions of the key features of innovations are critical to understanding key features of scientific grants, and in fact can be immediately applicable to scientific grants in terms of importance, usefulness, and impact. Along with the conception of **innovation**, the authors explicitly stressed the essential nature of scientific grant funding as a special type of **investment**, one of the most important concepts in the science of grants. Innovation is the goal of grants, while investment is the means of grants. Thus, a grant carries all the benefits and risks of an investment, a key to understanding and examining grants scientifically and practically, while a scientific grant as a scientific investment to support and sustain a scientific innovation should still follow the rules of science.

Fourth, the authors repeatedly specified another important concept, the **ecosystem** of scientific funding. This concept is important and profound for grantology, the science of grants. It suggests that a grant involves a complex dynamic system with multiple inputs, multiple processes, multiple layers, and multiple outcomes rather than one single element. Related to this, the authors distinguished the two historic eras: (1) the **traditional** grant system that features a patron-oriented, donor-oriented, and society-member-oriented system, mainly in Europe and (2) the **modern** grant system that features a government-oriented, investigator-initiated, institution-managed, and peer-reviewed system, mainly in the United States. It also discusses the extramural system with a decentralized process vs. the intramural system with a decision-making hierarchy.

Fifth, footnote #2 raises an interesting but debatable point. That is, for scientific research in general and basic research in particular, **private grantors** are more unlikely to provide the necessary funding than public grantors. More broadly, it is related to the view that national spending should be invested more in scientific research, national defense, or life improvement. Scientific grants vs. non-scientific grants as well as public grants vs. private grants are two pairs of concepts useful for us to understand and discuss the definition and typology of grants.

Sixth, the authors raise another interesting point on supporting **human capital** as the research infrastructure, while explaining why scientific research is funded through grants. Two examples are used to discuss the importance and necessity of grants. One is grants on **public goods** and another is grants on **training** (e.g. fellowship grants and training grants). These human capital grants are part of non-scientific grants and training grants are part of scientific grants.

Seventh, the authors provide a brief guideline for policymakers to design or improve grant programs in the six **major steps**, from developing goals to assessing impacts. Although this was written for funders to develop grant programs, it is particularly useful to study these six major steps as the general process of a grant cycle, an important concept that will be discussed in Chapter 2. This is related to the overall organization of the present book. Various concepts used in this section are useful to learn, such as horizontal vs. vertical (e.g. a series of grants awarding a set of diseases horizontally vs. a series of grants funding projects from early-stage to scaling up vertically), and upstream vs. downstream (e.g. funding projects upstream by providing seed grants to early-stage ideas vs. funding projects downstream by providing funding to support a mature finding for translation).

Eighth, the authors explicitly discuss "a **science** of scientific funding," an important research initiative launched by the **NBER** in 2018. As one of the outcomes of the NBER initiative, the authors focused on research with methods of evaluating the effectiveness of a program and on science funding and science policy. This discussion essentially concerns grantology formally, while it does not yet cover the entire field of grantology. Chapter 2 of this book contains a detailed discussion on grantology as a field of research.

Ninth, the references are comprehensive, including various major works by leading scholars (e.g. van Slyke, Price, Ottaviani), especially the literature on economics in science and the history of grants. For this and other reasons, it is ideal to read it as the first paper on grants to develop basic knowledge about grants.

Last, the paper has sixteen helpful footnotes. In the first footnote, while pointing out the limited literature on grants, the authors note: "Notable recent exceptions include the work of Price (2019), who offers a legal analysis of grant funding, and that of Ottaviani (2020), who provides a theoretical treatment of the challenges involved in allocating funds across heterogeneous fields." Here, Price (2019) is referred to in another theoretical paper (Price II, W. Nicholson. 2018. "Grants." *Berkeley Technology Law Journal 34*(1): 1–66), which will be discussed in the next section. However, Ottaviani (2020)[36] is not a theoretical paper, but rather an economic

---

[36] Ottaviani, M. (October 2020). Grantmaking. CEPR Discussion Paper No. DP15389, available at SSRN: https://ssrn.com/sol3/papers.cfm?abstract_id=3723581.

modeling paper that uses the supply and demand framework to characterize the grant-making equilibrium between applications and acceptance rates. Thus, it is too technical to discuss here.

3.2 Price (2019): Grants as Effective Innovation Levels

After discussing the first theoretical article, let us now study another.

Overview
This article[37] has a short title, "Grants." As of October 2023, it has been cited fifty-nine times based on Google Scholar. Like a small book, it is one of the longest journal articles on grants, with sixty-five print pages. It is also one of the earliest articles examining grants systematically and comprehensively from the legal perspective. Thus, this article is a must-read for scholars and students in grantology. It is one of the very few articles that exclusively and systematically discuss grants theoretically from the perspective of law.

The author Nicholson Price II is a professor of law at the University of Michigan Law School. His h-index is 30. His research areas are Patent Law, Innovation Policy, Pharmaceutical Industry, Genetic Testing, and Gene Patents. He had a JD and a PhD in biology from Columbia. The paper is his only journal article on grants published while he was an assistant professor at the University of Michigan.

Berkeley Technology Law Journal, established in 1985, is America's first technology law journal. It publishes four issues annually on a broad range of topics at the intersection of technology and the law. It is a student-produced publication of the University of California, Berkeley School of Law. It also published the *Annual Review of Law and Technology* and was founded and is still supervised by Peter Menell Koret, Professor of Law and Co-Director of Berkeley Center for Law & Technology. Among fifty-eight journals in science, technology, and computing law, Berkeley ranked second based on combined ranking scores in W&L Law Journal Rankings.[38]

Highlights
Nicholson Price's article is a legal paper. It has five major sections, with a clear and coherent structure: (1) Introduction; (2) Grants in the innovation law **literature**, focusing on three critiques (bureaucratic decision-making, unaccountable ex-ante incentives, problematic risk allocation); (3) Grants

---

[37] Price (2019), note 35 above.
[38] W&L Law Journal Rankings, *W&L Law*, available at: https://managementtools4.wlu.edu/LawJournals/.

in **practice** at the national institutes of health, using the NIH as a case, offering an overview of grants, testing the three grant-related critiques at the NIH; (4) Grants as innovation **levels**, discussing mismatches between social values and market value and defining grants as innovation enablers; and (5) Conclusion. This article helps us understand multiple aspects of grants from a law and policy perspective.

First, the title of the paper has only one word, **grants**. It could be among the shortest titles of all the existing journal articles. Why does it have such a short title? It is like a serious declaration. Based on personal communication (July 20, 2023), Price indicated that: "The law literature had so little on grants that I figured I'd go ahead and claim a big introduction (in that literature)." He further explained, based on personal communication (July 21, 2023), that: "I study how law shapes biomedical innovation generally. A lot of that is intellectual property (patents, trade secrets, etc.), but there are other areas too (tort, regulation, insurance reimbursement). And a chunk of the picture that wasn't discussed in any thorough way in the literature was grants, and how they fit in with other tools (especially since the little I'd read on them seemed to ignore their strengths). So I figured I'd fill that gap." He did exactly this in his 2019 paper!

Second, as indicated in the Abstract, the paper is built on **three** fundamental points: (1) innovation is a primary source of economic growth; (2) grants are a key tool to promote innovation; and (3) legal academic research is limited. This is very consistent with Azoulay and Li's paper, placing economics, innovation, and grants in a logic chain. Perhaps this is the reason why Azoulay and Li's 2020 article also cited Price's 2019 paper. It is important, insightful, and effective to examine grants from the perspective of scientific innovation rather than general research as a key to understanding grants. Despite the importance and uniqueness of grants, the grant research has been limited in all four of the law, economic, sociology, and psychology literatures. It should be a timely call to further develop grantology.

Third, the paper has a clear structure. It first focuses on three **wrong critiques** of the law literature on grant decisions, grant management, and grant impacts, namely: (1) grant allocation and funding decisions by governments are not optimal; (2) grant accountability is limited because funding mechanisms are based on purely ex-ante priorities and therefore lack accountability; and (3) grants misallocate risk by loading the government with all the risk and giving the innovator all the benefits. The paper then uses the NIH as an example to explain why these three critiques are wrong. Lastly, the author discusses how to use grants to leverage innovation in two unique and important ways (supporting social values and supporting people).

Fourth, Price points out that while extensive literature compares patents, prizes, tax R&D incentives, and grants, the **grant system** literature is limited. The grant system is important because considering grants as a system or an eco-system can help to understand, conceptually, the complexity behind grants in a **systematic** way.

Fifth, at the end of the Introduction, the author summarized that the current innovation literature on grants is far too simple. "Grants form their own **complex**, massive set of innovation tools, with their comparative strengths, and are a far larger, better, and more varied part of the innovation system than the innovation law literature has recognized." This point is critical and insightful to understand grants because he recognized that they actually are a **complex** system of grants rather than a simple system.

Sixth, the section on an **overview** of grants is an excellent concise summary of grants. The topics include mission-oriented funding vs. research-initiated funding, extramural grants vs. intramural grants, and different types of grants (e.g. governmental, federal, state, and local grants, private non-profit grants, internal grants, private industry grants, and national and international grants). The US government grants include basic research supported by the NIH and NSF, Department of Defense, Environmental Protection Agency, and DoE.

Seventh, the entire third section uses the **NIH** as an example to summarize the funding operation process, from seeking grant applications, and peer review, to grant decisions. It has over twenty print pages, one-third of the entire paper. It is a good section to read to find out how the NIH funds research projects. It is beautifully written.

Eighth, Price nicely describes a series of grant submissions (using the term **repeated players** for those researchers who will submit the next grant), a topic that is a little difficult to understand well, but important to know. Price explains that many researchers might submit a series of grant proposals, either an extension of the current grant, a new grant related to the current grant, or a totally different grant from the current one. Price further includes a helpful diagram showing a sequence of grants, from an F32 postdoc fellowship grant, to a K99/R00 career development grant at postdoc, an R03 small grant as junior faculty, and R21 and R23 exploratory grants, to R01 as an independent grant. This series of grants is dependent on the performance of previous grants.

Ninth, Price discusses in length how a grant can support exceptional researchers and young researchers to develop **human capital** (another important concept for the roles of grants). He used HHMI and MacArthur as two examples of organizations that select and fund exceptional researchers. He also uses the NIH's F31 (doctoral fellowship grants), F32 (postdoc fellowship grants), and F33 (senior fellowship grants) as three examples of training grants (rather than research grants) to show how the NIH focuses on training and funding young researchers. In particular, he lists major reasons to fund young researchers: (1) young scientists often produce their best work when they are young; (2) early career funding can support them to continue their career; (3) and it is a solid investment in human capital to produce more and better benefits.

Tenth, the author advances two important concepts: the **innovation ecosystem** and the **grant ecosystem**. These ecosystems suggest a complex view to examine scientific innovation and scientific grants from a systematic complex perspective.

Eleventh, the paper has 347 footnotes, with various rich information. These footnotes can be grouped into three types: (1) mostly, the annotated citations with Price's brief comments (e.g. #10 and #11); (2) simple direct citations of references used in the paper as a writing style in legal literature (e.g. #3 and #4); and (3) Price's own comments (e.g. #18 on the NIH and #19 on the grant cycle). Note that Price has cited multiple articles by Pierre Azoulay and Danielle Li at MIT, including, in footnote #22, their 2019 article.

3.3 May (1998): Grants as Scientific Investments

Let us now study the final theoretical article.

Overview

This article is titled "The scientific investments of nations."[39] As of October 2023, it has been cited ninety-five times based on Google Scholar. Compared with Price's sixty-five-page article, it is very short, just three print pages, but it is particularly rich and thoughtful in helping us understand grants.

The author, Robert May, was Chief Scientific Adviser to the UK Government, based in the Office of Science and Technology, London. He is also Professor of Zoology at the University of Oxford. His main research areas are in ecology and environment and financial systems. His h-index is 171, indicating a high impact of his work. Among his over 500 articles,

---

[39] May, R. M. (1998). The scientific investments of nations. *Science*, 281(5373), 49–51.

he has published three well-known short articles in grantology in science around 1995–97, which falls within the period he was chief adviser between 1995 and 2000.[40]

Highlights
This paper is an overview of scientific investment in the world. This three-page short report has five short sections: (1) Introduction; (2) R&D investment; (3) Investment in the science base; (4) Private sector R&D; and (5) Discussion, with detailed notes and brief references. Reading it, we can gain four major insights into scientific investments.

First, the title, "The scientific investments of nations," is very interesting. While "scientific investments" is the key phrase, "of nations" implies an international comparison approach that was used to study twelve countries for their national investment in R&D between 1981 and 1995. If we want to understand grants well at a macro level, it is necessary to have some basic knowledge about economics, especially scientific investments. Grants essentially concern an investment in science. This paper provides a large macro-level picture of grants as scientific investments.

In economics, investment is an important concept. It has three key points. First, it is traditionally defined as the commitment of resources to achieve later benefits, which concerns two key elements: expenditure and return. In finance, the purpose of investing is to generate a **return** from investment. If an investment involves money, then it can be defined as a "commitment of money to receive more money later." From a broader viewpoint, an investment can be considered the use of expenditure and resources to optimize the desirable return. Second, investment has **risks**. Investors generally expect higher returns from riskier investments and a low return from low-risk investments. Third, to deal with risks, investors, particularly novices, are often advised to diversify their **portfolios**. Diversification has the statistical effect of reducing overall risk.

As a special type of investment, scientific investment can refer to the investment in science to receive various types of returns, scientific, economic, social, or societal. Scientific investments also have risks. In general, high risk leads to high return and low risk leads to low return. And good scientific investment might have to develop a diverse portfolio for grantors and grantees.

---

[40] May, R. M. (1995). Science and everyday life. *Science, 269*(5228), 1199. Gs2; May, R. M. (1997). The scientific wealth of nations. *Science, 275*(5301), 793–6. Gs887.

Second, to measure and report scientific investment, R&D, or specifically gross expenditure on R&D (GERD), has been typically used. GERD is a ratio between R&D expenditure and gross domestic product (GDP). The average GERD was **2.2 percent** across twelve developed countries in 1996, while there is substantial variation in countries and years. Sweden, Japan, the United States, France, and Germany are the top five, with above 2.25 percent GERD, while Canada, Australia, and Italy are among the lowest, with around 1.75 percent GERD. Besides scientific investment, other national expenditures include defense spending, healthcare and medical research, infrastructure and investment, and public social spending. The general trends of R&D investment are that the public R&D investment has been substantially decreasing, while the private R&D investment has been substantially increasing.

Third, to measure and report a return on scientific investment, the article reports both journal articles published and patents approved. In 1996, in terms of articles published in natural science per £1 million of scientific investment, the top three countries were the United Kingdom (18.83 articles), Demark (16.35 articles), and Sweden (15.69 articles). In 1995, among all patents approved in the United States, the top two countries were the United States (55.0 percent) and Japan (21.5 percent); among all patents approved in Europe, the top three countries were the United States (34.3 percent), Germany (17.2 percent), and Japan (17.2 percent). We will discuss this topic further in Chapter 9.

4 Grantology vs. Journalology: Grant and Article

Put simply, grantology is the science of obtaining competitive grants and journalology is the science of publishing journal articles. We will discuss these two disciplines in detail in Chapter 2. For now, let us focus on comparing grants, the basic unit of analysis in grantology, and articles, the basic unit of analysis in journalology. It will be helpful to examine similarities and differences between a grant and an article from the perspectives of grantology and journalology so that we can develop a better understanding of grants.

4.1 Grant

A grant can be defined as a certain amount of money awarded to a grantee by a grantor to support a project. It is a basic unit of the grant-funding enterprise, like a brick in the large building of grant funding.

Conceptually, it is also a fundamental concept in grantology. In section 1.2, we have discussed ten examples of grants and presented a typology of grants. In section 1.3, we further discussed three theoretical articles on grants and synthesized the existing theoretical knowledge about grants. Here, we will briefly review the four basic elements of a grant: grant content, grantor, grantee, and grant purpose. It is particularly useful to study these four basic elements of a grant in order to help better understand grant funding.

Grant Amount
There are different meanings for the grant amount. Before the funding decision, the grant amount means the proposed amount in the grant budget, whereas after the funding decision, the grant amount means the committed amount of funding by funders. In terms of the size of grants, grants can have a small, medium, and large size. Grant size is also related to grant duration: there are short-term grants, one-to-two-year grants, and multi-year grants.

Grantee
There are various types of grantees, for example, individual vs. institutional grantees, junior vs. senior grantees, predoc vs. postdoc grantees, domestic vs. international grantees, and female vs. male grantees.

Grantor
There are various types of grantors, such as small vs. large grantors, and specialized vs. comprehensive grantors. The more common type is public vs. private grantors. Grants are offered by governmental public funding agencies (such as the NIH, NSF, European Commission, and Australian Research Council) and non-governmental private funding agencies (e.g. Bill & Melinda Gates Foundation, Andrew Mellon Foundation, Rockefeller Foundation, Wellcome Trust, and Howard Hughes Medical Institute). Each funding agency may have various grant programs, and each program may have various funding projects.

Grant Purpose
There are various types of grant purposes. As shown in Figure 1.1 on the typology of grants, for example, there are science vs. non-science grants, research vs. non-research grants, early-career vs. independent researcher grants, and intramural vs. extramural grants.

4.2 Article

Compared to a grant, an article can be defined as a written work published by an author in a journal or newspaper to disseminate various contents. For instance, in 1974, Tversky and Kahneman published a seminal article titled "Judgment under uncertainty: Heuristics and biases" in *Science* to report their early findings on biases in judgments and reveal some heuristics of thinking under uncertainty.[41] An article is the basic unit of the journal publication enterprise and a fundamental concept in journalology. Similar to a grant, an article could have four basic elements: article content, author, journal, and purpose. It is particularly useful to study these four basic elements in order to help us better understand the journal publication enterprise.

Article Content
Articles have multiple specific features in their contents – for example, published articles vs. unpublished manuscripts, news articles vs. scientific articles, articles in print vs. articles online, and short articles vs. major articles. The most common categories of scientific articles are empirical, theoretical, methodological, and review. The number of citations of an article is often used as its article-level quantitative indicator.

Author
There are various types of authors – for example, journalists vs. scholars, amateur vs. professional authors, junior vs. senior authors. In the scientific community, the h-index and its large family are often used to quantitatively indicate the impacts of an author at the author level.

Journal
There are various types of journals published by different publishers – for instance, different academic publishers, such as Springer Nature, Elsevier, Wiley, PLOS, or Frontiers, publish thousands of journals, such as *Nature, Cell, Child Development, PLOS Biology,* or *Frontiers in Psychology*. These journals publish millions of journal articles per year. Based on one estimation in 2018, 10,000 journal publishers globally, with 33,100 active scholarly peer-reviewed English-language journals in mid-2018 (plus a further 9,400 non-English-language journals), collectively published over 3

---

[41] Tversky, A., & Kahneman, D. (1974). Judgment under uncertainty: Heuristics and biases. Biases in judgments reveal some heuristics of thinking under uncertainty. *Science, 185*(4157), 1124–31.

million articles a year.[42] These specific articles become the bricks of the building of the journal publication enterprise. Impact Factor is often used as a journal-level quantitative proxy of a journal.

Scientific Contributions
There are various types of contributions to the literature. The common contributions include empirical, theoretical, methodological, synthesizing, synthetical, and practical contributions for empirical articles, theoretical articles, methodological articles, literature review articles, and practical articles, respectively.

In sum, there exist major **differences** between a grant and an article, especially a scientific grant and an academic article. First, a grant is an amount of money to invest in a project, whereas an article is an intellectual presentation to disseminate knowledge. Second, the aim of a grant is to achieve a specific purpose before a project is completed, whereas the aim of an article is to make scientific contributions and disseminate new knowledge after a project is completed. Thus, grants can be considered as the input of the scientific process, while articles are the output of this process. Third, a grant is an investment that has a risk of having no successful return, whereas an article is the final product of a completed project. If it has made significant contributions, it is almost certain that it will be recognized and published eventually. Fourth, there are different forms of products at different stages of the grant process (e.g. unsubmitted proposals, submitted proposals, reviewed proposals, rejected proposals, resubmitted proposals, awarded projects, implemented projects, completed projects). Similarly, there are different forms of products at different stages of the publication process (e.g. manuscripts in preparation, submitted manuscripts, reviewed manuscripts, rejected manuscripts, resubmitted manuscripts, accepted manuscripts, manuscripts in press, and articles published). Fifth, a grant is awarded by a grantor, whereas an article is published in a journal by a publisher, and a grant is received by a grantee, whereas an article is published by an author.

There also exist major **similarities** between a scientific grant and a journal article, especially a scientific grant and an academic article. First, in terms of typology, there exist different types of grants, grantors, grantees, and purposes (e.g. science vs. non-science, government vs. non-government, research vs. non-research). Similarly, there are different types of journal articles, different journals, different authors, and different contributions

---

[42] STM Report 2018, *STM*, available at: https://stm-assoc.org/document/stm-report-2018/.

(e.g. empirical, theoretical, methodology, and review). Second, in terms of elements, grants have four basic elements (grant program, grantors, grantees, grant purposes). Similarly, articles also have four basic elements (article authors, journals, publishers, and contributions). Third, both grants and journals rely on various evaluation systems (e.g. numerous peer review systems) to control quality and make decisions. Fourth, both grants and journals involve scientific communication (e.g. writing grant proposals for funding vs. writing manuscripts for publication).

5 Action Suggestions: Searching and Analyzing Two Existing Grants

5.1 Understanding Basic Elements and a Wide Diversity of Grants

At the end of the chapter, let us first summarize the previous four sections before offering action suggestions.

First, we have presented intuitive thoughts by new grant writers. From these intuitive thoughts, we can see that new grant writers do have considerable knowledge about grants (e.g. they know grants are a certain amount of money given by a grantor to a grantee). However, their knowledge is based on their own limited experience and thus has several limitations, especially in their incomplete and narrow understanding of the basic elements and wide diversity of grants (e.g. they often over-simplify diverse grants as grants for research by government agencies).

Second, we have outlined ten real-life cases of grants, showing not only the four basic elements of grants, but, more importantly, the extremely wide diversity of grants. These grants are either competitive grants or non-competitive ones, scientific grants or non-scientific ones, and research grants or non-research ones. Often, the term *grant* itself in daily conversation can refer to different things, for example, a funding program (e.g. a researcher applies for an NIH grant) or a funded project (e.g. a researcher receives an NSF grant).

Third, we reviewed three important theoretical studies by three leading scholars on grants to further illustrate important and complex knowledge of grants. These three articles have addressed a wide variety of issues behind grants and pointed out the defining feature of grants as a high-risk investment for innovation.

Fourth, we have compared two concepts, *grant* and *article*, in the broad context of grantology and journalology. Through the comparison, we can see not only basic similarities and differences between these two basic concepts, but, more importantly, unique functions and operations of grants more clearly.

5.2 Locating and Analyzing Public and Private Grants

Based on the above summary, here are a few action suggestions for new grant writers.

First, **develop a good understanding of the four basic elements of a grant**. Grant amount, grantor, grantee, and grant purpose are the four basic elements of a grant. A grant is essentially a financial investment. There may be other elements (e.g. grant review, grant decision, or grant impact), but a grant should have at least these four basic elements. Knowing these basic elements has important practical implications – for example, helping new grant writers to understand and focus on essential features of a grant or to synthesize and compare different grants.

Second, **develop a good awareness of the complex diversity of grants**. While a grant has four basic elements, enormous diversity exists in grant amount, grantor, grantee, and grant purpose. The typology of grants presented in Figure 1.1 illustrates the diversity of the grants. We should overcome popular myths about grants – for example, grants are quite similar in their amount, grantor, grantee, and purpose, or most grants are scientific research grants offered by one or two well-known governmental grantor(s). Understanding the diversity of grants also has an important practical implication. That is, if we as new grant writers have this diversity mindset, then we will not just focus on pursuing one grant or one kind of grant. Instead, we will be quite open-minded in searching and applying for various types of grants that fit our professional or personal needs well.

Third, **locate and analyze two real grant projects, one public and another private**. As a particularly useful practice, a new grant writer should visit the websites of at least two grantors (ideally, one public grantor and one private grantor), find their grant databases, enter keywords related to their interest in the databases, and locate two interesting or relevant grant projects funded by the grant agencies. For these two identified grant projects, thoughtful analyses should be conducted to examine the basic elements and unique features of these grants and then the grant writer should specify and justify why and how to pursue two similar grants in the near future.

CHAPTER 2

Grantology

Outline

1	Intuitive Knowledge: What Is Grantology?	39
	1.1 Responses from New Grant Writers	39
	1.2 Understand Grantology as a Specialized Field of Science	40
2	Real-Life Cases: From a Book on NIH Grants to a Workshop at Columbia University	40
	2.1 A Book on NIH Behavioral Grants: An Emerging Field	40
	2.2 A Book on the Economics of Science: An Interdisciplinary Field	41
	2.3 Three Organizations of Grant Practitioners: An Applied Field with Practical Challenges	42
	2.4 A New Book on the Science of Science	44
	2.5 A Comment by a Reviewer on the Next Grant Cycle	44
3	Scientific Knowledge: Five Features of Grantology	46
	3.1 Van Slyke (1946): Grantology as an Emerging Field	46
	3.2 Robert Merton (1968): Grantology as an Interdisciplinary Field (1)	50
	3.3 Thijs Bol, Mathijs de Vaan, & Arnout van de Rijt (2018): Grantology as an Interdisciplinary Field (2)	52
	3.4 Martin (2020): Grantology as an Applied Field with Practical Challenges	55
	3.5 Munafo *et al.* (2017): Grantology as a Branch of Metascience (1)	59
	3.6 Fortunato *et al.* (2018): Grantology as a Branch of Metascience (2)	62
	3.7 Laudel (2006): Grantology as a Field Examining Grant Cycles	64
	3.8 A Basic Dynamic Model of the Grant Process	69
4	Grantology vs. Journalology: The History of the Two Young Fields in Metascience	71
	4.1 Grantology	71
	4.2 Journalology	74
5	Action Suggestions: Identifying and Studying Journal Articles on Grantology	77
	5.1 Understand Five Features of Grantology	77
	5.2 Locating and Analyzing Five Journal Articles on Grantology	78

1 Intuitive Knowledge: What Is Grantology?

1.1 Responses from New Grant Writers

In preparation for writing this chapter, I also asked around for a quick and brief answer to a question: What is grantology? Below are four examples of various email responses that I have received from new grant writers.

- Response 1: Have never heard of this word. I guess this word refers to the scientific study of knowledge regarding applying for and regulating grants.
- Response 2: I have never heard about grantology, but I would imagine that grantology is the study of grants. This would not only include how to optimize one's chances of receiving grants, but also the mechanisms and behavior of grants.
- Individual 3: I have never heard about this term, but I can guess it must be related to grants. The suffix "-ology" always indicates a specific field or subject. Therefore, grantology might refer to the knowledge about the processes for identifying and applying the funds and also the strategies for successful grant applications.
- Response 4: I came across the term "Grantology" for the first time in your question. I infer that it may be a combination of "grant" and "ology" (a suffix that denotes a field of study or knowledge). If it exists, I guess that, in grantology, people could learn the techniques, knowledge, skills, and strategies involved in securing funding through grants. Especially, this might include writing effective grant proposals. If so, we can call the people who are experts in securing grants "grantologists"?

These four responses show several characteristics of initial knowledge about grantology among new grant writers. First, it is clear that none of them knows or has heard the term grantology before. Second, not surprisingly, they can easily guess what grantology means in general by breaking the term down into two lexical elements, "grant" and "ology." One can even generate a new term "grantologists" to label experts in developing, securing, and studying grants. Third, they can all outline some practical contents of grantology, from quite simply (e.g. "applying for and regulating grants") to more detailed (e.g. "… the techniques, knowledge, skills, and strategies involved in securing funding through grants. Especially, this might include writing effective grant proposals"). Last, and more importantly, these responses did not show their awareness or knowledge of grantology as an emerging field of study and are essentially related to grantsmanship (i.e. practical knowledge of writing and securing grants) rather than grantology (i.e. scientific understanding of grants). Many fields of study such as medicine, law, business, engineering, or education ultimately do address practical needs (e.g. how to treat cancer or how to win a lawsuit). However, these fields not only deal with practical purposes, but also develop broad and deep fundamental knowledge as a science (e.g. how cancer cells grow or how evidence should be used in a legal case). This chapter aims to discuss grantology as a field of science rather than just grantsmanship as an area of practice.

1.2 Understand Grantology as a Specialized Field of Science

In Chapter 1, we focused on the concept of *grant* by discussing the basic elements and wide diversity of grants and presenting a typology of grants. In this chapter, we will focus on the concept of *grantology*. Specifically, we will discuss the five basic features of *grantology* – namely, grantology as a field of research that is emerging, interdisciplinary, applied, metascience-related, and examining grant processes. In doing so, we would correct one of the common misconceptions about grantology that assumes grantology is equal to grantsmanship and considers it is all about how to get grants. In short, our goal is to understand the richness of grantology from a board perspective.

Similar to the structure of the first chapter, in this chapter, we will present five cases related to five basic features of grantology, discuss five studies to understand five features of grantology, compare grantology with journalology to show the uniqueness and similarities of grantology, and propose action strategies to understand and use grantology in the grant process.

2 Real-Life Cases: From a Book on NIH Grants to a Workshop at Columbia University

2.1 A Book on NIH Behavioral Grants: An Emerging Field

In 2008, I attended the American Psychology Association's Annual Convention in Boston. During the Convention, I passed by Press Booth #740 of Oxford University Press, and a thick book showcased on the display table drew my attention. It is about National Institutes of Health (NIH) grants. I have heard a lot about the NIH during both my doctoral program and my faculty work. Yet it has always been a mysterious thing

2 Real-Life Cases: From a Book to a Workshop

to me. As a recently tenured associate professor, I felt that it was time to consider submitting a grant proposal to the NIH. However, what shocked me was that: (1) Oxford University Press published such a book on grants rather than on typical academic topics; (2) it is titled *The Complete Writing Guide to NIH Behavioral Science Grants*,[1] and I didn't know that behavioral grants alone rather than typical biomedical grants offered by the NIH need nineteen chapters within 500 pages to provide a complete writing guide; and (3) it was written by nearly forty established authors rather than a few scholars, covering almost every major topic, from grant writing and peer review, to revision and resubmission. My doctoral program does not offer training on how to secure research grants, but we did attend various talks and workshops on how to publish journal articles. This is the first time I felt that knowledge about grants was much more sophisticated than I had initially thought. This was the first time I felt that I was facing a big ocean of knowledge. And this was the first time I was really exposed to grantology or the science of scientific funding as a field.

However, fifteen years later, I was surprised and disappointed to learn that this book has been cited only four times as of 2023 based on Google Scholar, and another similar book also released by the same publisher in 1992 has only thirteen citations.[2] I have been wondering if it is related to the emerging nature of the field.[3]

2.2 A Book on the Economics of Science: An Interdisciplinary Field

As a researcher of grantology, I am aware of Robert Merton's masterwork in the sociology of science. As a researcher on the psychology of technology, I am also aware of Paul Romer's Nobel-Prize-winning work on "integrating technological innovations into long-run macroeconomic analysis."[4] A few years ago, however, I accidentally and surprisingly learned about a book on the economics of science, titled *How Economics Shapes Science*.[5] The

---

[1] Scheier, L. M., & Dewey, W. L. (2008). *The Complete Writing Guide to NIH Behavioral Science Grants*. Oxford University Press.
[2] Schwartz, S. M., & Friedman, M. E. (1992). *A Guide to NIH Grant Programs*. Oxford University Press.
[3] Wang, J., Veugelers, R., & Stephan, P. (2017). Bias against novelty in science: A cautionary tale for users of bibliometric indicators. *Research Policy, 46*(8), 1416–36; Shibayama, S., Yin, D., & Matsumoto, K. (2021). Measuring novelty in science with word embedding. *PLoS One, 16*(7), article e0254034.
[4] Paul M. Romer: Facts, *The Nobel Prize*, available at: www.nobelprize.org/prizes/economic-sciences/2018/romer/facts/.
[5] Stephan, P. (2012). *How Economics Shapes Science*. Harvard University Press.

book was published by Harvard University Press, known to publish classic work. The author is Paula Stephan, an eminent economist at Georgia State University. Quickly and happily, I went onto the Amazon website and ordered the book.

I was surprised to learn the following from the Preface of her book. (1) Stephan as an economist had been studying the economics of science for over thirty years at the time the book was published, but she does not consider herself to be the first one in the field. (2) Many eminent economists began the field several decades ago and have made enormous contributions, for example, Kenneth Arrow (social choice), Paul David (computer technology), Zvi Griliches (technology and R&D), Richard Nelson (innovation, basic research), and Nathen Rosenberg (technology, innovation). (3) She also specified enormous impacts of Merton as a sociologist on her as an economist. The book addresses the relations between economics and science, including various issues related to scientific funding, especially chapter 6, which focuses on funding for research. It has been cited 1,323 times according to Google Scholar. It has been widely reviewed or featured in *Science, Nature, Inside Higher Education, The Times Higher Education, Genome Biology, Science Careers, Science and Public Policy, The New Physician, Chemistry World, Issues in Science and Technology*, and *Contemporary Sociology*.

Paula Stephan's book opened another beautiful door to deepen and broaden my knowledge of grantology. It is another opportunity for me to learn the interdisciplinary nature of grantology, since various factors affect grants and various lenses can be used to examine grants. Besides Merton's sociology of science and Stephan's economics of science, it is highly possible to discover more seminal books in different disciplines that might shape our understanding of grantology.

2.3 Three Organizations of Grant Practitioners:
An Applied Field with Practical Challenges

Several years ago, I accidentally saw a website of a professional association called the American Grant Writers' Association (AGWA).[6] It is the national association of professional grant writers, grant managers, and grant consultants. It has 1,200 active members working at government agencies, school districts, higher education institutions, corporations, foundations, native tribes, and non-profit organizations throughout the

[6] AGWA website, available at: www.agwa.us/.

United States and abroad. It offers a series of online courses on grant writing for project grants, grant writer certification, grant management, and grant consulting.

Later on, I learned another professional association, the National Grants Management Association (NGMA).[7] It supports over 5,000 professionals across grants management, including supervisory, support, accounting, and compliance roles. It aims to cultivate a community of excellence in grants management through education, certification, integrity, and professional connections. It offers a Certified Grants Management Specialist certification program. Its members include grants management specialists, grants management officers, grants coordinators, grants developers, grants administrators, grants compliance officers, grants policy analysts, chiefs of grants, directors of sponsored programs, budget analysts, financial managers, financial analysts, financial specialists, financial administrators, procurement officers, fiscal officers, and program officers.

I then learned about the third organization, the Grant Professionals Association (GPA).[8] It is an international membership association in the grants industry. It helps grant professionals seek to continually improve their professional knowledge and skills in grant research, proposal development, and post-award grant management. It has 3,000 current members internationally, and publishes three publications to serve the grant professional community: the annual *Journal of the Grant Professionals Association*, the quarterly *GPA Strategy Papers*, and the weekly *GPA Grant News*.

Professional organizations like the three presented above show the following. (1) There exists a wide variety of professional practitioners such as grant writers, grant managers, and grant consultants. They have been working as professionals to fulfill their daily jobs in grants. There also exist various professional organizations that organize practitioners into a professional community to meet their professional needs and fulfill their jobs. (2) These organizations show the practical nature or practical feature of grantology. Daily challenges faced by grant professionals will motivate and validate the research in grantology as sources of important research questions in grantology. At the same time, the findings of grantology researchers will inform and guide the daily practice among professional practitioners. In other words, the research in grantology and the practice in grantology should benefit mutually.

---

[7] NGMA website, available at: www.ngma.org/.
[8] GPA journal, *Grant Professionals Association*, available at: https://grantprofessionals.org/page/journal.

2.4 A New Book on the Science of Science

In 2021, I was excited and surprised to learn about the publication of a book titled *The Science of Science* by Dashun Wang and Albert-László Barabási.[9] I was excited because the publication of such a book is another strong indicator of the emergence or existence of the field of the science of science, with accumulated knowledge and significant recognition. I was also surprised for multiple reasons: (1) I was aware of the widely cited article on the science of science (Fortunato *et al.*, 2018), while Dashun Wang and Albert-László Barabási were among the eight authors.[10] However, I still did not fully expect a book with a relatively coherent framework of the field to be written and published in 2021, only three years after Fortunato *et al.* (2018). (2) Dashun Wang received his PhD in Physics in 2013 under the guidance of his advisor Albert-László Barsi at Northeastern University. It took only eight years for him to grow from being a PhD student into a well-established rising star. (3) In the acknowledgements section of the book, the authors indicated that Dr. Riq Parra, an officer from the Air Force Office of Scientific Research program, supported them as a true believer from the very beginning, at a time when few people knew what they meant by the "science of science." This vividly describes their authentic experience with a new field that is emerging, but not popular or well-known. (4) The book has chapters on career, collaboration, and impacts that are relevant to grantology. Although funding is not a major topic of the book, it cites a few major articles on grant research.[11]

2.5 A Comment by a Reviewer on the Next Grant Cycle

Many years ago, I submitted a federal grant proposal on cybersecurity risk judgment. It was rejected, but I was able to see all the detailed feedback from five grant reviewers. One reviewer not only pointed out the strengths and weaknesses of my proposal, but also encouraged me to fix existing problems and then submit a new proposal in "the next grant cycle." This

---

[9] Wang, D., & Barabási, A. L. (2021). *The Science of Science*. Cambridge University Press.
[10] Fortunato, S., Bergstrom, C. T., Börner, K., Evans, J. A., Helbing, D., Milojević, S. *et al.* (2018). Science of science. *Science, 359*(6379), article eaao0185.
[11] Yin, Y., Dong, Y., Wang, K., Wang, D., & Jones, B. F. (2022). Public use and public funding of science. *Nature Human Behaviour, 6*(10), 1344–50; Wang, Y., Jones, B. F., & Wang, D. (2019). Early-career setback and future career impact. *Nature Communications, 10*(1), article 4331; Yin, Y., Dong, Y., Wang, K., Wang, D., & Jones, B. (2021). *Science as a Public Good: Public Use and Funding of Science* (No. w28748). National Bureau of Economic Research.

was the first time I learned about the concept of *grant cycle*. I felt that I had an "aha!" moment when reading this comment. For many experienced grant writers like this reviewer, a rejected proposal can and should always be revised and resubmitted, and it is the most common practice to receive funding eventually. Professional grant writers might not often aim to be funded for the first submission, but rather, in most cases, resubmission is the key to successful funding. Afterward, I was highly motivated by that reviewer's wonderful suggestion, revised and resubmitted the original proposal, and indeed won a grant in the next cycle.

I did reflect on this critical learning moment. First, at that time, I had published around twenty journal articles. Having learned from my own successful and unsuccessful experiences in publishing, I fully understand that it is critical to revise and resubmit a manuscript. Typically, no manuscript would be accepted after the initial submission. Second, at that time, I had just started to submit research grants. I did not have experience in pursing external grants, especially successful experience in receiving external grants. Third, there exists a subtle but critical difference between article publication and grant writing. For a new manuscript, after external reviews are done, an editor will write a decision letter, either **rejecting** the manuscript or **inviting** major or minor resubmission. For a new proposal, after external reviews are done, a program officer will write a decision letter, either **rejecting** the proposal or **offering** the grant. Thus, as an experienced article writer but an inexperienced grant writer, I had a misconception about the grant process: if a program officer rejects a proposal and does not invite revision and resubmission implicitly or explicitly, then my only options were to throw the proposal away or submit it to another grant agency. (4) There also exists a major difference in understanding and implementing the concept of *grant cycle* from the perspective of grantors vs. from the perspective of grantees. For grantors, *grant cycle* is one of the most common concepts. For example, based on the grants.gov website,[12] the grant process of all federal grants follows a linear lifecycle that includes three phases: Pre-Award Phase, Award Phase, and Post-Award Phase. The NIH has three grant cycles:[13] Cycle I, Cycle II, and Cycle III. For instance, for Cycle I, the application due dates are between January and May, the scientific

---

[12] The Grant Lifecycle, *Grants.gov*, available at: www.grants.gov/learn-grants/grants-101/the-grant-lifecycle.
[13] Standard due dates, *NIH*, available at: https://grants.nih.gov/grants/how-to-apply-application-guide/due-dates-and-submission-policies/due-dates.htm.

merit review is between June amd July, the Advisory Council Round is in August or October, and the earliest project start date is in September or December. In contrast, for grantees or grant writers, the revision and resubmission cycle is critical, but it is not visible explicitly or formally on the websites of various grantors. Thus, for novice grant writers like myself at that time, I could formulate a misconception that the process of pursuing grants does not automatically include the revision and resubmission cycle.

Various potential confusions about the grant process are essentially rooted in the general understanding and presentation of the grant process. A typical model of the grant process is fixed, simple, and linear. However, the grant process in the real word is dynamic, complex, and non-linear, with various cycles. Thus, cycles as a general concept should be included in grantology to guide grantors and grantees, especially the model of the grant process, which we will discuss in the next section.

3 Scientific Knowledge: Five Features of Grantology

While there are limited published articles focusing on grantology as a field specifically, five features of grantology have emerged that have directly or indirectly contributed to the current knowledge about this field. That is, we can consider grantology as an emerging field, an interdisciplinary field, an applied field, a field within metascience, and a field examining complex grant processes. We will now discuss five important articles to illustrate each of these five features.

3.1 Van Slyke (1946): Grantology as an Emerging Field

Grantology, or the science of making and winning grants, is an emerging field of study. Although scientific research as a fundamental human behavior has a history of about 4,000 years, modern scientific research supported by research grants occurred only around 200 years ago (1825 in France and 1849 in the United Kingdom). In the United States, the modern grant system started around 150 years ago (e.g. the National Institutes of Health, NIH, and the National Science Foundation, NSF, were founded in 1887 and 1950, respectively). And the history of studying research grants is even shorter, around eighty years. Van Slyke's 1946 article, discussed below, could be considered the earliest journal article on modern scientific grants.

3 Scientific Knowledge: Five Features of Grantology

Overview

The author of the article is Cassius James Van Slyke.[14] He received his MD from the University of Minnesota in 1928 and immediately joined the US Public Health Service. In 1936, he began his distinguished career in experimental research in venereal disease. In 1946, he joined the NIH as first Chief of the Division of Research Grants until 1948. Note that the NIH created the Office of Research Grants (ORG) in 1945 and changed it to the Division of Research Grants (DRG). In the beginning, the ORG consisted of Van Slyke, his assistant Ernest Allen, who later became the DRG director in 1951–60, and two secretaries. This period was called the NIH's "the Good Old Days." Working diligently with a small staff, Van Slyke created the administrative structure and the grant procedures for NIH extramural funding. In 1948, he became the first Director of the National Heart Institute after the National Heart Act was signed. Dr. Van Slyke became Associate Director of the National Institutes of Health in 1952 and then the first NIH Deputy Director until his retirement in 1959. For his unique contributions in laying the foundation for a national program on medical research and training, he received the Albert Lasker Public Service Award in 1957. Often called "America's Nobels," the Lasker Award recognizes the major contributions of scientists, physicians, and public servants.

The article was titled "New horizons in medical research." It has been cited only twenty-two times to date based on Google Scholar in 2023. It was published in 1946, one year after the end of World War II in 1945, and two years after the passing of the Public Health Service Act in 1944. This was a tremendous period in developing American post-war biomedical research. Perhaps this was the reason for its title. Specifically, the enactment of the Public Health Service Act in 1944 provided a legislative basis for the provision of public health services in the United States. This kickstarted multiple horizons of modern public grant programs in the United States. For example, the Act granted the original authority for scientists and special consultants to be appointed "without regard to the civil-service laws," known as a Title 42 appointment, the normal civil service appointment.[15] The NIH was elevated from a Division to a Bureau, with a commitment to the production of scientific research as its first and foremost duty. The NIH was authorized to "make grants in aid to universities,

---

[14] Cassius James Van Slyke, *NIH*, available at: www.nhlbi.nih.gov/about/directorscorner/previous directors/van%20slyke-cassius-james.
[15] Snyder, L. P. (1994). Passage and significance of the 1944 Public Health Service Act. *Public Health Reports, 109*(6), 721–4.

hospitals, laboratories, and other public or private institutions, and to individuals." The National Cancer Institute became a Division of the NIH and its grants-in-aid program served as a model for a new grants program for researchers at non-government institutions, including universities and medical schools.

The article was published in *Science*, one of the best science journals since its founding in 1880 by the American Association for the Advancement of Science. Its impact factor in 2022 is 63.8. It is a weekly, peer-reviewed journal that publishes significant original research articles, as well as reviews and commentary on current research, science policy, and new issues of interest.

Highlights
This article was published in *Science* as an Article rather than a Review, a Commentary, a Letter, or an Insight.[16] The article has nine printed pages, which is rather generous in its length given that a research article should usually not exceed five printed pages. This article's contributions to modern grant research are highlighted below.

First, the article describes an **eight-step procedure** of research grant administration in the Research Grants Division: (1) authorizing research grants by the Congress; (2) making policy recommendations of National Advisory Councils; (3) proposing and reviewing grants by Special Study Sections; (4) administering by the Research Grants Division; (5) deciding funding priories; (6) interacting with institutional and individual grantees; (7) completing the application, assessment, and decision process; and (8) conducting grant administration and implementation. It also talks about the NIH's research fellowships program. It ends with four printed pages, the half-length of the entire paper detailing three National Advisory Councils and twenty-one Study Sections. Thus, we can see clearly from the content that this article is essentially about the grant policy and procedure of the Research Grants program. It addressed almost all the topics related to NIH funding policy that would remain in use by the NIH for decades. The major content relates to a program description of the NIH. Considering there were no websites or online resources at that time, the article is essentially a public announcement on available research grants. Thus, it is a policy article rather than an empirical article.

Second, it reveals **new horizons** in medical research in the United States. As Ven Slyke enthusiastically asserts at the start of his paper: "A large-scale,

---

[16] Information for authors, *Science*, available at: www.science.org/content/page/science-information-authors.

nationwide, peacetime program of support for scientific research in medical and related fields" is now a functioning reality. He reported that in its first year of operation, the NIH grant program invested $4 million to fund 264 projects at seventy-seven public and private institutes in twenty-six states. From the perspective of grantology, the rapid increase in federal health funding has motivated senior grant officers to describe and examine federal grants as a research effort. This paper published in *Science* is the earliest indicator of such an effort.

Third, it leads to the **first wave** of articles on grants by NIH senior officers.[17] The Van Slyke paper and other early articles between 1946 and 1954 share a few features: (1) Rather than grant professionals, grant writers, or grant researchers in other foundations or agencies, all articles were contributed by NIH senior officers (e.g. Cassius James Van Slyke, Director of Office of Research Grants, 1946–52; David Price, NIH Associate Director, 1950–52, Director of the Division of Research Grants,1948–50; Ernest Allen, Associate Director, 1960–63, Director of the Division of Research Grants, 1951–60). Interestingly, Alan Waterman, the first Director of the NSF, also published multiple articles on the NSF.[18] (2) The method used was descriptive, either describing funding programs or using some basic statistical data. This shows the humble beginning of grantology research. These studies did not use true experiments, randomized controlled trials, systematic surveys, rigorous sociometrics, or computational modeling with large data, but we begin to see these methods more and more often in later grantology literature. (3) These articles were all published in leading journals, mainly in *Science*, and are mostly about NIH medicine and health research. (4) These articles all had a low number of citations, between four and forty-one. This might be partly due to the nature of historical records, policy descriptions, or emerging grant research.

Fourth, these articles by NIH senior officers are the **earliest efforts** in grantology research. Despite a humble beginning in its first eight years, grant research has accumulated rapidly. There has been an exponential

---

[17] Van Slyke, C. J. (1946). New horizons in medical research. *Science, 104*(2711), 559–67; Reynolds, F. W., & Price, D. E. (1949). Federal support of medical research through the Public Health Service. *American Scientist, 37*(4), 578–86; Deignan, S. L., & Miller, E. (1952). The support of research in medical and allied fields for the period 1946 through 1951. *Science, 115*(2987), 321–43; Endicott, K. M., & Allen, E. M. (1953). The growth of medical research 1941–1953 and the role of Public Health Service research grants. *Science, 118*(3065), 337–43.

[18] Waterman, A. T. (1951). Federal support of fundamental research in the biological sciences. *AIBS Bulletin, 1*(5), 11–17; Waterman, A. T. (1953). Research for national defense. *Bulletin of the Atomic Scientists, 9*(2), 36–9; Waterman, A. T., Ward, J. C., & Kelly, M. J. (1954). Scientific research and national security. *Scientific Monthly, 78*(4), 214–24.

growth in the number of publications on research grants over a period of nearly eighty years. Based on an initial search of key words, "research grant*" on the Web of Science shows that, starting in 1977, on average, ten articles per year have been published; starting in 1992, the number of published articles went up to 100 per year; and starting in 2014, this number increased to 500 per year.[19]

3.2 Robert Merton (1968): Grantology as an Interdisciplinary Field (1)

The current literature on grantology is largely from diverse disciplines, such as sociology (Merton, 1968)[20] and economics (Stephan, 2012).[21] This reflects the internal and external complexity of grantology. Since it is widely recognized that sociology is among the earliest and best studies from the diverse disciplines, we will now discuss two articles examining the "Matthew effect" from the sociology perspective to illustrate the interdisciplinary feature of grantology. Let us start with the earliest one, which is perhaps the most frequently cited classic in the sociology of science.[22]

Overview
Robert Merton was a professor at Columbia University and a pre-eminent sociologist of the 1950s and 1960s. He is best known for his work on sociological theory and the sociology of science.[23] Based on Google Scholar, his total citation is 216,097 and his h-index is 133, all amazingly high, indicating from one angle his momentous impact on sociology as a whole and on the sociology of science in particular. Note that one of his sons, Robert Cox Merton, is also a pre-eminent scholar, and he won the Nobel Memorial Prize in Economic Sciences in 1997, together with Myron Scholes.)

The title of the article is "The Matthew effect in science: The reward and communication systems of science are considered." The Matthew effect in science refers to the effect of different reward allocations (e.g. receiving

---

[19] Yan, Z., Yang, P., Liu, Q., & Erickson, J. J. (2023). The science of research grants: A scoping review of journal articles in grantology published in 1970–2020, *OSF Preprints*, available at: https://ideas.repec.org/p/osf/osfxxx/ynepm.html.
[20] Merton, R. K. (1973). *The Sociology of Science: Theoretical and Empirical Investigations*. University of Chicago Press. Gs11686; Merton, R. K. (1968). The Matthew effect in science: The reward and communication systems of science are considered. *Science, 159*(3810), 56–63. Gs11550.
[21] Stephan, P. (2012). *How Economics Shapes Science*. Harvard University Press. Gs14078; Stephan, P. E. (1996). The economics of science. *Journal of Economic literature, 34*(3), 1199–235. Gs2108.
[22] Merton, R. K. (1968). The Matthew effect in science: The reward and communication systems of science are considered. *Science, 159*(3810), 56–63.
[23] Merton, R. K. (1968). *Social Theory and Social Structure*. Simon & Schuster; Merton, R. K. (1973). *The Sociology of Science: Theoretical and Empirical Investigations*. University of Chicago Press.

3 Scientific Knowledge: Five Features of Grantology 51

a Nobel Prize) and community visibility (e.g. publicizing a new book) of scientists' initial contributions to their future achievements, as Merton defines at the beginning of the article. This article is a seminal work on the effects of research rewards and a citation classic in the literature. It was published in 1968, five years before his 1973 book, and has been cited 11,550 times according to Google Scholar in 2023, which is among the highest in the field. While Merton's focus is on the Matthew effect in science broadly rather than in scientific funding particularly, the article concerns various central issues of the science of research grants and has a major influence on grantology research, and thus should be considered a classic work in grantology.

The article was published in *Science*, like Van Slyke's 1946 article. The journal has been publishing various types of work related to grantology. Thus, researchers and students in grantology should follow it closely.

Highlights
This article is a six-printed-page theoretical paper. It has eight sections: (1) a brief introduction on the central theme, as well as the main data resource; (2) the case of the 41st Chair of the French Academy of Science is used to introduce the reward system in science; (3) a discussion of the Matthew effect due to the reward system in science in detail; (4) a discussion of the Matthew effect due to the communication system of science, in detail; (5) a further explanation of the Matthew effect with multiple scientific discoveries; (6) a further analysis of the Matthew effect in terms of its social and psychological function of leading scholars; (7) a further analysis of the Matthew effect in terms of allocation of scientific resources; and (8) a brief summary. It also has one printed page of References and Notes with rich information, almost as rich as the main text, one feature of his writing. Craig Calhoun, an eminent American sociologist, writing in Merton's obituary, pointed out that he: "was among the clearest and most careful prose stylists in sociology. He edited each essay over and again, and left behind added footnotes and revisions both large and small to a host of his writings. It was easy to imagine that he might have been a professional editor had he not been an academic."[24]

There are several reasons why his seminal paper is so popular and impactful. First, Merton, as the father of the sociology of science, identified a

---

[24] Robert King Merton, *ASA*, available at: www.asanet.org/robert-k-merton/; Robert K. Merton, *Wikipedia*, available at: https://en.wikipedia.org/wiki/Robert_K._Merton#cite_note-Robert_K._Merton-2.

general human phenomenon, thoughtfully coined it the Matthew effect (i.e. the richer get richer and the poorer get poorer), and described it effectively for the first time in the research literature. As his Note #50 of the article stated: "Evidently the Matthew effect transcends the world of human behavior and social process."

Second, Merton uses a **series of concepts** in his framework of the sociology of science as his analytic tools to analyze and explain the Matthew effect effectively. These concepts include reward system, reward allocation, stratification of honor, social stratification, social selection, stratified distribution of chances, social structure, retractive effects, visibility, social function, redundancy, socialization process, social institution, character structure, delay gratification, social validation, and self-fulfilling.

Third, Merton examined **sociopsychological mechanisms** of the Matthew effect. Feedback is one of the most general mechanisms that leads to generating complex natural and social systems.[25] In essence, he revealed a critical process of how science develops through complex feedback loops rather than through simple linear paths.

Last, Merton has not focused directly on funding or grants, which is understandable. However, he does address **various issues** highly relevant to the grantology literature, including recognition, rewards, research career, scientific discovery, and visibility. Merton also includes one section on science resources allocation, while his focus was on human capital rather than finance capital to attract the best students, produce future Nobel winners, and develop centers of excellence.

3.3 Thijs Bol, Mathijs de Vaan, & Arnout van de Rijt (2018): Grantology as an Interdisciplinary Field (2)

Overview

The title of the article[26] is "The Matthew effect in science funding," straightforward and self-explanatory, examining the Matthew effect on science grants. This paper is a very beautiful empirical study, representing a high-level research design and generating convincing empirical evidence. Based

---

[25] Bar-Yam, Y. (2019). *Dynamics of Complex Systems*. CRC Press; Sterman, J. (2010). *Business Dynamics: Systems Thinking and Modeling for a Complex World*. Irwin/McGraw-Hill; Forrester, J. W. (1961). *Industrial Dynamics*. Martino Fine Books.

[26] Bol, T., de Vaan, M., & van de Rijt, A. (2018). The Matthew effect in science funding. *Proceedings of the National Academy of Sciences*, *115*(19), 4887–90. Gs439; Petersen, A. M., Jung, W. S., Yang, J. S., & Stanley, H. E. (2011). Quantitative and empirical demonstration of the Matthew effect in a study of career longevity. *Proceedings of the National Academy of Sciences*, *108*(1), 18–23. Gs226.

3 Scientific Knowledge: Five Features of Grantology 53

on Google Scholar, it has been cited 439 times. Based on the *Proceedings of the National Academy of Sciences of the United States of America* (PNAS) journal website, its total views are 62,570, and its total citations are 201. These data from the two sources indicate that the article has generated a broad impact.

Three scholars wrote the article. The first author, Thijs Bol, is a sociologist from the Netherlands. He is a Professor of Sociology, previously at Utrecht University, and then at the University of Amsterdam, with research areas on social stratification, inequality, and education. His h-index is 24. The second author, Mathijs De Vaan, is an Assistant Professor at UC Berkeley. His research areas are on social networks, medical sociology, and sociology of science. He received two PhDs – from Utrecht University in 2012 and from Columbia in 2015. His h-index is 14. The final author, Arnout van de Rijt, is from the European University Institute in Italy, studying social networks, social influence, and experiment methodology. His h-index is 24. Note that he and other co-authors published another PNAS paper on the Matthew effect on funding, review ratings received awards, and petition endorsement in 2014.[27] It appears that these three authors share an intellectual tie with the department of sociology at Utrecht University.

The article is published in *Proceedings of the National Academy of Sciences of the United States of America*. It is the official journal of the National Academy of Sciences, published since 1915. It is one of the most prestigious general science journals, along with *Nature* and *Science*. It has published multiple major empirical and review research on grantology, including multiple articles on the Matthew effect. Its 2022 impact factor is 11.1. Thus, researchers and students in grantology should follow PNAS closely. The most common types of publication in PNAS are Research Reports, which "describe the results of original research of exceptional importance" via direct submissions without solicitations or contributed submissions solicited from the PNAS members. The Bol, De Vaan, & van de Rijt article is under the category of Research Reports as a direct submission rather than a contributed submission. It was edited by Christopher Winship at Harvard University and accepted by Editorial Board Member Adrian Raftery.

Highlights
This article has four print pages. It follows PNAS's format for a research report, with four sections: (1) Introduction; (2) Data; (3) Results; and (4)

---

[27] Van de Rijt, A., Kang, S. M., Restivo, M., & Patil, A. (2014). Field experiments of success-breeds-success dynamics. *Proceedings of the National Academy of Sciences, 111*(19), 6934–9. Gs233.

Discussion. From the perspective of grantology, we will highlight a few interesting and important points.

First, this article was built directly on Merton's 1968 classic article. It used a clever design and unique data to **empirically testify the Matthew effect** on grant allocation. While there exists extensive literature in the sociology of science on the Matthew effect, these three sociology scholars made important contributions to the excellent tradition of research in the sociology of science by convincingly revealing the underlying mechanism of the Matthew effect on grants.

Second, the article had a **particularly thoughtful research design**. It focused on one single grant program, the Innovation Research Incentives Schedule, in the Netherlands between 2000 and 2018, with 3,660 early-career grantees. Furthermore, it used and analyzed funding decision threshold scores, the proposal evaluation scores above or below the funding decision threshold. For example, scores of –1 or –2 indicate that research proposals receive an evaluation score of one or two points below the funding threshold, and scores of +1 or +2 indicate that research proposals receive an evaluation score of one or two points above the funding threshold. Thus, the study focuses on a unique window for assessing the effects of winners vs. non-winners on their future grants, while their original threshold score differences are minimal, either –1/–2 or +1/+2, to demonstrate the Matthew effect.

Third, the article presents **two significant findings**. It was found that those who won an early career grant by the smallest margin (+1 or +2) were about three times more likely to *win* a mid-career grant later than those whose proposals were not funded with the early career grant by the smallest margin (–1 or –2), controlling other possible confounding factors (e.g. the number of publications and the number of citations). Thus, the Matthew effect on grants is confirmed. It was further found that those who won an early career grant by the smallest margin (+1 or +2) were about three times more likely to *apply for* a mid-career grant later than those whose proposals were not funded with the early career grant by the smallest margin (–1 or –2), controlling other possible confounding factors (e.g. exiting academia or moving to other countries). Thus, a participation mechanism was confirmed. That is, non-winners decide not to apply for later grant competitions. This participation mechanism was found to largely contribute to the Matthew effect in grants.

Grantology has been rapidly growing largely due to research advances in various disciplines such as sociology and economics. The two articles discussed above show that the line of research in the sociology of science represents one of the highest achievements in grantology.

3.4 Martin (2020): Grantology as an Applied Field with Practical Challenges

Grantology concerns how to pursue and manage grants. It is motivated by real-life practical issues, which demand researchers to address them. Thus, it is an applied science, like business or education, rather than a basic science, like physics or biology. This feature is not difficult for us to see and understand. However, this applied field has been facing various practical challenges. Various articles have been published which criticize the current grant system or the exiting grant process.[28] Jeffrey Martin's extensive commentary[29] is among the most practical and comprehensive criticisms on grants from a real-life, higher education practice perspective. His commentary is discussed below to illustrate how and why grantology is an applied field with various practical challenges.

Overview

The title of the article is "Grants: The good, the bad, the ugly, and thePuzzling." Note that *The Good, the Bad and the Ugly* is a popular 1966 Western film, starring Clint Eastwood as "the Good," Lee Van Cleef as "the Bad," and Eli Wallach as "the Ugly." Since then, this film's title has entered the English language as an idiomatic expression and has become one of the most popular titles among hundreds of academic articles.[30] It is typically used when breaking down something complex into three aspects: upsides, downsides, and the parts that should have been done better. According to Martin (personal communication, June 22, 2023), he loves Westerns and thus includes *The Good, the Bad, the Ugly* in the title. Because he felt that

---

[28] Price, W. N. (2019). Grants. *Berkeley Technology Law Journal*, 34(1), 1–66; Costello, L. C. (2010). Perspective: Is NIH funding the "best science by the best scientists"? A critique of the NIH R01 research grant review policies. *Academic Medicine*, 85(5), 775–9; Pier, E. L., Brauer, M., Filut, A., Kaatz, A., Raclaw, J., Nathan, M. J. et al. (2018). Low agreement among reviewers evaluating the same NIH grant applications. *Proceedings of the National Academy of Sciences*, 115(12), 2952–7; Shavers, V. L., Fagan, P., Lawrence, D., McCaskill-Stevens, W., McDonald, P., Browne, D. et al. (2005). Barriers to racial/ethnic minority application and competition for NIH research funding. *Journal of the National Medical Association*, 97(8), 1063–77; Erosheva, E. A., Grant, S., Chen, M. C., Lindner, M. D., Nakamura, R. K., & Lee, C. J. (2020). NIH peer review: Criterion scores completely account for racial disparities in overall impact scores. *Science Advances*, 6(23), article eaaz4868.
[29] Martin, J. J. (2020). Grants: The good, the bad, the ugly, and the puzzling. *Kinesiology Review*, 10(1), 18–28. Gs5.
[30] Pearson, H. (2007). The good, the bad and the ugly. *Nature*, 447(7141), 138–41; Tangney, J. P. (1991). Moral affect: The good, the bad, and the ugly. *Journal of Personality & Social Psychology*, 61(4), 598–607; Phillips, D. C. (1995). The good, the bad, and the ugly: The many faces of constructivism. *Educational Researcher*, 24(7), 5–12; Banerjee, S. B. (2008). Corporate social responsibility: The good, the bad and the ugly. *Critical Sociology*, 34(1), 51–79.

there were enough aspects that he initially found puzzling, he therefore added "puzzling" to the title. While Martin did start his article by outlining the benefits of external grants (i.e. "the Good"), his main focus is on "the Bad, the Ugly, and the Puzzling" to "outline the most common criticisms of grants to stimulate a conversation in kinesiology" (p. 1).

This article is published as a commentary rather than a review. As Martin explained: "To be honest I cannot recall the category of paper that *Kinesiology Review* had to select from, and it might have been labeled **Commentary** because I did not do an exhaustive review in any systematic way. I also likely shied away from a critical review label because I wanted to acknowledge that there are some benefits to grants" (personal communication, June 22, 2023). Although the article was cited only five times as of 2023 based on Google Scholar, it is particularly thoughtful and well-written, since Jeffrey Martin was a journal editor, a well-established writer, and a fine administrator.

The article was published in a specialized journal, *Kinesiology Review*. It is the official journal of the National Academy of Kinesiology and the American Kinesiology Association. Its focus is on scholarly reviews, such as integrative reviews, critical reviews, meta-analytic, and narrative reviews, as well as theoretical papers, critical analyses of significant issues and scientific methods, and position papers pertinent to kinesiology. It covers all sub-disciplines of kinesiology, such as sport and exercise psychology, motor behavior, exercise physiology, biomechanics, sports medicine, sports history, sports philosophy, sports sociology, physical education pedagogy, and sports management. It does not publish empirical articles. The impact factor of *Kinesiology Review* in 2022 is 0.93.

Dr. Martin is currently a Professor of Sport and Exercise Psychology at Wayne State University in Michigan, studying disability sports and Paralympics.[31] He has published over 250 research articles and book chapters, but this article is his only article on grants. His major research area has been on the psychosocial aspects of disability sport and physical activity. He has been the editor for two journals and associate or section editor for three journals. In addition, he has received over $8 million in federal and foundation funding. Based on Google Scholar, his total citations are 11,054 and his h-index is 61.[32] His extensive experience as a professor, an administration insider, a well-established scholar, a successful grant writer, and a veteran

---

[31] Jeffrey J Martin, PhD, *Wayne State University*, available at: https://education.wayne.edu/profile/aa3975.

[32] Jeffrey Martin, *Google Scholar*, available at: https://scholar.google.com/citations?user=Vd1j6NYAAAAJ&hl=en&oi=ao.

journal editor are represented well in this article. In addition, Dr. Martin represented Canada in the 1985 and 1987 World Cup Marathons.

Highlights
This article has seven major sections, plus an introduction and a conclusion. The major sections discussed the following topics: (1) Major benefits of grants; (2) The critical role of grants in higher education finance; (3) Grants are not always needed for research; (4) Complex relations between grant and research productivity; (4) Inefficient use of resources of faculty; (5) Negative impacts on teaching, service, mentoring, and clinical work; (6) Negative impacts on department climate and faculty morale; and (7) Weaknesses in the current grant system.

Martin starts the article by briefly outlining eight practical **benefits** of grants. These benefits include: (1) providing research funding; (2) offering additional salary; (3) supporting doctoral students; (4) generating income for the university via indirect costs; (5) creating grant administrator positions; (6) providing unique research opportunities, (7) marginally increasing doctoral program rankings; and (8) producing publications. Thus, he concludes that, in reality, receiving grants often becomes synonymous with advancing science, and obtaining grants is essential and prominent in various disciplines.

In the main body of the article, Martin criticizes practical issues of grants in four major categories.

First, the **purpose** of grants. Grants have been used as a critical strategy to address the financial challenges of increasingly corporatized universities. Researchers are becoming more fundraisers than scientists. Thus, grants are becoming the end rather than the means of scientific research.

Second, the **relationship** between grant inputs and grant output. Many important, high-cited, or innovative papers and projects are not funded. Public or private funders' mission of funding the best science by the best scientists is often not being realized; related to criticism #2, the relationship between grant inputs and grant outputs is mixed. Thus, advancing science via publications is not supported by robust evidence of grant impacts.

Third, the negative **impacts**. It is a systematic waste of time and resources to prepare, write, resubmit, and administrate grants for individuals, organizations, and society given that most submissions are rejected. Thus, there exist negative impacts of grant-seeking process on time and efforts of research; related to criticism #4, the grant system will damage the professional, institutional, and clinical services, and will harm the departmental culture and faculty wellbeing.

Last, **flaws** of the grant system. Besides the problematic impacts of grants, the grant system itself has various flaws and problems: (1) grant review has flaws and biases and predictive reliability; (2) the system inappropriately funds a small number of institutions; (3) there is age bias; and (4) the size of grants does not always correlate with the size of impact. He suggested four changes: spending less time, focusing on people, funding everyone, and using the lottery.

At the end of the article, Martin proposes correcting existing biases and problematic practices in five major areas: (1) It should be recognized that faculty feel pressured to pursue grants even if they might not need them or are pressured to change their line of research. (2) It should be communicated well how grant success is used for hiring, tenure, and promotion or eliminating grant activity as part of the process should be considered. (3) It should discourage and penalize those who have strong grants but weak publications. (4) Grants and publications should have equal status in faculty meetings. (5) It should be clarified that grants are part of scholarship or research, but are not equal to scholarship.

Martin's article is not only highly practical, but also particularly insightful. Below are several highlights of the paper from the perspective of grantology as an applied science.

First, this article is a good example of grantology as an **applied** science. It is the first to summarize various criticisms from high education daily practice, to show the complexity of grants in practice, and to demonstrate the applied science nature of grantology. While it does not exhaust all of the existing criticisms on practices, nor was it based on large and quality data: various **costs** of grants rather than various benefits of gran are what Martin intended to focus on. It challenged a popular view that grants are always beneficial and voiced four major types of concerns about grants in everyday professional practice.

Second, of course, the central theme is that grants have both **values** and **costs**. Various costs are associated with applying for grants, obtaining grants, and administrating grants because the majority of proposals will be rejected, even those proposals with positive reviews. He voices criticisms of the grant-funding process that is proliferating and wide-ranging across various disciplines such as biology, social work, psychology, and economics.

Third, Martin's points on **multiple puzzling aspects** of grants, frequently observed but rarely discussed, are particularly practical and thoughtful. For instance, he was first puzzled by his frequent observations in faculty meetings acknowledging and praising grants but not publications, wondering why higher education and reward systems appear to

3 Scientific Knowledge: Five Features of Grantology 59

value money over science. He was puzzled by the notion that researchers have to find their own pay (soft money) to pay themselves via grants in medicine as well as other fields, wondering why such a rare arrangement was made in the first place. He was also puzzled by his observation that administrators seem unwilling to simply admit that going after grants is to fund the university just as much as for research. He was also puzzled by the fact that all the praise goes for grants, even though grants often do not further science, wondering why grants still seem to have such high values in academia. He was puzzled that there is the strange silence on faculty wanting grants to increase their salary/income as a legitimate motive, but one that gets ignored. These are all important practical and scientific questions that need adequate research to be answered well.

In summary, the benefits of grants are widely perceived, but Martin's paper suggests that these benefits are less significant than commonly thought. As the title of the article suggests, Martin did present the good side, the bad side, the ugly side, and the puzzling side of grants in the real world, although his criticisms are specifically based on research grants rather than service grants, largely based on one discipline (kinesiology), directly based on one university (Wayne State University), essentially based on the observations and experiences of one individual in higher education (a scholar, a grantee, an editor, an administration insider). His article motivates research in grantology to better understand the challenges of grants and conduct research to address these challenges. To further advance grantology as an applied field, we should address existing problems and various challenges of grants to make grant research and grant practice more effective and efficient.

3.5 Munafò et al. (2017): Grantology as a Branch of Metascience (1)

Studying science itself as the objective of study has a long intellectual history. Some specific research areas include the history of science,[33] philosophy of science,[34] sociology of science,[35] economics of science,[36] and

---

[33] Kuhn, T. S. (1997). *The Structure of Scientific Revolutions* (Vol. 962). University of Chicago Press. Gs3472.
[34] Popper, K. (2005). *The Logic of Scientific Discovery*. Routledge. Gs42309.
[35] Bourdieu, P. (2004). *Science of Science and Reflexivity*. Polity Press. Gs5856.
[36] Stephan, P. (2012). *How Economics Shapes Science*. Harvard University Press. Gs 1407; Romer, P. M. (1990). Endogenous technological change. *Journal of Political Economy*, 98(5, Pt. 2), S71–S102. Gs41795.

scientometrics.[37] Over the past twenty years or so, a large wave of empirical research has surged, using rigorous methods and large data to study *metascience* or the *science of science*.[38] Munafo *et al.*'s 2017 article[39] and Fortunato *et al.*'s 2018 article are among the two most influential articles, both of which are discussed below.

Overview

The title of the article is "A manifesto for reproducible science," which emphasizes two of the article's key points: declaring an emerging field of metascience; and addressing the well-known reproducible crisis in science. This article is not a typical empirical or review article, but rather a *Perspective* article or an *Opinion* article. Based on Google Scholar, as of December 2023, it has been cited 2,426 times since 2017. It is a highly cited article.

There are ten authors for this article. The first author, Marcus Munafò, is a Professor of Psychology at the University of Bristol. Co-author Brian Nosek is at the University of Virginia investigating psychology and Open Science; Dorothy Bishop is at the University of Oxford studying experimental psychology; Katherine Button is at the University of Bath studying mental health disorders; Christopher Chambers is Professor of Cognitive Neuroscience at Cardiff University; Nathalie Percie du Sert is Head of Experimental Design and Reporting at NC3Rs (National Centre for the Replacement, Refinement and Reduction of Animals in Research) in the United Kingdom; Uri Simonsohn is Professor of Behavioral Science at ESADE of Spain; Eric-Jan Wagenmakers is a Professor of Mathematical Psychology at the University of Amsterdam studying Bayesian inference; Jennifer Ware worked in the Cure Huntington's Disease Initiative Foundation focusing on Huntington's disease research and drug development; and John Ioannidis is a Professor of Medicine at Stanford who is known as a leading pioneer of metascience. The majority of the authors are from the field of psychology. This article is not based on a conference,

---

[37] Price, D. (1963). *Little Science, Big Science*. Columbia University Press. Gs5456.
[38] Ioannidis, J. P. (2005). Why most published research findings are false. *PLoS Medicine*, 2(8), article e124. Gs13512; Wang, D., & Barabási, A. (2021). *The Science of Science*. Cambridge University Press. Gs221; Peterson, D., & Panofsky, A. (2023). Metascience as a scientific social movement. *Minerva*, *61*(2), 1–28. Gs52; Schooler, J. W. (2014). Metascience could rescue the "replication crisis." *Nature*, *515*(7525), 9. Gs284; Schooler, J. W. (2014). Turning the lens of science on itself: Verbal overshadowing, replication, and metascience. *Perspectives on Psychological Science*, 9(5), 579–84. Gs46.
[39] Munafò, M. R., Nosek, B. A., Bishop, D. V., Button, K. S., Chambers, C. D., Percie du Sert, N. *et al.* (2017). A manifesto for reproducible science. *Nature Human Behaviour*, *1*(1), 1–9.

a group project, or a workshop, and according to Marcus Munafò, "we were all collectively discussing these issues and thought it would be helpful to synthesize our discussions into a commentary/opinion piece. It wasn't anything more formal than that!" (personal communication, January 28, 2024 and August 22, 2023).

The article is published under the category of Perspective in *Nature Human Behaviour*. This journal's impact factor is 29.9 in 2022, which is high for a specialized journal. Launched in 2017, it is an online-only monthly journal in *Nature Portfolio*. While primarily publishing original research, *Nature Human Behaviour* also publishes non-research articles, for example, Reviews, Perspectives, Comments, News, Features, and Correspondence. Among them, Perspectives are intended to provide a forum for authors to discuss models and ideas from a personal viewpoint and to stimulate discussion and new approaches, and are more forward-looking and/or speculative than Reviews.

Highlights
Based on significant research in the field of *metascience*, the article first outlines various threats in research findings, including "reproducibility crisis" (i.e. low reproducibility of published studies exist extensively) and various cognitive biases (e.g. confirmation bias, hindsight bias, and experimenter effects). It then proposes to adopt five types of effective strategies to tackle the existing threats and biases in research and improve the reliability and efficiency of scientific publication and funding. These strategies are to optimize five key elements of the scientific process: methods, reporting and dissemination, reproducibility, evaluation, and incentives, corresponding to how to perform, communicate, verify, evaluate, and reward research, respectively.

From the perspective of grantology, we can highlight major relevant points below. (1) The article considers five key **stakeholders** in the scientific process – researchers, institutions, regulators, journals, and funders – in improving transparency, reproducibility, and efficiency of scientific research. Here, funders are included. (2) It suggests including independent **methodologists** in the design, monitoring, analysis, or interpretation of research outcomes to mitigate research biases that exist among researchers and funders. (3) It proposes that journals and funders adopt the **registered reports** initiative. Authors could submit a proposal for simultaneous review by both a funder and a journal to promote openness and transparency. (4) It suggests **replication** studies should be funded, besides other incentive strategies. Funders should adopt transparency requirements and pilot funding mechanisms to promote reproducibility, as the Netherlands Organisation for Scientific Research and the US National Science Foundation planned to fund replication studies. (5) It supports making **public access** to digital scientific data the standard or the requirement for funded research, as funding agencies such as Research Councils in the United Kingdom and the National Institutes of Health and National Science Foundation in the United States strived to do.

From these highlights, we can see that grantology is an integrative and important area of metascience. However, it is still a young research area compared with other areas of metascience, even including journalology. It is foreseeable that most studies in grantology will be produced and published within the broad framework of metascience.

3.6 Fortunato et al. (2018): Grantology as a Branch of Metascience (2)

Overview

This article is a review published in *Science*.[40] The title is simply "Science of science," which specifies a field that provides a quantitative understanding of the structure and evolution of science. According to Google Scholar, it has been cited 1,096 times after only five years – clearly a highly cited work.

The article has fourteen authors. These authors are from diverse disciplines across multiple countries and many authors are strong in using a computational approach to studying science. The first and corresponding author Santo Fortunato is known for his work on detecting a community with computational graphs. He and three other co-authors, Katy Börner, Staša Milojević, and Filippo Radicchi, are all from Indiana University, studying network science and information science. Carl Bergstrom is a Professor of Biology at the University of Washington. Roberta Sinatra, Alessandro Vespignani, and Albert-László Barabási are at Northeastern, studying complex systems. Brian Uzzi and Dashun Wang are at Northwestern. James Evans is a Professor of Sociology at Chicago. Dirk Helbing is at the Federal Institute of Technology Zurich (ETH Zurich), studying computational social science. Alexander Petersen is at the University of California, studying complex systems. Ludo Waltman is a Professor of Quantitative Science Studies at Leiden University and the founding editor of the journal *Quantitative Science Studies*. Given that the

---

[40] Fortunato, S., Bergstrom, C. T., Börner, K., Evans, J. A., Helbing, D., Milojević, S. *et al.* (2018). Science of science. *Science*, 359(6379), article eaao0185. GS1096.

fourteen authors seem to have rather diverse research backgrounds, how did they decide to get together and co-write the review? Fortunato recalled that he knew all the co-authors, he and Albert-Laszlo Barabasi organized this project and tried to involve as many experts as possible, with complementary expertise (personal communication, December 3, 2023).

Highlights
The article has a special Structure Abstract or Review Summary, outlining the background, advances, and outlook of the science of science. The main text synthesizes recent major findings in multiple areas of the science of science based on digital big data and specific data analysis with quantitative and computational approaches. The eight major findings include networks of science, problem selection, novelty, career dynamic, team science, citation dynamics, outlook for junior researchers, and review system.

Here, I highlight nine points of the paper that are related to grantology. (1) The article points out "the increasing availability of digital data on scholarly inputs and outputs," including that from research **funding**, and offers unprecedented opportunities to explore the structure and evolution of science. (2) It mentions how to improve the scientific enterprise, including the "discovery of novel effective **funding** vehicles." (3) It identifies an observed trend that more conservative but less innovative findings often get published and thus **funding** agencies should "proactively sponsor risky projects that test truly unexplored hypotheses." (4) It outlines one study suggesting that **funding** schemes that are tolerant of early failure and reward long-term success are more likely to generate high-impact publications. (5) Gender inequality in science remains prevalent and problematic – for example, women received less **funding**. (6) Small teams tend to disrupt science and technology with new ideas and opportunities, whereas large teams develop existing ones. Thus, it may be important to **fund** and foster teams of all sizes. (7) Although review panels acknowledge innovation, they ultimately tend to discount it. **Funding** agencies should ask reviewers to assess innovation. (8) The current external review system is subject to biases and inconsistencies in science **funding**. Five proposed alternatives include the random distribution of funding, person-directed funding without proposals and reviews, an open review process, allocating funds through a performance measure without human reviewers, and scientist crowd-funding to use community networks to raise funds for the community. (9) Interdisciplinary research proposals systematically receive lower scores for **funding**.

From these highlights, we can see that, while scientific funding is not a central or individual topic of the eight major areas of the science of science, the research in grantology has involved almost all of these eight areas. Thus, grantology plays a unique role in contributing to the science of science.

3.7 Laudel (2006): Grantology as a Field Examining Grant Cycles

We discussed the term *grant* as a fundamental concept in Chapter 1, examining the four basic elements of a grant (i.e. amount, grantor, grantee, and purpose), as well as the wide diversity of grants. In grantology, there is another fundamental concept, *grant cycle*, which has been widely used to describe the process of managing grants or pursuing grants.[41]

There are various models of grant cycles generated and presented from the **grantor's** perspective. For instance, the Grants Management Office of the US Department of Health and Human Services presents an operational model of the *HHS Grant Process*, a process of managing competitive grants. It has seven steps: (1) planning; (2) announcement; (3) Application Evaluation; (4) negotiation; (5) award; (6) post-award monitoring; and (7) closeout.[42] Clearly, this model is a multi-step linear forward workflow of how to manage grants (see Figure 2.1).

There are also various models of grant cycles generated and presented from the **grantee's** perspective. For instance, the University of Utah's Office of Sponsored Projects presents a thoughtful *Grant Life Cycle*.[43] It has six steps: (1) generate your idea; (2) find your funding; (3) develop your

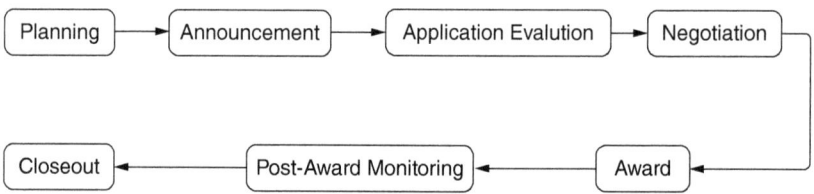

Figure 2.1 A multi-step linear forward workflow of how to manage grants

---

[41] Mole, B. (2013). NSF cancels political-science grant cycle. *Nature News*, available at: www.nature.com/articles/nature.2013.13501.pdf; Lammertse, D. P., Jackson, A. B., & Sipski, M. L. (2004). Research from the Model Spinal Cord Injury Systems: Findings from the current 5-year grant cycle. *Archives of Physical Medicine & Rehabilitation*, 85(11), 1737–9; Avin, S. (2015). *Breaking the grant cycle: On the rational allocation of public resources to scientific research projects*. Doctoral dissertation, University of Cambridge; Laudel, G. (2006). The "quality myth": Promoting and hindering conditions for acquiring research funds. *Higher Education*, 52, 375–403. Gs180.
[42] HHS grant process, *US Department of Health and Human Services*, available at: www.hhs.gov/grants-contracts/grants/get-ready-for-grants-management/grant-process/index.html.
[43] Grant life cycle, *University of Utah*, available at: https://osp.utah.edu/grant-life-cycle/.

3 Scientific Knowledge: Five Features of Grantology 65

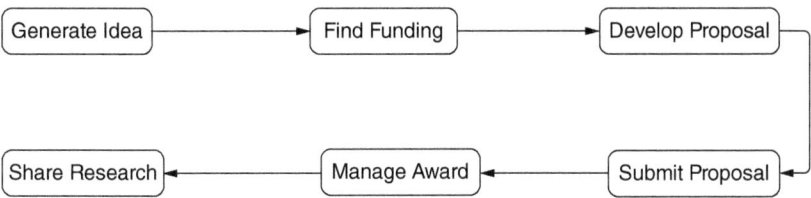

Figure 2.2 A multi-step linear forward streamline of how to pursue grants for grantees

proposal; (4) submit your proposal; (5) manage your award; and (6) share your research. Clearly, this model is another multi-step linear forward streamline of how to pursue grants for grantees to follow (see Figure 2.2).

There is **a comprehensive model** of the *Grant Lifecycle* that is presented by the program management office of Grants.gov to use in the Grants.gov system.[44] Grants.gov is a centralized platform for grant seekers to find and apply for federal funding opportunities in the United States and currently includes over 1,000 grant programs from around ternty-five federal grant-making agencies. The model divided the grant lifecycle into three major phases: pre-award, award, and post-award. It has **thirteen steps**: (1) planning an opportunity; (2) announcing an opportunity; (3) searching for an opportunity; (4) registering on Grants.gov; (5) completing an application; (6) retrieving the application; (7) staying in the loop; (8) finishing the review process; (9) notifying the award recipient; (10) beginning the hard work; (11) providing support and oversight; (12) reporting your progress; and (13) award closeout. The grant lifecycle travels down into **two streams**, the grantor actions (e.g. planning a funding program) and the grantee actions (e.g. searching and identifying available funding programs), along the thirteen steps of the grant lifecycle. While it is indeed a comprehensive model, it is a linear forward model without various pathways cycling back to its beginning – for example, grantees' grant resubmission or grantors' program revisions. Thus, it still presents a linear forward process rather than a non-linear complex grant cycle (see Figure 2.3).

The three models discussed above suggest that the concept of *grant cycle* might not be as simple as we would expect. In fact, *grant cycle* or *grant process* involves a complex dynamic process rather than a simple fixed process in the real-life world. Laudel's 2006 article[45] is one of the few articles

---
[44] The grant lifecycle, *Grant.gov*, available at: www.grants.gov/learn-grants/grants-101/the-grant-lifecycle.
[45] Laudel (2006), note 41 above.

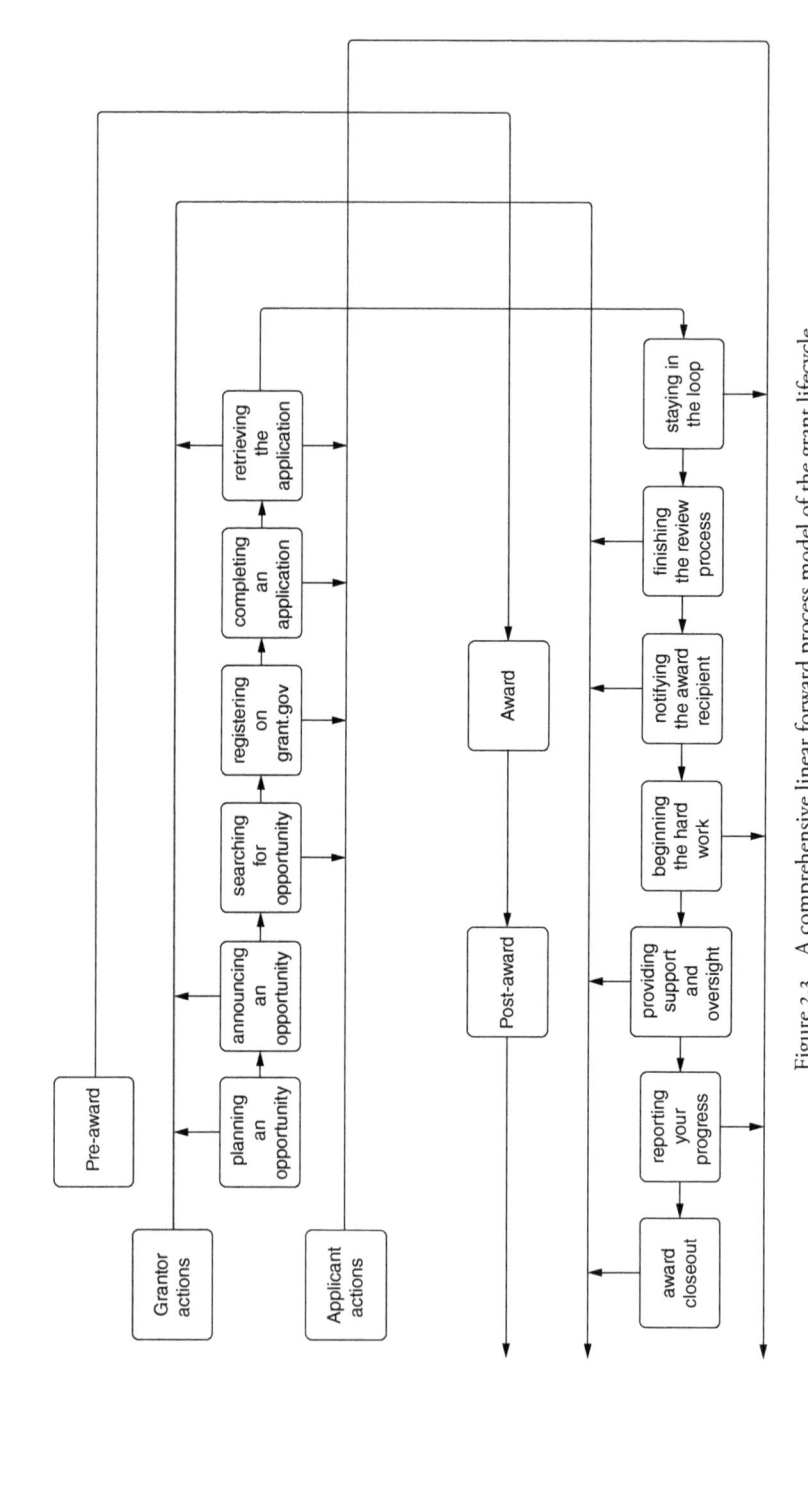

Figure 2.3 A comprehensive linear forward process model of the grant lifecycle

3 Scientific Knowledge: Five Features of Grantology

published in the grantology literature that presents a complex grant cycle model, as discussed below.

Overview
The author of the article, Grit Laudel, is a Senior Researcher at the Berlin University of Technology.[46] Her research area is on the sociology of science with quantitative methodology. Her h-index is 36 and total citations are 13,149. She has published multiple articles on grants.[47] Thus, she is an established scholar in grantology, and researchers and students in grantology should follow her work.

The article is titled "The 'quality myth': Promoting and hindering conditions for acquiring research funds." Here, "the quality myth" refers to the popular assumption that the best proposals receive funding; "Promoting and hindering conditions" refers to various factors that influence funding decisions. In this comparative qualitative study, Laudel interviewed forty-five German and twenty-one Australian experimental physicists. The major finding is that acquiring research funds is largely determined by the Matthew effect rather than by the quality of a proposal. Based on Google Scholar, as an empirical article it has been cited 187 times since 2006, which is quite high compared to similar articles. It is her second highest-cited work, indicating that this article has drawn considerable attention among researchers.

The article was published in *Higher Education*. Published by Springer, this journal is a bi-monthly, peer-reviewed, international journal on higher education research. The journal has a 2022 impact factor of 5.0. It is among the leading journals in higher education, along with *Studies in Higher Education*, *Research in Higher Education*, *The Journal of Higher Education*, and *The Review of Higher Education*.

Highlights
The article has seven major sections: (1) Introduction; (2) Analytic approach; (3) The object of study; (4) Data and methods; (5) Results; (6)

---

[46] Dr. Grit Laudel, *Technische Universität Berlin*, available at: www.tu.berlin/en/tis/ueber-uns/team/wissenschaftliche-mitarbeiterinnen/dr-grit-laudel.
[47] Laudel, G. (2006). The art of getting funded: How scientists adapt to their funding conditions. *Science and Public Policy*, *33*(7), 489–504. Gs320; Laudel, G., & Gläser, J. (2014). Beyond breakthrough research: Epistemic properties of research and their consequences for research funding. *Research Policy*, *43*(7), 1204–16. Gs164; Whitley, R., Gläser, J., & Laudel, G. (2018). The impact of changing funding and authority relationships on scientific innovations. *Minerva*, *56*(1), 109–34. Gs104; Laudel, G. (2023). Researchers' responses to their funding situation. In B. Lepori, B. Jongbloed, & D. Hicks (eds.), *Handbook of Public Funding of Research* (p. 261). Edward Elgar. Gs6.

Discussion; and (7) Conclusion, which is a relatively typical structure for an empirical article. We will discuss three highlights of the article related to the grant cycle from the grantology perspective.

First, the article focuses on **multiple specific factors** related to acquiring research funds to reveal the complexity of grant processes. As summarized in figure 2 of the article, Laudel analyzed her data from interviews with sixty-six physicists, identified eighteen factors, and categorized them into three types in terms of the relation to the quality of grant proposals. She found that, among the seventeen factors, only three factors are related to quality (e.g. quality of a proposal and quality of a scientist), seven factors are partly related to quality (e.g. availability of collaborators and amount of prior research), and seven factors unrelated to quality (e.g. diverse funding landscape and sufficient recurrent funding).

Second, the article specifies **multiple feedback loops** to conceptualize a complex non-linear model of the grant process, as illustrated in figure 1 of the article.

On the one hand, relatively similar to various linear forward models presented above, the main process of this model includes perceived demand of funds, actions for raising funds, decisions of reviewers, and funded projects. On the other hand, however, the model has four important features. (1) The model has a channel focusing on **grantees**. In this channel, the model specifies four feedback loops that *funded* projects will generate. That is, for grantees, their funding success can improve their reputation, their abilities and experiences in raising external funds, their new funding sources, and their research track records. These four loops will reconnect with the main grant submission and review process. However, the model does not include another important loop for *unfunded* proposals, namely, the revision and resubmission loop, even though it is rather common for grant writers to revise and resubmit their grant proposals and receive the funding eventually. (2) The model has another channel for **grantors**. In this channel, funding agencies take actions for raising external funds and manage grant reviews and grant decisions. However, the model does not include an important loop, namely, the revision and improvement loop for grant agencies to revisit a grant policy and to improve grant programs. (3) The model has a third channel for **institutions** that sponsor grant pursuit. In this channel, institutions provide internal recurrent seed funding, balance researchers' time, and sponsor and manage the actions for raising external funds. However, the model also does not include an important loop, namely, the revision and improvement loop for sponsor institutions to reflect on successes and failures and improve grant sponsor efforts. (4) Besides three exogenous variables, grantees, grantors, and sponsor institutions, the model has one extra **exogenous variable**, the field-specific characteristics. While a research field or an academic discipline (e.g. biomedical science, physics, computer science, engineering, mathematics, and anthropology) does play an important role in the grant process, however, we could consider this variable as an extended factor that can influence the three major exogenous variables: grantees, grantor, and sponsor institutions.

Third, of course, this article does not mainly focus on modeling grant processes. However, it does generate one of the **most sophisticated research-based complex dynamic models**. This is because complex elements (main and side processes with various pathways) and dynamic elements involve various feedback loops functioning over time (directions, forward vs. backward). This model is extremely inspiring and intriguing for further developing a complex dynamic model that maximizes inclusiveness and parsimony.

3.8 A Basic Dynamic Model of the Grant Process

Built on the above four models of the grant cycle, especially Laudel's model, a **basic dynamic model** of the grant process can be developed, as presented in Figure 2.4. It features: (1) four basic elements (grant writer, grant agency, grant decision, and grant impact) that are connected with four basic steps (grant writing, grant developing, grant reviewing, and grant managing); (2) two basic channels (grantor and grantee) as two key exogenous variables, while sponsor institutions and other external factors will be considered factors including these two key exogenous variables and included in an extension model; and (3) three basic cycles generated by three feedback loops, namely, the grantor management cycle, the grantee revision cycle, and the grantee new submission cycle.

This basic dynamic model can be extended to more complex models with: (1) multiple *factors* that influence the basic elements, steps, channels, and cycles (e.g. various factors influence grant writer or grant reviewing); (2) multiple *contexts* in which the basic elements, steps, channels, and cycles are situated (e.g. the social and scientific contexts of the grantor channel or the resubmission cycle in biomedical or mathematical research); and (3) multiple systems that link with the grant process system (e.g. a related dynamic system of journal publication or a related complex system of grant policy development).

Note that cycles or feedback loops should be considered as a general principle of the grant process and this should generate major practical implications. From the perspective of grantees, learning the resubmission cycle would help grant writers develop a better understanding of the

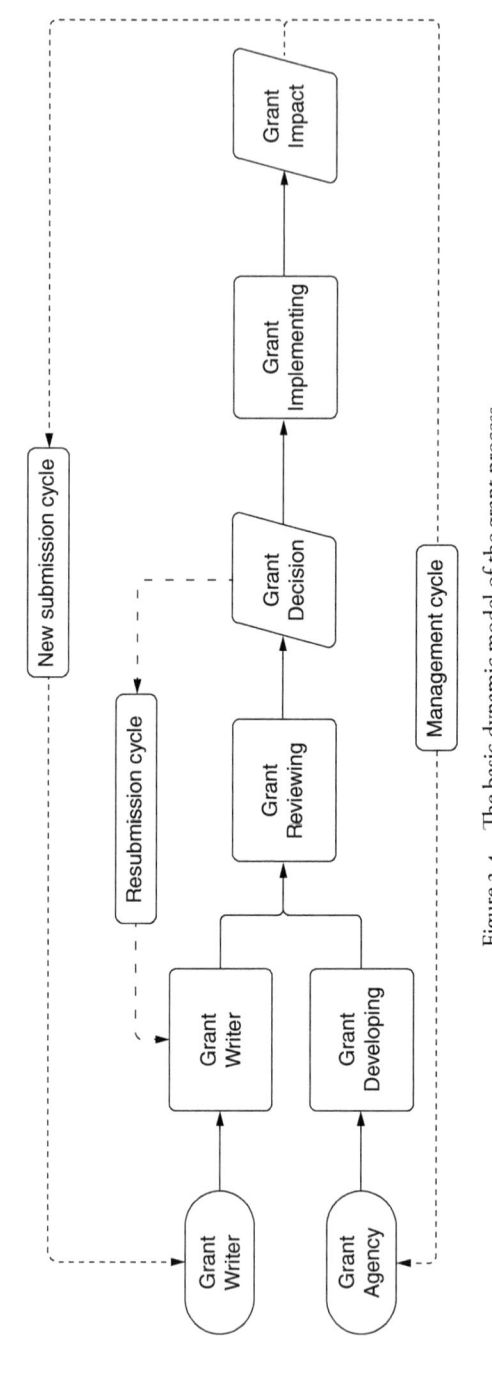

Figure 2.4 The basic dynamic model of the grant process

4 Grantology vs. Journalology: History 71

grant process, feel more positive about the rejection, read external reviews more carefully after a proposal is rejected, and be more motivated to revise and resubmit proposals. From the perspective of grantors, learning the management cycle would help grant managers and grant offices talk more about the grant cycle (like the NIH did on its website), reflect more on the grant management process, and improve further the grant policy and grant procedure (see Figure 2.4).

The present book uses this basic dynamic model to organize the presentation of core contents. Its ten chapters are divided into seven major chapters on seven major elements (i.e. writer, agency, writing, reviewing, decision, implementing, and impact) involved in the grant process, in addition to the two-chapter introduction and the one-chapter conclusion. The three cycles (the grant resubmission cycle, the new grant submission cycle, and the grant policy cycle) will be treated at the most relevant point of the grant process (e.g. the revision cycle will be discussed after a proposal receives a grant decision of rejection). Each chapter will have a five-step sequence: starting with people's intuitive thinking, followed by real-life cases, core concepts with supporting scientific evidence, a comparison between grantology and journalology, and ending with a summary and action suggestions for pursuing competitive grants and developing rational thinking.

4 Grantology vs. Journalology: The History of the Two Young Fields in Metascience

After the discussion of the five core features of grantology in the prior section, it will now be useful to compare two neighboring fields in metascience, namely, grantology and journalology, in a historical context. Grantology and journalology are like two brothers or sisters in a large family of metascience, one focusing on scientific funding to support research projects and the other on scientific publication to disseminate research findings. Comparing these two fields will help us further understand grantology as a field.

4.1 Grantology

Grants
The first modern grant system emerged after 1825 in France.[48] In 1825, the French Academy of Science decided not to award the annual grand prize

---
[48] Crosland, M., & Galvez, A. (1989). The emergence of research grants within the prize system of the french academy of sciences, 1795–1914. *Social Studies of Science, 19*(1), 71–100.

after several scholars delayed or avoided reporting their negative research results in order to increase their chances of winning the grand prize. In 1826, the French Academy of Science decided to award grants to promising research projects instead of highly successful scholars for the grand prize. Starting then from the 1890s, the French Academy of Science had gradually transited from the prize system to the grant system. This grant system led to a modern grant system model used by private foundations for years to come.

The modern grant system in the United Kingdom emerged after 1849, about ternty-three years later than the French one.[49] In 1849, the UK Government offered the Royal Society a large annual fund, called the Government Grant, to support scientific research in the long term. In 1850, the Royal Society created the Government Grant Committee to manage the fund and then the first research grants were awarded to seven fellows of the Society out of the first thirteen applications via the Government Grant Committee. From then to 1914, government grants rather than private funding played a central role in the endowment of research in the United Kingdom. The successful management system of the Government Grant Committee led to the model used in the NIH's grant management system.

Grant Research

Modern research examining grant practices as a research topic was published about 100 years after the emergence of modern grant systems. As discussed in the section above, in 1946, Van Kyle published one of the first grant research articles. This could be considered a starting point for formal grant research. This article was followed by a series of articles written by NIH senior officers. Gradually, highly influential empirical studies started to merge (e.g. Merton's 1968 classic article on the Matthew effect in science).[50] Starting in the early 2000s, major theoretical research was published (e.g. Azoulay & Li's 2000 article and Price's 2019 article).[51]

Grantology

Grantology as a field of research could be considered to start in 2019, seventy-three years later after the first published research article on grants in 1946. In 2019, led by Paula Stephan and Reinhilde Veugelers, the

---

[49] MacLeod, R. M. (1971). VI. The Royal Society and the government grant: Notes on the administration of scientific research, 1849–1911. *Historical Journal*, *14*(2), 323–58.
[50] Yan *et al.*, The science of research grants, note 19 above.
[51] Azoulay, P., & Li, D. (2020). *Scientific Grant Funding* (Vol. 26889). National Bureau of Economic Research; Price (2019), note 28 above.

National Bureau of Economic Research launched an initiative, *Science of Science Funding*.[52] In that summer, the first meeting was convened in Cambridge, Massachusetts. Although the term *science of science funding* rather than grantology was used, the research efforts organized under the initiative have made significant contributions to the development of the field of grantology in three important ways.

First, the research efforts under this initiative are **well-planned** rather than spontaneous. In 2018, a proposal to launch the initiative was submitted and approved by the Sloan Foundation.[53] Two continual grants were received in 2020 and 2024. With the support of these grants, the initiative has focused on a central goal: to build a research community on the economics of science. Specifically, it has strived to "improve understanding of effective methods of supporting scientific research" and to "promote analysis of the links between research funding models, management strategies, and scientific outcomes that can inform decision-making by both private and public funders." The wise vision (developing the science of economics) and specific focus (improving scientific grant funding) have been motivating and guiding the research under the initiative very well.

Second, the research efforts under this initiative are **collective** rather than individual-based. Given its goal of building a community of economics of science, the initiative has been striving to nurture a community of researchers, funders, and research administrators who can learn from one another and develop a research agenda. The three approaches to building the community are: convening research meetings; disseminating research; and supporting small-scale projects. The collective research efforts under the initiative have generated scientific and social impacts.

Third, the research efforts under this initiative are **continuous**, but intermittent. For instance, the annual conferences were held for six years, from 2019 to 2024. These conferences brought together economists, funders, researchers, and policymakers from around the world to discuss the latest work and recent findings, identify new areas for research, and examine methodological and data challenges. The conferences have continuously covered several themes, such as incentives in the current system, the effects of the structure of grants and review systems on scientific risk-taking, the costs and efficiencies of different research funding models, the scientific

---

[52] Economics of science, *NBER*, available at: www.nber.org/programs-projects/projects-and-centers/science-science-funding?page=1&perPage=50.
[53] Grants database, *Alfred P. Sloan Foundation*, available at: https://sloan.org/grants-database.

judgment of scientific quality, and measurement of return on investment in basic and applied science.

Because this initiative represents a series of well-planned, collective, and continuous effects on the economics of science in general and the science of science funding in particular, it has gathered a critical mass of researchers, disseminated the latest major studies in the field (e.g. Azoulay & Li's theoretical paper in 2000), and showcased leaders such as Paula Stephan at Georgia State University, Reinhilde Veugelers at KU Leuven in Belgium, and Pierre Azoulay and Danielle Li at MIT. Thus, the year 2019 when the initiative was launched can be considered the starting point of grantology as a field of science.

Note that while we discuss grantology today, we should distinguish *grantology* from *grantsmanship*, two seemingly similar terms. There exists an extensive literature on grantsmanship.[54] For example, Web of Science collected sixty-five articles and eight reviews on grantsmanship as of 2023. Grantsmanship focuses on skills of grant *writing* or on the *craft* of getting grants and is essentially about the practical skills of getting grants. In contrast, grantology is about the entire science of managing and pursuing grants as a field. It certainly includes grantsmanship as its applied contents. However, it also involves various empirical, theoretical, and methodological concepts. In short, grantology is larger than but not equal to grantsmanship.

4.2 Journalology

Having discussed grantology, it will be interesting to now examine journalology and highlight the similarities and differences between these two sister fields in metascience.

Journals

In January of 1665, the *Journal des Sçavans* ("Journal of the Learned" in English) was published in Paris by a French writer and lawyer, Denis de Sallo. After two months, in March of 1665, the *Philosophical Transactions* was published in London by the Royal Society of London, the United

---

[54] Roberts, J. A., & Kaack, M. B. (2000). Grantsmanship. *Journal of Urology*, *163*(5), 1544–8; Baker, K. (1975). A new grantsmanship. *The American Sociologist*, *10*, 206–19; Lorenz, P. H. (1982). The politics of fund raising through grantsmanship in the human services. *Public Administration Review*, *42*(3), 244–51; Falk, A. (2011). Teaching grantsmanship in a nonprofit leadership class. *Journal of the Grant Professionals Association*, *9*(1), 78–87; Sridhar, A. (2009). Grantsmanship and the university: Five strategies for grant professionals working with faculty. *Journal of the American Association of Grant Professionals*, *7*(1), 9–15; Gabbi, C., & Sauer, R. M. (2019). Grantsmanship writing tips: Background, hypothesis and aims. *European Journal of Internal Medicine*, *61*, 25–8.

Kingdom's National Academy of Sciences and the oldest continuously existing scientific academy in the world.[55] These two journals are generally considered to be the first scholarly journals in the history of journal publication. In other words, the emergence of scholarly journals in France and the United Kingdom is about 166 years earlier than the emergence of grant systems in France and the United Kingdom.

Journal Publication Research
Along with the journal publication practice, researchers started to examine the publication process itself as a subject of research in order to improve scientific communication. One of the earliest influential articles in journal publication is Eugene Garfield's 1964 classic article published in *Science*.[56] In this article, Garfield presented the concept of the "Science Citation Index," the first citation index as an *article*-level metric for articles published in academic journals. This eventually led to the concept of "impact factor," as a *journal*-level metric, which is frequently used as a proxy for the relative importance of a journal within a field. Garfield's work laid the foundation for the use of citation analysis to quantitatively assess the impact and importance of scientific articles. If we consider the Garfield 1964 paper as a formal starting point of journal article research, the grant research publication started eighteen years earlier than the journal publication research.

Journalology
In the spring of 1989, Stephen Lock or Stephen Penford Lock, the veteran editor of the *British Medical Journal* (1975–90), presented at the thirty-third annual meeting of the Council of Biology Editors and used the term journalology in his title for the first time. He later published the talk as an essay.[57] Eugene Garfield commented that the term "journalology" coined by Lock is an appropriate neologism for what became a widespread human activity of journal publication.[58]

---

[55] McCutcheon, R. P. (1924). The "Journal Des Scavans" and the "Philosophical Transactions of the Royal Society." *Studies in Philology*, *21*(4), 626–8; Brown, H. (1972). History and the learned journal. *Journal of the History of Ideas*, *33*(3): 365–78.
[56] Garfield, E. (1964). "Science Citation Index" – a new dimension in indexing. *Science*, *144*(3619), 649–54. Gs819.
[57] Lock, S. P. (1989). Journalology: Are the quotes needed. *CBE Views*, *12*(4), 57–9. Gs45.
[58] Garfield, E. (1990). Essays of an information scientist: Journalology, keywords plus, and other essays. *Current Contents*, *31*(3), 3–17; Asgarov, F. (2022). Journalology – academic publishing process. *Problems of Information Technology*, *13*(1), 43–8; Garfield, E. (2006). The history and meaning of the journal impact factor. *JAMA*, *295*(1), 90–3.

A few months later, in May 1989, while Lock was one of five key advisory board members, the first International Congress on Peer Review in Biomedical Publication was held in Chicago, with about 300 attendees and fifty talk abstracts presented by editors and researchers. It is widely accepted that this 1989 meeting marked the launch of journalology as a new field of research.[59] Since 1989, every four years, the Congress have been running for nine times and the tenth Congress will be held in 2025.[60] The latest ninth Congress was held in 2022, in Chicago, even with the impact of COVID-19, with 511 participants from thirty-seven countries, fifty-five podium speakers, fifty Plenary Session reports of original research, eighty-six Poster Session reports of original research, 125 poster presenters of sponsors and exhibitors and thirty-nine Virtual Poster Session reports of original research.

Besides the Congress, continuous community-scale research efforts in journalology have been increasing. A series of articles was published to study journalology since 1990.[61] In 2014, the Meta-Research Innovation Center was launched at Stanford University.[62] Next year, the Centre for Journalology as the first of its kind was launched at the Ottawa Hospital Research Institute.[63]

Comparing the emerging history of grantology and journalology discussed briefly above, we can see that, overall, these two fields are still very young, being only about thirty years old, compared to, say, classic physics (e.g. Isaac Newton's *Philosophiæ Naturalis Principia Mathematica* was published in 1687, about 337 years ago) or modern biology (e.g. Gregor Mendel's work was published in 1865, about 159 years ago). They will

---

[59] Burnham, J. C. (1990). The evolution of editorial peer review. *JAMA*, 263(10), 1323–9.
[60] International Congress on Peer Review and Scientific Publication website, available at: https://peerreviewcongress.org/.
[61] E.g. Lock, S. (1992). Journalology: Evolution of medical journals and some current problems. *Journal of Internal Medicine*, 232(3), 199–205; Boulos, M. N. K. (2005). On geography and medical journalology: A study of the geographical distribution of articles published in a leading medical informatics journal between 1999 and 2004. *International Journal of Health Geographics*, 4(1), 7; Kumar, R. (2013). The Science hoax: Poor journalology reflects poor training in peer review. *British Medical Journal*, 347, article f7465; Galipeau, J., Moher, D., Campbell, C., Hendry, P., Cameron, D. W., Palepu, A. et al. (2015). A systematic review highlights a knowledge gap regarding the effectiveness of health-related training programs in journalology. *Journal of Clinical Epidemiology*, 68(3), 257–65; Kumar, R. (2015). Journalology and authors: Bridging the divide. *Indian Journal of Urology*, 31(3), 163–4; Moher, D., & Ravaud, P. (2016). Increasing the evidence base in journalology: Creating an international best practice journal research network. *BMC Medicine*, 14, 1–4; Rennie, D., & Flanagin, A. (2018). Three decades of peer review congresses. *JAMA*, 319(4), 350–3; Krishan, K., & Kanchan, T. (2019). Open centres for journalology in universities and institutions. *Science & Engineering Ethics*, 25(4), 1259–60; Asgarov, F. S. (2022). Journalology – academic publishing process. *Problems of Information Technology*, 13(1), 49–55.
[62] METRICS website, available at: https://metrics.stanford.edu/.
[63] The Ottawa Hospital Research Institute website, available at: https://ohri.ca/journalology/.

continue to grow rapidly from their intellectual childhood to adolescence in the next thirty years or so. Here, grantology (about seven years old) appears to be younger than journalology (about twenty-three years old), like two brothers or sisters in the family of metascience.

5 Action Suggestions: Identifying and Studying Journal Articles on Grantology

5.1 Understand Five Features of Grantology

First, it is useful to understand grantology as an **emerging** field rather than an "intellectual baby" that has not yet been born. While formal grant systems have about 200 years of history since 1831 and grant research efforts have about eighty years of history since 1946, grantology as a branch of metascience has about forty years of history since 1990. It is important to have a sense of history when considering grantology.

Second, it is important to understand that grantology is an **interdisciplinary** field rather than a narrow area within a single discipline. Merton's 1968 paper on the Matthew effect is a good example of research from the sociology of science that has significantly contributed to grantology. We should be open-minded to pay attention to research in different fields, including sociology, economics, and other classic fields that have a long history of successful productive research, but also from scientometics, metascience, and other young fields that are rapidly developing and generating important findings.

Third, it is important to understand that grantology is an **applied** field rather than a theoretical field. Grantology needs to address a series of real-life challenges empirically, theoretically, methodologically, and practically rather than just focus on a few theoretical questions. Jeffrey Martin's 2020 article illustrates various existing practical challenges in grantology as an applied field. Researchers in grantology should continue to address them to make daily grant practice to research-based best practice.

Fourth, it is important to understand that grantology is a **subfield** of metascience. As presented by Munafo et al.'s 2017 article, grantology is a subfield largely residing within metascience, while metascience has grown rapidly in the past ten years. Just like self-concept development to better understand ourselves is important in human development, science should not only advance scientific knowledge in different fields, but also develop scientific knowledge about itself. Both grantology and journalology can and should help us understand science as a social system.

Last, it is important to understand that grantology focuses on the grant **process** that is both dynamic and complex rather than a simple concept. As shown in Figure 2.4, a basic grant process involves multiple basic elements, multiple basic steps, multiple basic cycles, and two channels. This basic process can be expanded to a more complex one, including multiple factors, multiple contexts, and multiple systems. The dynamic and complex grant process is the very target of research in grantology.

5.2 Locating and Analyzing Five Journal Articles on Grantology

As a practice to enhance our understanding of the five features of grantology, we could take the following actions. First, search several popular databases (e.g. the free-use ones, such as Google Scholar and PubMed, or the prescription-required ones, such as Web of Science and PsycINFO) by using keywords such as grant, funding, and grantsmanship. Second, identify five journal articles relating to both your research interest or home discipline and the five features of grantology. Third, analyze how these articles will help us understand the five key features of grantology and will potentially make scientific contributions to grantology. These articles could be empirical, theoretical, methodological, or review-based.

PART II
Grant Pursuit

CHAPTER 3

Grant Writers

Outline

1 Intuitive Knowledge: Who Is a Grant Writer?   82
   1.1 Responses from New Grant Writers   82
   1.2 Understand the Broad Diversity of Grant Writers   82
2 Real-Life Cases: From High School Students to Superstars   83
   2.1 Alyssa: A High School Student as a Quasi Grant Writer   83
   2.2 Madison: An Undergraduate Student as a Grant Writer   84
   2.3 Final Papers at Brown: Graduate Students as Grant Writers   85
   2.4 Sara: A Postdoc Grant Writer   86
   2.5 Dr. Qin Xu: An Outstanding Early Career Grant Writer   87
   2.6 Dr. Jill Rafael-Fortney: A Challenged Mid-Career Grant Writer   89
   2.7 Dr. Katalin Karikó: The Nobel Prize Winner as a Grant Writer   89
   2.8 Dr. Robert Sternberg: A Superstar Grant Writer with a Humble Beginning   90
   2.9 Dr. Emilie Rissman: A Professional Grant Writer in Medicine   91
   2.10 Lauren Steiner: A National Leader of Grant Writers   92
3 Scientific Knowledge: From Young Grant Writers to Super Grant Writers   93
   3.1 Kulage *et al.* (2015): Grant Writers in the Pre-Award Phase   93
   3.2 Enger & Castellacci (2016): Three Types of Institutional Grant Writers   97
   3.3 Chapman & McCauley (1993): Graduate Students as Grant Writers   99
   3.4 Wang, Jones, & Wang (2019): Early-Career Grant Writers   101
   3.5 Nguyen *et al.* (2022): Super Principal Investigators as Grant Writers   104
   3.6 Witteman, Hendricks, Straus, & Tannenbaum (2019): Grant Writers and Gender   107
   3.7 Ginther *et al.* (2011): Grant Writers and Race   110
   3.8 Pinto & Huizinga (2018): External Factors and Individual Factors of Grant Writers   113

4	Grantology vs. Journalology: Grant Writers vs. Article Writers	115
	4.1 Grant Writers	116
	4.2 Article Writers	116
5	Action Suggestions: Studying and Developing Profiles of Grant Writers	118
	5.1 Understanding Five Aspects of Grant Writers	118
	5.2 Studying at Least 100 Grant Writers and Drafting Your Grant CV	119

1 Intuitive Knowledge: Who Is a Grant Writer?

1.1 Responses from New Grant Writers

Who is a grant writer? This question appears to be simple and straightforward. Below are quick and brief responses from four new grant writers.

- Response 1: A person who writes and submits grant applications to the funders.
- Response 2: A person who writes to achieve available funding opportunities for a project or organization by writing grant proposals.
- Response 3: A person who writes a research or program proposal and tries to obtain funding or other resources for contributing to the world. The grant writers that first come to my mind are my department professors whom I often meet around.
- Response 4: A pioneer who charts his own area or defines his research objectives and receives funding in the land of scientific discoveries.

1.2 Understand the Broad Diversity of Grant Writers

It is useful to briefly analyze these responses. The first response focused on writing and submitting grant applications. The second response focused on writing proposals and receiving grants. The third response focused on writing proposals and attempting to receive grants, with professors in the department as examples of grant writers. The last response focused on scientists who pioneer uncharted areas of research and receive grants to make discoveries. Are these responses correct?

On the one hand, these brief, simple, and straightforward responses are correct because they all touch on two core elements of being a grant writer: writing proposals and seeking grants. These intuitive and authentic responses truly represent the initial knowledge of grant writers among these new grant writers.

On the other hand, these succinct and intuitive responses are not entirely correct because they reveal the existence of several popular myths and misconceptions about grant writers. Among the most popular ones are that a grant writer should: (1) be an **established** mature researcher rather than an early-career researcher such as an undergraduate or graduate student; (2) **successfully** get a grant rather than just write or submit a grant application; and (3) be a researcher or a scientist rather than a **non-science** or non-research professional (e.g. grant writers for local communities as non-profit organizations).

The main purpose of discussing grant writers in this chapter is not to determine which response is correct or wrong. Instead, the chapter is intended to demonstrate the diversity and complexity of grant writers and to motivate new grant writers to pursue grants bravely, as the title of this book suggests. Let us first examine a few real-life cases, then study the scientific literature on grant writers and compare grant writers to article writers, and finally learn a few practical suggestions for becoming grant writers and starting to pursue grants.

2 Real-Life Cases: From High School Students to Superstars

2.1 Alyssa: A High School Student as a Quasi Grant Writer

Alyssa, a rising junior high school student, is interested in learning more about brain diseases. In 2023, she completed and submitted her application for The Explorations in Neuroscience Summer Camp and then applied for The Explorations in Neuroscience Research Internship Program. To apply, she needed to complete a series of tasks, including listing what science courses she has taken, obtaining a letter from her guidance counselor, confirming that she obtained parental permission, presenting her career goals, and writing a 250-word essay on why she wanted to apply for this camp, what she wanted to gain from this experience, and why neuroscience was important to her personally. Her efforts paid off. She was accepted to both the summer camp and the internship program. She had an extremely useful experience that summer.

The summer camp and the internship program are based on an NIH R25 grant (Project # 5R25NS120282-04).[1] The R25 grant is the NIH

---

[1] Explorations in neuroscience research for high school students, *NIH*, available at: https://reporter.nih.gov/search/vR3aMzfmGUOeg2twDby4YA/project-details/10748356.

Research Education Program that supports creative educational activities with a primary focus on research experiences for high school students, undergraduate students, and/or science teachers during the summer. The grant recipient is Dr. Candice Askwith in the School of Medicine at Ohio State University. She has successfully received this grant for four consecutive years since 2021.[2] Specifically, The Explorations in Neuroscience Summer Camp runs for seven days in June, designed for rising junior and senior high school students who have an interest in learning more about the brain and spinal cord in health and disease. Following the camp, there is a seven-week paid research internship program opportunity in June and July to learn hands-on research in Neuroscience, Neurological Injury, or Neurodegeneration and to develop skills to be able to succeed in an undergraduate career in Neuroscience.

In this case, Alyssa is not only a successful summer camp applicant, but also a successful "quasi" grant writer. This is because she successfully went through the entire application process for the summer camp and the internship program that is related to a formal NIH training grant. During this competitive process, she had to think, plan, draft, write, revise, submit various paperwork, and develop various basic skills that are required for a grant writer. There are various summer camps, internship programs, and research scholarships for high-schoolers like Alyssa in STEM, biology, and computer AI. Applying for these opportunities even at the K-12 level is a wonderful way to become a grant writer at the undergraduate, graduate, and postdoc stages, and a successful grant writer in future professional careers.

Compared with Alyssa, Dr. Askwith is an experienced grant writer professionally. She has been a successful R25 grant writer for four years. She also received multiple grants from NIH such as P30 NS045758, R01 NS112805, R21 MH107021, and R21 H121744.

2.2 Madison: An Undergraduate Student as a Grant Writer

On April 13, 2023, Madison Tuohy, a senior majoring in geology at Binghamton University, was awarded the National Science Foundation Graduate Research Fellowships Program (GRFP) for her project in humanitarian demining geophysics. She will use aerial vehicles with hyperspectral

---

[2] New R25 grant shapes the future of neuroscience research with high school students, *The Ohio State University College of Medicine*, available at: https://medicine.osu.edu/news/r25-grant-shapes-future-of-neuroscience-research.

imaging for detecting landmines. With this fellowship funding, Madison will pursue this important research in her upcoming PhD program.[3]

The GRFP is one of the most esteemed and most competitive fellowships that an American undergraduate student or graduate student can receive for their research-based master's and doctoral degrees in the natural, social, and engineering sciences at US institutions. In 2015, 16,500 students applied and only 2,000 received the award, with a 7.8 percent success rate. Many National Science Foundation (NSF) GRFP alumni became Nobel laureates and members of the National Academy of Sciences – for example, Eric Cornell, Steven Chu, Jennifer Richeson, Sergey Brin, Amy Mainzer, Steven Levitt, and Burton Richter. As of 2024, the fellowship provides an honorarium of $16,000 to be placed towards the cost of tuition and fees at the university attended by the fellow and awards the student directly with an annual $37,000 stipend for three years.

Here, Madison is an undergraduate grant writer because she has successfully applied for and received this grant through a rigorous expert review procedure in a nationwide competition. She had to be first qualified for the fellowship requirements, then prepared all the application materials, including the purpose statement, the research proposal, the personal biography, and the letter of recommendation, and then went through the review process headed up by a panel of scientists, and eventually received the funding from the NSF. She went through almost all the key elements of a competitive grant process. However, she is not yet an independent grant writer because she is not yet a well-established scientist and this grant is a training grant rather than an independent research grant. It should be noted that education and training grants are always an important part of grant programs in the NSF, the NIH, and many public and private foundations. The GRFP is a competitive training grant awarded by the NSF and is significantly different from various university scholarships and assistantships for which an undergraduate student can apply.

2.3 Final Papers at Brown: Graduate Students as Grant Writers

More than ten years ago, by chance, I learned from a course syllabus online that a final term paper for a graduate student class at Brown University is

---

[3] NSF 101: High school students, undergraduate and post-baccalaureate scholar funding opportunities, *US National Science Foundation*, available at: https://new.nsf.gov/science-matters/nsf-101-high-school-students-undergraduate-post.

to write a grant proposal for the NSF GRFP. I was deeply impressed by the design of the final term paper and have never forgotten it.

This final term paper design is innovative and inspiring for two reasons. First, the design is authentic because it was based on the well-known, real-life NSF followership program. Second, the design is innovative because it asks graduate students to write a grant proposal to an NSF grant program as a term paper.

Now, should these students be called grant writers? Are they experienced enough in both research and grant experience to be called grant writers? Is a term too short for them to write, submit, or receive their grant proposals? If each of them did write an NSF grant proposal as their final papers for this class, they should be considered grant writers, regardless of whether they would submit the application or receive the grant.

2.4 Sara: A Postdoc Grant Writer

In one of the well-attended research group meetings, Sara, a recent doctoral graduate, shared with us great news that she had just received an NIH grant. We enthusiastically congratulated her for this impressive achievement. We then learned more about the NIH grant she received.

First, the grant she successfully received is a **K99/R00** grant. K99/R00 is called the Pathway to Independence Award. It is the NIH's high-level research training award. It is higher than the F series (e.g., F30, F31, F320), which is mainly for predoctoral students) and the K series (e.g., K01, K22, K25), which is mainly for postdoctoral students. It is a bridge award for a postdoc to transfer to a faculty position. It is the last award before a researcher becomes an independent investigator who will need to write an R01 application.[4] In short, besides research grants, like many other funders, the NIH has extensive training grants. Usually, based on the NIH's approach, if a researcher receives a doctoral degree after ten years, he or she will be considered an independent investigator. Before this point, a researcher needs to receive training at high school, undergraduate, predoctoral, and postdoctoral levels. The NIH has a series of training grants in place.

Specifically, the NIH Pathway to Independence Award (K99/R00) is for promising postdoctoral scientists seeking to complete needed **mentored** research career development that will facilitate their timely transition to an

---

[4] Choose an award by career stage, *NIH*, available at: www.niaid.nih.gov/grants-contracts/choose-award-career-stage.

independent tenure-track faculty position. The K99/Roo Award consists of two phases: the Mentored Phase (K99) supports one to two years of mentored postdoctoral research training; the Independent Research Phase (Roo) is a research project grant for up to three years. It is expected that Pathway to Independence Award recipients will be positioned to apply for independent NIH Research Project Grant support **during** or following the completion of the Independent Research Phase (Roo) period. The funding is relatively generous. The total cost per year for the initial mentored phase for K99 may not exceed $125,000. Salary is limited to $75,000, plus applicable fringe benefits and up to $25,000 for research support costs for a twelve-month budget period. The total cost for the independent investigator phase for Roo may not exceed $249,000 per year. This amount includes direct costs (personnel, research, and other expenses) and applicable facilities and administrative costs.

Sara is certainly a grant writer at the postdoc level. To receive the grant, she needs to submit a grant proposal with key materials such as a research plan and project budget. She needs to submit two unique materials: (1) The Candidate Section includes the Candidate's Background, Career Goals and Objectives, and Candidate's Plan for Career Development/Training Activities During the Award Period. (2) The Mentor Section includes Plans and Statements of Mentor and Co-mentor(s) for K99, Letters of Support from Collaborators, Contributors, and/or Consultants for Roo.[5] After submission, panel review and advisory council approval are needed. The success rate for the K99/Roo from different institutes varied, ranging between 16 and 33 percent in 2023. Through these rigorous processes, Sara has certainly made a very promising to being an excellent independent researcher in her career, as presented by a recent study on the effectiveness of the NIH K99/Roo grant.[6]

2.5 Dr. Qin Xu: An Outstanding Early Career Grant Writer

On May 17, 2004, I received an email regarding a virtual workshop on *A Causal Investigation of Heterogeneity in Mediation Mechanisms* taught by Dr. Qin Xu[7] during the AERA annual conference. I am interested in

---

[5] See the detailed application process on the NIH grants and funding webpage, available at: https://grants.nih.gov/grants/guide/pa-files/PA-24-194.html.
[6] Joël, B. (2023). Analysis of NIH K99/Roo awards and the career progression of awardees. *eLife*, 12. Gso.
[7] Xu Qin, *University of Pittsburgh*, available at: www.education.pitt.edu/faculty/directory/xu-qin/.

causality methodology and heterogeneity analysis, so I visited her website and quickly read her CV.

Her CV shows that she received her doctoral degree from the University of Chicago in 2018 and is currently an Assistant Professor at the University of Pittsburgh. I was immediately impressed by the details of her grant portfolio. As a junior faculty in statistics, she had already secured a total of ten grants: five as principal investigator (PI), two as Co-PI, and three as co-investigator (Co-I). Public and private funding agencies supporting her research include the NSF, the NIH, the IES, Spender, and Pitt Momentum Funds. The average grant amount is $600,000. In addition, she has received six Fellowships (e.g. National Academy of Education/Spencer Postdoctoral Fellowship, National Academy of Education/Spencer Dissertation Fellowship, and Social Science Division Fellowship of the University of Chicago) and fourteen Awards (e.g. Outstanding Dissertation Award of American Educational Research Association, Advanced Graduate Council Travel Fund Grant of the University of Chicago, National Award for the College Student Innovative Project of Ministry of Education of China) during her education.

Clearly, as shown in her CV, Dr. Qin Xu is an early-career grant writer with a strong grant portfolio. First, she has successfully received a series of important research grants from public and private funders. She plays various roles in these grants, as PI, who fully leads the project's scientific development and execution, Co-PI, who works under the PI in the project's scientific development or execution, and Co-I, who is a member of a grant project. Note that she did not list her unsuccessful grant applicants. (Often, scholars might list unfunded grants in their CVs as important evidence of grant experiences for tenure and promotion.) Second, she has also received a series of fellowships and awards since her undergraduate program. This means that she started competitive or non-competitive applications quite a bit earlier than when she began to pursue formal competitive research grants. We should never underestimate the usefulness of successful and unsuccessful experiences of participating in fellowship or scholarship applications in K-12 and undergraduate programs.

This case also shows the usefulness of studying the grant portfolio of a scholar to help us become effective and efficient grant writers. There are usually three useful ways to learn about grant writers: the grant section of a CV, a bio-sketch section of a grant proposal from grant databases, and the acknowledgment section of a journal article.

2 Real-Life Cases: High School Students & Superstars

2.6 Dr. Jill Rafael-Fortney: A Challenged Mid-Career Grant Writer

Dr. Jill Rafael-Fortney received her PhD at the University of Michigan and completed a postdoc at the University of Oxford.[8] Currently, she is a Professor of Physiology and Cell Biology in the College of Medicine at Ohio State University and the Director of the Center for Muscle Health & Neuromuscular Disorders and Cardiac Predoctoral T32 Training Program.

Back in 2008, however, at the age of nearly 40, she experienced a huge challenge in securing grants to keep her lab running. At that time, she had tried and failed to renew an R01 grant from the NIH that supported her work on mouse models of muscular dystrophy. She had also tried and failed to obtain a new R01 grant to study a genetic abnormality for human heart failure. With the unexpected rejection of her two R01 grants, in an email to inform her department chair about the bad news, she wrote in an almost hopeless tone: "My career in research seems to be over. It is all I ever planned to do from the age of six, so I don't really have another well-thought-out plan."

Dr. Jill Rafael-Fortney is a grant writer with a mid-career challenge. Based on the existing data, the NIH doubled its budget from 1998 to 2003, and then substantially reduced the success rates of R01-equivalent and research project grants around 2008.[9] This was the year when Dr. Rafael-Fortney experienced repeated rejections of grant proposals, like many other unfunded applicants.

2.7 Dr. Katalin Karikó: The Nobel Prize Winner as a Grant Writer

On October 1, 2023, Katalin Karikó,[10] along with Drew Weissman, received the Nobel Prize in Physiology/Medicine for her scientific groundwork on the mechanisms of the COVID mRNA vaccine. This research led to the successful development of the Pfizer and Moderna vaccines, the two most effective vaccines in the United States.

Katalin Karikó is a biochemist who specializes in ribonucleic acid (RNA), particularly in vitro-transcribed messenger RNA (mRNA). She was

---

[8] Wadman, M. (2009). Research funding: Closing arguments. *Nature*, 457(7230), 650–5. Gs13.
[9] Berg, J. M. (2020). Modeling research project grant success rates from NIH appropriation history: Extension to 2020. *bioRxiv*, 2020–11. Gs1; Modeling success rates from appropriations histories, *Science*, available at: www.science.org/content/blog-post/modeling-success-rates-appropriations-histories; Success rates: R01-equivalent and research project grants, *NIH*, available at: https://report.nih.gov/nihdatabook/category/10.
[10] Katalin Karikó, *Wikipedia*, available at: https://en.wikipedia.org/wiki/Katalin_Karikó.

initially an Assistant Professor at the University of Pennsylvania. However, during that time, the scientific community was skeptical of her innovative research, and grant reviewers were not impressed by her proposed projects. Her multiple grant proposals have been repeatedly rejected, and she failed to receive research grants for her lab. As a result, she was demoted to Adjunct Professor in 1995 and was then asked to retire from the University of Pennsylvania.

Certainly, Katalin is a grant writer because she has written, submitted, and received grants from various funding agencies many times. But she was not always a particularly successful grant writer because she had been suffering for many long years from being unable to secure research grants.

In the history of science, like Katalin, many well-established researchers are not always successful grant writers, and many successful grant writers are often not exceptional researchers. In some cases, scholars do not rely on grants for their significant artistic and scientific work. When we discuss grants or grant writers in grantology, it is important to remember that, despite grant funding being critical to support research, research is not equal to grants, and scientists are not equal to grant writers, let alone grant winners.

2.8 Dr. Robert Sternberg: A Superstar Grant Writer with a Humble Beginning

Robert Sternberg[11] is currently a Professor of Psychology at Cornell University and is one of the most productive psychologists in the world, with a h-index of 238 based on Google Scholar. After receiving his PhD at Stanford, he was on the faculty of Yale University from 1975 to 2005, directing the worldwide-known Center for the Psychology of Abilities, Competencies and Expertise. In the first paragraph of the first chapter of his edited book titled *Writing Successful Grant Proposals*, he briefly summarizes his experience of pursuing grants, with a tone of humor:

> When I started as an assistant professor in 1975, I was offered $5,000 in seed money from my university to start up my research. I had no extramural (outside) funding. A quarter century later, I had more than $6 million in extramural funding. But, there were some years that I seemed to have the golden touch in getting grants and other years in which everything I touched seems to turn to lead. Oddly, I never could predict which grant proposals would get funded, even after years of experience writing proposals.[12]

---

[11] Robert Sternberg, *Cornell University*, available at: https://psychology.cornell.edu/robert-sternberg.
[12] Sternberg, R. J. (ed.) (2013). *Writing Successful Grant Proposals from the Top Down and Bottom Up*. Sage Publications, p. 3.

Robert Sternberg is a grant writer. When he started teaching at Yale, he was an early-career grant writer, just with the $5,000 seed money. After twenty-five years or so, as the director of the Center, he became an outstanding grant writer, with multi-million extramural grants from various public and private funders. Once I met with him at Yale during a conference and asked him about his grants. He, as one of the most successful grant winners in psychology, told me that his success rate is about 30 percent. Here, we can call him a grant-writing superstar in psychology as there are always a few of these in any given field; we can see a growth curve from a new grant writer to an established grant writer in three decades; and we can even learn his success rate of 30 percent for a grant writing superstar.

2.9 Dr. Emilie Rissman: A Professional Grant Writer in Medicine

My husband and I are both scientists. We are PhDs working in a medical school. The university covers some of our salaries, paying us to perform tasks such as teaching graduate courses, the occasional lecture to medical students, and serving on various committees. However, our major role is to conduct research, and to perform this function, which is of course the reason we selected this career many years ago, we must write grants, many many grants.

This is a quotation from the beginning of a chapter written by Dr. Emilie Rissman[13] for the book edited by Sternberg in 2013. It vividly describes her professional grant writing experience as a medical scientist. Dr. Emilie Rissman is currently a Professor and the founding Chair of the Department of Biological Sciences at North Carolina State University. Before 2014, Rissman was a Professor of Biochemistry and Molecular Genetics at the School of Medicine at the University of Virginia. She has received nearly twenty major grants from the NIH covering thirty-six years between 1988 and 2024, and has published around 250 articles with 13,267 citations.

In this case, Dr. Emilie Rissman and her husband are another type of grant writer. They are not only grant writers, but also grant winners. They are professional grant writers in biomedicine. They "must write grants, many many grants" to keep their labs running and to pay themselves and their lab workers. This is quite common among scientists in the School of Medicine. Their job determined that writing and securing grants were a major part of their day-to-day job.

---

[13] Rissman, E. F. (2013). Guide to professional begging: Writing successful grant proposals from the top down and bottom up. In R. J. Sternberg (ed.), *Writing Successful Grant Proposals from the Top Down and Bottom Up* (pp. 25–36). SAGE Publications.

2.10 Lauren Steiner: A National Leader of Grant Writers

Lauren Steiner graduated with a degree in JD from Cleveland State University in 2001. She then worked as Manager of Foundation and Donor Relations in Achievement Centers for Children for nearly four years. In 2007, she founded Grants Plus[14] to help non-profits around the country raise grant funding and grow grant revenues strategically. Note that a non-profit organization might have a wide-ranging team to write grant proposals, including grant writers, development coordinators, fundraising directors, executive directors, board members, and other key stakeholders, such as staff and community members. To date, Grants Plus has secured more than $250 million in public and private grants for community-serving agencies, health organizations, schools and colleges, cultural institutions, and other entities nationwide. It has grown into a firm with more than thirty of the most experienced and talented grants professionals in the fundraising industry. As the founder and President of Grants Plus as well as the past President of the Grant Professionals Association Ohio-Northern Chapter, Lauren is committed to developing the field of grant-seeking by mentoring new professionals, championing equity in the sector, and speaking on best practices.

In this case, Lauren Steiner represents another type of grant writer. She has a professional career as a grant writer. She leads a successful firm of over thirty writing professionals. She has expertise in grant-seeking, grant writing, and fundraising for non-profit organizations.

To sum up, from the above ten cases, we can observe the following: (1) In the real world, grant writers could have diverse professional **titles**: Principal Investigator (PI), Program Director (PD), Co-PI, Multiple PI, Co-investigator (Co-I), Application PI, Non-PI Eligible Researcher, young researchers requiring faculty sponsors, senior personnel, grant administrators, university sponsor officers, grant writing professionals, or lead grant writing professionals. (2) Grant writers can also be at different education and career **stages**: high school students, undergraduate students, graduate students, postdoc researchers, early-career grant writers, mid-career grant writers, and senior grant writers. (3) In a specific grant cycle (Pre-Award, Award, and Post-Award), grant writers can perform different **tasks**: developing an idea for a grant, searching existing grants, writing grant proposals, submitting proposals to grant programs, resubmitting grant proposals, receiving funds, and completing funded projects. (4) In the real world,

---

[14] Grants Plus website, available at: https://grantsplus.com/.

there are also many unsuccessful grant writers, at one point in or throughout their entire careers. We even have non-grant writers as a special group of grant writers (see section 3.2 for details), and some researchers have never applied for or received internal or external grants.

3 Scientific Knowledge: From Young Grant Writers to Super Grant Writers

As shown in the cases presented above, existing literature reveals various aspects of the current scientific knowledge about grant writers. It shows that the concept of "grant writers" is complex, and we should understand this concept much more deeply and broadly in order to guide our grant writing practice successfully and enable us to become competent grant writers.

3.1 Kulage et al. (2015): Grant Writers in the Pre-Award Phase

It is generally acceptable to define grant writers as researchers who write grant proposals. However, this definition or conceptual understanding of grant writers is often too narrow as a stereotype and would misguide grant pursuit, especially for new grant writers. The existing literature indicates that we need to consider grant writers at different phases of a grant cycle, for example, planning, writing, submitting, resubmitting, winning, and implementing a grant. Let us now study one article that examines grant writers who are at the proposal preparation phase and focuses on the time these grant writers spent to submit their proposal.[15]

Overview
This article is one of the first and best descriptions of hours spent, costs incurred, and tasks performed by grant writers during the Pre-Award phase, but not at the Award or Post-award phases. It reports an empirical study, using a time-tracking protocol and a grant cost analysis to estimate the time and cost of preparing grants among five grant writers, three research administrators (RAs), and one grant editor. It has been cited twenty-three times as of 2023, based on Google Scholar. This citation is relatively high for an article published in a specific nurse-focused journal in a specific field of nursing research.

---

[15] Kulage, K. M., Schnall, R., Hickey, K. T., Travers, J., Zezulinski, K., Torres, F. *et al.* (2015). Time and costs of preparing and submitting an NIH grant application at a school of nursing. *Nursing Outlook*, *63*(6), 639–49. Gs23.

The article has eight authors, a research team mixed with senior and junior researchers in the various fields of nursing research, informatics, clinical management, and long-term care. They are all from Columbia University, either from the School of Nursing or the School of Public Health. The first and corresponding author is Kristine Kulage. She is the Director of Research and Scholarly Development. One of her research areas is grant writing and manuscript writing. She has published multiple articles on grants and nursing education.[16] She runs the Doctoral Student Federal Grant Writing Workshop, a known one-on-one grant writing mentorship program that we will study in Chapter 10.[17] Her h-index is 9.

It should be noted that Columbia University School of Nursing is ranked #1 among all US schools of nursing for total research funding received from the NIH in the fiscal year 2022, a rise from the school's #4 ranking in the three previous years of 2019, 2020, and 2021. In 2022, the school was awarded thirty-six NIH grants totaling over $18.7 million. The school's strong practice-based research in grantology could be a contributing factor to its strong grant funding achievements. Thus, researchers in grantology should follow Kristine and her colleagues at Columbia University to study their work on grant writing practice.

The article was published in *Nursing Outlook*, a bimonthly journal publishing innovative ideas for nursing leaders and examining current issues in nursing practice, education, and research. As the official journal of the American Academy of Nursing and the Council for the Advancement of Nursing Science, it aims to impact policy through nursing leadership, innovation, and science. Its impact factor is 3.3 in 2022. This journal has often published articles on grant research in nursing, like the one we are discussing here.

---

[16] Kulage, K. M., Stone, P. W., & Smaldone, A. M. (2020). Supporting dissertation work through a nursing PhD program federal grant writing workshop. *Journal of Professional Nursing, 36*(2), 29–38; Kulage, K. M., & Larson, E. L. (2018). Intramural pilot funding and internal grant reviews increase research capacity at a school of nursing. *Nursing Outlook, 66*(1), 11–17; Bevil, C. A., Cohen, M. Z., Sherlock, J. R., Yoon, S. L., & Yucha, C. B. (2012). Research support in doctoral-granting schools of nursing: A decade later. *Journal of Professional Nursing, 28*(2), 74–81; Gillespie, G. L., Vallerand, A. H., & Fairman, J. (2023). Characteristics of faculty mentoring in the Robert Wood Johnson Foundation Future of Nursing Scholars Program. *Nursing Outlook, 71*(2), article 101912; Munro, S., Hendrix, C. C., Cowan, L. J., Battaglia, C., Wilder, V. D., Bormann, J. E. *et al.* (2019). Research productivity following nursing research initiative grants. *Nursing Outlook, 67*(1), 6–12; Cepanec, D., Humphries, A., Rieger, K. L., Marshall, S., Londono, Y., & Clarke, T. (2016). Building graduate student capacity as future researchers through a research and training award program. *Journal of Nursing Education, 55*(5), 284–7.

[17] Kulage, K. M., Corwin, E. J., Liu, J., Schnall, R., Smaldone, A., Soled, K. R. *et al.* (2022). A 10-year examination of a one-on-one grant writing partnership for nursing pre-and post-doctoral trainees. *Nursing Outlook, 70*(3), 465–77.

Highlights

The article has five typical sections of an empirical study: Introduction, Materials and Methods, Results, Discussion, and Conclusion and Recommendations. From the perspective of grant writers, we can highlight the following points from the article.

First, the article shows a specific **institutional context** of a grant writer in the real world. Most grant writers are required to submit a grant proposal to a public or private funding agency through an institution rather than by an individual. This article briefly describes how a grant office of a school of nursing works. Specifically, it reports a funding portfolio in a large research-intensive academic health center in the School of Nursing at Columbia University. Using the fiscal year of 2015 as an example, the grant office had grant budgets totaling more than $5 million; managed sixty-four active grants in research, training, and career development; sponsored fifty-three applications; and had twenty faculty members actively seeking research funding, as well as ten doctoral students submitting federal grant applications to support their dissertation research.

Second, the article describes four **grant writers** as PIs who participated in the study: (1) a senior investigator as PI for the first submission of an R01 grant; (2) a junior investigator as PI for the first submission of an R01 grant with two subcontracts; (3) a junior investigator as PI for the resubmission of an R01 grant with two subcontracts; and (4) a doctoral student as PI for the first submission of an F31 Individual National Research Service Award Predoctoral Fellowship. They all prepared these federal research grants for submission to the NIH in the winter and spring of 2015. Besides PIs, two other types of grant writers, three RAs and one grant editor from the school of nursing also participated in the study.

Third, the article describes what **specific jobs** grant writers, including both PIs and RAs, do in the four phases during the Pre-Award period. (1) In the phase of Preparation Work, PIs worked on researching grant topics, planning statistical research, and reviewing the literature, while RAs worked on reviewing funding announcement guidelines and addressing questions about proposal compliance. (2) In the phase of Collaborative Work, PIs and RAs worked with research collaborators on communicating via emails, in-person meetings, or phone conferences. (3) In the phase of Grant Preparation and Writing, PIs worked on writing, revising, editing, and formatting grant applications, creating graphic presentations (e.g. tables, figures, flowcharts, and diagrams), and creating budgets and subcontracts, while RAs worked on completing administrative forms, uploading files, meeting research compliance requirements, and obtaining administrative approvals. (4) In the phase of Quality Assurance, PIs and RAs worked together on conducting internal grant reviews (e.g. reviewing and improving specific objectives and aims before due dates, running mock reviews), reviewing applications before submitting them to Grants.gov,[18] and reviewing the final application in eRA Commons.[19] In addition, RAs needed to review the quality of all applications and budgets. Here, we can see that the PIs and RAs must work together closely and seamlessly. In a sense, both groups should be considered as grant writers.

Fourth, the article calculated the **specific hours** spent by grant writers in preparing a grant. For preparing and submitting one grant proposal, each of the four PIs spent 69.8–162.3 hours, averaging 109.3 hours, equal to **three weeks** of full-time work for the PIs; each of the RAs spent 33.9–56.4 hours, averaging 41.45 hours, equal to **one week** of full-time work for the RAs. Specifically, the four PIs spent most of their time on writing (68.7 hours), literature review (17.5 hours), and meetings (17.0 hours), whereas RAs spent most of their time on writing (16.5 hours), meetings (6.55 hours), and forms (6.48 hours). There is a large variation in the four PIs' total hours among their four proposals (162.3, 84.8, 120.4, and 69.8 hours respectively), whereas the RAs' hours on these four proposals are relatively similar (38.2, 56.4, 37.4, and 33.8 hours respectively). Note that there is extensive literature on the time spent to write and submit grants in different disciplines.[20]

Fifth, the article also calculated the **costs** (e.g. salaries, fringe benefits, and indirect costs or finance/administration costs) for grant application preparation. For one submitted grant, the cost ranged from $4,784 to $13,512 per grant. For one funded R01 grant, the costs could be as high as $72,460 to $270,240.

---

[18] "Grants.gov" (www.grants.gov) is an e-government system that acts as a centralized location for applying for funding programs of twenty-seven federal grant-making agencies in the United States.
[19] "eRA Commons" (https://public.era.nih.gov/commons/) is the largest federal grants management system online used by the NIH and other federal agencies. It accounts for over 50 percent of the federal grant applications received by Grants.gov.
[20] Herbert, D. L., Barnett, A. G., Clarke, P., & Graves, N. (2013). On the time spent preparing grant proposals: An observational study of Australian researchers. *BMJ Open*, *3*(5), article e002800. Gs144; Herbert, D. L., Barnett, A. G., & Graves, N. (2013). Funding: Australia's grant system wastes time. *Nature*, *495*(7441), 314. Gs66; Herbert, D. L., Coveney, J., Clarke, P., Graves, N., & Barnett, A. G. (2014). The impact of funding deadlines on personal workloads, stress, and family relationships: A qualitative study of Australian researchers. *BMJ Open*, *4*(3), article e004462. Gs86; Arnett, A. G., Graves, N., Clarke, P., & Herbert, D. (2015). The impact of a streamlined funding application process on application time: Two cross-sectional surveys of Australian researchers. *BMJ Open*, *5*(1), article e006912. Gs21.

Last, the article has multiple **practical implications** for new grant writers. It shows various tasks that a grant writer needs to complete in the Pre-Award phase. This is hard work that demands substantial time and resources. Second, both PIs and RAs need to work closely together to complete the required process of grant submission. Rather than PIs working by themselves, both PIs and RAs work as a team, while PI plays a major role and RAs play a critical role.

3.2 Enger & Castellacci (2016): Three Types of Institutional Grant Writers

Overview

This article is titled "Who gets Horizon 2020 research grants? Propensity to apply and probability to succeed in a two-step analysis."[21] Horizon 2020 is a major grant program by the funding agency of the European Union. A two-step analysis here refers to two data analyses: analysis of the tendency to apply for grants and analysis of the tendency to receive grants. The article has been cited fifty-two times based on Google Scholar as of 2023.

This article is the product of a collaboration between one junior and one senior author from Norway. The first author, Simen Enger, was then a PhD candidate at the University of Oslo and worked at the Norwegian Ministry of Education and Research. The second author, Fulvio Castellacci, is a researcher in the Department of Research at the Norwegian Ministry of Education and Research. His h-index is 36. He has published several articles on grant research.

The article was published in *Scientometrics*, which is an international peer-reviewed journal that publishes original research on all quantitative aspects of the production, communication, and use of scientific and technological information. The impact factor was 3.9 in 2022. The publisher has been Springer since 1978. This is an important journal for researchers in grantology.

Highlights

This article is an empirical study. It analyzes which research institutions in Norway participated in Horizon 2020 and how they received EU funding.

---

[21] Enger, S. G., & Castellacci, F. (2016). Who gets Horizon 2020 research grants? Propensity to apply and probability to succeed in a two-step analysis. *Scientometrics*, *109*(3), 1611–38. Gs52.

It has five major sections: Introduction, Theory and Hypotheses, Context and Data, Results, and Conclusion. From the perspective of grant writers, we want to highlight the following points.

First, this article uses **research organizations** rather than individual researchers as a basic unit of analysis. It presents a data analysis of the participation and success of 1,402 research organizations in Norway in the Eighth European Framework Programme for Research and Innovation (i.e. Horizon 2020). In general, individuals and organizations participated in grant writing. Thus, a grant writer can be an individual or an organization. It is like a club that often has individual members and group members. A local organization, an international organization, or even a country can be considered a grant writer when studying grant writing behaviors at different social levels.

Second, this article distinguishes **three major types** of research institutions: non-applicants, unsuccessful applicants, and successful participants. This is interesting and important, because a common misconception is that grant writers are those who have successfully secured a grant. However, this article points out the importance of considering the three types of grant writers: (1) non-applicants are those research organizations which might wish to apply for EU funding, but have not yet decided to do so; (2) unsuccessful applicants are those research organizations which have submitted a grant proposal, but have received a rejection; and (3) successful applicants are those research organizations which have successfully secured a grant. In the existing literature, both unsuccessful and successful participants are most frequently studied, but **non-applicants** are often neglected. As discussed in the article, it is strategically critical for Norwegian policymakers to substantially increase their research institutions' applications for EU funding in the first place, given that around 50 percent of the research organizations are non-participants, in order to generate more successful participants.

Third, their major findings indicate that the propensity to apply is enhanced by prior participation in the European Framework Programme for Research and Innovation (EU FP) and the existence of complementary national funding schemes, and the probability of succeeding is strengthened by prior participation, as well as the scientific reputation of the applicant organization.

Fourth, the article focuses on Norway. Norway is not a large country among the twenty-seven member states in the European Union. However, funding systems and funding mechanisms in Norway are relatively similar to other small economies in Europe, like Denmark, Finland, Sweden,

3 Scientific Knowledge 99

the Netherlands, and Austria. Thus, the article, including the references provided at the end, helps us understand grant systems in Europe in general and grant writers in Europe in particular. It is critical to study grant writers throughout the world rather than grant writers in just one country or one region.

3.3 Chapman & McCauley (1993): Graduate Students as Grant Writers

Early-career grant writers are one of the most studied topics in grant writer research. Grant writers go through different career levels or stages, including undergraduate investigators, graduate investigators, predoc investigators, postdoc investigators, junior investigators, independent investigators, senior investigators, and super investigators. Here, we will discuss one study focusing on graduate students as grant writers.[22]

Overview
The article is titled "Early career achievements of National Science Foundation (NSF) graduate applicants: Looking for Pygmalion and Galatea effects on NSF winners," and focuses on the impacts of receiving an NSF grant on graduate students' careers. The Pygmalion effect generally refers to an observed psychological phenomenon that raising the expectations of teachers leads to good performance of students.[23] The Galatea effect refers to a psychological phenomenon observed further in the study of the Pygmalion effect that raising the expectations of trainees leads to their good performance.[24] It has been cited forty-four times based on Google Scholar as of 2023. It does not appear to be a well-cited article after over thirty years since its publication, perhaps due to a specific rather than a mainstream topic to applied psychologists.

Two senior researchers published this article. The first and corresponding author is Gretchen Chapman. She is currently a Professor of Psychology at Carnegie Mellon University. Her research areas are decision-making and health behavior. This paper is her first and only grant research paper. Her h-index is 64. The second author is Clark McCauley, a Research Professor

---
[22] Chapman, G. B., & McCauley, C. (1993). Early career achievements of National Science Foundation (NSF) graduate applicants: Looking for Pygmalion and Galatea effects on NSF winners. *Journal of Applied Psychology*, 78(5), 815–20. Gs44.
[23] Rosenthal, R., & Jacobson, L. (1968). Pygmalion in the classroom. *Urban Review*, 3(1), 16–20.
[24] Eden, D., & Ravid, G. (1982). Pygmalion versus self-expectancy: Effects of instructor- and self-expectancy on trainee performance. *Organizational Behavior & Human Performance*, 30(3), 351–64.

of Psychology at Bryn Mawr College. His research areas are group dynamics, genocide, politicide terrorism, and radicalization. His h-index is 59.

The article was published in 1993, over thirty years ago, in the *Journal of Applied Psychology*. This journal comes from the well-known journal publication program of the American Psychology Association (APA). It publishes empirical and theoretical studies that enhance understanding of cognitive, motivational, affective, and behavioral psychological phenomena in work and organizational settings related to applied psychology. Its impact factor was 9.9 in 2023.

Highlights

This is an empirical article reporting a nature experiment that examined 4,308 applicants of the NSF Graduate Student Fellowship Program in 1967 to 1976 and whether being a fellow or not impacted later early-career achievements. It has a typical structure for an empirical article: Introduction, Method, Results, Discussion, and Conclusion. From the perspective of grant writers, we can highlight the following major points.

First, the study used a **natural experiment** method to test the effect of being awarded by the NSF GRFP on early professional performance. Different from the traditional sense of a randomized controlled experiment, a natural experiment is a study in which participants are exposed to experimental and control conditions that are determined by nature or by other factors outside the control of the investigators. The GRFP is a **prestigious** national competition among outstanding graduate students in science, technology, engineering, and mathematics (STEM) or in STEM education. The success rate is about 10 percent. A panel of scientists reviews and rates applicants into two groups: Quality Group 1 (about 5 percent of top applicants) to award the fellowship, and Quality Group 2 (about 10 percent of top applicants) to either award the fellowship or offer honorable mentions without the award based on diversity goals and other factors. Among 4,308 Quality Group 2 applicants, 2,423 were awarded the fellowship and 1,885 were not. The study focused on Quality Group 2 because the applicants were divided randomly into two conditions by a natural process of selection and awarding, which offers a reasonable approximation of a natural experiment.

Second, the study generated **two major findings**. First, the award of an NSF fellowship leads to a relatively substantial improvement in the rate of PhD completion. Among 2,423 awardees, 1,689 (70 percent) completed a PhD, whereas among 1,885 non-awardees, 1,190 (63 percent) completed a PhD. Second, the award of an NSF fellowship leads to no substantial improvement in six types of post-PhD accomplishments, for example, gaining faculty status, top faculty status, applying for and receiving NSF research grants, and applying for and receiving NIH research grants. For example, 32 percent of awardees became faculty members, whereas 30 percent of non-awardees became faculty members; and 56 percent of awardees received NSF research grants, whereas 51 percent of non-awardees received NSF grants.

Last, given the unique prestige of an NSF fellowship and the substantial number of awards for multiple years, the authors found it challenging to explain the small award effect on PhD completion and non-award effect on post-PhD accomplishments using the Pygmalion and Galatea effects. For grant writer research, the important question remains: In addition to the Pygmalion and Galatea effects, how should we further examine possible impacts and underlying mechanisms of receiving or not receiving major prestigious grants among early-career investigators, conceptually, methodologically, and empirically? The following section offers another good example.

3.4 Wang, Jones, & Wang (2019): Early-Career Grant Writers

Early-career grant writers are important both for this chapter, because there exists extensive literature on this topic, and for the entire book, because our target readers are new grant writers. Here, we will discuss one of the best articles on early-career grant writers by Drs. Wang, Jones, and Wang.[25]

Overview

This article is titled "Early-career setback and future career impact," which suggests that the article focuses on the impact of early grant rejections on the late-career development of researchers. It used the existing data from the NIH and analyzed how the results of being funded or rejected impacted 1,184 early-career applicants who applied for the Research Project Grant Program (G01), the NIH's eldest and most standard research program for independent researchers.[26] The article has been cited 149 times based on Google Scholar as of 2023.

---

[25] Wang, Y., Jones, B. F., & Wang, D. (2019). Early-career setback and future career impact. *Nature Communications*, *10*(1), 1–10. Gs102.

[26] The NIH has multiple major funding mechanisms: for example, Research Grants (R series), Career Development Awards (K series), Research Training (T series), Fellowships (F series), and Program Project/Center Grants (P series). Each mechanism has several specific funding programs: for example, in G series, NIH Research Project Grant Program (R01), NIH Small Grant Program (R03), and NIH High Priority, Short-Term Project Award (R56).

The article has three authors. The first author is Yang Wang,[27] who did postdoc work with Dr. Dashun Wang at Northwestern University and is currently a Professor of Public Policy and Administration at Xi'an Jiaotong University, China. His relevant research is Computational Social Science and Science of Science. His h-index is 11. The second author is Benjamin Jones, a former Rhodes Scholarship winner and currently Gordon and Llura Gund Family Professor of Entrepreneurship at Northwestern University. His major research areas include innovation and development economics, and his h-index is 38. He has participated in the NBER Advancing the Science of Science Funding Meeting since 2018. Dashun Wang is the third and corresponding author. He is a Professor of Management at Northwestern University, with main interests in Science of Science, Computational Social Science, Network Science, Big Data, and Complex Systems. His h-index is 34. He has published a series of major studies related to grant research. Researchers in grantology should closely follow important work from his research group.

The article was published in *Nature Communications*, which is an open-access multidisciplinary journal publishing high-quality research in the biological, health, physical, chemical, Earth, social, mathematical, applied, and engineering sciences. It had an impact factor of 16.6 in 2022. The publisher is Springer-Nature. Note that, besides *Nature*, the leading international weekly journal of science first published in 1869, Springer-Nature publishes two types of *Nature* portfolio journals, subject-specific subscription journals (e.g. *Nature Genetics* and *Nature Physics*) and broad open-access journals (e.g. *Nature Human Behavior, Nature Communications*, and *Scientific Reports*). *Nature* and its portfolio journals have published multiple major articles on grantology and thus researchers in grantology should follow them.

Highlights
The article has four major sections: Introduction, Results, Discussion, and Methods, slightly different from the typical sequence of an empirical article. From the perspective of grant writers, the major points of this article are highlighted below.

First, the study is a **thoughtful secondary data analysis**[28] that uses the existing data to address new research questions via re-analysis. It had a

---

[27] Dashun Wang website, available at: www.dashunwang.com/group.
[28] Vartanian, T. P. (2010). *Secondary Data Analysis*. Oxford University Press; Johnston, M. P. (2014). Secondary data analysis: A method of which the time has come. *Qualitative & Quantitative Methods in Libraries*, *3*(3), 619–26.

particularly clever design: (1) The authors first used the existing NIH database to select all R01 grant applications submitted to the NIH between 1990 and 2005, given that R01 is the most common grant program for independent researchers.[29] (2) The authors then further focused on the first R01 applications being made within the previous three years so that these PIs should be junior scientists in their early careers. (3) They then focused on two specific groups: 561 near misses (i.e. PIs who just missed out on receiving funding) and 623 narrow wins (i.e. PIs who only just succeeded in getting funded). (4) They matched the NIH grant database with the database of the Web of Science, one of the major bibliometric databases, to study the relationship between the NIH R01 first grant applications and their publication and citation records. (5) They finally checked eleven demographic and performance characteristics (e.g. institutional reputation, number of previous publications) for these two groups of PIs, showing that, before treatment, these two groups were statistically indistinguishable for all the characteristics examined.

Second, the study generated **two important findings**. (1) The early grant rejection significantly reduced grant submission efforts, and the near misses had over a 10 percent more chance of disappearing permanently from the NIH system than the narrow wins. (2) The near misses significantly outperformed the narrow wins in publishing in the first and second five-year periods, with significantly more papers, but also significantly more high-impact papers. This is quite surprising because the narrow wins had the initial substantial NIH funding advantage (i.e. each receiving funding for around $1.3 million over five years), whereas the near misses did not receive the initial funding.

Third, the study performed further analysis and ruled out **four hypotheses** that might explain the observed performance gap between the near misses and the narrow wins: Early-career setbacks might (1) push persistent junior scientists to attempt more novel studies, (2) make them seek out advantageous collaborations, (3) generate intellectual or physical mobility (e.g. shifting research directions), and (4) motivate them to change institutions for better environments. Thus, the authors proposed future studies to examine various processes (e.g. a process involving researchers'

---

[29] In the NIH, the most common research grant mechanism is the R01. R01s are generally awarded for three to five years, and are used to support a "discrete, specified, circumscribed research project." The average annual budget was $460,000. All grant-awarding institutes and centers award R01s. Applications for R01s are complex and are typically over 100 pages by submission. In financial year 2016, the NIH received about 26,000 applications for new R01 grants; around 1,500 applications (the success rate is around 17 percent) were funded.

perseverance after setbacks) and methods (e.g. an econometric model with the fuzzy regression discontinuity design).

Fourth, the study focused on the **early career of grant writers**, developed a beautiful design, and demonstrated the significant impact of early setbacks on future grants and future publications. Thus, it makes an important contribution to the literature. However, it focuses on a special grant (i.e. the NIH's G01 grant) rather than various other grants from various funders, and also a special early-career group (i.e. those who might become independent scientists) rather than other early-career groups, such as postdocs, graduate students, and undergraduate students. Thus, whether the findings can be generalized to other grants by other funders and to other early-career groups of grant writers still needs further examination.

Last, this article has a **few practical implications** for new grant writers. For instance, for those who are not successful in the early grant efforts, be aware of the significant negative impact of early failure, be aware that there is sometimes only one small distance between failure and success, and be aware of the importance of being persistent and resilient to use different innovative strategies to overcome the failure. For those who are successful in the early grant efforts, be aware that securing a grant is the beginning of the process of completing funded projects and generating scientific and societal impacts.

3.5 Nguyen et al. (2022): Super Principal Investigators as Grant Writers

Overview

This article is titled "Gender, racial, and ethnic and inequities in receipt of multiple National Institutes of Health research project grants."[30] It takes a special angle to examine the hot topic of funding inequity among a special group of elite grant writers who receive multiple NIH G01 grants. It has been cited forty-six times since 2023 and has already generated a good impact.

Six scholars in medicine from four different universities wrote this article. The first and corresponding author is Mytien Nguyen, an MD/PhD candidate at Yale. Her h-index is already 16. She has published at least three

---

[30] Nguyen, M., Chaudhry, S. I., Desai, M. M., Dzirasa, K., Cavazos, J. E., & Boatright, D. (2023). Gender, racial, and ethnic and inequities in receipt of multiple National Institutes of Health research project grants. *JAMA Network Open*, 6(2), e230855–e230855. Gs34.

other good articles on grant research and is a rising star in the field of grantology.[31] Sarwat Chaudhry is a Professor of Medicine at Yale, Mayur M. Desai is a Professor of Epidemiology at Yale, Kafui Dzirasa is an Associate Professor of Psychiatry and Behavioral Sciences at Duke University, Jose Cavazos is a Professor of Neurology, Neuroscience & Physiology at the University of Texas Health, and Dowin Boatright is an Associate Professor of Emergency Medicine at New York University.

The article was published in *JAMA Network Open*. This journal is an open-access medical journal published by the American Medical Association covering all aspects of the biomedical sciences. It was established in 2018 and has a 2021 impact factor of 13.353. The journal has published multiple articles on grantology.

Highlights
This is an empirical article. It includes five typical major sections: Introduction, Methods, Results, Discussion, and Conclusion. While the article focuses on gender, racial, and ethnic diversity, we highlight a few points from the perspective of grant writer research.

First, the most interesting concept in this article is **super principal investigators (SPIs)** or elite PIs. The authors defined SPIs as those receiving three or more concurrent active research project grants (G01) in a given fiscal year from the NIH **simultaneously**. Holding three or more G01 grants was considered a status of exceptional or elite grant writers. They are approximately the top 10 percent of all NIH principal investigators in 2020. They found that among 33,896 investigators in the fiscal year 2020, SPIs were 3,942 (11.6 percent), whereas 8,695 (25.6 percent) were early-stage investigators. Furthermore, between 1991 and 2020, the proportion of **SPIs** tripled from 704 (3.7 percent) to 3,942 (11.6 percent).

Second, the authors found that **SPIs were unequally distributed** across gender, ethnic, and racial groups. Women and Black PIs were significantly underrepresented among SPIs, even after adjusting for career stage and

---

[31] Nguyen, M., Panyadahundi, A., Olagun-Samuel, C., Chaudhry, S. I., Desai, M. M., Dardik, A. *et al.* (2023). Transition from mentored to independent NIH funding by gender and department. *JAMA, 329*(24), 2189–90. Gs8; Nguyen, M., Gonzalez, L., Newman, A., Cannon, A., Zarebski, S. A., Chaudhry, S. I. *et al.* (2023). Rates of National Institutes of Health funding for surgeon-scientists, 1995–2020. *JAMA Surgery, 158*(7), 756–64. Gs8; Nguyen, M., Gonzalez, L., Chaudhry, S. I., Ahuja, N., Pomahac, B., Newman, A. *et al.* (2023). Gender disparity in National Institutes of Health funding among surgeon-scientists from 1995 to 2020. *JAMA Network Open, 6*(3), e233630–e233630. Gs11.

degree, and were 34 and 40 percent less likely than their male and White colleagues to be an SPI. Furthermore, Black female PIs were the least likely to be represented among SPIs and were 71 percent less likely to attain SPI status than White male PIs. That is, Black female PIs were significantly underrepresented in this group, even after adjusting for career stage and degree, suggesting that persistent gender, race, and ethnic inequity exists among an elite class of SPIs.

Third, in addition to this study, a **few other interesting studies** have also been published examining this category of elite grant writers.[32] Clearly, it is a much-needed but less-studied area in grant writer research, contrasting with the extensive literature on early-career grant writers. For grantology research, it is particularly important to understand who elite grant writers are, how they become elite grant writers, and what early-career and mid-career grant writers can learn from the elite grant writers.

Fourth, perhaps because of the nature of the topic, the article ends with **three notes**. While the first note on Conflict of Interest Disclosures and the third note on Role of the Funder/Sponsor indicate no conflict of interest for the authors and funders, the second note indicates that this article received support from four grants: three from National Institute of General Medical Sciences (**T32**GM136651, PI Ms. Nguyen; **R01**GM137411, PI Dr. Boatright; **T32**GM113896, PI Dr. Cavazos); and one from the National Institute of Allergy and Infectious Diseases (**F30**AI157227, PI Ms. Nguyen).[33] This typical grant information note is informative, specifying funding institutions, funding mechanisms, grant IDs, and grant PIs. New grant writers should and can learn a significant amount of information about relevant grants from the grant note when they read relevant articles in their own fields.

---

[32] Abramo, G., D'Angelo, C. A., & Soldatenkova, A. (2016). The ratio of top scientists to the academic staff as an indicator of the competitive strength of universities. *Journal of Informetrics, 10*(2), 596–605. Gs24; Larivière, V., Macaluso, B., Archambault, É., & Gingras, Y. (2010). Which scientific elites? On the concentration of research funds, publications and citations. *Research Evaluation, 19*(1), 45–53. Gs125; Stavropoulou, C., Somai, M., & Ioannidis, J. P. (2019). Most UK scientists who publish extremely highly-cited papers do not secure funding from major public and charity funders: A descriptive analysis. *PLoS One, 14*(2), article e0211460. Gs19; Van Arensbergen, P., & Van Den Besselaar, P. (2012). The selection of scientific talent in the allocation of research grants. *Higher Education Policy, 25*(3), 381–405. Gs46.

[33] Note that T32 = Training Programs, Institutional National Research Service Award to individuals selected for predoctoral and postdoctoral research training in specified shortage areas; F30 = Individual Fellowships Programs for predoctoral training which leads to the combined MD/PhD degrees; and F31 = Predoctoral Fellowships to Promote Diversity to enhance the diversity of the biomedical, behavioral, and clinical research workforce by supporting the research training of predoctoral students from diverse backgrounds.

*3.6 Witteman, Hendricks, Straus, & Tannenbaum (2019):
Grant Writers and Gender*

Gender differences in funding have an extremely extensive research literature.[34] We will study one article that has a good design and good results.[35]

Overview
This is an empirical article, using a natural experiment to examine whether gender differences truly exist in the grant review focusing on the applicant or on the science in the national funding agency of Canada. It has been cited 503 times in Google Scholar as of 2023, among the highest cited articles in the already extensive literature. The second most cited study was undertaken in the Netherlands.[36]

The paper was written by four Canadian prolific researchers in medicine. Holly Witteman is an Associate Professor of Digital Health at Université Laval. Her h-index in 2023 is 44. Michael Hendricks is an Associate Professor of Biology at McGill University. His h-index in 2023 is 16. Sharon Straus is a Professor of Geriatric Medicine at the University of Toronto. She is in the top 1 percent of highly cited clinical researchers based on the Web of Science. Her h-index is 120. She is an expert in scoping reviews and published an influential article on the PRISMA extension for scoping reviews (PRISMA-ScR).[37] The final author is Cara Tannenbaum, a Professor of Medicine and Pharmacy at the Université de Montréal. Her h-index is 42.

The paper was published under the category of Articles in *The Lancet*. The journal is a world-leading general medical journal, like *NEJM, JAMA,*

---

[34] Jagsi, R., Motomura, A. R., Griffith, K. A., Rangarajan, S., & Ubel, P. A. (2009). Sex differences in attainment of independent funding by career development awardees. *Annals of Internal Medicine*, *151*(11), 804–11. Gs364; Karukstis, K. K. (2009). Women in science, beyond the research university: Overlooked and undervalued. *Chronicle of Higher Education*, *55*(41), n41; Feller, S. E., Ronco, S. E., Rowlett, R. S., Elgren, T. E., & Karukstis, K. K. (2009). Barriers to seeking external research funding: Perceptions and facts. *Journal of Chemical Education*, *86*(7), 788–90; Ley, T. J., & Hamilton, B. H. (2008). The gender gap in NIH grant applications. *Science*, *322*(5907), 1472–4. Gs250; Van der Lee, R., & Ellemers, N. (2015). Gender contributes to personal research funding success in The Netherlands. *Proceedings of the National Academy of Sciences*, *112*(40), 12349–53. Gs279.
[35] Witteman, H. O., Hendricks, M., Straus, S., & Tannenbaum, C. (2019). Are gender gaps due to evaluations of the applicant or the science? A natural experiment at a national funding agency. *The Lancet*, *393*(10171), 531–40. Gs347.
[36] Jagsi, R., Motomura, A. R., Griffith, K. A., Rangarajan, S., & Ubel, P. A. (2009). Sex differences in attainment of independent funding by career development awardees. *Annals of Internal Medicine*, *151*(11), 804–11. Gs364.
[37] Tricco, A. C., Lillie, E., Zarin, W., O'Brien, K. K., Colquhoun, H., Levac, D. *et al.* (2018). PRISMA extension for scoping reviews (PRISMA-ScR): Checklist and explanation. *Annals of Internal Medicine*, *169*(7), 467–73. Gs23861.

and *Annals of Internal Medicine*. It publishes the best science from the best scientists worldwide, especially high-impact studies on global health practice and global health policy. *The Lancet* publishes Articles (including randomized controlled trials and meta-analyses), Review, Seminar, Health Policy, Therapeutics, Comments, Clinical Pictures, Correspondence, and World Reports. Its impact factor is 168.9 in 2023.

Highlights
The paper has a typical structure of an empirical article with four sections: Introduction, Methods, Results, and Discussion. From the perspective of grant writer research, several interesting strengths of the article are highlighted below.

First, the research design is **innovative**. One of the most active research areas in grantology is gender gaps in funding. Across countries and disciplines, extensive studies have indicated that male researchers receive more research funding than their female peers. However, it is challenging to develop a scientific understanding of gender gaps partly because a wide variety of factors are involved directly and indirectly. For instance, if a grant proposal is rejected, is it mainly based on the gender of the applicant or the quality of the proposal? To address this challenge, the authors creatively designed a nature experiment, a ubiquitous research design that differs from the randomized control trial and uses random treatment assignments without planned manipulations to determine a causal impact.[38] Specifically, in 2014, the Canadian Institutes of Health Research (CIHR) decided to divide investigator-initiated funding applications (like G01 grants by the NIH) into two new grant programs: one with an explicit review focus on the caliber of the PI and another without. This created a natural experiment or quasi-experiment situation by using random treatment assignments without experimental manipulations to determine a causal impact of gender gaps in funding. That is, they first analyzed the baseline data in 2011–14 with the review focusing on the quality of proposals to estimate gender gaps. They then analyzed the national experimental data in 2014–16, with half of the applications with a review focusing on the quality of proposals and another half with a review

---

[38] Dunning, T. (2012). *Natural Experiments in the Social Sciences: A Design-Based Approach.* Cambridge University Press; Sekhon, J. S., & Titiunik, R. (2012). When natural experiments are neither natural nor experiments. *American Political Science Review, 106*(1), 35–57; Craig, P., Cooper, C., Gunnell, D., Haw, S., Lawson, K., Macintyre, S. *et al.* (2012). Using natural experiments to evaluate population health interventions: New Medical Research Council guidance. *Journal of Epidemiology & Community Health, 66*(12), 1182–6.

focusing on the quality of applicants to estimate gender gaps. This innovative design is mixed with two methods, the pre- and post-test and natural experiment, which makes the findings convincing.

Second, the database used in the study is **sound**. The data were from the CIHR, a federal agency responsible for funding health and medical research in Canada – the Canadian version of the NIH. The authors analyzed 23,918 grant applications from 7,093 PIs in all investigator-initiated grant programs of the CIHR between 2011 and 2016. Because the data are confidential due to Canadian privacy legislation, the internally held data were analyzed by staff at the CIHR within their mandate as a national funding agency.

Third, the major finding is **convincing**. With a large dataset and a large sample size, the study demonstrated robust experimental evidence of the gender gap in funding. Given that the overall application success across competitions was 15.8 percent, after adjusting for age and research domain, the predicted probability of success in traditional programs was 16.3 percent for males and 15.4 percent for females, 0.9 percentage points lower for female applicants than male applicants. In the new program in which the reviewers focused on the quality of grant proposals, males were 12.9 percent vs. females 12.1 percent (i.e. the gap was 0.8 percentage points). However, in the new program with an explicit review focus on the quality of PIs, males were 12.7 percent (similar to 12.1 percent) vs. females at 8.8 percent (much higher than 0.8 percent), the gap being 3.9 percentage points. Here, the study provides clear empirical evidence from a natural experiment that gender gaps in grant funding stem from women being evaluated less favorably as PIs, not from differences in the quality of proposals by these PIs.

Fourth, the result interpretation is **systematic**. The authors considered three types of explanations for the observed gender gap. (1) Individual bias might exist, such that grant reviewers might have conscious or unconscious gender bias in evaluating female PIs. (2) Systemic bias might exist when grant review criteria introduce gender bias (e.g. leadership is used as one criterion: women PIs might be perceived to lack competent or ambitious leadership). (3) Weak applications of female applicants might be observed during the grant review (e.g. female applicants might unconsciously or implicitly use modest language to present their proposals and describe their accomplishments).

Last, the suggested strategies are particularly **useful**. To address the first explanation discussed above, the authors suggested a few thoughtful solutions, including funders instituting reviewer anti-bias training, using blind review, or having automatic adjustments to correct for known biases. To address the second explanation, the authors proposed a few sensible solutions. Funders could use more equitable review criteria or automatic adjustments, journals and societies could ensure equitable publication and awards processes, and institutions could provide all faculty with equitable resources and support. To address the third explanation, the authors considered that female PIs should seek leadership opportunities and describe their accomplishments in compelling language.

3.7   Ginther et al. (2011): Grant Writers and Race

There is also relatively extensive literature on race differences in funding.[39] Here, we will discuss one of the best.[40]

Overview

This article is titled "Race, ethnicity, and NIH research awards." It presents an empirical study, collecting the existing data to systematically and exclusively examine how race/ethnicity is associated with the probability of receiving the NIH's G01 grants.

This article was contributed by seven authors, a strong group with one leading scholar, two NIH researchers, and four professional analysts from Discovery Logic, a data analysis unit of Thomson Reuters. The first author is Donna Ginther, Regents Distinguished Professor of Economics at the University of Kansas. Her main expertise area is in labor economics and science policy. Her h-index is 33 as of 2023. She has published multiple major articles on research funding and gender and race. Thus, researchers in grantology should closely follow her work. The second author is Walter Schaffer, a Senior Advisor to the deputy director of extramural research at

---

[39] Shavers, V. L., Fagan, P., Lawrence, D., McCaskill-Stevens, W., McDonald, P., Browne, D. *et al.* (2005). Barriers to racial/ethnic minority application and competition for NIH research funding. *Journal of the National Medical Association, 97*(8), 1063–77. Gs122; Ginther, D. K., Kahn, S., & Schaffer, W. T. (2016). Gender, race/ethnicity, and National Institutes of Health R01 research awards: Is there evidence of a double bind for women of color? *Academic Medicine: Journal of the Association of American Medical Colleges, 91*(8), 1098–107. Gs204; Nelson, D. J., & Rogers, D. C. (2003). *A National Analysis of Diversity in Science and Engineering Faculties at Research Universities.* National Organization for Women. Gs298; National Science Foundation, Division of Science Resources Statistics (2009). Women, minorities, and persons with disabilities in science and engineering: 2009. NSF 09-305. ERIC Clearinghouse. Gs15; DiPrete, T. A., & Eirich, G. M. (2006). Cumulative advantage as a mechanism for inequality: A review of theoretical and empirical developments. *Annual Review of Sociology, 32*(1), 271–97. Gs2536.
[40] Ginther, D. K., Schaffer, W. T., Schnell, J., Masimore, B., Liu, F., Haak, L. L. *et al.* (2011). Race, ethnicity, and NIH research awards. *Science, 333*(6045), 1015–19. Gs1098.

the National Institutes of Health. He has published multiple major articles on grants and gender and race. Thus, researchers in grantology should also follow his work. Among them, the third author is Joshua Schnell, a former Discovery Logic Analyst and now a Clarivate Analytics Researcher, specializing in the research areas of bibliometrics, scientometrics, and science policy. His h-index is 16. He has published articles on grants and publications using bibliometrics, especially his highly cited papers about the Web of Science.[41]

The article was published in 2011 in *Science*, one of the world's top academic journals. Its rival is *Nature*, and both journals cover the full range of scientific disciplines. *Science* has been publishing a long list of articles, letters, reviews, news, and policy perspectives on grantology. Thus, researchers in grantology should closely follow this journal. *Science*'s 2020 impact factor was 47.728.

Highlights
The article is one of the best on the race gap in funding. It has been cited 1,098 times as of 2023 based on Google Scholar. It is among the highest cited articles on this topic, suggesting the major impact it has generated. This is a data analysis report with just five print pages in *Science*, along with twenty-five pages of supplemental materials online. Roughly, it has six sections, typically without subheadings, including abstract, introduction, methods, results, references and notes, with supporting online material. From the grant writer research perspective, it is useful to highlight the following important points.

First, the authors conducted **rigorous analysis** through meticulous data mining across multiple databases. The main database was the application data for Type 1[42] R01 Research Project Grants submitted between financial years 2000 and 2006 from the NIH. It includes 83,188 applications and 40,069 unique investigators, due to investigators being able to submit multiple grants for different projects. Among them, 21 percent of applicants are Asian, Black, Hispanic, and Native American investigators,

---

[41] Birkle, C., Pendlebury, D. A., Schnell, J., & Adams, J. (2020). Web of Science as a data source for research on scientific and scholarly activity. *Quantitative Science Studies*, 1(1), 363–76. Gs619; Schnell, J. D. (2017). Web of Science: The first citation index for data analytics and scientometrics. In F. J. Cantu-Ortiz (ed.), *Research Analytics: Boosting University Productivity and Competitiveness through Scientometrics (Data Analytics Applications)* (pp. 15–30). Auerbach Publications. Gs13.
[42] Note that the NIH uses nine types of codes in the application number to identify various stages in the lifecycle of a grant (https://grants.nih.gov/grants/how-to-apply-application-guide/prepare-to-apply-and-register/type-of-applications.htm). Type 1 is for a new submission, namely, the initial request for support of a project that has not yet been funded.

whereas Asian investigators were 16.2 percent, Blacks were 1.4 percent, Hispanics were 3.2 percent, Native Americans were 0.05 percent, Whites were 69.9 percent, and others/unknown were 9.2 percent.

Interestingly and ironically, one unusual challenge of this study is to identify race and ethnicity. Although applicants self-identify race and ethnicity, this information does not appear in the grant application, unlike other information, such as names and affiliations. However, because of the difficulty in identifying, determining, and confirming race/ethnicity, they used at least **five various databases** to code the applications' race/ethnicity as one of five types, Asian, Black, Hispanic, White, and Native American, but the analysis focused only on Asian, Black, Hispanic, and White PIs due to the small sample of Native American PIs. Technically, the study used a combination of self-reported responses in three databases, IMPAC II, the DRF, and the Faculty Roster, to intelligently gather this key information by looking at the undergraduate or doctoral institution attended and applicant names contained in the application bio sketch, which may in some cases be used as a proxy for race/ethnicity.

Second, the article presents **strong evidence** of the race gap in findings. No race difference was found in the grant priority scores during the panel review. Applications with good priority scores were more likely to be funded, regardless of race. However, significant race difference was found in grant funding after the panel review. Specifically, White PIs' award probability is 29 percent, Asian PIs' award probability is 25 percent, and Black PIs' award probability is 17 percent. In other words, Asians are 4 percentage points and Blacks are 12 percentage points less likely to receive NIH research funding compared with Whites.

Third, the article found two **significant predictors** after further analyses of various possible reasons to explain this race gap. (1) Resubmission: The authors examined the average number of grants per person, the proportion of investigators submitting single and multiple grants, and the likelihood of application resubmission. On average, investigators submitted/resubmitted three to four Type 1 R01 grant applications to receive the funding eventually. The data show that (a) Blacks and Asians resubmitted significantly more times before being awarded an R01 (2.01 and 1.85 times, respectively) compared with Whites (1.58 times); and Blacks (45 percent) and Hispanics (56 percent) were significantly less likely to resubmit an unfunded application compared with White investigators (64 percent). (2) Early scientific training: Participation in training grant programs significantly improved subsequent R01 award probability for both applications and applicants of the NIH's F, T, or K series of grants[43] to support young PIs effectively. Specifically, comparing R01 applicants who had no previous participation in these NIH training programs, fellowships, traineeships, and career development awards were associated with a 2.5, 2.2, and 4.8 percentage point increase, respectively, in the probability of an R01 award. However, for all applicants who received F or T training, Blacks were 27.4 percentage points, Asians were 6.9 percentage points, and Hispanics were 9.5 percentage points *less likely* to ever receive an R01 award compared with Whites.

Fourth, the author suggested **two policy-level strategies** to address the two significant factors discussed above. (1) To improve efforts and results in resubmission, institutions should provide strong assistance with the grant submission and resubmission process. (2) To improve training opportunities, institutions should further investigate the impact of training programs on differences in R01 award probability and generate more targeted training programs for underrepresented investigators. A cumulative effect may exist that minor advantages in access to research resources and mentoring during training or at the beginning of a career may be accumulated to generate major impacts.

3.8 Pinto & Huizinga (2018): External Factors and Individual Factors of Grant Writers

The research on external and internal factors influencing grant writers is quite extensive.[44] We will now discuss a good empirical study.[45]

---

[43] NIH pre- and postdoctoral fellowships (F), NIH pre- or postdoctoral traineeships (T), and NIH career development awards (K) are largely awarded to early-career investigators as grant funding for research.

[44] Goff-Albritton, R. A., Cola, P. A., Pierre, J., Yerra, S. D., & Garcia, I. (2022). Faculty views on the barriers and facilitators to grant activities in the USA: A systematic literature review. *Journal of Research Administration*, *53*(2), 14–39. Gs2; Karukstis, K. K., Elgren, T. E., Ronco, S. E., Feller, S. E., & Rowlett, R. S. (2009). Barriers to seeking external research funding: Perceptions and facts. *Journal of Chemical Education*, *86*(7), 788–90. Gs3; Jonisch, A. I., Kligerman, S., Nagy, E., Bhargavan, M., Forman, H. P., & Sunshine, J. (2006). What characterizes academic radiology departments that secure large amounts of external funding for research? *Academic Radiology*, *13*(12), 1513–16. Gs9; Boyer, P. G., & Cockriel, I. (2001). Grant performance of junior faculty across disciplines: Motivators and barriers. *Journal of Research Administration*, *2*(1), 19–24. Gs25; Liebert, R. J. (1977). Grant getting and productivity among scholars: Recent national patterns of competition and favor. *Journal of Higher Education*, *48*(2), 164–92. Gs52; Goff-Albritton, R. A., Cola, P. A., Pierre, J., Yerra, S. D., & Garcia, I. (2022). Faculty views on the barriers and facilitators to grant activities in the USA: A systematic literature review. *Journal of Research Administration*, *53*(2), 14–39. Gs4.

[45] Pinto, K. M., & Huizinga, D. (2018). Institutional barriers and faculty persistence: Understanding faculty grant-seeking at a predominantly undergraduate institution. *Journal of Faculty Development*, *32*(1), 65–72. Gs9.

3 Grant Writers

Overview

The title of the article is "Institutional barriers and faculty persistence: Understanding faculty grant-seeking at a predominantly undergraduate institution," suggesting that the study focused on both external factors and individual factors that increase and decrease the grant-seeking activities of the faculty at an undergraduate university. It has been cited nine times since 2018. While its citation might not high in number, the article is one of the well-organized and well-written studies on the topic of external factors impacting on grant writers.

The first author of the article is Katy Pinto, a Professor of Sociology at California State University at Fullerton. The second author is Dorota Huizinga, a Professor of Information and Decision Sciences and Associate Provost for Academic Research at California State University at Fullerton. She is well appraised for her leadership in both increasing proposal submissions from $29 million to $140 million and growing grant awards from $29 million in 2018–19 to $47 million in 2021–22.

The article was published in the *Journal of Faculty Development*. Founded in 1983, it publishes important topics relevant to educational developers, deans, department chairs, executives, and faculty. Each issue of the journal includes a general section with three to five articles and a special section with six to eight articles edited by one or more invited editors. The publisher is MAGNA Publications. No impact factor information can be found.

Highlights

The study is an interview study. The setting is California State University at Fullerton, a predominantly undergraduate institution. It experienced a major decrease in external grant submissions, from 105 in 2008–09 to only thirty-six in 2013–14. During these years, some faculty applied for grants regularly, but others stopped seeking grants. In this context, the first author interviewed fifteen of the **most persistent grant seekers** at the university to understand the faculty capacity of grant-seeking and examine how the faculty maintains research productivity in external grant-seeking and how institutional support and leadership affect their grant-seeking behavior.

The article has four major sections: Context, Approach and Methods, Results, and Conclusion. From the grant writer research perspective, the key points from this study are highlighted below.

First, the faculty interviews show **four individual factors** that increased faculty grant seeking: (1) individual drive for funding (e.g. a tenured faculty stated that he did not have to apply for a substantial grant, but he wanted the success of knowing he could be a PI on a very competitive major research grant); (2) prior experience (nine out of fifteen interviewees recalled their previous successful experiences); (3) presence of collaborators (eleven out of fifteen interviewees considered collaboration on and off campus to be part of their grant-seeking success); and (4) knowing the audience (e.g. junior faculty were more likely to only know of one or two external granting agencies, while experienced faculty often had at least four external granting agencies or programs they routinely targeted for funding). The faculty interviews also revealed **two individual factors** that decreased faculty grant-seeking: (1) faculty workload (e.g. faculty members had decreased their grant-seeking activities due to workload in teaching and service) and (2) lack of support for grant activities in retention, tenure, and promotion process.

Second, the faculty interviews indicate **three institutional factors** that increased faculty grant-seeking: (1) working with grant writers (e.g. a faculty stated that he has worked with a grant writer with 100 percent success); (2) having a pre-award faculty research liaison (e.g. the liaison person who can identify grants, review proposals, and meet program officers from external agencies); and (3) offering internal grants (e.g. to support pilot studies and manuscript publication). The interviews also show **four institutional barriers** that decreased grant-seeking activities: (1) a poor administration system; (2) decentralized pre-award and post-award offices; (3) lack of post-award support (e.g. preparing the annual reports, paying contractors, getting accurate budget reports); and (4) broken promises by the university (e.g. lab space commitments and course releases).

Finally, the article has **important implications** for new grant writers. We should be aware that grant writers do not work alone and various internal and external factors can increase or decrease their grant-seeking performance. Thus, we should always maximize successful factors and minimize challenging factors in our grant writing.

4 Grantology vs. Journalology: Grant Writers vs. Article Writers

In the real-life world, we can see many scholars, researchers, and professionals are strong grant writers who have won twenty, thirty, and more large grants, but who are not strong article writers. We can also see strong article writers who published 200, 300, or more influential articles, but who have not obtained even one or two large grants. At other times, we also see some who excel or perform poorly in both securing grants and publishing articles. What are the similarities and differences between grant writers and article writers?

4.1 Grant Writers

Grant writers can generally be defined as anyone who writes to pursue grants. The term "grant writers," by its name, has two defining features: grant and writers. For the first feature of "grant," all grant writers share the same major purpose: pursuing and securing grants. Their writing is to convince grant reviewers, grant officers, or grant agencies to invest in their proposed projects with funding. For the second feature of "writer," while they need to write different types of proposals for different grant programs, all grant writers share the same process of involving argumentative writing or scientific writing. They should excel in scientific communication. Content knowledge and methodological knowledge are often prerequisites for grant writers. But all their knowledge is reflected in their proposal writing.

However, grant writers are very diverse. First, they might have other different names: for example, awardees, grantees, PIs, Co-PIs, project managers, senior personnel, project leaders, contractors, freelance grant writers, or grant professionals. Second, grant writers can be at different stages in a grant cycle. At a given time, grant writers could engage in initiating, planning, developing, drafting, submitting, and resubmitting grant proposals at the Pre-Award phase. They further engage in receiving, negotiating, and finalizing grants at the Award phase. They also engage in implementing, completing, and managing funded projects and producing scientific and social impacts at the Post-Award phase. Third, grant writers can also be at different stages of their professional careers. They can be professionals in early career, mid-career, or later career. Some grant writers can be as early as students in high school or undergraduate programs when they apply for small student grants to conduct a small study or attend a local conference.

4.2 Article Writers

Article writers can be defined as those who draft, write, submit, and publish journal articles. Article writers can be identified by various terms, for example, authors, co-authors, first authors, last authors, corresponding authors, manuscript writers, or owners of a copyright of an article.

4 Grantology vs. Journalology

Comparing grant writers and article writers, we can see several similarities. First, they are all writers, engaging in writing to produce professional work in a writing form. Second, they are all involving scientific communication, communicating scientific or professional ideas to target readers. Third, there are different types of grants (fellowships, postdoc grants, seed grants, major grants, R03, R01, and P01); likewise, there are different types of articles (empirical, theoretical, methodological, and theoretical). Fourth, there are different levels of grant writers (graduate students, early career grant writers, or superstar grant writers); likewise, there are different levels of article writers (high-schoolers, new writers, junior writers, senior writers, or writing masters). These **similarities** are not difficult to understand. However, grant writers and article writers **differ** from each other in multiple major ways. These differences might not be easy to know at first glance.

First, the **purpose** of writing is particularly different. The goal of grant writers is to obtain funding, the means is a grant proposal, and the outcome is scientific and social impacts via finished projects. In contrast, the goal for article writers is to get published and communicate research findings with readers. The means is a journal article, and the outcome is knowledge dissemination and citation impacts via the published article. Note that patents and publications are two major impacts of scientific grants.

Second, the **contents** of writing are different. To achieve their goal of pursuing grants, grant writers write grant proposals, along with the budget and justification, to convince grant reviewers that their projects are fundable. In contrast, to achieve their goals of disseminating knowledge, article writers write manuscripts to show peer reviewers that their manuscripts are publishable. In a sense, grant writers work at the beginning of a scientific process, securing grants to support research, whereas article writers work at the end of a scientific process, publishing articles to publicize science.

Third, the **success** rates of writing are different. A grant writer might not always be successful, with a low funding rate (e.g. 20 percent) due to the increasingly competitive grant process. However, an article can almost always be published; the rejection rate or acceptance rate is relatively lower if it is not for top journals such as *Nature* and *Science*. Even for the same researcher, the number of grant proposals submitted, resubmitted, or funded is usually much lower than the number of manuscripts/articles submitted, resubmitted, or accepted. We could say there are four levels of competition in writing: resumeable (work can be included in our resume), presentable (work can be presented at a conference), publishable (work can be accepted by a journal), and fundable (work can be funded by a funder).

Fourth, the **ownership** of writing is different. Grant writers do not usually have a formal way to claim the copyright for their grant proposals. However, article writers own the copyright of their journal articles and can transfer it to publishers if needed.

5 Action Suggestions: Studying and Developing Profiles of Grant Writers

In the final section of this chapter, let us review what we have discussed so far and then consider possible future actions.

5.1 Understanding Five Aspects of Grant Writers

First, grant writers are at **different stages** of the grant process. We know now that there are different steps in a grant process, from developing a fundable idea to submitting a proposal, from receiving a grant to generating impacts. Thus, we should overcome one misconception that grant writers are grant winners. Once we have fundable ideas, we should learn, develop, write, and submit grant applications as soon as we can. Our goal is to become a grant winner, but we should first start as a grant writer, a grant applicant, and a grant resubmitter.

Second, grant writers are at **different stages** in their careers. We know now that there are different stages in our careers, from early career, mid-career, and late career. Thus, we should overcome the misconception that grant writers have to be independent established researchers. We could identify who and where we are in terms of our career and decide to apply accordingly to the relevant types of grants, including training grants, postdoc grants, early career grants, independent grants, large grants, and center grants. If we are a grant writer in our early career, there will be a large learning curve when we plan to apply for an independent grant such as the NIH's G01. Be prepared to learn from failure and to learn how to resubmit. Most importantly, as new grant writers, we should find mentors, join other research teams, and/or become Co-PI with experienced grant winners first, rather than investing heavily and hastily in applying for a large grant on our own.

Second, grant writers are in **different disciplines** of knowledge. We know now that they are from different disciplines, and different disciplines have different types of grant systems. Thus, we should overcome the misconception that grant writers are generic or from a typical discipline such as basic medicine or public health. We should be clear about what discipline we are in (e.g. nature or social science, medicine or anthropology), what grant systems the discipline operates (e.g. specific grantors, specific grant programs, or specific funding patterns), and what strategies we should use effectively and efficiently.

Fourth, grant writers have **diverse internal factors**. We know now that various internal factors (e.g. gender, age, race, personality, motivation, and time allocation) influence grant writers. Thus, we should overcome the misconception that grant writers are a homogeneous group of people rather than many different types of people with different internal factors. We should identify where our strengths and weaknesses are, understand what type of grant writers we are, know what type of support or barriers we have, improve our strengths and tackle our weaknesses, and use different strategies to pursue and secure grants.

Fifth, grant writers deal with **diverse external factors**. We know now that grant writers will be influenced by multiple external factors (e.g. institutions, communities, societies, and socio-economic facts). Thus, we should overcome the misconception that grant writers mainly work individually rather than in various contexts with different external factors. We should know our departments, schools, institutions, and countries (e.g. a history department vs. a biological department, a community college vs. a large research university, a developed country vs. a developing country), learn what general and specific external supports we can have and what general and specific external barriers we should overcome, and thus choose different strategies to be successful.

5.2 Studying at Least 100 Grant Writers and Drafting Your Grant CV

In addition to learning the complexity and diversity of grant writers and overcoming the five misconceptions outlined above, here are two suggestions you can action now to help you become a successful grant writer.

First, search and study at least **100 grant writers** besides reading more grant programs and grant proposals, just like we should search and study tens of journal articles before writing and publishing our own journal articles. For these grant writers, we could search and study: (1) the grant section of investigators' CVs; (2) the bio-sketch section of grant proposals from funders' databases; and (3) the grant acknowledgment section of journal articles to see **professional profiles** (e.g. grant steps, career stages, research disciplines, and internal and external features of a grant writer) and **grant portfolios** (e.g. the number of grants received, the name of funders, and types of grant programs). We can save all these found materials in one special folder or dossier titled "Grant writers." We can learn various strategies used by these grant writers. We can gain various inspirations from these grant portfolios. For example, we can find the CV of Fei-Fei Li, one of the leading AI scientists in the world, when she was an Assistant Professor of Computer Science at Stanford University in 2011.[46] Six years after she received her PhD in 2005, she had a strong professional profile as a computer scientist and a strong grant portfolio as a grant writer, including ten grants from public and private agencies, such as the NIH, the NSF (CAREER),[47] DOC, IARPA,[48] Google, and Kodak; most were large grants and she acted as PI.

Second, develop and draft your own professional profiles and grant portfolios in your **grant CV**, a type of CV that specifically focuses on grants, like various types of CVs for various purposes (e.g. for admission, scholarship, job, tenure, promotion, executive recruitment). In your grant CVs, you can develop and analyze your own professional profiles as grant writers (e.g. listing grant steps, career stages, research disciplines, and internal and external features of grant writers). Be mindful of your strengths and weaknesses. Make sure to include your potential mentors and experienced collaborators (ideally having informal interviews or formal meetings with them). You can also develop and analyze your grant portfolios (e.g. listing your grants at federal, state, local, and institutional levels that are complete, current/active, pending, submitted, resubmitted, unfunded, drafting, and planning). You can include your publications or patents as the outcome of grants.

---

[46] Fei-Fei Li, *Stanford University*, available at: https://cs.stanford.edu/people/feifeili/LiFei-Fei_ProfessionalCV_noref.pdf.

[47] Faculty Early Career Development Program (CAREER), *US National Science Foundation*, available at: https://new.nsf.gov/funding/opportunities/faculty-early-career-development-program-career.

[48] High-risk high-payoff research, *IARPA*, available at: www.iarpa.gov/.

CHAPTER 4

Grant Agencies

Outline

1	Intuitive Knowledge: What Is a Grant Agency?	122
	1.1 Responses from New Grant Writers	122
	1.2 Understand the Complexity of Funding Agencies	122
2	Real-Life Cases: From Grant Agencies to Grant Portfolio	124
	2.1 The Pat Connaughton Foundation: A Sport Grant Agency	124
	2.2 The SUNY Research Foundation: A Grant-Managing Grant Agency	125
	2.3 The National Institutes of Health: The Largest Public Grant Agency Worldwide	126
	2.4 The Institute of Education Sciences: One of the Thirty-Eight Federal Grant Agencies	127
	2.5 The Howard Hughes Medical Institute: A Private Biomedicine Grant Agency	129
	2.6 The American Psychological Association: A Professional Organization with a Grant Program	130
	2.7 A Harrow Agenda and Four Grants: Developing Grant Portfolio	132
3	Scientific Knowledge: From Largest Funders to Grant Portfolio	133
	3.1 Viergever & Hendriks (2016): The Ten Largest Funders	133
	3.2 James McCullough (1994): The NSF as a Public Funder	137
	3.3 McCoy *et al.* (2009): The Gates Foundation as a Private Funder	141
	3.4 Huang & Huang (2018): Funders across Disciplines	143
	3.5 McGovern (2012): Build a Solid Grant Portfolio	146
4	Grantology vs. Journalology: Grant Agencies vs. Journal Publishers	150
	4.1 The NIH: An American Public Research Funder	150
	4.2 Elsevier: A Dutch Private Academic Publisher	152
5	Action Suggestions: Understanding Grant Agencies and Developing Grant Portfolios	154
	5.1 Understanding the Complexity and Diversity of Grant Agencies	154
	5.2 Studying and Developing Grant Portfolios	155

4 Grant Agencies

1 Intuitive Knowledge: What Is a Grant Agency?

1.1 Responses from New Grant Writers

What is a grant agency? What are examples of grant agencies? What kinds of professionals work in a grant agency? Below are quick responses to these questions from four new grant writers.

- Response 1: I think a grant agency is an organization that can provide funding for a research project. For example, APA, AERA, and NSF. I think some university faculty members, researchers, and scholars who specialize in a specific area are working in an agency.
- Response 2: From my understanding, grant agencies offer money to support researchers in completing their research projects. They could be government departments (e.g. New York State Education Department, NSF), non-profit organizations (e.g. United States Fund For UNICEF), and companies (e.g. ETS). The agents who work in the agency should be familiar with the process of applying for a grant, should have experience applying for a grant before, and have qualities such as good judgment, without bias.
- Response 3: I think that a grant agency is a place to provide and manage to fund a research project. These are usually public or not-for-profit funding such as state government entities that provide the grant. Examples include the Institute of Education Sciences (IES) and the National Science Foundation (NSF). Professionals who work in an agency include those in Grants Management (e.g. answer questions, award funds, design grant policies, and serve as liaisons between the government and external parties) and in Financial Management (e.g. the Chief Financial Officers or specialists dealing with a variety of financial partnerships with non-profits and public–private collaborations).
- Response 4: From my understanding, a grant agency is an organization that provides funding for supporting a research project to create some valuable and meaningful research products for society. For example, NSF and NIH. Professional work in NSF or NIH could be academic work like reviewing project proposals, administrative work such as financial budget, and technical work such as technology innovation with some engineers or scientists.

1.2 Understand the Complexity of Funding Agencies

Various terms have been used to name an agency that provides grants, such as grant agency, funding agency, funder, foundation, sponsor, donor,

1 Intuitive Knowledge: What Is a Grant Agency? 123

and philanthropist. This variation partially reflects the complexity of grant agencies as a core concept in grantology. The quick responses presented above from the four new grant writers reveal their intuitive knowledge and understanding of the complexity of grant agencies. Let us briefly analyze these intuitive responses.

The first response reveals that: (1) this new grant writer was partially correct in their understanding of the core mission of grant agencies because research funding is important, but many grant agencies support non-science activities (e.g. supporting community development) and non-research activities (e.g. training science teachers); (2) the grant writer provided *some* correct examples of grant agencies because the NSF is a typical grant agency, but the American Psychology Association (APA) and the American Educational Research Association (AERA) are professional associations with small funding programs; and (3) the grant writer was partially correct about whom they considered to be grant agency professionals because university faculty and staff could be grant reviewers, panel chairs and even rotated program officers (e.g. in the NSF), but they are not grant agency professionals.

The second response shows that this grant writer had a better knowledge than the first one, but still revealed partial knowledge about grant agencies. Specifically, this grant writer: (1) still narrowly focused on grant agencies supporting research and researchers; (2) thoughtfully classified three types of grant agencies (federal/state agencies, non-profits, and corporations); however, the Educational Testing Service (ETS) is not a grant agency, but rather than one of the largest testing companies worldwide with only a small number of grant programs for research, training, and internship; and (3) correctly pointed out that grant agency professionals should have good judgment and no bias, but many of them do not need to have successful or unsuccessful experiences of grant applications. There is a wide variety of professionals working in grant agencies, from senior leaders such as board members, presidents, and program directors to regular operations such as program officers, award accountants, and office assistants.

The third response reveals that this grant writer has relatively good knowledge with some limitations. Specifically, the grant writer: (1) still narrowly considered that a grant agency is to fund research projects, while thoughtfully classifying public or not-for-profit agencies. (2) gave two great examples, the NSF (a very popular federal grant agency) and the IES (a much less popular federal grant agency); and (3) described two major types of professionals in an agency in Grants Management and Financial Management.

The final response shows the highest level of knowledge about grant agencies among the four. Specifically, this new grant writer (1) mentioned the societal impacts while still narrowly limiting grant agencies to funding research projects; (2) specified two examples, the National Science Foundation (NSF) and especially the National Institutes of Health (NIH) (the largest public funder in the world) – this grant writer is the only one among the four to specify this agency; and (3) thoughtfully classified three types of grant professionals in grant agencies, including "reviewing project proposals" (note that this is partially correct because most program officers usually manage but do not participate in the review process), administering the financial budget, and handling "technology innovations."[1]

Overall, we can see that these new grant writers do have basic knowledge about grant agencies, but often their knowledge is partially correct. They all narrowly considered grant agencies as agencies to provide funding for research rather than to provide grants for both scientific and nonscientific projects (see the typology of grants in Chapter 1 for details). They are all unclear about grant-making funders vs. grant-making programs. For instance, the APA, AERA, or ETS essentially are not grant-making funders, but do offer some grant programs to serve these organizations' central missions. None of them mentions program officers, who are the key professionals in a grant agency for managing external reviews and recommending grant funding.

Building on these intuitive responses as our baseline knowledge, this chapter will present real-life cases, discuss scientific research, compare funders and publishers, and provide action suggestions to new grant writers. Our learning objective is to understand the complexity and diversity of grant agencies and use this new understanding to guide our research-based practice of grant applications.

2 Real-Life Cases: From Grant Agencies to Grant Portfolio

2.1 *The Pat Connaughton Foundation: A Sport Grant Agency*

On June 11, 2024, I received an email from the Pat Connaughton Foundation (PCF),[2] perhaps because my son had attended its popular basketball summer camp a few times previously. It said that the Foundation is

---

[1] Note that this could be related to the NSF's small business innovation research and technology transfer programs. To accelerate the impact of research, the NSF created a new Directorate for Technology, Innovation and Partnerships (see Technology, Innovation and Partnerships, *US National Science Foundation*, available at: https://new.nsf.gov/tip/latest).

[2] Pat Connaughton Foundation website, available at: www.patconnaughtonfoundation.org.

2 Real-Life Cases

proud to announce a $400,000 donation to Fidelity House in Arlington, Massachusetts, to support the renovation of their basketball facility. Pat Connaughton is currently an American professional basketball player for the Milwaukee Bucks of the National Basketball Association (NBA). He is an Arlington native and started his basketball journey in Fidelity House, a local community center that has two basketball courts. Pat Connaughton wanted to give back to a place that meant so much to him. He founded the Pat Connaughton Foundation in 2016 with the mission of creating access to athletics for the next generation of student-athletes.

The PCF, as its name indicates, is a grant agency that gives out money for a good cause, one of thousands of foundations of this type in the world, including in the United States. But more specifically, it is a private grant agency rather than a public one; it is a grant-making agency rather than a grant-managing one; and it offers social or developmental grants (i.e. supporting children of a community to play basketball) rather than scientific grants (e.g. conducting a research project or training young researchers). From this case, we can see that grant agency is a very complex concept that concerns an extremely wide variety of scientific or non-scientific grant agencies worldwide, including private development-oriented ones like the PCF.

2.2 The SUNY Research Foundation: A Grant-Managing Grant Agency

On February 13, 2024, the State University of New York's Office of Research, Innovation, and Economic Development[3] made a brief announcement that the SUNY's next *Research Forward* webinar will be on Tuesday, February 13, 2024. Dr. Bindu Nair, Director of the Department of Defense (DoD) Basic Research Office, would give an overview of funding priorities and research programs and discuss how to best partner with them.

I always enjoy reading and attending a series of exciting grant-related events run by SUNY's Office of Research, Innovation, and Economic Development and SUNY Research Foundation (SUNYRF). However, for years, I have always been puzzled by an irrelevant question: What is SUNYRF? Does this foundation offer grant opportunities like the NIH or NSF for which we can apply?

After a brief search and study, I came to develop two understandings. First, the Office of Research, Innovation and Economic Development

---

[3] The Research Foundation for SUNY, *LinkedIn*, available at: www.linkedin.com/company/rfsuny/about/.

(ORIED) provides strategic direction to the Research **Foundation** for SUNY. It is responsible for designing, directing, and expanding SUNY's research, innovation, and economic development activities. Second, SUNYRF serves sixty-four campuses of the State University of New York by providing essential sponsored programs administration and innovation support services to SUNY faculty, students, and staff. It manages SUNY's research portfolio, assists SUNY faculty, students, and staff through the research grant process, and ensures compliance with SUNY, grant sponsor and government requirements. In short, ORIED concerns research leadership and SUNYRF concerns research management.

The SUNYRF, as indicated by its name, is indeed a grant agency. However, it is primarily not a grant-making agency that provides research funding, even though it does make various internal awards and seed funding with a small budget. Instead, it is essentially a grant-managing agency that receives and administers external grants for research. From this case, we can see that various foundations only manage research grants (e.g. the SUNYRF) rather than make research grants (e.g. the NIH, NSF).

2.3 The National Institutes of Health: The Largest Public Grant Agency Worldwide

I heard about the National Institutes of Health (NIH) during my doctoral program. However, it learned for the first time about the complexity of the NIH when I attended the an APA convention on August 31, 2010. When passing a booth in the hallway, I saw a book titled *The Complete Writing Guide to NIH Behavioral Science Grants*.[4] I was surprised by its thickness, a total of 506 pages, especially given that it only covers the NIH's small behavioral science grants rather than its primary biomedicine grants. What struck me most was its long, comprehensive list of various funding mechanisms and funding programs, from grants for high school students and undergraduate students to early-, middle- and late-career independent scientists.

After the conference, I have learned that the NIH is a gigantic universe and requires an ocean of knowledge. The National Institutes of Health is plural rather than singular because it has twenty-seven separate institutes and centers of different biomedical disciplines. The NIH has the intramural component (around 80 percent of its funding) and the extramural

---

[4] Scheier, L. M., & Dewey, W. L. (2008). *The Complete Writing Guide to NIH Behavioral Science Grants*. Oxford University Press.

component (around 20 percent of its funding). As of 2013, the intramural research program had over 1,200 principal investigators and over 4,000 postdoctoral fellows in basic, translational, and clinical research. As of 2011, the extramural research program consisted of about 50,000 grants to more than 325,000 researchers at more than 3,000 institutions, with an annual budget of about $20 billion. The NIH is the largest governmental funding agency in the world. It is also the most studied funding agency worldwide due to its importance, its impacts, and especially its public access policy that allows its huge data to be studied.

I further learned that the NIH needs to go through a complex 1.5-year process to obtain its funds from Congress. Specifically: (1) Directors of Institutes and Centers, collaborating with scientists, determine the most important and promising research areas within their fields. (2) The NIH Director develops a budget request for continuing projects, new research proposals, and new initiatives. (3) The Department of Health and Human Services (HHS) considers this request as a portion of its budget, after many adjustments and appeals occur between the NIH and HHS, and submits the NIH's budget request to the Office of Management and Budget (OMB). (4) The OMB determines what amounts and research areas are approved for incorporation into the President's final budget. (5) The President then sends the NIH's budget request to Congress for the next fiscal year's allocations. (6) The House and Senate Appropriations Subcommittees deliberate and appropriate funding.

From this case, we can see that the NIH is not only one of the public grant agencies, but also the largest public funder of health research in the world.

2.4 The Institute of Education Sciences: One of the Thirty-Eight Federal Grant Agencies[5]

Over the past ten years, I had quite a few great opportunities to learn from my colleagues about their successful experiences of securing grants from various grant agencies in the field of education and psychology. Among them is a young faculty member who successfully received multiple research grants from the Institute of Education Sciences (IES). To me, it is an eye-opening learning experience because the NSF and NIH are the

---

[5] The National Center for Education Statistics: Who we are, *Institute of Education Sciences*, available at: https://ies.ed.gov/aboutus/; Funding opportunities, *Institute of Education Sciences*, available at: https://ies.ed.gov/funding/.

grant agencies that people talk about all the time, and the past decade has been the first opportunity for me to find out more about the IES.

I first learned that the IES is not an institution of education as suggested by its name. Instead, like the NIH, it both runs research in education and funds research in education. It is the statistics, research, and evaluation arm of the US Department of Education. It has four major units, like the NIH's research institutes: the National Center for Education Research (NCER); the National Center for Education Statistics (NCES); the National Center for Education Evaluation and Regional Assistance (NCEE); and the National Center for Special Education Research (NCSER).

I then learned that the IES funds thirteen types research and research training programs that contribute to improved education outcomes for all learners: (1) education and special education research programs; (2) transformative research in the education sciences; (3) research training programs; (4) statistical and research methodology in education; (5) partnerships and collaborations focused on problems of practice or policy; (6) national research and development centers and special education research and development centers; (7) research networks focused on critical problems of education and special education policy and practice; (8) low-cost, short-duration evaluation of education and special education interventions; (9) research grants focused on systematic replications; (10) using longitudinal data to support state education policymaking; (11) research grants focused on National Assessment of Educational Progress process data for learners with disabilities; (12) research to accelerate pandemic recovery in special education; and (13) improving pandemic recovery efforts in education agencies.

I further learned a similar case from another colleague of mine who consistently received multiple large research grants in psychology from the Department of Veterans Affairs (VA). She was generous enough to share her successful grant proposals with me so I could learn from them.

The IES and VA are just two of the twenty-six federal funding agencies and twelve small agencies in the United States.[6] The federal grant agencies are not just the NIH and NSF. Many other countries in the world have various popular and unpopular governmental grant agencies to support scientific and non-scientific activities and research or non-research projects. In a sense, each of them should be a gigantic universe that requires an ocean of knowledge.

---

[6] Grants.gov website, available at: www.grants.gov/.

2.5 The Howard Hughes Medical Institute: A Private Biomedicine Grant Agency

On December 13, 2023, a jury of six members delivered a unanimous verdict in favor of the Howard Hughes Medical Institute (HHMI), finding that it did not discriminate against Dr. Vivian Cheung, a disabled physician-scientist and pediatric neurologist at the University of Michigan, in declining to renew her seven-year, $9 million major grant. Both *Science* and *Nature* reported this unprecedented, significant, and complicated case of alleged disability discrimination.[7]

After reading this case, I briefly studied the famous HHMI from the grant agency perspective. I learned that: (1) The HHMI is one of the largest private funding organizations for biological and medical research in the world. Its signature funding program is the Investigator Program, identifying the most promising biological and medical scientists as HHMI investigators and giving them generous and stable financial support (usually $9 million in no-strings-attached funding over seven years). This unique funding model is intended to fund researchers rather than fund projects.[8] (2) The HHMI is not only a private funder, but also a non-profit funder for the taxing purpose of the Inland Revenue Service (IRS) – which is another unique and complicated issue where private funders are concerned.[9] The IRS has ruled that the HHMI did not qualify as a public medical research charity for taxing purposes, even after the ruling was appealed to the IRS by HHMI. (3) While 70 percent of its funding is on medical research, surprisingly, 13 percent of its funding is on **science education** and other scientific programs, enabling undergraduate and graduate students at all types of colleges and universities to engage in high-impact and inclusive research projects (e.g. its Science Education Alliance, the Gilliam Fellows Program). This is similar to the Burroughs Wellcome Fund (BWF),[10] another of the largest private funders in the United States. The BWF supports not only biomedical scientists in their significant research, but

---

[7] Wadman, M. (2023). Researcher loses disability lawsuit against major science funder, *Science*, available at: www.science.org/content/article/hhmi-prevails-disability-lawsuitm; Wadman, M. (2023). Trial puts Howard Hughes Medical Institute – and disabled scientists – in the spotlight, *Science*, available at: www.science.org/content/article/trial-puts-howard-hughes-medical-institute-and-disabled-scientists-spotlight; Heidt, A. (2023). Disability lawsuit lands Howard Hughes Medical Institute in court, *Nature*, available at: www.nature.com/articles/d41586-023-03848-z.
[8] Ioannidis, J. P. (2011). Fund people not projects. *Nature*, 477(7366), 529–31.
[9] HHMI fundamentals, *HHMI*, available at: www.hhmi.org/about; Howard Hughes Medical Institute, *Wikipedia*, available at: https://en.wikipedia.org/wiki/Howard_Hughes_Medical_Institute.
[10] Burroughs Wellcome Fund website, available at: www.bwfund.org/.

also K-12 students, science and mathematics teachers, institutions, and academic scientists.

From this case, we can see that the HHMI is a large, private, and complex funder rather than a public research grant agency.

2.6 The American Psychological Association: A Professional Organization with a Grant Program

In a research group meeting three years ago, I asked four to five doctoral students who have not yet developed a dissertation topic if they know of any potential grant opportunities to support their potential dissertation research in psychology. To my surprise, they were all unable to name such grants at that time. I then asked them to do a quick search online. To my surprise, and to their surprise too, they have all found various wonderful grant opportunities to support their dissertation research. One of them ended up presenting an informative talk to the group on how to apply for funding for dissertation research. In the end, he recommended three grants by the American Psychological Association (APA) that they could prepare to apply for now: the APA Dissertation Research Award, the Early Graduate Student Researcher Award, and the E.R. Hilgard Best Graduate-Level Academic Thesis Award.

The APA is a professional association in the United States, like the AERA, the APS, and the Society for Research in Child Development. They are primarily not grant-making agencies like the NIH and NSF. However, many professional associations offer various grants to support various scientific projects.

Take the APA as an example. If we search the APA website, it might give us at least fifteen hits on dissertation grants, travel grants, and awards: (1) Early Career Service Grants: To support direct services/programs that are not eligible or likely to receive financial support from other funding agencies *and* are not likely to be delivered without the funding support. (2) Travel Grants for Students of Color in Psychology: Awarded to students of color in psychology to serve as a source of funding for graduate students to help defray travel expenses associated with attending and presenting research at a professional conference. (3) Board of Educational Affairs (BEA) Conferences and Workshops Grant: Block grants support conferences and workshops on graduate and postdoctoral education and training to enhance the quality of teaching. (4) Commission on Ethnic Minority Recruitment, Retention and Training Grants: Seed funds to energize, empower, and support interested individuals, organizations, and educational institutions committed to enhancing ethnic minority recruitment, retention, and training in psychology. (5) Early Career Global Psychology Grants: These grants provide funding to support psychologists conducting work directly related to international psychology. Funds must be utilized to support services/programs not eligible or likely to receive financial support from other funding agencies, and are not likely to be delivered without the funding support. (6) BEA Grants for Precollege and Undergraduate Teaching Conferences: These grants support pre-college and undergraduate teaching conferences to enhance the quality of teaching and learning outcomes. (7) APA Dissertation Research Award: This award program assists science-oriented doctoral students of psychology with dissertation research costs. The Science Directorate of the APA sponsors an annual competition for dissertation research funding. The purpose of the Dissertation Research Award program is to assist science-oriented doctoral students of psychology with research costs. The current program offers three grants of $10,000 and seven grants of $5,000 to students whose dissertation research reflects excellence in scientific psychology. (8) APA Summer Undergraduate Psychology Experience in Research Fellowships: The APA offers fellowships to support undergraduate students from underrepresented groups interested in psychology research experience during the summer. (9) Professional Development Awards for High School Psychology Teachers: The purpose of these awards is to help high school psychology teachers travel to and attend psychology conferences or meetings. (10) APA Early Career Convention Grant: The goals of this grant are to support early career psychologists' professional development and their ability to make meaningful personal and inter-professional connections by reducing barriers to attending the APA convention. (11) Interdivisional Grant Program: The purpose of this program is to support joint activities that enhance the work, interests, or goals of two or more divisions. (12) The MOU Partner Collaboration and Exchange Program: The APA will support the travel for psychologists to attend the Fourth Annual Congress of the Portuguese Order of Psychologists in Braga, Portugal. (13) BEA Grant for Innovation in Career and Professional Skill Development for Psychology Graduate Students, Interns, and Postdoctoral Trainees/Scholars: This award supports departments and programs of psychology in developing new and innovative practices to support career and professional development. (14) Early Career Psychologist Champion Award: To recognize groups or individuals who champion the interests of early career psychologists. (15) Promoting Psychological Research and Training on Health Disparities at Ethnic Minority Serving Institutions: This supports early career faculty for activities related to the preparation of a federal or foundation funding proposal.

From this example, we can see that many good grant opportunities not only come from public and private funders, but also from various professional associations.

2.7 A Harrow Agenda and Four Grants: Developing Grant Portfolio

On July 18, 2019, *Times Higher Education* posted a feature article online on how to win a research grant.[11] Six distinguished scholars gave their golden tips that are among the most useful and usable advice I have seen so far. However, what really caught my eye is a comment by a reader posted three years later by its amusing username, "harrowagenda21," on September 4, 2022 at 5:57 am: "It is quite clear to me after thirty years, and reading this, that repeatedly applying for larger grants is a pathway to nowhere. In my field of social science, it is expected, but I never get past the 'internal starter grant' stage. I have not got the bigger ones, prefer to do the research myself rather than palm it off to funded students and RAs which is what happens when you have a bigger budget."

Last year, I also read an inspirational article published in *Science*, examining how scientific policy and scientific research interacted during the COVID-19 pandemic.[12] However, again, what really caught my eye was the acknowledgment note at the very end of the article, specifying four grants that support their research: the Air Force Office of Scientific Research grant FA9550-17-1-0089, the Air Force Office of Scientific Research grant FA9550-19-1-0354, the NSF grant SBE 1829344, and the Alfred P. Sloan Foundation grant G-2019-12485.

The reader "harrowagenda21" advised not to stick to a big grant from a big grant agency. The article in *Science* showed they relied on four grants from three grant agencies for their research. These two anecdotal cases not only suggest the importance of broadening our knowledge of various types of grant agencies, but also indicate the importance of understanding the concept of grant portfolio in grantology. Just like financial investment, a good investigator needs to develop a diversified investment

---

[11] How to win a research grant, *Times Higher Education*, available at: www.timeshighereducation.com/features/how-win-research-grant.

[12] Yin, Y., Gao, J., Jones, B. F., & Wang, D. (2021). Coevolution of policy and science during the pandemic. *Science*, 371(6525), 128–30. Gs87.

portfolio rather than rely on a single investment in order to maximize the return and minimize the risk. Likewise, it is critical for a new grants writer to develop a diversified grant portfolio rather than rely on a single, substantial, famous grant to maximize the return and minimize the risk. We should not build a "harrow agenda" or a distressing grant pursuit. We will further discuss the concept of a grant portfolio later in this chapter.

In summary of the above discussion of the seven cases, we can understand a little more about the complexity of agencies in the real world. To understand grant agencies, we should focus not only on their missions, organization, policy and procedure, and daily operation, but also on their grant priorities, grant programs, and grant officers.

3 Scientific Knowledge: From Largest Funders to Grant Portfolio

After discussing the seven short real-life cases presented above, it is now time for us to study published journal articles in order to further develop our scientific knowledge of grant agencies.

3.1 Viergever & Hendriks (2016): The Ten Largest Funders

When studying grant agencies, it is a good idea to learn from some large funders first to gain some good exposure to this topic. Here, let us study a well-cited article.[13]

Overview
This is an empirical article, surveying the largest public and philanthropic funders of health research in the world. It has been cited 183 times in Google Scholar as of 2023. It is one of the first comprehensive surveys of health-related funders at the global level.

The first author is Roderik Viergever. He was a researcher in the Department for Health Evidence at the Radboud University of the Netherlands and is now a researcher in the Department of Health Services Research, London School of Hygiene and Tropical Medicine. His research area is health policy and systems research, with an h-index of 16. He has

---

[13] Viergever, R. F., & Hendriks, T. C. (2016). The 10 largest public and philanthropic funders of health research in the world: What they fund and how they distribute their funds. *Health Research Policy & Systems*, *14*(1), 1–15. Gs183.

published another two articles on grant funders.[14] The second author is Thom Hendriks. He was also a researcher in the Department for Health Evidence at Radboud University and is now a general surgery resident at Vrije Universiteit Amsterdam, the Netherlands.

The article was published in 2016 in *Health Research Policy & Systems*. This journal covers all aspects of the organization and use of health research. It had an impact factor of 4.0 in 2022. The publisher is BioMed Central (BMC), a part of Springer Nature, in collaboration with the World Health Organization (WHO).

Highlights

It is an empirical study and has a typical structure, including background, methods, results, discussion, and conclusion. From the perspective of the funder or funding agencies, highlights of this paper are discussed below.

First, this article develops for the first time the list of **fifty-five largest funders** of health research in the world, based on the annual research expenditures. It paints a good macro-level picture of the worldwide landscape of health research funding as of 2016. The top ten largest public and private funders include: (1) the NIH; (2) the European Commission (EC); (3) the UK Medical Research Council (MRC); (4) the French National Institute of Health and Medical Research (*Institut national de la santé et de la recherche médicale*, or Inserm, in French); (5) the US DoD; (6) the Wellcome Trust; (7) the Canadian Institutes of Health Research; (8) the Australian National Health and Medical Research Council (NHMRC); (9) the HHMI; and (10) the German Research Foundation (DFG). Among them, eight organizations were public funding bodies and the Wellcome Trust and the HHMI were the only two philanthropic funders. Other noticeable names among the fifty-five largest funders include: (11) the National Natural Science Foundation of China; (14) Japan Society for Promotion of Science; (16) Bill & Melinda Gates Foundation; (38) the Russian Foundation for Basic Research; (50) the Ministry of Health Care of the Russian Federation; and (53) the Rockefeller Foundation.

Besides the top public and private funders, the article also reports two types of funders, Official Development Assistance (ODA) and

---

[14] Viergever, R. F. (2011). Aid alignment for global health research: The role of HIROs. *Health Research Policy & Systems*, 9(1), 12. Gs11; Kieny, M. P., Viergever, R. F., Adam, T., Boerma, T., & Røttingen, J. A. (2016). Global platform to inform investments for health R&D. *The Lancet*, *387*(10024), 1157. Gs10.

multilateral funders, given that the expenditures of ODA and multilateral funders on health research were substantially smaller than the expenditures of the largest public and philanthropic funding organization. Note that ODA is a category used by the Organisation for Economic Co-operation and Development to measure foreign aid. It is widely used as an indicator of international aid flow, as the donor government agency may disburse grants or low-interest loans to the government of the recipient country. The largest funder of health research through ODA includes the US Agency for International Development and the UK Department for International Development. The largest multilateral funder includes the WHO, the World Bank, the Pan American Health Organization, and the Global Alliance for Vaccines and Immunization (GAVI, the recipient of the largest grants from the Gates Foundation).

Second, this article meticulously presents funding **distribution mechanisms** in the funding patterns. It shows considerable diversity in organizations' funding distribution mechanisms with three pairs of basic features: (1) Extramural mechanism vs. intramural mechanism (including a hybrid mechanism that is a mix of both). Among the top ten funders, five funded research fully extramurally, five allocated at least a proportion of their funding to intramural research institutes, and one funder, the Inserm, funded research almost exclusively intramurally. (2) Targeted prioritized mechanism vs. un-targeted competitive mechanism (including mixed one). Six of the top ten funding organizations that provided extramural funding allocated funding through untargeted competitive grants or investigator grants. The European Commission's Cooperation Programme, however, used a more targeted approach and issued calls under prioritized areas. Two funders, the UK MRC and the Deutsche Forschungsgemeinschaft (DFG), used a mixed approach to allocate funding. (3) Project grants. vs. people grants. Most funders mainly dispensed funding via project grants. However, others (e.g. the HHMI) placed more focus on individual excellence for people grants.

Third, the article further describes specific **funding areas** or funding priorities under diverse funding mechanisms. For example, the NIH spent less on infectious disease research than on cancer research alone, while the Wellcome Trust spent much more on infectious disease research. The NIH also prioritized the HIV/AIDS funding, while the Australian NHMRC contributed much less in comparison.

Fourth, there exists an **extensive literature** on health research funding. Two excellent examples are articles by Hamilton Moses, Earl Ray Dorsey, and their collaborators.[15] Their analysis suggests six types of funders for the US biomedical research based on the data in 2007: (1) the NIH and other federal funders; (2) state and local government; (3) private not-for-profit funders (e.g. foundations, public charities, medical research organizations); (4) industry support (pharmaceutical firms, biotechnology firms, medical devise firms); (5) colleges and universities; and (6) funders for health policy and service research (e.g. the Agency for Healthcare Research and Quality and the Robert Wood Foundation). Industry firms and the NIH are the two largest funders.

Fifth, the article shows the **technical complexity** of estimating health research expenditures, the most basic estimation in studying funding organizations in the world. Individual funding organizations' expenditures are often limited to one or several countries or a select group of diseases. There exist substantial differences in how health research expenditures are reported, with three examples outlined here. First, expenditures are reported as actual expenditures, committed expenditures, or budgeted expenditures. Second, an organization's total expenditures on health research might include or exclude costs for managing the funding organization. Third, training support and research education might be included or excluded from the overall amount of health research expenditures. Fourth, organizations' expenditures in the national currency of a given country should be deflated for a given year based on the International Monetary Fund.

Last, the article has several **practical implications** for new grant writers. (1) We should learn more in breadth about funders, especially the wide spectrum of funders. There exist diverse funding sources rather than just one or two, which means we can develop and diversify our own grant portfolio. (2) We should learn more in-depth information about funders, especially their funding missions, mechanisms, and areas, so that we can be prepared for our grant applications. (3) We should pay attention to the differences in funding across disciplines. This article, as well as many others, focuses on health research or biomedical research. There are similarities and differences between natural sciences, life sciences, social sciences, and interdisciplinary sciences. (4) We should also pay attention to the change in funding trends, whereas this article focused on funding patterns in one year only.

---

[15] Moses, H., Dorsey, E. R., Matheson, D. H., & Thier, S. O. (2005). Financial anatomy of biomedical research. *JAMA*, *294*(11), 1333–42. Gs533; Dorsey, E. R., De Roulet, J., Thompson, J. P., Reminick, J. I., Thai, A., White-Stellato, Z. et al. (2010). Funding of US biomedical research, 2003–2008. *JAMA*, *303*(2), 137–43. Gs418.

3.2 James McCullough (1994): The NSF as a Public Funder

The public or governmental funders are the major types of grant agencies in the world. Different countries have different public grant agencies to award scientific funding. Here, we will study the NSF,[16] the United States' lead governmental agency through one unique article.[17]

Overview
This article is a nine-page unique review. Instead of presenting general operations and functions of the NSF, it focuses on a specific and critical topic: how the NSF's program officers manage and award grants.

The author of this well-written article is James McCullough (1942–2015).[18] He was the NSF's director of program evaluation. In 1989, he led the NSF in introducing a new type of award known as **Small Grants for Exploratory Research**. He received an NSF Meritorious Service Award and was elected a Fellow of the American Association for the Advancement of Science. He served as a senior analyst for the President's Council of Advisors for Science and Technology and then as Senior Policy Officer in the National Science Board office, including assistance on the Strategic Policy and Planning Committee and the Merit Review Task Force.[19] He retired in 1997 after thirty-five years of government service. He is known for his strong analytical skills and work ethic, unassuming brilliance, optimistic disposition, natural leadership, and perpetual quest for knowledge. This well-written article is one good example of his high-level professionalism.

The article was published in 1994 in *Higher Education*. This journal is recognized as the leading international journal of Higher Education studies. Since its establishment in 1972, *Higher Education* has actively

---

[16] Holbrook, J. B. (2005). Assessing the science–society relation: The case of the US National Science Foundation's second merit review criterion. *Technology in Society*, 27(4), 437–51. Gs166; Kevles, D. J. (1977). The National Science Foundation and the debate over postwar research policy, 1942–1945: A political interpretation of Science – the endless frontier. *Isis*, 68(1), 5–26. Gs255; Bush, V. (1945). *Science, the Endless Frontier: A Report to the President on a Program for Postwar Scientific Research*. Gs6226; McLellan, T. (2021). Impact, theory of change, and the horizons of scientific practice. *Social Studies of Science*, 51(1), 100–20. Gs31.
[17] McCullough, J. (1994). The role and influence of the US National Science Foundation's program officers in reviewing and awarding grants. *Higher Education*, 28(1), 85–94. Gs24.
[18] James M. McCullough, *Dignity Memorial*, available at: www.dignitymemorial.com/obituaries/washington-dc/james-mccullough-6426132.
[19] McCullough, J. (1989). First comprehensive survey of NSF applicants focuses on their concerns about proposal review. *Science, Technology, & Human Values*, 14(1), 78–88. Gs55; Russell, S. H., Hancock, M. P., & McCullough, J. (2007). Benefits of undergraduate research experiences. *Science*, 316(5824), 548–9. Gs1835.

endeavored to report on developments in both public and private Higher Education sectors. The publisher is Springer. Its impact factor is 5.0 in 2022.

Highlights

This review article focuses on program officers of the NSF. It has eight major sections: Introduction, The NSF and federal research support, Internal organization and staffing, Program Officers' roles, Recommendation, Deciding small grants, Communicating with Applicants, and Oversight of program officers. Note that the article was published in 1994, over thirty years ago. There have been various changes in the NSF since then. However, the NSF's general structure and major procedure remain unchanged. McCullough's major points presented in the article are still extremely helpful. From the grant agency research perspective, the following key points can be highlighted.

First, the NSF has four major **governing** features. (1) The NSF's principal mission is comprehensive. It supports basic research through grant-making in all fields of sciences and engineering (even including social and behavioral sciences), and the improvement of education in the sciences, mathematics, and technology at all grade levels (including K-12 education). Put briefly, the NSF focuses on all non-medical sciences. As the NSF's medical counterpart, the NIH focuses on medical and health sciences. (2) The NSF, as an independent agency of the federal government, operates more flexibly and less bureaucratically than other federal agencies. Its budget is part of the federal research and development budget. Its fundamental legislation (the National Science Foundation Act of 1950) gives the Foundation broad authority to create and administer programs. It reports directly to the President, through the White House Office of Science and Technology Policy and the Office of Management and Budget. Except for NASA and the Environmental Protection Agency, other US research agencies are parts of larger departments (e.g. the NIH is part of the Public Health Service) and are known as mission agencies. This is because their efforts are directly related to the missions from their home departments. (3) The NSF is governed by a Board of Directors like a private grant-making organization. The Board comprises twenty-four members appointed by the President for six-year terms to establish and approve its overall policies. (4) The NSF's director and deputy director are appointed by the President of the United States and confirmed by the US Senate. They are responsible for administration, planning, budgeting, and day-to-day operations of the Foundation.

Second, the NSF has a five-level **organization** structure. The first level is the National Science Board. The second level is the NSF's director and deputy directors. The third level is directorates. The NSF has seven grant-making directorates that are organized along fields of science (e.g. Mathematical and Physical Sciences; Geosciences; Biosciences; Social, Behavioral and Economic Sciences; Computer and Information Science and Engineering; Engineering; and Education and Human Resources).[20] The fourth level is divisions. Each directorate has divisions covering several fields of research. For example, the Directorate of Mathematical and Physical Sciences makes grants in physics, mathematics, astronomy, and chemistry. Altogether, there are around thirty-five divisions. A division may make grant decisions about proposals, from typical individual investigator proposals to large research projects or interdisciplinary centers. The final level is programs. The thirty-five divisions operate around 170 programs. Each program may have one or two program officers.

Third, NSF reviews and makes decisions about 30,000 proposals a year, around one-third of which are funded. The Foundation's fiscal year 1993 budget is $2.7 billion, with its research grant programs making up around $2 billion, its education grant programs $0.5 billion, and its administrative costs $0.1 billion. Most grants from the NSF go to Principal Investigators (PIs) at various colleges and universities, although the NSF makes limited awards to small research firms, school districts, and local governments. There are three levels among the colleges and universities receiving the funding: around twenty-five **extremely strong** institutions at the top of receiving funding, such as MIT, Stanford, the University of California-Berkeley, the University of California-San Diego, the University of Wisconsin, and the University of Washington; around fifty **very strong** institutions in a middle band that includes notable universities with several strong departments, such as the University of Arizona and the University of Maryland; and a third group of around 100 institutions that have a few **strongly competitive** departments, such as Wayne State University in Ohio (strong in chemistry) and the University of Delaware (strong in chemical engineering).

Fourth, the article presents the NSF's **program officers** (POs) in detail. POs are the heart and soul of the NSF or the most fundamental professionals in the NSF, like doctors in a hospital, teachers at a school, or lawyers at a legal firm. In other foundations, they are also called program

---

[20] In 2022, the NSF added a new directorate: Technology Innovation and Partnerships.

officials or program administrators. Of 1,200 full-time staff, around 350 are POs and another fifty or so are the division and directorate officials who supervise them. Most programs are typically managed by one or two POs. A PO's portfolio may range from around 150 new grant proposals for reviewing and around 150 funded projects for monitoring. Each PO is an expert in his or her field of research or education, and has usually operated a laboratory or directed major projects in their career.

The PO has four principal responsibilities: (1) to manage the proposal review process, including forming and facilitating merit review panels; (2) to make a funding recommendation by integrating the views of external reviewers with his or her own views and with the NSF's policies; (3) to communicate with the PI community; and (4) to decide small grants. POs may also be involved with a broad spectrum of national scientific programs and initiatives. Note that, in the NSF, program **directors** but not program **officers** make final decisions about whether to fund research proposals based on the opinions of external peer reviewers, their own views and scientific judgment, and general NSF policies.

Different from other funders, the NSF has full-time **permanent** POs and **temporary** rotators. Around two-fifths of the POs and division directors are rotators or visiting scientists, namely, experienced researchers and educators on leave from their institution, usually for two years, specifically to come to Washington in mid-career to help administer a program in their field. Rotators make recommendations about which proposals to fund; influence new directions in the fields of science, engineering, and education; support cutting-edge interdisciplinary research; and mentor junior research members. This rotator system has mutual benefits: rotators constantly bring new energy to contribute significantly to the vitality of the NSF, and at the same time, the NSF enables rotators to greatly broaden the horizons of their own fields and significantly develop their insights into the NSF's grants-making process.

Fifth, the article points out at the end that the NSF uses various strategies to **monitor and oversee** POs. Such strategies include that a final decision needs to be signed off by a higher-level manager; the Committee of Visitors reviews the programs every three years; and the NSF's Inspector General's Office randomly examines proposals every year and audits grantees for conflict of interest, fraud, and plagiarism.

Last, new grant writers can gain several practical insights from this article, the best of which is probably the demystification of the NSF in general and the program office in particular. Another obvious benefit is that the information in the article can help new grant writers understand the role of POs and how best to communicate with them before, during, and after a grant application.

3.3 McCoy et al. (2009): The Gates Foundation as a Private Funder

Private funders are another major type of grant agency. Compared with public grant agencies, private grant agencies are much more diverse and have much less research literature. Let us now study one good example, the Bill & Melinda Gates Foundation, which is the largest private funder on health, by reviewing an article by McCoy *et al.*[21]

Overview
This article is an analysis of the Foundation's grant-making program from the perspective of global health. Here, the article does not present the general contributions of the Foundation to global health. Instead, it explicitly focuses on the "grant-making" program of the Foundation, specifically, the 1,094 grants awarded from 1998 to 2007. It has been well cited, a total of 353 times as of 2023, based on Google Scholar.

Four authors wrote this article. They are from the Centre for International Health and Development, University College London. Based on the contribution note of the article, the first author, David McCoy, is the project leader, with his three co-authors as project assistants. He has published several articles on global health research funding.[22]

The article was published in *The Lancet*. One of *The Lancet*'s features is to publish major studies on public health and global health. Again, *NEJM, JAMA, BMJ, The Lancet*, and *Internal Medicine Annual* are considered among the best medicine and public health journals. The publisher is Elsevier.

Highlights
The article is a health policy report. It has three major sections: Introduction, which briefly presents the Foundation; Analysis, which describes the data

---

[21] McCoy, D., Kembhavi, G., Patel, J., & Luintel, A. (2009). The Bill & Melinda Gates Foundation's grant-making programme for global health. *The Lancet, 373*(9675), 1645–53. Gs353.
[22] McCoy, D., & McGoey, L. (2011). Global health and the gates foundation – in perspective. In S. Rushton & O. D. Williams (eds.), *Partnerships and Foundations in Global Health Governance* (pp. 143–63). Springer. Gs66; McCoy, D., Chand, S., & Sridhar, D. (2009). Global health funding: How much, where it comes from and where it goes. *Health Policy & Planning, 24*(6), 407–17. Gs348.

analysis method used in the study; and The Gates Foundation's grant-making program, which discusses its global health funding program in detail. From the grant agency research perspective, several important points are highlighted below.

First, there is a long history of private philanthropic funding in global health, notably by the Rockefeller Foundation and the Ford Foundation a century ago. The Gates Foundation has currently emerged as the **most influential** global health funder. Its spending on global health in 2007 was $1.22 billion, close to the WHO's annual budget of $1.65 billion. The Gates Foundation has approximately 733 employees with $264 million in operating and administrative expenses in 2007. As the largest private grant-making foundation in the world, the Gates Foundation has three main programs: the US program, which focuses on secondary and post-secondary education; the global development program, which focuses on hunger and poverty; and the global health program, which is the main focus of the article.

Second, the article presents the **trend of increase in funding** in the period 1998–2007. During these nine years, the number of grants awarded annually increased from 34 to 129, with a total of 1,094 awarded; the annual value of grants increased from $151 million to $1,079 million, with the total value of grants awarded or committed being $8,949 million; and the annual amount of money disbursed increased from $686 million to $1,220 million, with the total amount being $6,602 million. Note that grants awarded/committed vs. grants disbursed/spent (the two seemingly similar terms used here) have different financial meanings. For example, when a grantee receives a grant of $2 million in 2001 for two years, financially, that means that the Foundation awards or commits $2 million. However, half of the grant will be disbursed in 2001, namely, the grantee will receive the first $1 million to use for the proposed project in 2001. The other half of the grant will be disbursed in 2002, namely, the grantee will receive another $1 million to use in 2002.

Third, the **size of individual grants** varied substantially. The smallest grant was $3,500, whereas the largest was $750 million. The largest individual grants awarded include: GAVI Alliance in 1999, $750 million, to purchase new vaccines; Aeras Global TB Vaccine Foundation in 2007, $201 million to develop and license an improved vaccine against tuberculosis; and the Program for Appropriate Technology in Health (PATH) 1998, $125 million to support the Children's Vaccine Program. The largest organizations that received grants included GAVI Alliance, Path, the WHO, and seven universities, including the University of Washington,

Johns Hopkins University, Harvard University, Columbia University, and the London School of Hygiene and Tropical Medicine.

Fourth, the Bill & Melinda Gates Foundation **distributed its global health grants** during the 1998–2007 period to six types of **recipients**: (1) non-governmental/non-profit organization (e.g. PATH), 36.8 percent; (2) global health partnerships (e.g. GAVI Alliance, Global Fund to Fight AIDS, Tuberculosis and Malaria), 32.5 percent; (3) universities (e.g. University of Washington, Johns Hopkins, Harvard, Columbia), 20.2 percent; (4) intergovernmental organizations (e.g. the WHO, UNICEF), 7.9 percent; (5) public organizations (e.g. the NIH), 1.4 percent; and (6) private for-profit organizations (e.g. Beth Israel Deaconess Medical Center), 0.9 percent. In addition, the Foundation allocated its funding across six types of **activity**: (1) research and development and basic science, 36.5 percent; (2) healthcare delivery, 24.1 percent; (3) enabling supply and purchasing, 17.6 percent; (4) applied health research, 11.4 percent; (5) public awareness and advocacy (e.g. food fortification and agricultural research), 3.5 percent; and (6) program and policy development, 1.9 percent.

Fifth, significantly different from public funding agencies such as the NIH and NSF, the Gates Foundation relies on **direct solicitation** for grant applications and **non-review selection** for grant decisions. Grant-making by the Gates Foundation seems to be largely managed through an informal system of personal networks and relationships rather than by a more transparent process. How the Foundation solicits, judges, and funds individual grant proposals is not informed publicly.

Last, this article may have a few practical pointers for new grant writers. The knowledge about private grant agencies is complex, as we can see from the Gates Foundation, and many operate in their own unique ways, significantly different from public grant agencies like the NIH or NSF, which operate a standard and open process. Thus, for new grant writers, it is always useful to first study grant portfolios of a few researchers in our own areas and then identify targeted private foundations before applying to them.

3.4 Huang & Huang (2018): Funders across Disciplines

Funders in biomedical and public health have been dominant. However, it is important to learn about funders in different disciplines. The article by Huang and Huang allows us to do just this.[23]

---

[23] Huang, M.-H., & Huang, M. J. (2018). An analysis of global research funding from subject field and funding agencies perspectives in the G9 countries. *Scientometrics*, *115*(2), 833–47. Gs48.

4 Grant Agencies

Overview

This is an analytic paper, titled "An analysis of global research funding from subject field and funding agencies perspectives in the G9 countries." It is one of the very few articles comparing funding and funding agencies across multiple disciplines at the global level, while there is extensive research on global funding.[24] Here, the G9 refers to Canada, China, France, Germany, Italy, Japan, Russia, the United Kingdom, and the United States.[25]

Two authors wrote this paper, the first being Mu-Hsuan Huang, who is currently a Professor of Library and Information Science at National Taiwan University.[26] She has published extensively on informatics, including research funding and patent searching.[27] She is the editor of the *Journal of Informatics* and the *Journal of Library and Information Studies*.

The paper was published in 2018 in *Scientometrics*. The journal, again, is an international journal for quantitative studies in the science of science, communication in science, and science policy. Its impact factor was 3.5 in 2023. The publisher is Springer. The journal has published a long list of interesting articles in grantology and thus students and researchers in grantology should follow it closely.

Highlights

This article is a special empirical study that analyzes bibliometric data. It has four regular sections: Introduction, Methods, Results, and Conclusion.

---

[24] Luukkonen, T. (2014). The European Research Council and the European research funding landscape. *Science & Public Policy*, *41*(1), 29–43. Gs74; Lepori, B., Masso, J., Jabłecka, J., Sima, K., & Ukrainski, K. (2009). Comparing the organization of public research funding in central and eastern European countries. *Science & Public Policy*, *36*(9), 667–81. Gs59; Morillo, F. (2019). Collaboration and impact of research in different disciplines with international funding (from the EU and other foreign sources). *Scientometrics*, *120*(2), 807–23. Gs22; Zhou, P., Cai, X., & Lyu, X. (2020). An in-depth analysis of government funding and international collaboration in scientific research. *Scientometrics*, *125*(2), 1331–47. Gs29; Chankseliani, M. (2023). Who funds the production of globally visible research in the Global South? *Scientometrics*, *128*(1), 783–801. Gs16; Gök, A., Rigby, J., & Shapira, P. (2016). The impact of research funding on scientific outputs: Evidence from six smaller European countries. *Journal of the Association for Information Science & Technology*, *67*(3), 715–30. Gs105; Wang, X., Liu, D., Ding, K., & Wang, X. (2012). Science funding and research output: A study on 10 countries. *Scientometrics*, *91*(2), 591–9. Gs160.

[25] There are different groups of countries in discussing and coordinating economic policies and strategies, such as the G7, the G8, the G9, the G10, and the G20. For details, see G-7 and G-20, *US Department of the Treasury*, available at: https://home.treasury.gov/policy-issues/international/g-7-and-g-20; and The difference between G-7, G-8, and G-20 – and why they matter, *CNBC*, available at: www.cnbc.com/2018/06/08/difference-between-g7-g8-g20-world-economy.html.

[26] Chair Professor Huang, Mu-Hsuan, Department of Library and Information Science, *National Taiwan University*, available at: www.lis.ntu.edu.tw/english/?page_id=230.

[27] Fan, H. L., Huang, M. H., & Chen, D. Z. (2019). Do funding sources matter? The impact of university–industry collaboration funding sources on innovation performance of universities. *Technology Analysis & Strategic Management*, *31*(11), 1368–80. Gs33.

From the grant agency research perspective, we can highlight the following important points.

First, it is a **challenging** task to directly or indirectly compare funding and funding agencies across major fields, while existing studies have primarily focused on one specific discipline within or between countries. The authors used thoughtful methods in data collection and data analysis to compare funding and funding agencies across major fields. For the data collection, they chose to use the bibliometric database of Webs of Science. They first identified 5,856,744 articles published in the G9 countries, then narrowed this down to 3,693,488 articles that have information about the funding agency, with substantial labor of cleaning, checking, and correcting for different languages, and then classified all the articles into the seven major fields primarily based on the categories used on the Web of Science while handling overlapping issues. For data analysis, the authors developed three indexes, the funded paper ratio, the relative funded paper ratio, and sponsorship surplus, to analyze the data and discover potential patterns.

Second, the major finding paints an **informative** picture of funding by funders across seven major fields. It was found that, for the G9 countries, the average funded article ratios, which were estimated based on the number of funded articles within the total number of published articles, are (in order from highest to lowest): 77.67 percent in life sciences, 72.16 percent in agriculture, 70.42 percent in natural sciences, 66.33 percent in engineering, 53.30 percent in clinical medicine, 22.82 percent in social sciences, and 4.44 percent in humanities. Here, across the seven major fields, life sciences are the highest and humanities are the lowest. Specifically, for the United States, the average funded article ratios are (in order from highest to lowest): 79.14 percent in life sciences, 70.98 percent in agriculture, 67.90 percent in natural sciences, 65.88 percent in engineering, 55.78 percent in clinical medicine, 21.30 percent in social sciences, and 3.70 percent in humanities. The same pattern remains: across the seven major fields, life sciences are the highest and humanities are the lowest.

One interpretation for this empirical evidence could be that research in life sciences has a high demand in running labs and thus receives a larger amount of funding and produces the largest number of funded articles, whereas humanities might have a small need for research equipment and thus demands a small amount of funding and produces a small number of funded articles. While further research is needed to verify the findings, the central message is that significant differences in grant funding and grant impact might exist across different major fields. Research in grantology in general and grant funders specifically must consider the context of diverse disciplines.

Last, there are **important implications** for new grant writers. We must know funding patterns and funding agencies of our own disciplines well before developing a grant portfolio.

3.5 McGovern (2012): Build a Solid Grant Portfolio

After reviewing a few articles on different types of grant agencies, it is now helpful to study grant agencies from the integrated perspective to guide our grant applications. Let us study a short but well-written article by a senior grant professional.[28]

Overview

The article has a simple title, "Getting grants," but includes extremely rich contents. Different from hundreds of practical articles of this kind, it not only effectively addresses the practical issues of new grant writers securing grants, but also systematically synthesizes key knowledge of securing grants. There is no wonder it was published as the lead article of the January/February issue of 2012 under Editor's Corner. It has only six citations after a decade, perhaps due to its specific topic for a specific readership.

The author is Victoria McGovern. She received her PhD in biochemistry at the University of Alabama at Birmingham. She has been with the BWF for just under thirty years, since 1997, initially as a Program Officer, then as a Senior Program Officer, and now as Chief Strategy Officer. As an American extension of the England-based Wellcome Trust, the BWF is a US-based non-profit biomedical research organization with an endowment of $780 million. McGovern's specialties include non-profit program management and development and infectious diseases. She has been a science writer for around thirty years, known for her content knowledge and writing skills. She is among the few foundation directors who writes well and publishes well. Her h-index is 10.

The article was published in a specialized journal, *Virulence*. The term virulence means the degree to which a virus causes disease. The journal is affiliated with the American Society for Virology. Virology is the scientific study of biological viruses to address challenges in infectious diseases. It has been an open-access journal since it was launched in 2010 by Taylor & Francis. Its impact factor is 5.428 in 2021.

---

[28] McGovern, V. (2012). Getting grants. *Virulence, 3*(1), 1–11. Gs6.

Highlights

The article is a narrative review, with three major sections to address three key questions about how to secure grants: (1) How do you build a funding portfolio? (2) Which grant fits? (3) What does it take to get a grant? From the perspective of grant agencies, we discuss only the first two questions (the next chapter addresses how to write a grant proposal in detail) and highlight other interesting points.

First, the author covered a wide variety of **core knowledge** of securing grants, as we can see from the long list of abbreviations at the very beginning of the article: BSSD =Biological Systems Science Division of the DOE; BWCo = Burroughs Wellcome Company; BWF = Burroughs Wellcome Fund; CAREER = NSF Faculty Early Career Development Program; CSR = NIH Center for Scientific Review; DARPA = Defense Advanced Research Projects Agency; DOE = Department of Energy; ECR = CSR Early Career Reviewer Program; EPSCoR = Experimental Program to Stimulate Competitive Research; IDSA = Infectious Disease Society of America; K22 = NIH Research Scholar Development Award; K23 = NIH Career Transition Award; K99/R00 = NIH Pathway to Independence Award; NIAID = National Institute of Allergy and Infectious Diseases; NIH = National Institutes of Health; NSB = National Science Board; NSF = National Science Foundation; PA = Program Announcements; PECASE = Presidential Early Career Award for Scientists and Engineers; R01 = NIH Research Project Grant; R03 = NIH Small Research Grant; R21 = NIH Exploratory/Developmental Grant; RFA = Request for Applications; SGER = NSF Small Grants for Exploratory Research; VA = Department of Veterans Affairs.

Second, the author proposed to use the terms **productive** and **successful** to redefine grant application efforts. This is because funding resources are getting scarcer, the number of applications has increased substantially, and the success rate of grant proposals has dropped over the past decade. With these factors, even high-quality proposals end up being unfunded. Thus, it should be appropriate and thoughtful for us to redefine our application efforts as productive without funding or successful with funding.

Third, the author stressed the particular importance of building a **funding portfolio** for grant writers. This is the critical theme of this article, like the critical strategy of diversifying financial investment in business. She immediately stresses this at the beginning of the article: "For researchers just beginning their independent careers, building a diversified funding portfolio is a good strategy for keeping a laboratory financially healthy for the long term." She further points out that, even for researchers at mid-career and beyond, building a diversified funding portfolio is also important because "researchers who have several lines of funding, even if some of those lines are small, should be more able to thrive in tough times than those who rely entirely on the National Institutes of Health (NIH)" (p 1). As someone who has been in the grant management profession for nearly thirty years, she stressed enough that understanding and developing a diversified funding portfolio or a spectrum of diverse funders rather than sticking to one or two popular funders will help us to make successful grant applications. For those who are interested in this topic, here is an outstanding reference.[29] To build a funding portfolio, the author made four important suggestions.

The first suggestion is to pursue **small grants from small funders first**. There could be six types of small grants. (1) Our own institutions offer start-up funds negotiated as part of the hiring process so that we can have initial support for pilot studies before our first independent research grants. (2) Our own institutions may have various other funding available for encouraging collaborations, stimulating the use of core facilities, developing new research projects, or participating in relevant research centers. (3) Local professional organizations may have small funding opportunities. (4) Local community foundations might have philanthropic services or permanent endowments to support science. This potential funding source has often been overlooked. (5) State-level funding is often useful for research. (6) Some funding organizations support small but important projects (e.g. the Morris Animal Foundation). Pay attention to the funding acknowledgments in published articles in your own field to identify other good funding resources.

The second suggestion is to pursue **large grants from large funders later**. Seven common large funders have been specified. (1) NIH R01, known for new and established PIs. (2) The NSF's Faculty Early Career Development Program (CAREER) and small grants for exploratory research. (3) Various federal agencies such as the Departments of Defense, Commerce, Veterans Affairs, Homeland Security, Centers for Disease Control and Prevention, and Food and Drug Administration, besides the NIH and NSF. (4) Various private foundations such as the Gates Foundation, the Starr Foundation, the BWF, and the James McDowell Foundation, as well as the HHMI, which is not incorporated as a private foundation.

---

[29] Franko, M., & Ionescu-Pioggia, M. (2004). *Making the Right Moves: A Practical Guide to Scientific Management for Postdocs and New Faculty*, Burroughs Wellcome Fund and Howard Hughes Medical Institute.

These foundations are significant supporters of research and many have programs aimed at supporting early-career researchers. (5) Various public charities (e.g. the Heart Association). Note that private foundations support research with income from endowments or with direct donations, whereas public charities make grants with money raised from the public. (6) Various new foundations that could emerge and evolve rapidly (e.g. the Ellison Medical Foundation).

The third suggestion is to pursue **high-risk-high-reward** grants. The NIH and NSF both have mechanisms that support exploratory research and pilot work. Foundations and public charities have followed the Bill & Melinda Gates Foundation in creating "Grand Challenges" programs to stimulate the development of new approaches to fundamental questions or critical challenges. The Defense Advanced Research Projects Agency (DARPA) has a Young Faculty Award to support untenured faculty and help research career development.

Fourth, the author presented three practical strategies to **find a grant program that fits**, after discussing how to build a grant portfolio. The first strategy is to learn each funder's mission. Each funder has its **goals** and **missions**, and missions drive its policies and procedures. We can find the mission statement on a funder's website or through its grant database. The second strategy is to study each funder's **grant priorities**. This is often through planning activities by senior leaders and the advisory councils. For instance, the NIH's funding priorities are decided by the director along with congressional oversight. The NSF's funding priorities are decided by a twenty-five-member National Science Board. The Gates Foundation's funding priorities and strategies are guided by a six-member panel. And the BWF's funding priority is determined by a twelve-member board. The third strategy is to further investigate specific **grant programs**. For example, in the NIH, G01 is the most standard research grant program and K99/R00 is the most regular program to support mentored postdoctoral training. The fourth strategy is to look into **funding opportunities** via (1) funders' grant databases and (2) funders' grant solicitations (e.g. the NIH uses Requests for Applications (RFAs) and Program Announcements (PAs), and the NSF uses Program Descriptions, Program Announcements, and Program Solicitations). The last strategy is to communicate with POs because one of their daily jobs is to help us understand whether our planned proposal fits into their program and thus is the best resource to assess the grant fit.

Last, new grant writers can glean critically important tips and advice from reading this article. The most important point is that while learning

150   4 Grant Agencies

more about diverse grant agencies, it is critical to build a portfolio and find a program that fits. This is essentially why we need to study grant agencies in this chapter.

4 Grantology vs. Journalology: Grant Agencies vs. Journal Publishers

Grant agencies and journal publishers seem to have more differences than similarities. Given the complexity and diversity of grant agencies, we will focus on comparing one example of grant agencies, namely, the NIH, with one example of publishers, namely, Wiley.

4.1 The NIH: An American Public Research Funder

History

The NIH is one of the world's foremost medical research centers. It has a history of around 136 years if we trace its roots to the year 1887 when the one-room Hygienic Laboratory was created in New York. In 1930, the Hygienic Laboratory was renamed as the National Institute of Health. In 1937, the National Cancer Institute (NCI) was created and started to award research grants to non-federal scientists and to fund fellowships for young researchers. In 1944, the Public Health Service Act gave the NIH the authority to conduct and support medical research, award grants for research projects and fellowships, and make the NCI a division of the NIH. Thus, the formal history of the NIH as both a research center and a grant agency might start in 1944, seventy-nine years from now. In 1948, with new research institutes, the NIH was renamed as the National Institutes of Health.[30]

Mission

According to the NIH, its mission is "to seek fundamental **knowledge** about the nature and behavior of living systems and the **application** of that knowledge to enhance health, lengthen life, and reduce illness and disability."[31] It has two key elements: seeking knowledge of health; and applying knowledge of health. This is an NIH-wide mission, while each institute or center has its own mission and research priorities focusing on

---

[30] A short history of the National Institutes of Health, *NIH*, available at: https://history.nih.gov/display/history/A+Short+History+of+the+National+Institutes+of+Health.
[31] Mission and goals, *NIH*, available at: www.nih.gov/about-nih/what-we-do/mission-goals.

specific diseases, body systems, life stages, or fields of science. Every five years, the NIH releases the Strategic Plan to outline its vision for biomedical research direction, capacity, and stewardship, by articulating its highest priorities. In addition, it provides illustrative examples of accomplishments under the last plan.[32]

Strategies
To achieve this mission, the NIH operates twenty-seven Institutes and Centers. It receives its annual funding (e.g. $47.68 billion in 2023) from the US Congress. More than 80 percent of the funding is passed on to researchers and research institutions around the country via the extramural research program, through a rigorous competitive process, while less than 20 percent of the funding goes to the intramural research program conducted by scientists in the NIH's own laboratories, which are also subject to an equally rigorous review.

The extramural program supports research across the United States and beyond. Every year, the NIH receives more than 54,000 research project grant applications and funds almost 50,000 new and continuing grants. These grants support more than 300,000 researchers at all career stages, including more than 43,000 PIs at approximately 2,500 universities, medical schools, and other research institutions in every state of the United States and around the world. The NIH relies on the expertise of more than 25,000 external reviewers annually to assess the scientific merit of grant applications in the first stage of peer review, followed by a second-level review for mission relevance by members of national advisory councils for Institutes and Centers. Final funding decisions are made by Directors of Institutes and Centers.

The intramural program supports research on NIH campuses. The program supports approximately 8,000 basic, translational, and clinical researchers at NIH research facilities. The research program includes an estimated 1,200 PIs, 1,800 staff clinicians and staff scientists, and 5,000 trainees. Around 1,600 clinical research studies are in progress at the NIH Clinical Center. Approximately half are studies of the natural history of the disease, while most of the other studies are clinical trials, often the first tests of new drugs and therapies in people.

As a grant agency, the NIH uses a variety of funding mechanisms, including research grants, cooperative agreements, research contracts, prize competitions, and other less frequently used systems.

---

[32] NIH-wide strategic plan, *NIH*, available at: www.nih.gov/about-nih/nih-wide-strategic-plan.

Impacts

The NIH's impact can be seen in revolutionizing science and improving health. Hundreds of scientists have received Nobel Prizes for their groundbreaking achievements. For more than a century, 171 scientists who won 102 Nobel Prizes conducted their work at the NIH or were supported by NIH funds. Their studies have led to the development of MRI, an understanding of how viruses can cause cancer, insights into cholesterol control, and knowledge of how our brain processes visual information, among dozens of other advances.

4.2 Elsevier: A Dutch Private Academic Publisher

Background

The academic publishing industry generates around $19 billion annually and globally. However, around 50 percent of that revenue is distributed between only five major players or the Big Five: Elsevier, Springer Nature, John Wiley & Sons, Taylor & Francis, and SAGE. The academic publishing industry has one of the biggest profit margins, sometimes amounting to 40 percent (i.e. a company retains $40 million for its revenue of $100 million). The large profit margins are more than some of the most successful tech companies, like Google and Amazon. Like the NIH, Elsevier was founded in 1880, around 150 years ago. It is a Dutch academic publisher specializing in scientific, technical, and medical content. Its products and services include prestigious journals (e.g. *The Lancet*, *Cell*), *ScienceDirect* (its collection of electronic journals), and Scopus (its online citation database).

Mission

As a global leader in information and analytics, Elsevier's mission is to "help researchers and healthcare professionals to advance science and improve health outcomes for the benefit of society."[33] This mission has one keyword, "help," and two important phrases, "advance science" and "improve health outcomes." If one interprets it correctly, this mission means that Elsevier does not advance science and improve health outcomes directly. Instead, it **helps** researchers and professionals to advance science and improve health outcomes.

---

[33] Elsevier website, available at: www.elsevier.com/.

Strategies

Elsevier uses various strategies to achieve its mission. First, Elsevier has around 100 **offices** around the world, with 9,500 employees, to serve academic and government institutions, research and development intensive corporations, healthcare institutions, and medical and nursing students in over 170 countries and regions. Second, as the largest academic publisher in the world, Elsevier published 2,928 **journals** in 2022, the most among all academic publishers, while Springer published 2,920 journals, Taylor & Francis published 2,508 journals, Wiley published 1,607 journals, and SAGE published 1,151 journals. In 2023, Elsevier received nearly 3.2 million article submissions, publishing over 630,000 new research articles following peer review. Third, Elsevier launched **Scopus**, a multidisciplinary metadata database of scholarly publications on November 10, 2004, after the Web of Science in 1997 and before Google Scholar on November 20, 2004.

Outcomes

Elsevier published around 702,217 academic **articles** through its journals in 2022, the most among all academic publishers, and accounts for over 13 percent of all published academic articles per year. Elsevier generated over $3.35 billion in **revenue** per year, while Springer Nature and Wiley around $2 billion each annually. It had a reported **profit** before tax of $2,929 billion, with an adjusted operating margin of 33.1 percent in 2023 ($967 million). Globally, Elsevier journal articles accounted for over 17 percent of global research output and 28 percent of citations, demonstrating its commitment to quality significantly ahead of the industry average. More than 99 percent of the Nobel Laureates in science have been published in Elsevier journals.

In summary, taking the perspective of grantology and journalology, we can see similarities and differences between the NIH and Elsevier.

In terms of **similarities**, both the NIH and Elsevier as two social organizations are extremely complex. They have their long and complex histories. They have core missions, major strategies, and major impacts. Through a complex operational process, they use their major strategies to generate major impacts and achieve their missions. The NIH and Elsevier showcase that grant agencies and journal publishers are two types of knowledge-based organizations: the former is essentially to invest in science and advance knowledge; and the latter is essentially to publish articles and disseminate knowledge. In addition, they have a series of compatible pairs: for example, grants vs. articles, grantors vs. journals, POs vs. journal editors, grantees vs. authors, and grant review panels vs. manuscript peer reviewers. Personnel-wise, the NIH has various types of staff, such as directors, assistant directors, program directors, staff scientists, secretaries, and assistants, while POs are its basic staff, whereas Elsevier also has different types of staff, such as president, publishers, managers, production editors, and associate editors, while editors are its basic staff.

In terms of **differences**, the NIH is a public funder, whereas Elsevier is a private publisher. The NIH's aim is essentially to give out money, whereas Elsevier's aim is essentially to make money. The NIH's mission is "to seek fundamental knowledge about the nature and behavior of living systems and the application of that knowledge to enhance health, lengthen life, and reduce illness and disability," whereas Elsevier's mission is to "help researchers and healthcare professionals to advance science and improve health outcomes for the benefit of society." The NIH uses its extramural and intramural programs to conduct and support biomedical research, whereas Elsevier uses its various publication programs to help advance health science. The NIH's impacts are shown in scientific breakthroughs and health improvements, whereas Elsevier's impacts are demonstrated through knowledge consumption and global readership.

5 Action Suggestions: Understanding Grant Agencies and Developing Grant Portfolios

5.1 Understanding the Complexity and Diversity of Grant Agencies

At the end of the chapter, let us first summarize the previous four sections, intuitive knowledge, real-life cases, scientific knowledge, and funder-publisher comparison, before offering suggestions for action going forward.

From the intuitive knowledge presented by four new grant writers, we can see that they do have basic knowledge about grant agencies, but often their knowledge is partially correct. For example, their understanding of grant agencies was narrowly defined, all of them over-concentrating on grant agencies that provide research grants. Their examples of grant agencies tended to over-concentrate on popular public agencies such as the NSF, with confusion about grant funders (e.g. the NSF and NIH) vs. professional organizations (e.g. the APA, AERA, or ETS). They did not specify POs, who are the key grant professionals in any grant agency. In short, their intuitive knowledge did not yet show a good understanding of the complexity and diversity of grant agencies.

5 Action Suggestions

From the seven real-life cases, we can see the diversity of grant agencies, among them a sport grant agency, a grant-managing grant agency, a large public grant agency, one of the thirty-eight federal grant agencies, a private biomedicine grant agency, and a professional organization with a grant program. We learned the importance of developing grant portfolios.

From five journal articles, we have learned the complexity of: various kinds of grant agencies, including that of the ten largest funders; the NSF as a public funder; the Gates Foundation as a private funder; and funders across disciplines. We learned again the importance of building a solid grant portfolio.

From the funder-publisher comparison, we have learned that grant agencies, such as the NIH, give out money to support research at the beginning of the research process, typically having the specific mission of funding different proposed projects via peer review, and generating impacts to achieve the missions. Journal publishers, such as Elsevier, publish articles at the end of the research process, typically having the specific mission of publishing different journal articles via peer review, and generating impacts to achieve the dissemination of knowledge.

5.2 Studying and Developing Grant Portfolios

Based on the above summary, here are a few action suggestions for new grant writers.

First, **develop a good understanding of the complexity and diversity of grant agencies**. To understand the complexity of grant agencies, as an intellectual exercise, we can identify five to ten grant agencies and analyze their central missions, funding priorities, funding programs, funded projects, and key grant officers. To understand the diversity of grant agencies, we can identify three to five different types of funding agencies (e.g. public funders, private funders, and professional associations) and compare major differences in their central missions, funding priorities, funding programs, and funded projects.

Second, **collect grant portfolios of investigators and develop our own grant portfolios**. First, we can search and collect ten to fifty grant portfolios of investigators in our area by searching online CVs (check the grant section), published articles (check the grant acknowledgment note), and grant databases (check the biographical sketch section in the grant summary). We can then study these collected grant portfolios by analyzing completed grants, current grants, pending grants, and unfunded grants, identifying various grant agencies and grant programs, and classifying major grants, small grants, research grants, training grants, internal grants, or seed grants. Second, we can draft our own grant portfolios as soon as we can and gradually improve them over time. In our grant portfolios, we should make sure to diversify our grant agencies and grant programs rather than focusing on only one or two. We can continue improving and refining our grant portfolios in our careers, along with the development of our experiences, abilities, and insights in pursuing grants.

CHAPTER 5

Grant Writing

Outline

1	Intuitive Knowledge: How to Write a Grant Proposal	158
	1.1 Response from New Grant Writers	158
	1.2 Understand the Uniqueness of Writing Grants	159
2	Real-Life Cases: From Common Mistakes to Successful Tips	160
	2.1 George Hazelrigg: Winning Proposals and Losing Proposals	160
	2.2 Robert Porter: It Reads Like a Journal Article	161
	2.3 Lyn Yates and Dame Athene Donald: Satisfying Two Types of Reviewers	163
	2.4 Diana: Let Us Discuss My Specific Aims Page	164
	2.5 The NIH: Cut the Project Description from Twenty-Five to Twelve Pages	164
	2.6 Adam Putnam: Three Basic But Fundamental Strategies	165
3	Scientific Knowledge: From Common Shortcomings to Grant Writing Coaching	166
	3.1 Allen (1960): Common Shortcomings of Rejected Grant Writing	166
	3.2 Monte & Libby (2018): A Critical Element of Grant Writing	170
	3.3 Inouye & Fiellin (2005): Specific Steps of Grant Writing	174
	3.4 Markowitz & Shulman (2021): Word Choice in Grant Writing	176
	3.5 Hoppe *et al.* (2019): Topic Choice of Grant Writing	179
	3.6 Connor & Mauranen (1990): Ten Typical Moves in Grant Writing	180
	3.7 Weber-Main *et al.* (2020): Grant Writing Coaching	182
4	Grantology vs. Journalology: Grant Writing vs. Article Writing	185
	4.1 Similarities between Grant Writing and Article Writing	185
	4.2 Differences between Grant Writing and Article Writing	185
5	Action Suggestions: Studying Six Grant Proposals and Outlining One Grant Proposal	187
	5.1 Understanding the Uniqueness of Grant Writing	187
	5.2 Studying Grant Proposals and Outlining a Grant Proposal	188

1 Intuitive Knowledge: How to Write a Grant Proposal

1.1 Response from New Grant Writers

Below are quick responses from four new grant writers to my question about how to write a grant proposal.

- Response 1: Have a promising and meaningful research idea; follow the criteria and purposes of the target grant; check the previous proposals that have applied for the funding successfully; have a great statement of the proposal.
- Response 2: I think a winning grant proposal must include four elements. First, it should have a strong **cover letter** with a clear and fascinating summary. Second, the proposal should state the goals and the strong significance of the study. Then, the method and designed progress should be appropriate. Finally, the description of funding use should be organized and persuasive. These four elements are important and necessary for a grant application.
- Response 3: To write a winning grant proposal, we need to make sure that the proposal is both appropriate procedurally and great in content. Being appropriate procedurally means we need to finish and submit the proposal in time and make sure the research area and the researchers included in the research fit the requirements of the grant. Being great in content means the proposal should show innovation and (practical and theoretical) values of the research which make it worth being funded. Another thing I can think about is to be prepared for rejection and revisions. A **winning** grant proposal is very likely to be written with several rounds of revisions based on feedback and suggestions from relevant experts and grant reviewers.
- Response 4: I think that a winning grant proposal can be a challenging process for everyone. If I should come up with some tips based on my experience, these are as follows. (1) First of all, we need to clearly define our project and its objectives. We should start by outlining the goals and objectives of our project in a clear and concise manner. This will help the grant reviewers understand what we are trying to accomplish and how their funding can help. (2) On top of that, we need to demonstrate the need for our project. We should clearly articulate the problem or need our project is addressing and provide evidence to support our claims. This will help the grant reviewers understand why our project is important and necessary. (3) We need to provide evidence of our qualifications.

1 Intuitive Knowledge: How to Write a Grant Proposal 159

We should demonstrate that we have the skills and experience necessary to complete the project successfully. To do this, we need to provide relevant experience or careers, awards, or qualifications to show that you are the best candidate to carry out the proposed project. (4) We must check carefully the grant application guidelines. We should make sure we follow the grant application guidelines carefully and submit our proposal on time. We would better review our proposal carefully and repeatedly before submitting it to ensure that it is complete and free of errors. (5) Besides these things, there would be other things to set up a detailed budget, but I am not sure about its process.

1.2 Understand the Uniqueness of Writing Grants

What can we learn from these four responses? Let us analyze each of them briefly.

The first response is relatively general, mentioning grant ideas, grant criteria, grant statements, and especially previous successful grant proposals for study.

The second response is also relatively general. It mentions four general elements, including the cover letter (which is not common), goal and significance, research method, and budget justification. Note that this respondent mentioned having a "clear and fascinating summary" (in the cover letter, though) and being "persuasive" (in budgeting, though) – two important topics that will be discussed later in the chapter.

The third response is longer than the first two, but is still quite general. It focuses on the general procedure (i.e. timely submission and project fit) and general content (i.e. being innovative practically and theoretically). However, it does point out a critical issue in grant writing: several rounds of revisions and resubmissions for a final winning proposal – another major critical topic for the next chapter.

The final response is long, detailed, and inclusive, showing this respondent did have some prior experience involving grant applications. It summarizes five tips: outlining project goals and objectives well, demonstrating evidence of need and importance, providing evidence of applicants' qualifications, checking the grant application guidelines carefully, and developing a detailed budget. This response touches on three profound insights: it is "challenging" for everyone to write a winning grant proposal; it is critical to "provide evidence" to support claims; and it is important to "help the grant reviewers to understand" a grant proposal.

In summary, these four responses, from brief to detailed, are particularly interesting because the responses represent certain common strengths and weaknesses of intuitive knowledge of grant writing among new grant writers. These responses also clearly show quite a large variation of knowledge about grant writing among them, indicating that they do lack solid systematic training to improve their scientific knowledge.

Thus, the intellectual objective of this chapter is to build on the intuitive knowledge and deepen and broaden conceptual and procedural knowledge of the **uniqueness** of grant writing, by learning a series of cases, studying existing empirical evidence, comparing grant writing vs. article writing, and considering suggestions for action points.

2 Real-Life Cases: From Common Mistakes to Successful Tips

2.1 George Hazelrigg: Winning Proposals and Losing Proposals

George Hazelrigg is currently a Research Professor of Mechanical Engineering at George Mason University. Starting in 1983, he worked at the National Science Foundation (NSF) for thirty-five years. He has served as program officer and division director for the Division of Electrical, Communications, and Systems Engineering and the Division of Civil, Mechanical, and Manufacturing Innovation. He was known for offering proposal-writing workshops over five times a year. These workshops were based on his supervision of reviewing 50,000 proposals and his analysis of what made proposals successful and what turned panelists off.[1]

In 2000, George Hazelrigg, as the NSF's veteran program officer, made two observations. The first one is based on his experience of administering the review of 3,000 proposals and being involved in the review of another 10,000 proposals. He has come to see that there exist real and clear differences between winning proposals and losing proposals, but these differences are rather straightforward: losing proposals simply miss something basic that winning proposals don't. The second observation is based on his experience of having lunch with a young faculty member. This young person came to the NSF to be a review panelist for the first time. Hazelrigg asked her what she had learned from the process. She quickly summarized

---

[1] Personal communication on July 8, 2024.

2 Real-Life Cases: Common Mistakes & Successful Tips 161

major observations based on common mistakes that many losing proposals made. Hazelrigg reiterated with one line: "Don't make the mistakes that the losing proposals made."

He summarized his two observations into a well-received essay,[2] in which he presented multiple simple steps to write a winning research proposal: Know yourself; Know the program from which you seek support; Read the program announcement; Formulate an appropriate research objective; Develop a viable research plan; State your research objective clearly in your proposal; Frame your project around the work of others; Grammar and spelling count; Format and brevity are important; Know the review process; and Proof read your proposal before it is sent.

Here, George Hazelrigg's message is strong and loud: Don't make the mistakes that the losing proposals made. From the grant writing perspective, it is basic mistakes rather than a lack of central strengths that often kill a possible winning proposal. Thus, it is critical for new grant writers to avoid basic mistakes in writing grant proposals, especially given the increasingly competitive trend of securing grants.

2.2 Robert Porter: It Reads Like a Journal Article

Robert Porter was Director of Program Development at Virginia Tech from 2001 to 2009. One day, he received a phone call from a well-known senior scholar at Virginia Tech, criticizing a funder who declined his recent grant proposal. On the phone, he suggested a meeting for a discussion and asked the scholar to bring the rejected proposal with the reviewers' comments to the meeting. At the beginning of the meeting, the scholar placed the proposal and the reviews on the desk. Robert immediately saw that on top was the lead reviewer's evaluation summary, which began "Reads like a journal article."[3]

Inspired by this killer remark of "Reads like a journal article," in the summer of 2006, Robert Porter presented a paper titled "Why academics have a hard time writing good grant proposals" at the 2006 Annual Meeting of the Society of Research Administrators International. He received the Best Paper of the Year award.[4] In 2007, he published this

---

[2] Hazelrigg, G. A., Twelve steps to a winning research proposal, *US National Science Foundation*, available at: www.cs.rpi.edu/~trink/HazelriggWinningResearchProposal.pdf.
[3] Porter, R. (2017). Reprint 2007: Why academics have a hard time writing good grant proposals. *Journal of Research Administration, 48*(1), 15–25.
[4] Porter, R. (2007). Why academics have a hard time writing good grant proposals. *Journal of Research Administration, 38*(2), 37–43.

paper in the *Journal of Research Administration*, the official journal of the Society of Research Administrators International. The article is a short and practical essay, presenting eight contrasting perspectives between grant writing and academic writing and five remedial strategies. It is well received, with a citation of 83 times, one of the highest on the topic. In 2017, ten years later, his paper was selected for reprinting in the special issue of the journal for the 50th anniversary of the Society of Research Administrators International.

One of the major reasons why his 2007 paper has been so well received is that it shows the unique style of grant writing, which is one of the major reasons why many grant writers, including the scholar who met with Robert Porter that day, have not used the correct style to write winning grant proposals. Based on his thirty years' experience as a tenured professor, private consultant, and research administrator in winning over $8 million in awards from government agencies and private foundations, Robert Porter observed that this phenomenon is "universal" across the world.

In addition, this case also delivers three extra messages for grantology research in general. (1) Like Dr. Robert Porter, thousands of grant professional practitioners have published a great number of articles. While these articles might not have a high citation, they are always insightful, practical, and invaluable (e.g. Porter's other wonderful articles[5]). (2) Like the *Journal of Research Administration*, several practical journals have contributed to the field of grantology for decades. One example is the *Research Management Review*.[6] (3) Like the Society of Research Administrators International, multiple professional organizations in the world have organized, led, and assisted a large number of grant professionals in multiple ways. Examples include the National Council of University Research Administrators (NCURA), the Association of Research Managers and Administrators (ARMA), and the European Association of Research Managers and Administrators (EARMA).[7]

---

[5] Porter, R. E. (2005). What do grant reviewers really want, anyway? *Journal of Research Administration*, 36(1/2), 47–56; Porter, R. (2011). Crafting a sales pitch for your grant proposal. *Research Management Review*, 18(2), 79–84; Porter, R. (2009). Can we talk? Contacting grant program officers. *Research Management Review*, 17(1), 10–17; Porter, R. (2011). More paper out the door: Ten inexpensive ways to stimulate proposal development. *Research Management Review*, 18(1), 64–72.

[6] Research management review, *NCURA*, available at: www.ncura.edu/Publications/ResearchManagementReview.aspx.

[7] NCURA website, available at: www.ncura.edu/Home.aspx; ARMA website, available at: https://arma.ac.uk/; EARMA website, available at: https://earma.org/.

2.3 Lyn Yates and Dame Athene Donald: Satisfying Two Types of Reviewers

On July 18, 2019, *Times Higher Education* published a forum article online, titled "How to win a research grant."[8] Among six schools, two scholars offered an interesting tip for writing a successful grant proposal: Consider two types of reviewers instead of just one.

Lyn Yates is Redmond Barry Distinguished Professor Emeritus at the University of Melbourne.[9] Over the years, she has worked on more than twenty funded projects from a wide variety of sources, including the Australian Research Council (ARC), the US Department of Education, and UNESCO. Between 2011 and 2016, she was one of the chief investigators of a large ARC-funded project on globalization and elite schools. As a grant reviewer and grant applicant, she has found that one of the trickiest issues in writing applications is to **satisfy two types of assessors**. On the one hand, we should demonstrate the specialist sophistication that satisfies reviewers in your own field; and on the other, we should make a compelling easy-to-read case for why your research matters to reviewers outside your direct field. Likewise, on the one hand, we should show that our proposal builds on and expands the work we have done before; and on the other, we should demonstrate our proposal will address new and significant issues. Too many applicants either over-claim or under-claim the "why it matters" story.[10]

Dame Athene Donald is a Professor Emeritus of Experimental Physics and Master of Churchill College at the University of Cambridge. She is also a former scientific member of the European Research Council. The Council is composed of eminent scientists and scholars, appointed by the European Commission.[11] She suggests that one of the critical challenges of writing grant proposals is "to target the customer." What complicates matters is that there are **at least two different customers**, **peer reviewers** and the **review panel**, with different requirements. Our sales pitch should be detailed enough to convince peer reviewers that you know what you are doing, but it also needs to be exciting enough to convince the panel to select your application ahead of other proposals that are equally valid scientifically.

---

[8] How to win a research grant, *Times Higher Education*, available at: www.timeshighereducation.com/features/how-win-research-grant.
[9] Honorary staff, *Faculty of Education*, available at: https://education.unimelb.edu.au/stesh/people/honorary-staff.
[10] How to win a research grant, note 8 above.
[11] Athene Donald, *European Research Council*, available at: https://erc.europa.eu/erc_member/dame-athene-donald.

2.4 Diana: Let Us Discuss My Specific Aims Page

A few years ago, Diana, a wonderful visiting professor, emailed everyone in our research group that she would love to get feedback on her one-page Specific Aims for a National Institute of Child Health and Human Development grant proposal. While I admired her for sharing her work and soliciting feedback, I was a little surprised about why she wanted to discuss the Specific Aims page only, rather than the entire grant proposal. I have attended quite a few grant proposal talks before submission and always participated in discussing these proposals with great interest. But it was the first time for me to hear that someone wanted to discuss the Specific Aims page.

Through her presentation and group discussion, I learned several reasons why the Specific Aims page is critically important for a proposal for an NIH grant.[12] First, the Specific Aims page is one of the most widely read sections of an NIH grant and creates the first impression of the grant. Second, we can create specific aims that are clearly significant and achievable in three to five years so that our reviewers can understand clearly what the specific important outcomes of the project will be. This way, we can effectively pitch our proposal to our reviewers and program officers. Third, drafting and discussing the Specific Aims page is the appropriate starting point for writing a proposal. We can then use it to develop different sections of the proposal. Fourth, it is often read by the program officer before selecting reviewers and it helps recruited reviewers to determine whether she or he will review a proposal from a list of proposals for review. Note that this section could be confused with three other relevant parts in an NIH grant proposal: Project Summary, Project Narrative, and Project Abstract. One of the best descriptions has been provided by the NIH: "The Specific Aims page is a key element of a grant proposal. It is widely recommended to start early on the Specific Aims page and send it around to solicit feedback before submission."[13]

2.5 The NIH: Cut the Project Description from Twenty-Five to Twelve Pages

In 2010, the National Institutes of Health (NIH) implemented significant changes in its grant application guidelines. One of the striking changes

---

[12] Draft specific aims, *National Institute of Allergy and Infectious Diseases*, available at: www.niaid.nih.gov/grants-contracts/draft-specific-aims.
[13] Project summary/abstract and project narrative: What's the difference and what to include, *NIH*, available at: https://nexus.od.nih.gov/all/2019/06/28/project-summary-abstract-and-project-narrative-whats-the-difference-and-what-to-include/.

2 Real-Life Cases: Common Mistakes & Successful Tips 165

was reducing the number of pages for the project descriptions of research grants (e.g. R01) from twenty-five to twelve pages. The NIH's goal is to increase the efficiency of the peer review process while decreasing the administrative burden (e.g. now it might take two to three hours rather than five to six hours for a reviewer to review a proposal).[14] The practical implications for grant writing are significant. More than ever before, the process requires grant writers to write more concisely, while still presenting a very persuasive argument in a winning grant proposal. It makes grant writing more unique and more challenging.

To respond to this major change, for example, eleven editorial board members of the *Western Journal of Nursing Research* came together to discuss strategies to write competitive shorter research proposals.[15] They concluded with a list of nearly fifty specific strategies (e.g. determine whether the study meets the requirements for funding, such as being innovative and addressing the mission of the funding agency; ensuring each sentence makes the key points stated in the outline; reading the proposal backward to find typographical errors and to check for logical progression of ideas) at three writing stages, namely, preparation, construction, and editing and reviewing.

This case reconfirms that a precise and compelling writing style is essential for any successful grant application.

2.6 Adam Putnam: Three Basic But Fundamental Strategies

Adam Putnam is currently an Associate Professor of Psychology at Furman University.[16] Twelve years ago, he won an NSF Graduate Research Fellowship Program. As a second-year graduate student, she shared ten wonderful strategies for drafting a polished competitive application for an extremely competitive award like this one.[17] Among them, three strategies directly concern writing grant proposals: **(1) Write, rewrite, and then rewrite again.** This is perhaps the most important rule. This is because

---

[14] Page limits, *NIH: Grants and Funding*, available at: https://grants.nih.gov/grants/how-to-apply-application-guide/format-and-write/page-limits.htm; Wadman, M. (2010). Shorter NIH grant form launches. *Nature*, 463(7277), 12–14. Gs5.
[15] Groves, P. S., Rawl, S. M., Wurzbach, M. E., Fahrenwald, N., Cohen, M. Z., McCarthy Beckett, D. O. *et al.* (2012). Secrets of successful short grant applications. *Western Journal of Nursing Research*, 34(1), 6–23. Gs13.
[16] Adam Putnam, *Furman University*, available at: www.furman.edu/people/adam-putnam/.
[17] Ten tips for applying to the NSF Graduate Research Fellowship Program, *Association for Psychological Science*, available at: www.psychologicalscience.org/observer/ten-tips-for-applying-to-the-nsf-graduate-research-fellowship-program.

strong writing comes from rewriting. Start writing early enough to leave time for several revisions. **(2) Have as many readers as you can manage.** Good readers are those you trust to be critical, and their perspective may be like that of grant reviewers. **(3) Write clearly and concisely.** This is because vigorous writing is concise. Write concisely so an undergraduate can understand.

These tips appear to be simple and common, but they are truly fundamental and critical for successful grant writing.

3 Scientific Knowledge: From Common Shortcomings to Grant Writing Coaching

In this section, we will discuss five articles on shortcomings, unique elements, writing genres, revision, and innovative training. The topic of peer reviewers and review criteria will be discussed in detail in Chapter 6, which covers grant review. The topic of revision and resubmission will be discussed in detail in Chapter 7, which covers grant decisions.

3.1 Allen (1960): Common Shortcomings of Rejected Grant Writing

The first article[18] of note concerns common shortcomings of writing a grant proposal rather than effective strategies for writing a grant proposal. There are two major ways to learn how to write a winning grant proposal: learning from the successful stories, as most of the published articles do, and learning from the unsuccessful stories, as few major studies do. For new grant writers, it could be effective and efficient to learn unsuccessful lessons as early as possible, even before learning successful experiences. The motivation for doing this here is like Popper's falsification idea that we should falsify rather than verify: while it is impossible to verify that every swan is white, finding a single black swan proves that not every swan is white.

Overview

This is an analytic paper. Its title is: "Why are research grant applications disapproved? Characteristic shortcomings of rejected applications to the National Institutes of Health." It has been cited 110 times since 1960. It is among the earliest and best in the literature on grant rejection analysis.

---

[18] Allen, E. M. (1960). Why are research grant applications disapproved? Characteristic shortcomings of rejected applications to the National Institutes of Health are described. *Science, 132*(3439), 1532–4. GS115.

3 Scientific Knowledge: From Shortcomings to Coaching 167

The author, Ernest Mason Allen (1914–99),[19] was named as the third Chief of the NIH division of research grants in 1951, after Cassius Van Slyke and David Price. During his tenure, he oversaw the virtually logarithmic growth of the funds appropriated for grants by Congress. In 1960, he was named Associate Director for Research Grants. Just three years later, in 1963, he was named as Grants Policy Officer in the Office of the Surgeon General – a newly created position. He received the Distinguished Services Award from the Department of Health, Education and Welfare, and the Lasker Award from the American Public Health Association. He has published approximately ten articles on grants, most of them in the 1950s and 1960s.[20] He is one of the true pioneers in grantology and among the first to publish articles on grantology.[21]

The article was published in *Science*. *Science* and *Nature* have both published short grant-related editorials, news, letters, and articles. The initial search in the Web of Science indicates that *Nature* has published around 1,500 short articles (mainly editorial material, news, and letters)[22] and

---

[19] Person record: Allen, Ernest Mason, *Office of NIH History*, available at: https://onih .pastperfectonline.com/byperson?keyword=Allen%2C%20Ernest%20Mason.
[20] Allen, E. M., & Endicott, K. M. (1953). Public Health Service research grants in biology. *AIBS Bulletin*, *3*(2), 19–21; Endicott, K. M., & Allen, E. M. (1953). The growth of medical research 1941–1953 and the role of Public Health Service research grants. *Science*, *118*(3065), 337–43. Gs33; Allen, E. M. (1961). Submission of research grant applications to the public health service. *Academic Medicine*, *36*(6), 737–8; Em, A. (1960). How the National Institutes of Health carry on the extensive PHS grant and award programs. *Journal of the Kentucky Medical Association*, *58*, 1060–1; Allen, E. M. (1961). *Research in Biological Sciences Related to Agriculture*, University of Missouri, Agricultural Experiment Station; Lindsay, D. R., & Allen, E. M. (1961). Medical research: Past support, future directions: Aims of the National Institutes of Health are surveyed as its annual budget passes the half-billion mark. *Science*, *134*(3495), 2017–24; Allen, E. M. (1968). Fiscal relations between the medical schools and the federal government. *Academic Medicine*, *43*(6), 697–705; Allen, E. M. (1980). Early years of NIH research grants. *NIH Alumni Association Newsletter*, *2*, 6–8.
[21] Schneider, W. H. (2015). The origin of the medical research grant in the United States: The Rockefeller Foundation and the NIH extramural funding program. *Journal of the History of Medicine & Allied Sciences*, *70*(2), 279–311.
[22] Myers, N., Mittermeier, R. A., Mittermeier, C. G., Da Fonseca, G. A., & Kent, J. (2000). Biodiversity hotspots for conservation priorities. *Nature*, *403*(6772), 853–8. Gs29034; Landis, S. C., Amara, S. G., Asadullah, K., Austin, C. P., Blumenstein, R., Bradley, E. W. *et al.* (2012). A call for transparent reporting to optimize the predictive value of preclinical research. *Nature*, *490*(7419), 187–91. Gs1207; Bromham, L., Dinnage, R., & Hua, X. (2016). Interdisciplinary research has consistently lower funding success. *Nature*, *534*(7609), 684–7. Gs581; Tannenbaum, C., Ellis, R. P., Eyssel, F., Zou, J., & Schiebinger, L. (2019). Sex and gender analysis improves science and engineering. *Nature*, *575*(7781), 137–46. Gs539; Plerou, V., Amaral, L. A. N., Gopikrishnan, P., Meyer, M., & Stanley, H. E. (1999). Similarities between the growth dynamics of university research and of competitive economic activities. *Nature*, *400*(6743), 433–7. Gs185; Nicholson, J. M., & Ioannidis, J. P. (2012). Conform and be funded. *Nature*, *492*(7427), 34–6. Gs215; Ioannidis, J. P. (2011). Fund people not projects. *Nature*, *477*(7366), 529–31. Gs193; Rylance, R. (2015). Grant giving: Global funders to focus on interdisciplinarity. *Nature*, *525*(7569), 313–15. Gs139.

Science has published around 1,200 short articles (mainly news, editorial material, and letters).[23] These two journals have been contributing to grantology as an invaluable resource for decades. Note that the editorials, news, and letters published in journals are not traditional research articles and the citations are usually low mainly due to the nature of narrow topics on grants, but they are still tremendously invaluable for grantology research.[24] Thus, students and researchers in grantology should pay special attention to these types of non-traditional publications.

Highlights
This is a short article in *Science*, only 2.5 print pages, a total of ten paragraphs. It consists of Introduction, Method, Results, Discussion, and Notes, with its structure and sequence slightly different from a typical empirical study. From the grant writing perspective, we can highlight several important points.

First, Allen's design and approach were **innovative**. He adapted ideas from symptomatology (a branch of medicine dealing with the signs and symptoms of a disease) and epidemiology (the study of the distribution patterns and determinants of health and disease conditions in a defined population). He focused on rejected proposals, just as medical doctors would focus on a disorder or an illness.

Second, Allen's method was **clever**. In 1959, the NIH had nearly 6,000 applications (4,600 new submissions and 1,200 continuations); 2,000 were disapproved by the study sections, which is roughly a 30 percent success rate. Among the 2,000 disapprovals, Allen studied 605 applications that were discussed, rated, voted, and disapproved through the thirty-three study section meetings. He collected and analyzed comments summarized in the review minutes from these study section meetings.

---

[23] Ginther, D. K., Schaffer, W. T., Schnell, J., Masimore, B., Liu, F., Haak, L. L. *et al.* (2011). Race, ethnicity, and NIH research awards. *Science, 333*(6045), 1015–19. Gs1140; Fortunato, S., Bergstrom, C. T., Börner, K., Evans, J. A., Helbing, D., Milojević, S. *et al.* (2018). Science of science. *Science, 359*(6379), article eaao0185. Gs1308; Ley, T. J., & Hamilton, B. H. (2008). The gender gap in NIH grant applications. *Science, 322*(5907), 1472–4. Gs292; Li, D., & Agha, L. (2015). Big names or big ideas: Do peer-review panels select the best science proposals? *Science, 348*(6233), 434–8. Gs271; Margolis, R. M., & Kammen, D. M. (1999). Underinvestment: the energy technology and R&D policy challenge. *Science, 285*(5428), 690–2. Gs292; Li, D., Azoulay, P., & Sampat, B. N. (2017). The applied value of public investments in biomedical research. *Science, 356*(6333), 78–81. Gs201.

[24] Giles, J. (2005). Research grants: The nightmare before funding. *Nature, 437*(7057), 308–12. Gs7; Perrault, C. (2009). Grant-writing offices would let scientists get on with research. *Nature, 458*(7236), 281. Gs2; Poirazi, P. (2017). The perfect grant and how to get it. *Nature, 543*(7644), 151. Gs5; Else, H. (2018). Scientists' early grant success fuels further funding. *Nature, 556*(7701), 416–18. Gs2.

Third, the core finding is **interesting**. Basically, the 605 criticisms raised in the study sections are classified into four major types. (1) 58 percent of criticisms focus on "**Problems**," the research question that the proposed research seeks to answer, with seven minor types. Examples of criticisms included the proposal problem being of insufficient importance or being unlikely to produce new knowledge. (2) 73 percent of criticisms focus on the "**Approach**" by which the answer is to be sought, with nine minor types. Examples included the proposed tests, methods, or scientific procedures being unsuited to the stated objectives. (3) 55 percent focus on "**Man**," investigators' scientific judgment and technical skills, with six minor types, one examples being the investigator not having adequate experience or training. (4) 16 percent focus on **Other**, with four minor types, one example being that the requirements for equipment or personnel are unrealistic. In total, these four types consist of twenty-six minor types of criticisms. Note that these twenty-six shortcomings are not mutually exclusive.

Fourth, this is a **classic** article for multiple reasons. Although it is not a citation classic (Gs = 110, WOS = 38), it is the first analysis of common shortcomings of disapproved or rejected applications. Its scientific contribution to grantology is that it pioneered and created a new promising and feasible line of research on grant writing, from a negative angle rather than a positive one.

Fifth, Allen's list of twenty-six criticisms under four major types was based on the data from **fifty-seven years ago**, although it is still useful and comprehensive. In addition, it particularly focuses on grant writing rather than general grant quality. In 2023, the NIH posted a useful list of common mistakes under seven major types.[25]

Last, this article has **important tips** for helping new grant writers to write a winning proposal. We can write a successful proposal in two ways: 50 percent is to avoid mistakes; and 50 percent is to enhance strengths. From the grant writing perspective, the 1960 Allen paper opened a line of productive research to answer why a proposal is rejected.[26] This is in contrast to the dominating literature, which discusses why a grant proposal

---

[25] Common mistakes in writing applications, *National Institute of Mental Health*, available at: www.nimh.nih.gov/funding/grant-writing-and-application-process/common-mistakes-in-writing-applications.

[26] Levenson, R. W. (2013). Mistakes that grant proposers make. In R. J. Sternberg (ed.) *Writing Successful Grant Proposals from the Top Down and Bottom Up* (pp. 37–48). Sage Publishing. Gs2; Ward, D. (2002). The top 10 grant-writing mistakes. *Principal*, 81(5), 46–7. Gs1; Henson, K. T. (1997). Writing for publication: Some perennial mistakes. *Phi Delta Kappan*, 78(10), 781–4. Gs20.

is successful.[27] No grant writers, not even the most successful and accomplished ones, can 100 percent guarantee the success of the grant proposals they submit. However, every grant writer can easily check the common reasons leading to rejections in proposals before submission.

3.2 Monte & Libby (2018): A Critical Element of Grant Writing

After discussing common shortcomings of rejected grant proposals, let us focus on an impactful article[28] about how to write one short but critical section of a proposal.

Overview

The article is titled "Introduction to the specific aims page of a grant proposal." The authors used their own experience as grant writers, grant reviewers, and grant mentors to numerous investigators, and have characterized effective specific aims pages with a meticulously developed "recipe." This paper has been cited twenty-six times since 2018, according to Google Scholar. It is relatively normal to have such a citation number, perhaps due to the narrow nature of the specific topic on grantology.

The first author, Andrew Monte, is currently a Professor of Emergency Medicine at the University of Colorado, and was an Associate Professor in 2018 when the article was published. His research and publication areas are Precision Medicine and Substance Abuse. His h-index is 34 as of 2023. Regarding grant writing experience, Dr. Monte has been funded by pharmaceutical industry grants, the Emergency Medicine Foundation Career Development Award, a departmental pilot grant, a Colorado Clinical and Translational Science Institute early career investigator grant, an NIGMS K23 career development award, the Colorado Department of Public Health and Environment, the Department of Defense, and now an NIGMS R35 Maximizing Investigators Research Award. He has reviewed

---

[27] Wisdom, J. P., Riley, H., & Myers, N. (2015). Recommendations for writing successful grant proposals: An information synthesis. *Academic Medicine*, *90*(12), 1720–5. Gs24; Guyer, R. A., Schwarze, M. L., Gosain, A., Maggard-Gibbons, M., Keswani, S. G., & Goldstein, A. M. (2021). Top ten strategies to enhance grant-writing success. *Surgery*, *170*(6), 1727–31. Gs17; Groves, P. S., Rawl, S. M., Wurzbach, M. E., Fahrenwald, N., Cohen, M. Z., McCarthy Beckett, D. O. *et al.* (2012). Secrets of successful short grant applications. *Western Journal of Nursing Research*, *34*(1), 6–23. Gs13; Brownson, R. C., Colditz, G. A., Dobbins, M., Emmons, K. M., Kerner, J. F., Padek, M. *et al.* (2015). Concocting that magic elixir: Successful grant application writing in dissemination and implementation research. *Clinical & Translational Science*, *8*(6), 710–16. Gs34.

[28] Monte, A. A., & Libby, A. M. (2018). Introduction to the specific aims page of a grant proposal. *Academic Emergency Medicine*, *25*(9), 1042–7. Gs26.

grants for NIH study sections and numerous foundations and has sat on the Scientific Advisory Board for the NIH. He directed a grant writing workshop from 2014 to 2018. Dr. Monte and Dr. Libby are supported by an NIH/NCATS Colorado CTSA Grant. Anne Libby is a Professor of Emergency Medicine at the University of Colorado. Her research expertise is patient-oriented outcomes research. She served four years on the study section for the Agency for Healthcare Research and Quality (AHRQ). Her research and mentored training programs have been funded by federal funders (e.g. the NIH and AHRQ) and national foundations (e.g. Robert Wood Johnson Foundation and Doris Duke Charitable Foundation). Based on ResearchGate, she published 127 publications and received 3,400 citations.

The article was published in 2018 in *Academic Emergency Medicine*, a journal with an impact factor of 5.4 in 2023. It is the official publication of the Society for Academic Emergency Medicine and publishes information relevant to the practice, educational advancements, and investigation of emergency medicine. It is the second-largest peer-reviewed scientific journal in the specialty of emergency medicine. Its regular major sections include Original Contributions, Systematic Reviews (With or Without Meta-Analyses), Research Methods and Statistics, Invited Commentaries, Unsolicited Commentaries and Research Letters, Special Contributions, and Biros Section on Research Ethics. This article is marked as an "Original Contribution."

Highlights
This article is a short six-page tutorial rather than an empirical article. "Introduction to the **specific aims page** of a grant proposal" is the first subheading – a repeat of the article title. Clearly, this article focuses explicitly on one element of a grant proposal. This is rather rare and perhaps quite surprising to many new grant writers. It is one of the very few articles on the specific aims page, while thousands of articles of this type usually discuss all the key elements of a proposal.

Its structure is also a little unusual. It has three major sections: Introduction, Summary, and References. However, the Introduction section covers all the major contents, taking up five of a total of six pages, with six subsections, the introductory paragraph, the rationale paragraph, the specific aims paragraph, the overall impact paragraph, format and writing style, and additional resources.

From the grant writing perspective, we can highlight three related questions to help us better understand this article.

First, **what** is the specific aims page? The two authors focus on the specific aims page strategically based on their extensive experiences as grant writers, grant reviewers, and grant mentors. A complete NIH application is a large package, has multiple sections and various forms, and usually includes more than 100 single-spaced pages. For a sample proposal of ninety-seven pages,[29] for instance, besides various required forms and materials, the essential narrative materials include Project Summary (half page), Abstract (one paragraph), Introduction (one page), Specific Aims (one page), and Research Strategy (twelve pages). Specific Aims and Research Strategy are the two key narrative parts of the research plan section. Here, we can see that the specific aims page is short, and typically it is not the first or longest section of an NIH grant proposal, but rather the first section of a research plan. An effective aims page should make three points: (1) the research is important; (2) the methods will be successful; and (3) the applicant is the right person and has the right team to undertake the project. While these goals seem simple, it is challenging to convey these elements efficiently and coherently in order to engage reviewers.

Second, **why** is the specific aims page important? The article specifies the three important functions of the page for the entire grant proposal: (1) Grant writing starts with the **iterative** (i.e. repetition of a sequence yields results successively closer to a desired result) development of a specific aims page. (2) The specific aims page serves as a **concept sheet**, with project milestones, hypotheses, and the most important elements of the approach. (3) This page also serves as a **master plan** for the research proposal and ideally engages the reader as an advocate during the review process. Here, the grant reviewers, specifically the review panel members, often have significantly different training, experience, and expertise. Thus, the specific aims page should give the diverse reviewers a basic understanding of the proposal and at the same time provide just enough technical details to indicate mastery of the proposed project.

Third, **how** can you write it well? The specific aims section is the most **fundamental** part of any NIH grant application. It is one of the most **difficult** sections to write well. It should quickly gain the reviewers' trust and confidence, while effectively convincing them that a proposed project is important to fund. The key strategy is to strike a delicate balance

---

[29] For other sample applications of major mechanisms, see Sample applications & more, *National Institute of Allergy and Infectious Diseases*, available at: www.niaid.nih.gov/grants-contracts/sample-applications.

between being concise and being persuasive, and avoid over- or underpresentation to reviewers.

The authors suggested specific strategies. (1) The aims page should be written to an educated **non-expert** audience, saving the field-specific details for **content experts** in later sections of the proposal. (2) It should make the plan as simple as possible, but not simpler, including only "need to know" information. Demonstrating the **depth** of expertise and fine details of pilot data are best deployed in later sections of the grant. Instead, identify the problem to study, educate the reader with background knowledge, and describe why the proposed study will successfully solve the problem. (3) It should minimize citations so as not to distract the reviewers. Detailed references can be included in the background section. (4) It should obey the "cultural norms" that vary by discipline or review groups – for example, whether hypotheses or short descriptive approach statements are listed by **aim** or as an opening paragraph. (5) A figure could be included on the specific aims page. Simple figures, such as conceptual models or relationships among key variables, are encouraged in order to provide visual reinforcement. (6) It should educate the **non-expert** reader on existing literature, identify a knowledge gap, propose a solution grounded in the aims themselves, and demonstrate the impact of the work, while specific sequence and format may vary.

Fourth, **how** should you write each of the four major paragraphs for the aims page? This article explains meticulously the four key components of an effective specific aims page: (1) The introductory paragraph, including how to write the first and the sentences. (2) The rationale paragraph for reviewers: solution, gap, objective, goal, and hypothesis. (3) The specific aims list. Think of each aim as generating a result after the project is complete, about each of which a paper can be written. Two to four is acceptable, but three is optimal. (4) The overall impact paragraph: use two to three sentences to address the innovation, impact, and importance of a large research agenda. In addition, the article discussed both technical details of formatting and writing style (e.g. font, verb use, topic sentence) and useful resources (e.g. grant example databases, writing checklist, grant writing workshops, useful webinars).

Last, for new grant writers, learn to write the specific aims page as the core section well. The skill developed in writing the section could be generalizable to other sections of a proposal. Furthermore, there exists extensive literature on how to write other specific elements of a grant proposal, such as how to write a budget, an abstract, a CV, a description, and an entire application. We should study these as well.

3.3 Inouye & Fiellin (2005): Specific Steps of Grant Writing

Grant writing involves not only elements and structures, but also steps and procedures. Many grant writing guides exist,[30] but few are evidence-based and systematic. Let us study a well-known evidence-based systematic guide.[31]

Overview

This article introduces an evidence-based guide to writing grant proposals for clinical research. The words "evidence-based guide" mean that this article is based not only on the authors' own general experiences of writing grants, reviewing grants, and mentoring grant writers, but also the authors' specific synthesis of sixty-six NIH G01 applications submitted to one study section of the NIH. It has been cited 116 times, among the highest cited, indicating that this work is well-received.

The first author is Sharon Inouye, a Professor of Medicine at Harvard Medical School and Director of the Aging Brain Center at the Hinda and Arthur Marcus Institute for Aging Research. She is the Editor-in-Chief of *JAMA Internal Medicine* and served as Associate Editor for *JAMA Network Open* from 2020 to 2023. Her research focuses on delirium dementia cognition. Dr. Inouye has been continuously funded by the NIH since 1989 and has received more than ninety grants, including a current $13 million NIH-P01 grant and a $10 million PCORI contract.[32] She has published over 400 articles, many in the highest-impact journals. Her h-index is 121, among the highest in the field. The second author, Dr. Fiellin, has focused his scholarly work on the interface between primary care, general healthcare settings, and addiction. He is an Internal Medicine physician in Addiction Medicine and serves as the inaugural Director of the Yale Program in Addiction Medicine.

---

[30] Wisdom, J. P., Riley, H., & Myers, N. (2015). Recommendations for writing successful grant proposals: An information synthesis. *Academic Medicine, 90*(12), 1720–5. Gs32; Sathian, B., Simkhada, P., van Teijlingen, E., Roy, B., & Banerjee, I. (2016). Grant writing for innovative medical research: Time to rethink. *Medical Science, 4*(3), 332–3. Gs74; Guyer, R. A., Schwarze, M. L., Gosain, A., Maggard-Gibbons, M., Keswani, S. G., & Goldstein, A. M. (2021). Top ten strategies to enhance grant-writing success. *Surgery, 170*(6), 1727–31. Gs14; Blanco, M. A., & Lee, M. Y. (2012). Twelve tips for writing educational research grant proposals. *Medical Teacher, 34*(6), 450–3. Gs25.

[31] Inouye, S. K., & Fiellin, D. A. (2005). An evidence-based guide to writing grant proposals for clinical research. *Annals of Internal Medicine, 142*(4), 274–82. Gs116.

[32] The Patient-Centered Outcomes Research Institute (PCORI) is an independent, non-profit research funding organization that seeks to empower patients and others with actionable information about their health and healthcare choices. It funds patient-centered comparative clinical effectiveness research. For details, see the PCORI website, available at: www.pcori.org/for.

3 Scientific Knowledge: From Shortcomings to Coaching

The article was published in 2005 in the *Annals of Internal Medicine*. Established in 1927 by the American College of Physicians, *Annals* is the most-cited general internal medicine journal and one of the most influential journals in the world. Its impact factor was 19.6 in 2023.

Highlights
This article is a comprehensive summary of grant writing, specifically focusing on clinical research. It has two major sections, background information on grants (summarizing general advice) and major review issues identified in NIH grant proposals (discussing specific problems), along with a summary, a conclusion, and an appendix on the specific aims section. From the grant writing perspective, we can highlight the following interesting points.

First, the authors' characterization of grant reviewers is **insightful**. The grant reviewers have two general characteristics. At one end of the scale, in general, as good medical scholars, they are intelligent, savvy about research, successful in research, have broad scientific knowledge, and are committed to providing thorough and fair reviews. At the other end, typically, as busy clinical researchers, they might only have time to review a grant in a few hours at the most and often not be in the exact field to review a specific proposal. Thus, grant writers must help but not hinder these smart but busy reviewers to understand a proposed project. Furthermore, grant writers should do their best to know the reviewers. For instance, for the NIH, search and study the members of relevant study sections on the Centers for Scientific Review website. Likewise, for other foundations, we should also search and study the potential reviewers, including foundation staff, to make our proposals understandable to reviewers.

Second, the grant writing timeline drawn by the authors is **extremely useful**. They listed sixteen specific tasks (interesting tasks are in bold): conceptualize the project, initiate the pilot work, contact program **officers**, obtain all application forms and instructions, review the funding agency's priorities, review recently funded **grants**, determine potential **reviewers**, outline and draft proposals, work with mentors and collaborators, get input from a **biostatistician**, review and obtain required IRB approvals, finalize the budget and budget justification, request and obtain letters of support, complete full draft for review by mentor, collaborators, and experienced **investigators**, write and revise **abstract**, and revise, revise, and revise the final grant. For each of the sixteen tasks, the authors suggested an interesting timeline within twelve months before submission, backward from the submission to conceptualization. New grant writers can readily adopt this timeline for effective grant writing.

Third, the authors discussed **grant writing problems** that exist in the seven major sections of a proposal among sixty-six submitted G01 applications they collected. For instance, in the section on specific aims/hypotheses, the most important section of the grant, the common critiques from reviewers are that the specific aims are poorly focused, underdeveloped, or overly ambitious. In addition, they created a checklist targeting major sections and topics of a proposal and asking questions for grant writers to consider during grant writing. For instance, in the checklist on the specific aims section, three questions are asked: "Are the aims well-focused and fully conceptualized?" "Are the hypotheses clearly articulated?" "Do the aims appear balanced, not overly ambitious or unrealistic?" Reviewing and following these discussions should be extremely important and useful in writing a good grant proposal.

Fourth, its appendices are particularly **informative**. For example, appendix 2 provides a real example of the specific aims section to show how to write it. Appendix table 1 offers a detailed list of major issues raised by NIH reviewers. The appendix figure provides a five-year timeline of ten major activities that are closely related to the specific aims section.

Last, one important implication for new grant writers is that there is a wide variety of ways to write grant proposals, but the **highly systematic** approach presented in the article will make our grant writing effective and efficient.

3.4 Markowitz & Shulman (2021): Word Choice in Grant Writing

After discussing a few articles on grant writing, let us now examine an article showing counter-intuition results with gigantic data.[33]

Overview

This article is titled "The predictive utility of word familiarity for online engagements and funding." Here, the term predictive utility can simply refer to usefulness in prediction. It reports a study to verify the popular simpler-is-better phenomenon and to demonstrate how well simple or complex language patterns predict meaningful behaviors in two contexts: social media participation and grant success. It has twenty-three citations since its publication in 2021.

---

[33] Markowitz, D. M., & Shulman, H. C. (2021). The predictive utility of word familiarity for online engagements and funding. *Proceedings of the National Academy of Sciences*, *118*(18), article e2026045118. Gs23.

3 Scientific Knowledge: From Shortcomings to Coaching

The first author, David Markowitz, is an Associate Professor of Communication at Michigan State University. In 1922, he was selected as a "Rising Star" of the Association for Psychological Science. His main research areas are language deception and persuasion, text analysis, and computer-mediated communication. His h-index is 24. He published another important article on NSF grant writing.[34] The second author is Hillary Shulman, an Associate Professor of Communication at Ohio State University, with research and publication areas on political communication, science communication, and social cognition. Her h-index is 24 in 2023. She has published multiple articles relevant to grant writing.[35] These two authors are productive and impactful and thus should be followed in terms of grant writing research.

The article was published in 2021 in the *Proceedings of the National Academy of Sciences* (PNAS). It is through "Direct Submission" rather than "Contributed Submission." Its action editor is Susan Fiske, a renowned social psychologist at Princeton. PNAS is the official journal of the National Academy of Sciences, published since 1915, and is the second most-cited scientific journal, like *Science* and *Nature*. It has a 2023 impact factor of 9.4. PNAS has consistently published multiple influential and rigorous articles on grantology and thus researchers and students in grantology should follow it closely.

Highlights

This is an empirical article presenting two studies. It has four major sections: Introduction, Study 1, Study 2, and General discussion. From the grant writing perspective, we can highlight the following points.

First, the most interesting point of the article, of course, is its **findings** about grant writing. It is widely believed that effective writing should use simple language and avoid jargon, so-called the simpler-is-better phenomenon. However, the strong evidence generated from this study paints a

---

[34] Markowitz, D. M. (2019). What words are worth: National Science Foundation grant abstracts indicate award funding. *Journal of Language & Social Psychology, 38*(3), 264–82. Gs49.

[35] Bullock, O. M., Colón Amill, D., Shulman, H. C., & Dixon, G. N. (2019). Jargon as a barrier to effective science communication: Evidence from metacognition. *Public Understanding of Science, 28*(7), 845–53. Gs90; Shulman, H. C., Dixon, G. N., Bullock, O. M., & Colón Amill, D. (2020). The effects of jargon on processing fluency, self-perceptions, and scientific engagement. *Journal of Language & Social Psychology, 39*(5–6), 579–97. Gs97; Bullock, O. M., Shulman, H. C., & Huskey, R. (2021). Narratives are persuasive because they are easier to understand: Examining processing fluency as a mechanism of narrative persuasion. *Frontiers in Communication, 6*, article 719615. Gs46; Shulman, H. C., & Bullock, O. M. (2020). Don't dumb it down: The effects of jargon in COVID-19 crisis communication. *PLoS One, 15*(10), article e0239524. Gs34.

more complete picture: while readers respond more positively to simple and non-technical language when giving their time and attention (e.g. simple online language receives more social engagements), readers tend to respond positively to complex and technical language when giving their money (e.g. complex language in grant abstracts generates more money). This finding is consistent with the emerging grant writing literature on genre systems[36] and different styles in different proposal elements.[37] It could have useful implications for new grant writers to use multiple writing strategies flexibly and thoughtfully rather than stick to a single strategy to write competitive grants.

Second, the **method** used in the study is both effective and promising. The study first collected gigantic data, a total of 1,064,533 words, from twelve diverse settings (e.g. 32,062 words from *PLoS One* article titles and 226,452 words from NIH grant abstracts). It then used automated text analysis (e.g. Linguistic Inquiry and Word Count, a neural network model in R) to identify and quantify common vs. uncommon words. It ends with regression analysis and correlation analysis to estimate the relation between the use of common words vs. complex words and outcomes of positive vs. negative behaviors in social engagement or grant funding. This type of computational big data analysis will be very useful for grantology research, especially current research in grantology that often lacks large-scale data sets and relies on personal experience reflections.

Last, of course, the study only focuses on one aspect of grant writing (i.e. word choice), four funders (e.g. the NIH), small vs. large money amounts rather than the more important aspect of rejection vs. award, and publicly available materials (e.g. campaign blurbs or grant abstract) rather than on the entire application packages. Further research in this promising line is needed to further develop a complete scientific understanding of effective grant writing. For example, another promising topic of research is how HYPE, a form of intensive publicity or promotion, uses trends in NIH grant applications.[38]

---

[36] Ding, H. (2007). Genre analysis of personal statements: Analysis of moves in application essays to medical and dental schools. *English for Specific Purposes*, 26(3), 368–92. Gs325.

[37] Monte, A. A., & Libby, A. M. (2018). Introduction to the specific aims page of a grant proposal. *Academic Emergency Medicine*, 25(9), 1042–7. Gs26.

[38] Millar, N., Batalo, B., & Budgell, B. (2022). Trends in the use of promotional language (hype) in abstracts of successful national institutes of health grant applications, 1985–2020. *JAMA Network Open*, 5(8), e2228676–e2228676. Gs19; Millar, N., Batalo, B., & Budgell, B. (2023). Promotional Language (hype) in abstracts of publications of National Institutes of Health – funded research, 1985–2020. *JAMA Network Open*, 6(12), e2348706–e2348706. Gs2; Millar, N., Batalo, B., & Budgell, B. (2022). Trends in the use of Promotional Language (hype) in National Institutes of Health funding opportunity announcements, 1992–2020. *JAMA Network Open*, 5(11), e2243221–e2243221. Gs5.

3 Scientific Knowledge: From Shortcomings to Coaching 179

3.5 Hoppe et al. (2019): Topic Choice of Grant Writing

Overview

The article is titled "Topic choice contributes to the lower rate of NIH awards to African-American/black scientists."[39] Obviously, the article focuses on race bias in NIH funding, an extremely hot topic in grantology research. This might explain why it has been highly cited, 529 times since 2019, as the second highest after the influential Ginther *et al.* study.[40] However, from the perspective of grant writing, it raises an important and thought-provoking issue, topic choice vs. word choice.

A team of eleven NIH officers contributed to this article. The first author, Travis Hoppe, is currently Assistant Director of AI Research and Development at the Office of Science and Technology Policy of the White House and was a data scientist in the Office of Portfolio Analysis, National Institutes of Health. His h-index is 14.

The article was published in 2019 in *Science Advances*. The journal is the American Association for the Advancement of Science's open-access multidisciplinary journal, publishing impactful research papers and reviews in all fields of science. It uses evolving digital publishing technologies to extend the capacity of *Science*. In 2019, it surpassed *Science* and became the journal with the largest number of monthly submissions in the *Science* family of journals. Its impact factor was 11.7 in 2023.

Highlights

This empirical article has a typical structure used in *Science*: Introduction, Results, Discussion, and Methods. The following key points can be highlighted from the perspective of grant writing.

The first highlight is that the authors built up previous studies and came up with a thoughtful analysis design. They identified **six decision points** at which differential outcomes might contribute to an overall difference in funding: (1) application submission; (2) application selection for discussion by a study section; (3) assignment of impact scores; (4) final funding decisions made; (5) resubmission for unfunded applications; and (6) choice of topic that has not been studied before. Data analysis at these six decision points of the grant process was performed with 157,549 new and renewal R01 applications from 2011 to 2015.

---

[39] Hoppe, T. A., Litovitz, A., Willis, K. A., Meseroll, R. A., Perkins, M. J., Hutchins, B. I. *et al.* (2019). Topic choice contributes to the lower rate of NIH awards to African-American/black scientists. *Science Advances*, 5(10), article eaaw7238. Gs542.
[40] Ginther, D. K., Schaffer, W. T., Schnell, J., Masimore, B., Liu, F., Haak, L. L. *et al.* (2011). Race, ethnicity, and NIH research awards. *Science*, 333(6045), 1015–19. Gs1124.

The second and foremost highlight is the **unexpected major findings** of the study on race differences in the topic choice of grant proposals. Both descriptive statistics and multivariate analysis indicate significant differences at three of the six decision points: two (decision to discuss and impact score assignment) have been studied before, but one (topic choice) has not been studied before. Notably, African American applicants tend to propose research on topics with lower award rates. These topics include research at the community and population level, as opposed to more fundamental and mechanistic investigations. Topic choice alone accounts for over 20 percent of the funding gap after controlling for multiple variables, including the applicant's prior achievements.

Last, one of the **practical implications** to new grant writers is to develop a clear awareness that topic choice matters when designing and developing a grant proposal, while various aspects of grant writing (e.g. word choice or genre use), as discussed extensively in the literature, are also useful. The former is essentially strategic, and the latter is largely tactical. This applies to all grant writers, especially for African American writers. Of course, public and private funders need to pay specific attention to this issue to design interventions and reduce the funding gaps.

3.6 Connor & Mauranen (1990): Ten Typical Moves in Grant Writing

Overview

This article, titled "Linguistic analysis of grant proposals: European Union research grants,"[41] is a classic study on linguistic analysis of grant proposals. It has been cited 473 times. The article is clearly written and can be easily read, which is probably one of the reasons why it is so well-received.

The first author, Ulla Connor, is a Professor in the English department at Indiana University-Purdue University Indianapolis. She is one of the pioneers of linguistic analysis of grant writing. She has 158 publications with 6,457 citations. She has published multiple articles on genre analysis and grant writing.[42] The second author, Anna Mauranen, is a Professor

---

[41] Connor, U., & Mauranen, A. (1999). Linguistic analysis of grant proposals: European Union research grants. *English for Specific Purposes, 18*(1), 47–62. Gs473.

[42] Connor, U. (2000). Variation in rhetorical moves in grant proposals of US humanists and scientists. *Text & Talk, 20*(1), 1–28. Gs179; Connor, U., & Upton, T. (2004). The genre of grant proposals: A corpus linguistic analysis. In U. Connor & T. Upton (eds.), *Discourse in the Professions: Perspectives from Corpus Linguistics* (pp. 235–56). John Benjamins. Gs103.

3 Scientific Knowledge: From Shortcomings to Coaching 181

Emeritus of Languages, English, and Philology at the University of Helsinki. She has 100 publications with 4,872 citations.

The article was published in 1999 in *English for Specific Purposes*. This is an international peer-reviewed journal that publishes studies on the teaching and learning of English for academic, occupational, business, industrial, scientific, technical, or other specific purposes. Its impact factor was 3.2 in 2023. Its publisher is Elsevier.

Highlights

The article is an empirical study, with six major sections: Grant proposals as persuasive writing, Data, Development of moves, Identification of moves, Moves (the main section), and Conclusion. We have the following major highlights.

First and foremost, the authors identify and specify **ten rhetorical moves** that regularly appear in grant proposals. They defined a move in a text as a functional component used for some identifiable rhetorical purposes. A move should have function indicators and boundary indicators. Based on their genre analysis (i.e. analysis of texts to find recurrent patterns of structure and behavior for better communications) of thirty-four EU research grants, a grant proposal includes ten typical functional moves. Among them, six general moves for any **persuasive writing** include: territory (establishing practical or scientific territory); gap (indicating a knowledge gap); goal (stating aims); means (specifying how to achieve goals); reporting previous research (presenting previous work); and competence (introducing capable researchers); and four specific moves that **grant proposals** seem to have are achievements (presenting anticipated results); benefits (specifying benefits); importance (specifying importance); and compliance (meeting grant requirements).

Second, the article has a special **theoretical** implication for grantology researchers. Grantology is heavily influenced by the sociology of science and economics of science. This article as well as other articles on linguistical analysis of grant writing demonstrate another line of theoretical influence on grantology made by linguistics. Grantology is an interdisciplinary field and this article is another good example of this.

Last, writing grant proposals, like writing for sale letters, applying for job applications, or introducing a research paper, uses a **promotional genre** and concerns **ten typical functional moves**. For new grant writers, knowing the general genre and the ten functional moves will benefit our writing of a grant proposal from a new linguistic perspective.

3.7 Weber-Main et al. (2020): Grant Writing Coaching

After studying several articles on grant writing, now let us study a comprehensive and ambitious study on the impacts of a large grant writing coaching program.[43]

Overview

This article is titled "Grant application outcomes for biomedical researchers who participated in the National Research Mentoring Network's Grant Writing Coaching Programs." It reports a large complex study, assessing how well six grant writing coaching programs improve grant submission and grant success among 545 early-career biomedical investigators from 187 different institutions across the United States between 2015 and 2018.

A team of nineteen authors from fourteen schools of medicine or health sciences wrote the article. Four of them had grants to support the study.[44] The first and co-corresponding author is Anne Marie Weber-Main, a Professor of Medicine at the University of Minnesota Medical School. Her expertise is in research faculty development, with concentrations in scientific/medical writing and mentoring models. In her teaching, she developed the Proposal Preparation Program, a longitudinal grant writing workshop series for early-career faculty. She adapted this successful curriculum for national dissemination through the NIH-funded National Research Mentoring Network (NRMN), a nationwide consortium of biomedical professionals and institutions to support the career advancement of trainees from under-represented groups in biomedical disciplines. Her h-index is 17 as of 2023 based on Google Scholar. She has published multiple articles on grant writing programs.[45] Researchers in

---

[43] Weber-Main, A. M., McGee, R., Eide Boman, K., Hemming, J., Hall, M., Unold, T. *et al.* (2020). Grant application outcomes for biomedical researchers who participated in the National Research Mentoring Network's Grant Writing Coaching Programs. *PLoS One*, *15*(11), article e0241851. Gs27.

[44] This information is based on the grant acknowledge note at the end of the article, another good example of using the grant acknowledge note to learn and build grant portfolios.

[45] Jones, H. P., McGee, R., Weber-Main, A. M., Buchwald, D. S., Manson, S. M., Vishwanatha, J. K. *et al.* (2017, December). Enhancing research careers: An example of a US national diversity-focused, grant-writing training and coaching experiment. *BMC Proceedings*, *11*(12), 183–92. Gs35; Weber-Main, A. M., Engler, J., McGee, R., Egger, M. J., Jones, H. P., Wood, C. V. *et al.* (2022). Variations of a group coaching intervention to support early-career biomedical researchers in Grant proposal development: A pragmatic, four-arm, group-randomized trial. *BMC Medical Education*, *22*(1), 1–16. Gs11; Harwood, E. M., Jones, A. R., Erickson, D., Buchwald, D., Johnson-Hemming, J., Jones, H. P. *et al.* (2019). Early career biomedical grantsmanship self-efficacy: Validation of an abbreviated self-assessment tool. *Annals of the New York*

grantology, especially applied grantology, should follow her work. The last and co-corresponding author is Kolawole S. Okuyemi, a Professor of Family Medicine at Indiana University School of Medicine. His research has focused on cancer- and smoking-related health disparities experienced by African Americans, Sub-Saharan African immigrants, and persons experiencing homelessness. He was also one of the Principal Investigators awarded the NIH Common Fund grant to establish the NRMN. His research has been continuously funded for more than twenty years by the NIH, with grant awards totaling more than $50 million. It would be useful to study his grant portfolio and learn his winning strategies.

The article was published in *PLoS One*. The journal is a multidisciplinary open-access mega journal published by the Public Library of Science (PLoS), a non-profit publisher of open-access journals in science and technology. Its impact factor was 2.9 in 2023.

Highlights
The article is an empirical article, with a typical structure, Introduction, Methods, Results, and Discussion, with a detailed note on the authors' contributions to this team project. From the grant writing perspective, we can highlight two major points.

First, the article presents **particularly interesting** grant writing coaching programs. These programs share several key features. (1) The **programs** have three core curricular elements of the NRMN Grant Writing Coaching Program: two or three days of kickoff in-personal meetings, biweekly or monthly virtual or in-person coaching sections for four to ten months, and a mock review session. (2) The programs also used relatively different **models** in different institutions (e.g. some programs extensively engaged with NIH program officials). (3) **Participants** are assistant professors or postdocs and may be at different phases of grant writing, from being ready to write and submit grants within six months after the program to just starting to collect data. (4) Participating **coaches** are mid-career and late-career scientists as associate or full professors who have successful experience in grant writing and grant reviewing and have

Academy of Sciences, *1445*(1), 17–26. Gs11; Weber-Main, A. M., Thomas-Pollei, K. A., Grabowski, J., Steer, C. J., Thuras, P. D., & Kushner, M. G. (2022). The proposal preparation program: A group mentoring, faculty development model to facilitate the submission and funding of NIH grant applications. *Academic Medicine*, *97*(1), 53–61. Gs4; Weber-Main, A. M. (2010). Conquering the mega grant: An approach to editing proposals for centers or program. *Science Editor*, *33*(4), 135–7. Gs0.

a strong interest and sufficient time to mentor early-career researchers, especially underrepresented groups. In short, the grant writing coaching programs essentially engage early-career participants both in multiple months of sustained and intensive coaching by experienced investigators and in working within a small cohort of peers actively writing grant applications.

Second, the article reports the **two major results** from Phase 1 of the programs. (1) Among 545 participants, 328 submitted at least one proposal within eighteen months after the program, with a submission rate of 59 percent. Reasons for not achieving a 100 percent submission rate are lacking institutional support, lacking research capacity, lacking time commitment, and being too early for grant writing and submission. (2) Among 328 submissions, 134 proposals were awarded, with a success rate of 41 percent. Among these grants, ninety-three were from the NIH, including sixteen NIH G01 grants. The remaining forty-one are from the NSF and various professional associations. Thus, the Phase 1 study has generated compelling preliminary evidence that the programs can help participants achieve the important goals of proposal submission and grant funding. Note that several members of the team have received **Phase 2 funding** from an NIH U01 grant to more rigorously study intervention effects of the grant writing coaching programs, using randomized trial designs and mixed methods analytic approaches.

Third, there exist extensive publications which present and assess various ways of grant writing training.[46] This article not only showcases this line of research, but also provides multiple important leads in its literature review and references.

Last, the direct **practical implication** to the new grant writers is obvious: we can and should follow these models or some fine elements of these models (e.g. learning from experienced grant writers or working as a cohort in writing grants) in our own grant writing efforts to improve submission rates and success rates of our grant writing.

---

[46] Kulage, K. M., Corwin, E. J., Liu, J., Schnall, R., Smaldone, A., Soled, K. R. *et al.* (2022). A 10-year examination of a one-on-one grant writing partnership for nursing pre-and post-doctoral trainees. *Nursing Outlook*, *70*(3), 465–77. Gs2; Ding, H. (2008). The use of cognitive and social apprenticeship to teach a disciplinary genre: Initiation of graduate students into NIH grant writing. *Written Communication*, *25*(1), 3–52. Gs164; Jones *et al.* (2017), note 46 above; Reynolds, C. F., Martin, C., Brent, D., Ryan, N., Dahl, R. E., Pilkonis, P. *et al.* (1998). Postdoctoral clinical-research training in psychiatry: A model for teaching grant writing and other research survival skills and for increasing clarity of mentoring expectations. *Academic Psychiatry*, *22*(3), 190–6. Gs24.

4 Grantology vs. Journalology: Grant Writing vs. Article Writing

After discussing several research articles on grant writing, let us compare grant writing to article writing. While there are different variations of grant writing (e.g. public and private grant proposals, major research grant proposals, and career development grant proposals) and article writing (e.g. empirical, theoretical, methodological, and review articles), grant writing is a major topic of grantology, while article writing is a key topic of journalology.[47] We can take the perspective of grantology and journalology to examine major similarities and differences between grant writing and article writing so that we can understand grant writing better and write grant proposals better.

4.1 Similarities between Grant Writing and Article Writing

It is not difficult to see various similarities between grant writing and article writing. Briefly, the major similarities include: (1) Grant writing and article writing essentially are all scientific writing, produced by professionals and consumed by a wide variation of target readers. (2) Grant writing and article writing are all going through major steps of a scientific writing cycle, from planning, writing, revising, to completion. (3) Grant writing and article writing are all assessed against professional criteria by peer reviewers to ensure scientific quality. (4) The final product of grant writing and article writing should have core elements, strong contents, coherent structures, and acceptable styles. (5) Grant writing and article writing all require a professional team to manage and assist the process. Among all the professionals involved in grant writing and article writing, grant officers and journal editors are the most critical decision-makers.

4.2 Differences between Grant Writing and Article Writing

It is not easy to immediately see the fundamental differences between grant writing and article writing. However, it is critical to understand the uniqueness of grant writing to generate a winning grant proposal. Some

---

[47] Inouye, S. K., & Fiellin, D. A. (2005). An evidence-based guide to writing grant proposals for clinical research. *Annals of Internal Medicine*, *142*(4), 274–82. Gs 121; Bem, D. J. (2021). Writing the empirical journal article. In J. M. Darley, M. P. Zanna, & H. L. Roediger III (eds.), *The Compleat Academic* (2nd edn., pp. 171–201). Psychology Press. Gs 533.

of the unique important aspects of grant writing that distinguish it from article writing are highlighted as follows.

First, the **direct goal** of grant writing essentially is to write in order to secure a grant. It is an investment to seek the highest possible scientific or societal returns. Certainly, securing a grant broadly is to complete a proposal project, advance scientific knowledge, and, ultimately, improve human life. This direct goal largely determines elements and structures of a grant proposal, genres and styles of grant writing, criteria and process of assessment, and outcomes and impacts of grant writing to see if the goal is achieved. In comparison, the direct goal of article writing is to write for publishing or disseminating an intellectual product. Likewise, this direct goal largely determines all other aspects of article writing, from input to output.

Second, driven by its direct goal, content-wise, grant writing primarily specifies and justifies **why the proposed project is significant and how it is feasible**. It is like writing the Introduction and Method of an empirical paper, while a full empirical paper typically consists of Introduction, Method, Results, and Discussion. Put differently, a grant proposal focuses on the beginning of a project, and a journal article focuses on the end of a project. In addition, grant writing has to include extra elements such as investigator capacity and grant budget besides the project plan.

Third, a grant proposal is often reviewed by a **panel of ten to twenty peer reviewers** to make sure the assessment process is rigorous and the decision for funding or rejecting is sound, while a manuscript is usually reviewed by two to three peer reviewers and then an editor makes an editorial decision. Thus, grant writing needs to satisfy the ten to twenty panelists who have various backgrounds, experience, and expertise.[48]

Next, the review of grant writing essentially is **norm-referenced** rather than **criteria-referenced**. In other words, because of the limitation in funding slots in a given fiscal year, the funding decision is based on whether a grant proposal is ranked at the top against others in a pool rather than whether a grant proposal passes certain criteria. In contrast, the review of article writing is criteria-referenced, but not norm-referenced. If two to three reviewers offer consistently positive reviews against the journal publication standard, a manuscript will be accepted and published sooner or

---

[48] Marsh, H. W., & Ball, S. (1981). Interjudgmental reliability of reviews for the Journal of Educational Psychology. *Journal of Educational Psychology, 73*(6), 872–80. Gs112; Cicchetti, D. V. (1991). The reliability of peer review for manuscript and grant submissions: A cross-disciplinary investigation. *Behavioral & Brain Sciences, 14*(1), 119–35. Gs592.

later. For new grant writers, this aspect of grant writing is important and challenging: It is not enough to write a good grant proposal to be funded; it has to be at least among the best, if not the best.

Fourth, one interesting aspect of grant writing is that a funded or rejected grant proposal is an **internal product**. It is not publicly available and often treated as confidential, with two exceptions: a few full grant proposals are presented publicly as illustrative examples; and many grant proposal summaries are accessible in federal grant databases. This aspect is completely different from article writing: all accepted manuscripts are published in the journal and are accessible publicly, either free or unfree. Thus, new grant writers should proactively collect and carefully study various real grant proposals, rejected or approved.

Last, a grant proposal differs from **other types of proposals**, such as a dissertation proposal, a project proposal, or a research proposal. The grant proposal pursues a grant and requests funding for a proposed project, whereas other types of proposals present a project plan that guides the completion of a project. For example, a doctoral student needs to develop a dissertation proposal and needs to receive approval from the dissertation committee before following the plan and completing a dissertation study.

5 Action Suggestions: Studying Six Grant Proposals and Outlining One Grant Proposal

5.1 Understanding the Uniqueness of Grant Writing

At the end of the chapter, let us first summarize the previous four sections before offering suggestions for action.

First, we have seen the intuitive knowledge of four new grant writers. These new grant writers do have general knowledge of grant writers (e.g. mentioning terms such as fundable ideas and grant criteria, and knowing several elements of a grant proposal, such as grant objectives, research methods, and grant budget). Some of them even have good insights into the importance of grant proposal resubmission, the style of persuasion, the challenging nature of winning a grant via writing, and the need to use evidence to justify projects. The major weakness is their knowledge was that it was too general, and without a clear scientific understanding of both common problems that lead to rejected proposals and unique features of grant writing that lead to successful proposals.

Second, we have examined six real-life cases of grant writing, learning: (1) basic differences between winning proposals and losing proposals;

(2) the importance of writing a grant proposal in a persuasive style, but not a genre of journal articles in a narrative style; (3) the existence of two types of reviewers in assessing a proposal; (4) the key element of a proposal – the specific aims page; (5) the trend of writing precisely and persuasively; and (6) three basic but fundamental strategies. These cases show some of the unique elements of grant writing, which are useful for us to improve our intuitive understanding.

Third, we reviewed and studied seven inspirational empirical studies – some are classic, and others are latest advances. These studies show: (1) common shortcomings of rejected grant writing; (2) detailed strategies of writing the specific aims page as the most critical element of writing an NIH grant; (3) specific steps and strategies for writing a grant proposal; (4) the new understanding of word choice in grant writing; (5) the discovery of the importance of topic choice in grant writing; (6) ten typical functional moves in a grant proposal; and (7) useful training programs to improve grant writing. These studies further demonstrate the uniqueness of grant writing and can help us write grant proposals more productively and successfully.

Fourth, we have compared two concepts, grant writing and article writing, in the broad context of grantology and journalology. Through this comparison, we can see not only basic similarities and differences between grant writing and article writing, but more importantly, unique processes and strategies of grant writing more clearly.

5.2 Studying Grant Proposals and Outlining a Grant Proposal

To better understand the scientific knowledge of grant writing and better apply scientific knowledge to grant writing practice, the following actions can be suggested.

First, search, identify, and study five successful grant proposals and five rejected grant proposals. At least one successful and one rejected grant proposal should be training grants or early-career grants. Make sure to compare the strengths and weaknesses of these real examples. Having around ten real examples of grant proposals in mind will develop a good baseline knowledge of writing a grant proposal. In addition, it will be really useful to find two versions of the same proposal – one being an original submitted and rejected proposal, and the other being a resubmitted and successful one – and compare them to see how errors in the original submission are corrected and how the resubmitted submission is improved.

Second, with a research topic in mind, draft the specific aims section, expand it to an outline of the entire proposal, and develop a timeline to plan your grant writing process. Use various strategies discussed in this chapter, as well as others you have learned from alternative sources. We will have time to finish a full version of a grant proposal, hopefully, a winning one, after reading the next two chapters on grant review and grant decision.

CHAPTER 6

Grant Review

Outline

1 Intuitive Knowledge: What Is Grant Review? 191
  1.1 Responses from New Grant Writers 191
  1.2 Understanding the Complexity and Diversity of Grant Review 192
2 Real-Life Cases: Positive and Negative Sides of Grant Review 194
  2.1 European Union: Annual Call for Grant Reviewers 194
  2.2 The NIH: Removing Disqualified Grant Reviewers 195
  2.3 The NSF: The Broader Impacts Criterion 196
  2.4 The NIH: The New Change from the Five Review Criteria to the Three Review Criteria 197
  2.5 The MRC: The Medical Research Council's Grant Review Process 197
  2.6 The NEA: Post-Review Decisions 198
  2.7 Twenty-Eight Funders, the NIH, and the ERC: Administrative Burden in Grant Review 199
  2.8 Hong Kong vs. Thirty Countries: Gender Biases in Grant Review 201
3 Scientific Knowledge: From Grant Review Features to Grant Review Biases 201
  3.1 Cole *et al.* (1981): Funding Is Determined by Chance in Grant Review 202
  3.2 Wessely (1998): A Complex Picture of Grant Review 204
  3.3 Davis *et al.* (2020): Twenty-One Core Review Skills for Panel Reviewers 209
  3.4 Ardern *et al.* (2023): Outstanding Reviewers vs. Poor Reviewers 211
  3.5 Falk-Krzesinski & Tobin (2015): Review Criteria by Ten US Federal Agencies 214
  3.6 Hug & Aeschbach (2020): Review Criteria by Diverse Funders across the World 216
  3.7 Martin *et al.* (2010): Impacts of Panel Review Discussion 218
  3.8 Tamblyn *et al.* (2018): Various Biases in Grant Review 219
4 Grantology vs. Journalology: Grant Review and Manuscript Review 222
  4.1 Comparing the History 222

	4.2 Comparing Similarities	223
	4.3 Comparing Differences	224
5	Action Suggestions: Reading and Writing Grant Reviews	226
	5.1 Understanding Grant Review as a Complex Multifaceted Assessment System	226
	5.2 Reading Many Grant Reviews and Writing Many Grant Reviews	227

1 Intuitive Knowledge: What Is Grant Review?

1.1 *Responses from New Grant Writers*

Below are quick responses to the question "What is grant review?" from five new grant writers.

- Response 1: From my understanding, a grant review is a process to evaluate and assess applications for grants. A committee will be in charge of the review according to certain criteria to determine which applications should be funded.
- Response 2: I think grant review is similar to the publication peer review. Peer reviewers will evaluate the grant applications and provide fair and objective feedback. If the peer reviewers think the paper has reached the basic requirements, the grant manager will then make the final decision.
- Response 3: Grant review is a review process in which reviewers evaluate the grant in a fair, equitable, and objective way. Before reviewing the grant proposals, it is necessary to set some criteria/ principles for how to review grant proposals. Then, follow the criteria/ principles to review each part of the proposal. Further, in this process, a proposal will need to be reviewed by more than two reviewers.
- Response 4: Grant review is a process where proposed projects are reviewed to decide which should be funded without knowing who applies for the grant during the review. The grant review procedure is conducted by a group of experts. Some of them should be familiar with the research area in which the projects will be conducted, while others may be funding officers. From a chronological perspective, only a few proposals are likely to "survive" the grant review process to become finalists and eventually get funded.
- Response 5: I think that grant review is the assessment of applicants' (e.g. students, researchers, organizations, and institutions) proposal for the next step after submitting their application for a grant successfully. Ultimately, grant review aims to identify the most promising proposals

for funding, based on their potential impact and the likelihood of success. From what I know, typically, grant review involves a panel of experts who assess proposals based on their own criteria, such as the scientific merit of the proposed research, the feasibility of the project, the potential impact of the proposed work, and the qualifications of the applicant or team. The review process tends to be quite rigorous and thorough. Normally, proposals may be initially screened for basic eligibility and relevance, and then subjected to more detailed scrutiny by a panel of reviewers. And then, the financial part is also reviewed. Each grant reviewer team has its own different timeline and generally lists the processing times publicly on its website.

1.2   *Understanding the Complexity and Diversity of Grant Review*

Let us briefly analyze the above five quick responses and see what initial knowledge of grant review among new grant writers could be.

The first response is brief and general. It shows that this individual knows about the basic procedure of grant review. However, grant reviews are conducted in different ways by different grant agencies; some use a review panel and others use individual reviewers.

The second response clearly is general, with several partial misunderstandings. It starts with a partial misconception that considers grant review to be similar to article review. In fact, although these two types of reviews partially overlap, they essentially are very different from each other, which will be discussed later in this chapter in the section on grantology and journalology. Another partial misconception is to consider fairness and objectivity as the criteria or requirements for evaluating grant applications. One might easily get confused with two types of criteria: general criteria for assessing a review process and specific criteria used to assess a grant proposal. In the real world, fairness, objectivity, equity, or unbiasedness are **general** criteria for any good assessment. However, regarding **specific** criteria of grant review, funders and reviewers will usually not assess whether a submitted proposal is fair or objective. Instead, they often use importance and feasibility as the two core criteria, while the criteria vary among different funders – a topic to be discussed later in this chapter. The third partial misconception is that grant managers make the final decision. Usually, it is program officers who recommend a funding decision for final approval by their supervisors.

The third response is a little more specific than the first two and also contains partial misunderstandings. It mentions three major goals of

1 Intuitive Knowledge: What Is Grant Review?

review, the predetermined criteria for review, the need to review each part of a grant proposal, and the number of reviewers needed for review.

The fourth response mentions more details about grant review, with some partial misunderstandings. For instance, the review needs to be anonymous, but actually, the assessment of researchers is an important part of the review process; reviewers are a group of expert reviewers as well as funding officers, but actually, review panels are just one type of review and grant officers usually only manage but not conduct the review. This responder did correctly point out a competitive process of grant review: a proposal needs to pass the grant review, needs to be among finalists, and finally receives the funding.

The last response clearly is the most knowledgeable among the five; perhaps the responder had previous experience of grant applications. It is correct for this responder to state that (1) "grant review aims to identify the most promising proposals for funding," (2) "typically, grant review involves a panel of experts who assess proposals," (3) some criteria include "the scientific merit of the proposed research, the feasibility of the project, the potential impact of the proposed work, and the qualifications of the applicant or team," and (4) the normal review procedure includes initial screening, rigorous panel review, and budget review.

In summary, these five intuitive responses demonstrate that these new grant writers do have a certain understanding rather than very little knowledge of grant review (e.g. knowing that the grant review involves grant reviewers, grant criteria, and grant review processes). However, their knowledge is often (1) inaccurate (e.g. considering "requirements" rather than criteria in assessing a grant proposal, believing the "grant managers" make the final funding decision, saying some reviewers are "funding officers"), (2) incomplete (e.g. saying "the committee" or more than three reviewers will review the proposal), and (3) unspecific (e.g. indicating "each part" of the proposal will be reviewed, but not specifying various elements in a proposal such as abstract, statement, plan, team, or budget, and saying "only a few proposals" get funded rather than general successful funding rates). They have some partial misunderstandings (e.g. considering grant reviews are similar to journal reviews and grant reviews as double-blind or single-blind reviews). They are aware of neither the current debates on review bias, nor the diversity of grant review (e.g. funding with or without review, formal vs. informal reviews, diverse reviewers, and criteria). Obviously, there exists a large variation in their levels of knowledge, from quite limited to rather strong, showing that systematic training is needed for many of them.

The grant review essentially concerns scientific assessment, a critical topic in grantology and a specific area in the science of science.

Considering the above intuitive knowledge, the chapter is intended to focus on the current scientific understanding of grant review, especially on key concepts and challenging issues (e.g. reviewers, review criteria, review processes, review outcomes) to help prepare the grant proposal writing and achieve success in grant applications. While there are different funding agencies and diverse grant review procedures, this chapter does not exhaust all the grant review approaches. Instead, it focuses on major important and challenging issues in grant review. It focuses on the complexity and diversity of grant review.

2 Real-Life Cases: Positive and Negative Sides of Grant Review

2.1 European Union: Annual Call for Grant Reviewers

On January 1, 2024, the European Union released its annual Call for Expression of Interest, indicating that it needs experts mainly for (1) assessing applications for EU funding (including prizes and tenders) and (2) monitoring of EU-funded projects and contracts. It states that experts act in their capacity to assist the EU services with the implementation of EU funding and tenders managed through the Portal. If an individual has extensive professional experience and proven domain-knowledge, he or she can register as an expert online first before the procedure of selection, appointment, assignment, and payment.[1] Selected experts are usually paid no more than €90,000 (around $99,173) during four consecutive calendar years, excluding allowances and travel costs.

This case delivers at least two basic messages regarding grant reviewers. First, grant review performed by reviewers is widely used in grant funding. For instance, for Horizon Europe alone, 63,898 proposals by 17,176 researchers were evaluated between 2021 and 2023.[2] Second, grant reviewers are in great demand. For example, for Horizon Europe Frontier Research Grants by the European Research Council (ERC), the peer review evaluation is carried out through panels of independent scientists and scholars. The review process usually consists of two steps: (1) proposals are reviewed by at least three peer reviewers individually and

---

[1] EU Funding and Tenders Portal, *European Commission*, available at: https://ec.europa.eu/info/funding-tenders/opportunities/portal/screen/how-to-participate/how-to-participate/3.
[2] Horizon Europe – performance, *European Commission*, available at: https://commission.europa.eu/strategy-and-policy/eu-budget/performance-and-reporting/programme-performance-statements/horizon-europe-performance_en#performance-assessment.

2 Real-Life Cases: Positive & Negative Sides

(2) proposals are further assessed by a review panel consisting of a panel chair and eleven to seventeen panel members.[3] This is significantly different from the journal article review performed by two to three peer reviewers. Thus, widely used review procedures and highly demanding two-step panel review have made reviewer recruitment a special challenge for many funding agencies such as the EU, the National Institutes of Health (NIH), and the National Science Foundation (NSF).

2.2 The NIH: Removing Disqualified Grant Reviewers

On April 6, 2020, Jeffrey Mervis, Senior Correspondent at *Science* who has covered science policy for more than thirty years, posted an article on the *Science* website.[4] Based on a newly released report[5] of the Office of Inspector General of the Department of Health and Human Services, as well as previous statements by the NIH, Jeffrey Mervis summarized that the NIH had taken disciplinary action against external reviewers who violated research integrity: for example, seventy-seven reviewers have been put on a "Do Not Use" for breaching confidentiality, forty-seven were flagged for not reporting their affiliations with foreign institutions, and fifty-five scientists were removed from the reviewer pool who were facing allegations of sexual harassment.

This news shows two sides of grant reviewers. The positive side is that the NIH enlists nearly 30,000 scientists every year to review over 80,000 grant proposals. The reviewers volunteer their time and knowledge to ensure the quality of funding decisions. The negative side is that a small number of disqualified reviewers have broken rules and damaged the quality of grant reviews, another challenge for responsible funding agencies worldwide.[6]

---

[3] Horizon Europe, European Research Council (ERC) Frontier Research Grants: Guide for peer reviewers starting and consolidator grant calls, *European Commission*, available at: https://ec.europa.eu/info/funding-tenders/opportunities/docs/2021-2027/experts/guide-for-peer-reviewers_he-erc-stg-cog_en.pdf.
[4] NIH's process for removing reviewers remains a mystery, watchdog finds, *Science*, available at: www.science.org/content/article/nih-s-process-removing-reviewers-remains-mystery-watchdog-finds; NIH Director pledges to move quickly on recommendations to stop sexual harassment, *Science*, available at: www.science.org/content/article/nih-director-pledges-move-quickly-recommendations-stop-sexual-harassment; NIH looks to punish reviewers who violate confidentiality, *Science*, available at: https://www.science.org/doi/abs/10.1126/science.360.6384.17.
[5] NIH has acted to protect confidential information handled by peer reviewers, but it could do more, *US Department of Health and Human Services, Office of Inspector General*, available at: https://oig.hhs.gov/oei/reports/oei-05-19-00240.pdf.
[6] Merit review process, *US National Science Foundation*, https://nsf-gov-resources.nsf.gov/2023-06/FY_2021_Merit_Review_Digest.pdf. The NSF receives about 44,000 proposals each year for research, education, and training projects, the reviewer community has completed nearly 240,000 reviews per year.

2.3 The NSF: The Broader Impacts Criterion

In 1997, nearly thirty years ago, the NSF formally introduced broader impacts as a key criterion for evaluating grant proposals. This was after the National Science Board approved the NSF's revised criteria for evaluating proposals. All NSF proposals are evaluated through the use of the two merit review criteria. First, the **intellectual merit** of the proposed activity is evaluated. Core questions are: How important is the proposed activity to advancing knowledge and understanding within its own field or across different fields? How well qualified are the proposed individuals or teams to conduct the project? To what extent does the proposed activity suggest and explore creative and original concepts? How well conceived and organized is the proposed activity? Is there sufficient access to resources? Second, the **broader impacts** of the proposed activity are evaluated. Core questions include: How well does the activity advance discovery and understanding while promoting teaching, training, and learning? How well does the proposed activity broaden the participation of underrepresented groups (e.g. gender, ethnicity, disability, geographic)? To what extent will it enhance the infrastructure for research and education? Will the results be disseminated broadly to enhance scientific and technological understanding? What may be the benefits of the proposed activity to society?

In 2002, after five years, the NSF Director issued an Important Notice titled "Implementation of new grant proposal guide requirements related to the broader impacts criterion." This Important Notice reinforces the significance of addressing both criteria in the preparation and review of all proposals submitted to the NSF. For instance, Principal Investigators (PIs) must address both merit review criteria in separate statements within the one-page Project Summary and reiterate the broader impacts in the Project Description. On the other hand, the NSF continues to strengthen its internal processes to ensure that both of the merit review criteria are addressed when making funding decisions. For instance, the NSF will return without review proposals that do not separately address both merit review criteria within the Project Summary.[7]

This case from the NSF suggests that grant review criteria are critical to grant writing, they often undergo continuous adjustment and improvement, and some are more difficult than others to implement in grant writing, grant review, and grant funding.

---

[7] Grant proposal guide, *US National Science Foundation*, available at: www.nsf.gov/pubs/2003/nsf032/032_3.htm.

2 Real-Life Cases: Positive & Negative Sides

2.4 The NIH: The New Change from the Five Review Criteria to the Three Review Criteria

On December 8, 2022, Mike Lauer, NIH Deputy Director for Extramural Research, and Noni Byrnes, Director of NIH Center for Scientific Review, posted a blog, updating the NIH's progress in simplifying its grant review criteria. Specifically, the five review criteria (Significance, Investigators, Innovation, Approach, and Environment) will be simplified to the three review criteria (Importance of the Research, Rigor and Feasibility, Expertise and Resources).[8] On January 25, 2025, the NIH implemented this simplified framework for the peer review of the majority of competing research project grant applications.[9] The NIH hopes this change will help to better identify the strongest, highest-impact research, and especially to better assess the scientific and technical merit, mitigate the effect of reputational bias,[10] and reduce reviewer burden.[11]

Like the previous case, this case again suggests that review criteria significantly impact grant writing, grant review, and grant decisions, and it is not uncommon to see radical and incremental changes in the review criteria, even in the well-established review systems in the NIH and NSF.

2.5 The MRC: The Medical Research Council's Grant Review Process

On May 10, 2016, the United Kingdom's Medical Research Council (MRC) posted a video on YouTube titled "Peer review process: From submission to final funding decision."[12] It has had over 95,000 views since 2016. Using animated illustrations, this video is one of the most unique and humorous introductions to the grant review process. It is one of 203 videos about news and features produced by the MRC and attracted 29,000 subscribers.

---

[8] Update on simplifying review criteria: A request for information, *NIH*, available at: https://nexus.od.nih.gov/all/2022/12/08/update-on-simplifying-review-criteria-a-request-for-information/.
[9] Simplifying review of research project grant applications, *NIH*, available at: https://grants.nih.gov/policy/peer/simplifying-review.htm.
[10] Kaiser, J. (2023). To reduce "reputational bias," NIH may revamp grant scoring. *Science (New York, NY)*, *379*(6629), 223.
[11] Guthrie, S., Ghiga, I., & Wooding, S. (2017). What do we know about grant peer review in the health sciences? *F1000Research*, *6*, article 1335. Gs105; Schroter, S., Groves, T., & Højgaard, L. (2010). Surveys of current status in biomedical science grant review: Funding organisations' and grant reviewers' perspectives. *BMC Medicine*, *8*, 1–9. Gs44.
[12] The MRC peer review process: From submission to final funding decision, *YouTube*, available at: www.youtube.com/watch?v=_DErve4aoIA&t=159s.

Based on this video, the MRC is a public funding agency in the United Kingdom, quite like the NIH in the United States, which manages and funds medical research. Each year, it receives about 18,000 proposals and funds about 23 percent of them through a review process aimed at being fair, rigorous, objective, and transparent. The MRC's review process consists of two steps: (1) External Peer Review. At least three independent experts worldwide review a proposal. The reviewers will use three core criteria (Importance of the question, Scientific potential/feasibility of the work, and Resources requested) to write comments and rate with an overall score (1 = poor quality, 6 = exceptional). (2) Internal Board and Panel Assessment. First, each board member will individually review the comments and overall scores of the external reviewers and write their written **comments**. Second, all proposals will be discussed at a triage **meeting** with a panel of six board members (one chair, one deputy chair, and four regular members). If a proposal is assessed as uncompetitive, it will be declined, and anonymous comments will be sent to applicants for their use in future submission; if a proposal is found to be the highest score for competitive, anonymous comments will be sent to applicants for their responses before the full board meeting. Third, each proposal will be assessed in the full board **meeting** of around twenty members. Three board members will first present a proposal; there will be a full board discussion; each member gives a **score** (1 = unacceptable, 10 = exceptional); a median of all scores given by all the members will be determined; and finally the board decides to fund – a median of 9 or 10 will usually be funded. This two-step peer review process is the cornerstone of the MRC's work and is relatively similar to the review process in the NSF and NIH.[13]

From this case, we can see the complexity of the review process in public funding agencies, which is much more complicated than the normal journal peer review.

2.6 The NEA: Post-Review Decisions

On May 25, 1992, over thirty years ago, the *Los Angeles Times* published an article by Diane Haithman, a veteran staff writer. It reported a story that a public funder's chairman reversed initial grant recommendations.[14]

---

[13] The NIH has an excellent four-part video on the peer review process at the NIH on YouTube, available at: www.youtube.com/watch?v=LsaChVs-VXk&t=9s; www.youtube.com/watch?v=Es1KkFO5Aow&t=127s; www.youtube.com/watch?v=KYlECxn63vs&t=219s; and www.youtube.com/watch?v=KKViraEcIp8.

[14] NEA peer panels face issues of art ethics, *Los Angeles Times*, available at: www.latimes.com/archives/la-xpm-1992-05-25-ca-140-story.html.

Basically, Anne-Imelda Radice, then acting chair of the National Endowment for the Arts (NEA), had overturned two $10,000 grants that had been recommended by review panels (it cost the NEA $7,000 to run the panel review) and the advisory National Council on the Arts (NCA), which reviews and makes recommendations on applications for grants. The two grants are Virginia Commonwealth's Anderson Gallery and the Massachusetts Institute of Technology's List Gallery, proposing to display exhibitions exploring sexual themes and depicting body parts. Anne-Imelda Radice considered that the exhibitions lacked artistic quality and thus decided to reverse initial funding decisions. Of course, this generated a series of strong reactions. Note that the chairman does have the authority to overturn grant recommendations, but Radice was criticized for being politically motivated to some extent, namely, keeping controversial grants from becoming embarrassments to the Bush Administration.

Like the NIH and NSF, the NEA is the largest federal funder of the arts and arts education in communities nationwide and a catalyst of public and private support for the arts. The NEA's primary activities include grant-making to non-profit arts organizations, public arts agencies and organizations, colleges and universities, federally recognized tribal communities or tribes, and individual writers and translators. The NCA advises the Chairman of the NEA and reviews and makes recommendations to the Chairman on applications for grants, funding guidelines, agency policies, and leadership initiatives.[15]

This case, although it seems to be uncommon, shows the complexity of the real-life grant review and decision process, especially after panel review and initial funding decisions were completed.

2.7 Twenty-Eight Funders, the NIH, and the ERC: Administrative Burden in Grant Review

In 2023, Sara Schroter, Senior Researcher at the *British Medical Journal* (*BMJ*), Trish Groves, **Deputy Editor and Head of Research at the *BMJ*, and Editor-in-Chief of *BMJ Open***, and Liselotte Højgaard, Professor at the University of Copenhagen and a member of the Scientific Council of ERC, published a large-scale international survey study on the current status of biomedical science grant review. They found that twenty-eight funders in nineteen countries reported five major problems, including the

---

[15] NCA, *National Endowment for the Arts*, available at: www.arts.gov/about/leadership-staff/national-council-arts.

administrative burden of the review process, that had increased substantially over the previous five years. Administrative burden generally refers to the extra time and work required for non-research-related tasks (e.g. filing forms, setting up meetings, and getting signatures) for funders, reviewers, applicants, and institutions during the pre- and post-award phase.[16]

It was estimated that PIs of federal research grants spend 42 percent of their time on administrative tasks.[17] Major funders of biomedical research have reported recently that they are becoming overburdened by workloads and by the complexity and slowness of grant review processes, and they have attempted to address this burden. For example, the NIH is changing its five criteria to three, one of the reasons being to adjust the administrative burden.[18] The ERC plans to give researchers a "lump sum" to carry out their funded projects without actual cost reporting, time sheets, and financial audits.[19] Multiple studies have been published to examine the administrative burden.[20]

---

[16] What is administrative burden in research, and how can you reduce it? *Cayuse*, available at: https://cayuse.com/blog/research-funding-administrative-burdens; Mosley, L., Forsberg, J., & Ngo, D. (2020). Reducing administrative burden in federal research grants to universities, *IBM Center for the Business of Government*, available at: www.businessofgovernment.org/report/reducing-administrative-burden-federal-research-grants-universities. Gs5.

[17] Reducing investigators' administrative workload for federally funded research, *US National Science Foundation*, available at: www.nsf.gov/pubs/2014/nsb1418/nsb1418.pdf; 2012 faculty workload survey research report, *Federal Demonstration Partnership*, available at: https://sites.nationalacademies.org/cs/groups/pgasite/documents/webpage/pga_087667.pdf; Report recommends 14 ways to reduce administrative burden, *American Association for the Advancement of Science*, available at: www.aaas.org/taxonomy/term/7/report-recommends-14-ways-reduce-administrative-burden; How to actually reduce the administrative burden on research, *Good Science Project*, available at: https://goodscienceproject.org/articles/how-to-actually-reduce-the-administrative-burden-on-research/.

[18] Tag: Administrative burden, *NIH*, available at: https://nexus.od.nih.gov/all/tag/administrative-burden/.

[19] Bid to cut grant administrative burden "may have opposite effect," *Times Higher Education*, available at: www.timeshighereducation.com/news/bid-cut-grant-administrative-burden-may-have-opposite-effect; Lump sums in advance grants 2024, *European Research Council*, available at: https://erc.europa.eu/news-events/news/lump-sums-advanced-grants-2024.

[20] Guthrie et al. (2017), note 11 above; Schiller, J. L., & Lemire, S. D. (2023). A survey of research administrators: Identifying administrative burden in post-award federal research grant management. *Journal of Research Administration*, 55(3), 9–29. Gs1; Decker, R. S., Wimsatt, L., Trice, A. K., & Konstan, J. A. (2007). *A Profile of Federal-Grant Administrative Burden among Federal Demonstration Partnership Faculty: A Report of the Faculty Standing Committee of the Federal Demonstration Partnership*; Heinrich, C. J. (2016). The bite of administrative burden: A theoretical and empirical investigation. *Journal of Public Administration Research & Theory*, 26(3), 403–20. Gs256; Schiller, J. L. (2022). *A Survey of Research Administrators to Identify Areas of Administrative Burden in Federal Research Grant Management* (Doctoral dissertation, University of North Dakota); Leyland, B., Jackson, G., Godard, K., Taggart, K., Nalevanko, A., & Capor, R. (2020). Structuring a departmental research administration office to combat a high-demand workload and offset administrative burden. *Research Management Review*, 24(1), n1; Chun, M. B. (2010). Building a research administration infrastructure at the department level. *Journal of Research Administration*, 41(3), 77–84. Gs17.

The information presented above is a case of administrative burden in the grant process, as one of the various negative outcomes of grant review.

2.8 Hong Kong vs. Thirty Countries: Gender Biases in Grant Review

In August 2020, Paul Yip and his three colleagues published an article titled: "Is there gender bias in research grant success in social sciences? Hong Kong as a case study."[21] Since existing research on the gender gap in funding has focused on biomedical, science, technology, engineering, and mathematics in the West, they decided to examine the gender biases in social sciences and Asia. It was found that women had a higher grant submission rate, a higher grant success rate, and a higher amount per award than their male counterparts. This might be due to good practices and distinctive contextual factors in social science funding in Hong Kong.

In 2024, Alex James and his three colleagues in New Zealand posted a preprint titled: "Female-dominated disciplines have lower evaluated research quality and funding success rates, for men and women."[22] They used data from thirty countries (e.g. Australia, Canada, the European Union, and the United Kingdom) and found that the more women in a specific discipline, the lower the quality of the research in that discipline is evaluated to be, and the lower the funding success rate is. In short, in the scope of an entire discipline, women's work is valued less. An open review states that this study provides **convincing** evidence that the quality of research in female-dominated fields of research is systematically undervalued by the research community.

These two recent studies provide contrasting evidence surrounding the current debate on the gender gap in funding, showing the complexity of positive and negative outcomes of grant review.

3 Scientific Knowledge: From Grant Review Features to Grant Review Biases

Grant review is central to research grants because it assesses the quality of grant proposals and determines the chance of funding or not. A process

---

[21] Yip, P. S. F., Xiao, Y., Wong, C. L. H., & Au, T. K. F. (2020). Is there gender bias in research grant success in social sciences? Hong Kong as a case study. *Humanities & Social Sciences Communications*, 7(1), 1–10. Gs17.

[22] James, A., Buelow, F., Gibson, L., & Brower, A. (2024). Female-dominated disciplines have lower evaluated research quality and funding success rates, for men and women. *bioRxiv*, 2024–03. Gs2.

6 Grant Review

of evaluation generally involves the four basic elements: reviewers, review criteria, review process, and review outcomes. In this section, we will first introduce two classic studies of grant review. We will then discuss six articles representing the latest development of the research in grant review.

3.1 Cole et al. (1981): Funding Is Determined by Chance in Grant Review

There exists an extensive literature on grant review. Let us start with a classic seminal paper.[23]

Overview

The article, titled "Chance and consensus in peer review," is one of the earliest and highest cited articles on grant review. The central theme of the article is whether a research proposal gets funded to a significant extent depends on chance rather than other factors (e.g. quality, importance, or feasibility). The article has a high citation of 295, indicating its broad impact.[24]

The first author of the article, Stephen Cole (1941–2018), was a Distinguished Professor of Sociology at SUNY Stony Brook from 1968. Supported by the NSF for twenty years, he has studied the grant review process and significantly contributed to the development of the NSF peer review process. He published two volumes on peer review in the NSF.[25] He also published a long list of major articles on grant review.[26] He was a founding member of Columbia's Program in the Sociology of Science, along with Robert Merton, Harriet Zuckerman, and his younger brother Jonathan R. Cole. As the second author of the article, Jonathan Cole is John Mitchell Mason Professor of Sociology of Science at Columbia University and was the provost of Columbia University for fourteen years. The third author, Gary Simon, is a Professor Emeritus of applied statistics at New York University.

---

[23] Cole, S., Cole, J. R., & Simon, G. A. (1981). Chance and consensus in peer review. *Science*, 214(4523), 881–6. Gs870.
[24] Cole, J. R., & Cole, S. (1973). *Social Stratification in Science*. University of Chicago Press.
[25] Cole, S., Rubin, L., & Cole, J.R. (1978). *Peer Review in the National Science Foundation: Phase One of a Study*. National Academy Press. Gs295; Cole, S., Rubin, L., & Cole, J.R. (1981). *Peer Review in the National Science Foundation: Phase Two of a Study*. National Academy Press. Gs88.
[26] Cole, S., Rubin, L., & Cole, J. R. (1977). Peer review and the support of science. *Scientific American*, 237(4), 34–41. Gs199; Cole, J. R., & Cole, S. (1979). Which researcher will get the grant? *Nature*, 279(5714), 575–6. Gs39; Cole, S., Simon, G., & Cole, J. R. (1988). Do journal rejection rates index consensus? *American Sociological Review*, 53(1), 152–6. Gs84; Cole, S., Cole, J. R., & Simon, G. A. (1982). Response: NSF peer review (continued). *Science*, 215(4531), 346–8. Gs5.

The article was published in 1981 in *Science*. The journal has published many strong articles on grantology, including Merton's 1968 classic on the Matthew effect.[27]

Highlights
This is one of the first major empirical studies or experiments on grant review. It has four major sections: The COSPUP experiment, Reversals, Consensus, and Conclusions. It is the Phase II report after the Phase I report was published. The study is a cleverly designed experiment in which the same 150 proposals in three fields submitted to the NSF were evaluated independently again by a new set of reviewers. The authors examined whether disagreement exists in the review results of the original review group vs. the new reviewer group and where sources for disagreement are located. From the perspective of grant review, we highlight four key points below.

First, the major finding of the study is **truly shocking**. The authors found that securing an NSF research grant to a significant extent depends on chance. In other words, based on the study, the fate of a particular grant application is half determined by the characteristics of the proposal and the PI, and half by apparently random elements that might be characterized as the "luck of the reviewer draw."

Second, comparing the review rating results by the original reviewers and the newly recruited reviewers, substantial disagreement/variability was found. The authors then identified the **four types of sources** for the variability and offered a statistical estimation: (1) **proposals** differ in quality (estimated variation = 35.48); (2) the original and new reviewer groups did not follow completely identical review **procedures** (estimated variation = 2.53); (3) systematic **bias** in rating proposals by the two reviewer groups (estimated variation = 0.45); and (4) **reviewer** variation among the reviewers (estimated variation = 66.22). Among the two largest variations, the reviewer variation is twice as large as the proposal variation.

Third, the authors offered a **careful interpretation** of the findings. Although the finding of a proposal submitted to the NSF is to a significant extent dependent on the applicant's luck in the program director's choice of reviewers, this should not be interpreted that the entire review process unfolds randomly or that each reviewer assesses a proposal randomly. In practice, it is important to examine the sources of reviewer disagreement. The reviewer disagreement could be that two reviewers translate their

---

[27] Merton, R. K. (1968). The Matthew effect in science: The reward and communication systems of science are considered. *Science, 159*(3810), 56–63. Gs11560.

judgment excellently or poorly or they have true disagreement in assessing the same proposal, just like two good physicists have two different theories to explain one physical observation.

Last, the shocking results have **usable implications** for new grant writers. Given that funding decisions are largely determined by what reviewers we will have for our submitted proposal, it is practical and realistic to submit more proposals, solicit reviews from multiple experienced colleagues before submission, and use diverse reviewers during grant review than rely on submitting just one single proposal and being hopeful for successful funding.

3.2   Wessely (1998): A Complex Picture of Grant Review

Let us study another classic article on grant review. This second article is different from the first as it is a review article rather than an empirical article.[28]

Overview

This article, titled "Peer review of grant applications: What do we know?", synthesizes the existing knowledge about grant review. It is among the earliest and most-cited review articles on grant review. Although it was written close to thirty years ago, it is wise, insightful, comprehensive, and still particularly useful today. It is a classic in grant review and has been cited 216 times in Google Scholar as of 2023.

The author, Simon Wessely, or Sir Simon Wessely, is Regius Professor of Psychiatry at King's College London. He was knighted in 2013 for his services to military healthcare and psychological medicine. From 2014 to 2017, he was elected as President of the Royal College of Psychiatrists and then President of the Royal Society of Medicine as the first psychiatrist to be elected in 200 years. His research area is in psychiatry, epidemiology, and mental health. His h-index is 152. This review article is his only work on grantology among his 1,000+ articles.[29]

---

[28] Wessely, S. (1998). Peer review of grant applications: What do we know? *The Lancet, 352*(9124), 301–5. Gs216.

[29] The full-length version of this review was published as a book chapter: Wood, F., & Wessely, S. (1999). Peer review of grant applications: A systematic review. In F. Godlee & T. Jefferson (Eds.), *Peer Review in Health Sciences*, BMA Books. Note that the book is an authoritative text on health sciences peer review and contributions are from the world's leading figures. For the two book editors, Fiona Godlee was the editor in chief of the *British Medical Journal* (BMJ) from 2005 to 2021 and Tom Jefferson was a well-known epidemiologist in Cochrane Collaboration. The book has the second edition in 2003.

3 Scientific Knowledge: Grant Review Features & Biases

The article was published in 1998 in *The Lancet*, which is one of the oldest and highest-impact general medical journals. It was founded in England and its impact factor is 98.4, the highest among general and internal medicine journals worldwide. Its current publisher is Elsevier.

Highlights

The article is a narrative review, synthesizing sixty-one empirical articles selected from an initially identified 121 journal articles on grant review. It first provides an overview of the literature on grant review: Starting in the 1940s, peer review has become the principal mechanism for assessing grant applications. Starting in the 1980s, empirical studies on peer review emerged rapidly, but most are related to journal publication rather than grant application. Even among the existing grant review research, randomized controlled trials are highly limited, which is ironic when we consider that scientific funding decisions are made routinely without robust evidence to support them. It then focuses on addressing six important questions surrounding grant review, regarding fairness, reliability, costs, impact, improvement, and replacement of the peer review. The remainder of this section highlights how the author addressed these six questions.

1. Is peer review fair? Based on Wessely's review, this is a central and complex question about which scientific knowledge is still limited, and the main charges against peer review (e.g. institutional bias, sex bias, and age bias) are generally unfounded, with a few exceptions. Wessely thoughtfully broke this central and complex question into six specific questions and used the existing literature to address each of them.

1.1 Do researchers believe that peer review is a fair system? This question is related to a series of published survey studies of grant applicants carried out by multiple funding agencies worldwide. Overall, participants in these surveys do overwhelmingly endorse the principle of peer review, whereas many have practical criticisms that the grant reviews are "incomplete, inaccurate, or careless" among successful applicants or "inconsistent, inadequate, or unfair" among unsuccessful applicants.

1.2 Is there a bias against lesser-known individuals and institutions? Overall, the literature indicates that institutional bias has limited evidence to support it. In the 1970s, for example, reviewers at the NSF were more likely to be from top-ranked departments. But in the 1980s, the situation was reversed. Thus, the current choice of reviewers from different institutions does not lead to institutional bias against lesser-known institutions.

1.3 Is there an issue of "cronyism"? Literally, cronyism means one favors only companions and friends, while nepotism means one favors only relatives, and patronage means that officers favor promoting their friends and relatives. There is evidence showing that this type of "old-boy social network" or conflicts of interest between reviewers and applicants exist worldwide. We need to deal with a fundamental dilemma in practice, namely, choosing good reviewers and avoiding a conflict of interest.

1.4 Is peer review biased against women? Based on Wessely's review, the evidence of gender bias has been mixed. On the one hand, strong evidence of sex bias was generated by a study of applications for postdoctoral fellowships through the Swedish MRC,[30] indicating that female applicants received significantly lower scores than their male counterparts. On the other hand, various studies found no evidence of sex bias (e.g. Cole's 1981 NSF experiment).

1.5 Does the peer-review system operate against younger researchers? Overall, studies confirm that age has a minor role in grant success at various public and private funding agencies worldwide. Age is also confounded by experience. Note that, taking the NIH as an example, the number of younger applicants has decreased and the age at which a person secures their first research grant is increasing.

1.6 Are there other biases? There are some other biases based on observational data, but not robust evidence. For instance, reviewers might favor a proposal that is within their own specialty. Reviewers might favor basic biomedical research rather than clinical research. Grants discussed early in a review session might be assessed more critically than those reviewed later. Wessely argued thoughtfully that perceptions of bias are common and individual and institutional injustices do occur, just as with all human systems. The strategy should be to recognize them, improve transparency, and introduce due procedure.

2. What is the reliability of peer review? Specifically, are the **ratings** of peer reviews reliable? Based on Wessely's review, this question can be answered in four aspects. (1) There was strong reliability among 75 percent of the **decisions** to fund or reject made by the review panel. (2). There was substantial variation in the reviewers' **ratings**. That is, the reliability

---

[30] Breen, G. (1997). Nepotism and sexism in peer-review. *Nature*, *389*(6649), 326. Gs27; Wenneras, C., & Wold, A. (1997). Nepotism and sexism in peer-review. *Nature 387*(6631), 341–3. Gs2307; Wenneras, C., & Wold, A. (2008). Nepotism and sexism in peer-review. In M. Wyer, M. Barbercheck, B. Cookmeyer, H. Ozturk, & M. Wayne (eds.), *Women, Science, and Technology: A Reader in Feminist Science Studies* (pp. 64–70). Routledge.

among most **reviewers'** ratings of grant proposals was weak. (3) Reviewers show greater reliability in the decision to **reject** rather than accept. (4) Wessely cited Stephene's book[31] to point out insightfully that the expectation for high reliability is **unrealistic**. This is because high reliability among reviewers is possible only when all reviewers agree on a single unanimous view, which is untrue and undesirable. Consensus at the frontiers of science is frequently elusive, and likewise, true honest disagreement among reviewers often exists.

3. What are the costs of peer review? Based on Wessely's review, answering this question is straightforward: (1) The burden of reviewing more submissions with less funding for a funder is **tremendous**. Over 160,000 reviews are provided by 50,000 reviewers to the NSF. The NIH receives 40,000 applications every year, which necessitates each panel reviewer to devote thirty to forty days for review. The UK Research Council used 25,477 days of reviewer time or 115 reviewer years as of 1989. (2) Recruitment of reviewers is **challenging**. Many funding agencies encounter difficulties in persuading scientists to give up time to review grant applications. The Australian Research Council now asks applicants to undertake reviewing duties as a condition of awarding a grant.

4. Does peer review serve the best interests of science? Wessely summarized three aspects of the effectiveness of peer review. (1) Peer review is frequently criticized for its inherent conservatism against **innovative** research. Evidence exists both supporting and rejecting this criticism. (2) Rejection of research proposals through peer review is **harmful**. Evidence exists supporting the claim. In a sample of projects rejected by the NIH in 1970–1, 22 percent of proposals were carried out without substantial changes and 43 percent were abandoned. Similarly, 48 percent of researchers who were not awarded funds by the NSF halted their proposed line of research. (3) No direct experimental evidence showing peer review results, funded or unfunded, causally generate **specific outcomes**

---

[31] Cole, S. (1992). *Making Science: Between Nature and Society*, Harvard University Press. Gs935. The link at www.barnesandnoble.com/w/making-science-stephen-cole/1117249427 provides the book's table of contents (the bold text indicates the most relevant points to Wessely's review): Preface, 1. Nature and the Content of Science, 2. Constructivist Problems in Accounting for Consensus, 3. Constructivist Problems in Demonstrating Causality, 4. **Luck and Getting an NSF Grant**, 5. Consensus in the Natural and Social Sciences, 6. Evaluation and the Characteristics of **Scientists**, 7. Is Science Universalistic?, 8. Conceptualizing and Studying Particularism in Science, 9. Social Influences on the Rate of Scientific Advance, 10. The Future of the Sociology of Science, Appendix: **The COSPUP NSF Peer Review Experiment**, Notes, References. Chapter 4 and the appendix are the most relevant to grantology.

and **impact** of research, while some evidence does suggest that successful grant applicants are more productive than unsuccessful ones.

5. Can peer review be improved? Wessely summarizes various ways that have been proposed and piloted to improve the grant review. First, relevant to grant **reviewers**, efforts include: (1) blinding proposals to reviewers so they will not know applicants and their institutions; (2) asking reviewers to sign their reports to increase their accountability; (3) increasing the number of reviewers or making rating criteria more explicit to improve inter-rater reliability; and (4) adjusting individual reviewers' scores according to their previous performance. Relevant to grant review **procedure**, efforts include: (1) implementing triage processes to review applications as the most popular way of improving efficacy; (2) using interviews as well as written evaluations, as undertaken by the Australian National Health and Medical Research Council; (3) randomly allocating reviewers to meet the PI; (4) removing the fixed deadlines, as implemented by the Engineering and Physical Sciences Research Council; and (5) reducing the workload of the applicants by not submitting the budget request until the grant is awarded.

6. Should peer review be replaced? Wessely's review does not substantiate claims that peer review is so flawed, biased, or corrupt that it needs to be replaced. However, various alternatives to peer review have been suggested. These alternatives include using bibliometrics to assess researchers' scientific productivity, awarding grants at random with a lottery, using cash prizes to stimulate research in key areas, randomly selecting reviewers from a pool, and using a system of professional reviewers.

Last, the article reviews the positive and negative sides of the complex grant review process, and is informative for new grant writers. The grant review process is arguably the best available option and has been widely used for assessing the quality of grant proposals. Furthermore, enormous efforts have been made to improve the system. However, new grant writers should: develop a good awareness of the complexity of the review system; know that grant review involves various unanswered questions or controversial issues; and understand that various existing review systems used by funders are imperfect rather than perfect. Having a balanced and realistic view of the grant review process will help us to generate innovative and feasible strategies in grant writing. If Cole's classic study is strong on depth, then Wessely's classic review is strong on breadth, and both provide remarkable insights into the grant review process.

3.3 Davis et al. (2020): Twenty-One Core Review Skills for Panel Reviewers

After studying two classic articles on grant review, let us now discuss an empirical study on panel reviewers.[32]

Overview
The article we will study here is titled: "What makes an effective grants peer reviewer? An exploratory study of the necessary skills." It is unique and interesting because it focuses on what makes a good grant reviewer rather than what makes a good grant review process. The phrase "An exploratory study" perhaps refers to the fact that their article has two studies: the first study was conducted successfully, interviewing seven program officers and five review panelists, but the second study only received fifty-one survey responses after various efforts to reach 8,868 individuals via LinkedIn and 748 university faculty members.

The article has four authors: Miriam Steiner Davis, Tiffani Conner, Kate Miller-Bains, and Leslie Shapard. They are specialists in the division of Research, Reviews, Evaluation, and Technology at Oak Ridge Associated Universities, a Tennessee-based not-for-profit scientific and technical management organization that has been working with government agencies, universities, and corporate entities since 1946.

The article was published in *PLoS One*, which is a peer-reviewed open-access mega journal published by the Public Library of Science (PLoS) since 2006. The journal covers primary research from any discipline within science and medicine. The PLoS began in 2000 with an online petition initiative by Nobel Prize winner Harold Varmus, formerly Director of the NIH, Patrick O. Brown, a biochemist at Stanford University, and Michael Eisen, a computational biologist at the University of California at Berkeley and the Lawrence Berkeley National Laboratory. Its impact factor was 3.7 in 2022.

Highlights
This exploratory study used mixed methods to identify core skills that are required to be an effective member of review panels conducted for federal funding agencies. It first interviewed seven program officers who worked

---

[32] Steiner Davis, M. L., Conner, T. R., Miller-Bains, K., & Shapard, L. (2020). What makes an effective grants peer reviewer? An exploratory study of the necessary skills. *PLoS One*, *15*(5), article e0232327. Gs8.

for the NIH, NSF, Department of Energy (DoE), and US Geology Survey, and five expert peer-review panelists who reviewed for seven federal agencies and identified twenty-one review skills. It then surveyed fifty-one respondents who had grant review experiences to assess the importance of these twenty-one review skills. From the grant review perspective, we will several interesting points of the study are highlighted below.

First, the authors focused only on **panel reviewers**, the most common, standard, sophisticated review type in the federal funding agencies. The grant review systems are diverse in the real world, for example, with vs. without review, peer vs. expert review, external vs. internal review, and individual vs. panel review. Generally, there are two types of grant reviewers. First, individual reviewers review grant proposals individually (face-to-face or remotely) and submit ratings and comments. Some funders only use individual reviewers, like those reviewing manuscripts for academic journals. Second, panel reviewers, also called review panel members or simply panelists, often review grant proposals individually first and then join the panel discussion to develop final scores and panel review summaries. A panel will usually have a chair and a program officer. The NIH, NSF, and various governmental funders use the panel reviewers.

Second, the most important finding of the study is that they identified and confirmed the **twenty-one review skills** for panel review. These twenty-one review skills, divided into three levels, in an order based on perceived importance, are as follows: (1) extremely common: Subject matter expertise, Openness to other opinions, Impartiality (i.e. fairness), Preparedness, Put proposed research into context, Articulate ideas clearly, Analytical thinking, Collegially disagree, Open to novel ideas and diverse opinions, Broad scientific understanding, and Active listening; (2) very common: Stay on topic, Sustain attention, Sensitivity towards bias, Clear and concise writing; and (3) common: Confidence in own opinion, Redirect conversation, Knowledge of specific agencies' peer review process, Familiarity with the peer review process, Build rapport, and Interpret body language.

Third, the study also found **thirteen activities** that helped improve review skills. These activities, divided into three levels, in an order of most endorsed by the survey results, were as follows: (a) most useful: Being the chair responsible for running a discussion, Listening to panelists making arguments, Sharing thoughts during discussions, and Serving as a peer reviewer of manuscripts for publication; (2) very useful: Participating on more than one panel, Writing and submitting research proposals, Casual discussions with senior colleagues, Reading reviews of our own research proposals, Being mentored by colleagues experienced in panel reviews, Mentoring others concerning participation in panel reviews, Observation of other panelists; and (3) useful: Academic training (e.g. attending graduate programs or training workshops), and Receiving training or instructions from funding agencies.

Last, new grant writers can gain practical tips from this article. First, volunteer to be a grant reviewer for some funding organizations soon, even before writing a grant proposal. Second, choose from the thirteen useful activities and twenty-one core review skills identified in the study that you want to work on in order to develop skills for grant review. These skills of effective peer reviewers are related to the professional skills needed by successful scientists.

3.4 Ardern et al. (2023): Outstanding Reviewers vs. Poor Reviewers

Overview

The article is titled: "Three years of quality assurance data assessing the performance of over 4000 grant peer review contributions to the Canadian Institutes of Health Research Project Grant Competition."[33] The title suggests three key elements of the study: (1) The data were from the Canadian Institutes of Health Research (CIHR). (2) It analyzed over 4,000 grant reviews. (3) It focused on assessing the quality of reviewers. Overall, it is an interesting article on how well reviewers review grant proposals. It has just one citation, perhaps because it was published fairly recently in 2023.

The authors are a team of medical experts and funding agency officers from Canada. Clare Ardern is a scholar in orthopedic sports medicine at the University of British Columbia (UBC). Her h-index is 49. She and her colleagues have published another three preprints and one article related to grantology in the past two years.[34] Nadia Martino works as Executive

---

[33] Ardern, C. L., Martino, N., Nag, S., Tamblyn, R., Moher, D., Mota, A. *et al.* (2023). Three years of quality assurance data assessing the performance of over 4000 grant peer review contributions to the Canadian Institutes of Health Research Project Grant Competition. *FACETS*, *8*, 1–14. GSI.

[34] Lasinsky, A., Wrightson, J., Khan, H., Kitchin, V., Khan, K. M., & Ardern, C. L. (2024). If at first you don't succeed: Biomedical research grant resubmission rates, and factors related to success – a scoping review, available at SSRN 4803560; Wrightson, J. G., Lasinsky, A., Snell, R. R., Hogel, M., Mota, A., Khan, K. M. *et al.* (2024). What factors are important to the success of resubmitted grant applications in health research? A retrospective study of over 20,000 applications to the Canadian Institutes of Health Research. *medRxiv*, 2024–05; Lasinsky, A., Ardern, C., Kitchin, V., Khan, H., Wrightson, J., Khan, K. *et al.* (2022). Grant resubmissions scoping review, *OSF Registries*, available at: https://osf.io/fxdz4/resources; Tamblyn, R., Girard, N., Hanley, J., Habib, B., Mota, A., Khan, K. M. *et al.* (2023). Ranking versus rating in peer review of research grant applications. *PLoS One*, *18*(10), article e0292306.

Director of the College of Reviewers for CIHR. Sammy Nag worked as Lead of Peer Reviewers Recruitment for the CIHR. Robyn Tamblyn is a Professor of Medicine at McGill University, Epidemiologic Studies. David Moher at Ottawa Hospital Research Institute is known for his work on journalology and systematic reviews, with a high h-index of 188. Adrian Mota is the Associate Vice-President of Research Programs and Operations at the CIHR. Karim M. Khan is a Professor of Sports Medicine at UBC, with a h-index of 114.

The article was published in 2023 in *FACETS*, which is Canada's first multidisciplinary open-access science journal. *FACETS* is published by Canadian Science Publishing, Canada's independent publisher of twenty-four international scientific journals. Its impact factor was 3.1 in 2023.

Highlights
This is an empirical article, consisting of six major sections: Introduction, Context, Methods, Results, Discussion, and Conclusion. From the perspective of grant review, especially grant reviewers, we highlight the following interesting points.

First, the study thoughtfully collected a **large dataset** to examine the quality of reviewers. The CIHR commenced a Quality Assurance Program in 2019 to monitor the quality of peer review in its Project Grant Competition Peer Review Committees. The performance of CIHR grant peer reviewers was assessed by CIHR peer review leaders and scientific officers during the four grant competitions in three years of the Research Quality Assurance Program in 2019, 2020, and 2021, who completed Reviewer Quality Feedback forms immediately following Peer Review Committee meetings. Each CIHR Peer Review Committee comprises a Chair, a Scientific Officer (committee leaders), and up to twenty committee members (peer reviewers). Leaders will assign three reviewers who review one application; each reviewer receives up to ten applications per competition. Each committee handles a median of forty applications per competition. Data were collected after four CIHR Project Competition Peer Review Committee meetings (fall 2019, fall 2020, spring 2021, and fall 2021). The performance of peer reviewers was evaluated with 4,438 proposal reviews. Specifically, fifty-nine committees had 991 peer reviewers in fall 2019, fifty-seven committees had 1,123 peer reviewers in fall 2020, sixty-one committees had 1,230 peer reviewers in spring 2021, and fifty-seven committees had 1,094 peer reviewers in fall 2021. Across the four competition rounds, 2,459 unique reviewers participated.

3 Scientific Knowledge: Grant Review Features & Biases 213

Second, since it is unclear how the authors calculated and presented their major statistics, re-calculation was done here based on the raw data presented in the study. Relatively different from the results presented in the study, the **major finding** is close to 70 percent (3,104 of 4,438) of peer reviewers submitted **outstanding** reviews beyond the regular review quality expectation. Around 13 percent (561 out of 4,438) demonstrated potential as a future Peer Review Committee **leader**. However, around 18 percent (785 out of 4,438) of peer reviewers were **unqualified** to review concerning review quality (e.g. lacks robustness), participation (e.g. lacks professionalism), or responsiveness (e.g. late submitting review). Around 12 percent (549 out of 4,438) of grant reviewers are qualified reviewers who performed **adequately** between the two ends of the scale (i.e. outstanding reviewers vs. inadequate reviewers). Thus, while it is pleasing to see that 3,104 of 4,438 reviewers demonstrated outstanding performance, as many as 785 unqualified reviewers certainly are a major concern. Prevention and intervention efforts are really needed to address this problem of quality.

Finally, there exists an extensive literature on the quality of the grant reviewers. Various studies have examined several diverse aspects of grant reviewers, such as their perceptions of panel discussions,[35] their expertise,[36] their motivations,[37] their understanding of review criteria,[38] and reviewing **experience** to reduce disagreement,[39] in addition to general investigations of grant reviews.[40] For grantology researchers, a series of studies[41] on grant reviews by Stephen Gallo and his collaborators deserve special attention.

---

[35] Gallo, S. A., Schmaling, K. B., Thompson, L. A., & Glisson, S. R. (2020). Grant reviewer perceptions of the quality, effectiveness, and influence of panel discussion. *Research Integrity & Peer Review*, 5, 1–9. Gs5.
[36] Gallo, S. A., Sullivan, J. H., & Glisson, S. R. (2016). The influence of peer reviewer expertise on the evaluation of research funding applications. *PLoS One*, 11(10), article e0165147. Gs70.
[37] Gallo, S. A., Thompson, L. A., Schmaling, K. B., & Glisson, S. R. (2020). The participation and motivations of grant peer reviewers: A comprehensive survey. *Science & Engineering Ethics*, 26(2), 761–82. Gs11.
[38] Hug, S. E., & Ochsner, M. (2022). Do peers share the same criteria for assessing grant applications? *Research Evaluation*, 31(1), 104–17. Gs12.
[39] Seeber, M., Vlegels, J., Reimink, E., Marušić, A., & Pina, D. G. (2021). Does reviewing experience reduce disagreement in proposals evaluation? Insights from Marie Skłodowska-Curie and COST actions. *Research Evaluation*, 30(3), 349–60. Gs12.
[40] Gallo, S. A. (2021). The science of peer review: Grant review feedback. *BioScience*, 71(5), 431; Marsh, H. W., Jayasinghe, U. W., & Bond, N. W. (2008). Improving the peer-review process for grant applications: Reliability, validity, bias, and generalizability. *American Psychologist*, 63(3), 160–8. Gs331; Shepherd, J., Frampton, G. K., Pickett, K., & Wyatt, J. C. (2018). Peer review of health research funding proposals: A systematic map and systematic review of innovations for effectiveness and efficiency. *PLoS One*, 13(5), article e0196914. Gs31.
[41] Gallo, S. A., Pearce, M., Lee, C. J., & Erosheva, E. A. (2023). A new approach to grant review assessments: Score, then rank. *Research Integrity & Peer Review*, 8(1), 10. Gs1; Schmaling, K.

3.5 Falk-Krzesinski & Tobin (2015): Review Criteria by Ten US Federal Agencies

We are lucky to be able to study a well-written article[42] which is the best summary of review criteria used by public funders in the United States. This will save us much time and energy.

Overview

The article is titled: "How do I review thee? Let me count the ways: A comparison of research grant proposal review criteria across US federal funding agencies." It is a synthesis of proposal review criteria across ten US federal funding agencies. The first part of the title is related to Elizabeth Barrett Browning, a celebrated English poet, who counted **twenty-five ways** in which she loves her husband in her poem, "How do I love thee? Let me count the ways." The article identified **eight ways** to evaluate the potential for success of a federal research grant proposal.

As the first author of the article, Holly Falk-Krzesinski is Vice President of Research Intelligence at Elsevier. Her main research area is team science, and her h-index is 15. The second author, Stacey Tobin, is a well-admired biomedical writer and editor, and the founder of the consulting firm Tobin Touch.

The article was published in the *Journal of Research Administration*. It is, again, the official journal of the Society of Research Administrators International. It has published a long list of practical and thoughtful articles on grant management.

Highlights

This review article has three major sections: Introduction, Observation, and Discussion. The ten federal funding agencies reviewed in the

---

B., & Gallo, S. A. (2023). Gender differences in peer reviewed grant applications, awards, and amounts: A systematic review and meta-analysis. *Research Integrity & Peer Review, 8*(1), 2. Gs17; Gallo, S. A., Sullivan, J. H., & Croslan, D. R. (2022). A seat at the table: Minority-serving institutions and grant review. *BioScience, 72*(3), 219–20; Gallo, S. A., Sullivan, J. H., & Croslan, D. R. (2020). Scientists from minority-serving institutions and their participation in grant peer review, *BioScience, 72*(3), 289–99. Gs3; Gallo, S. A., Schmaling, K. B., Thompson, L. A., & Glisson, S. R. (2021). Grant review feedback: Appropriateness and usefulness. *Science & Engineering Ethics, 27*(2), 1–20. Gs9; Gallo, S. A., Carpenter, A. S., & Glisson, S. R. (2013). Teleconference versus face-to-face scientific peer review of grant application: Effects on review outcomes. *PLoS One, 8*(8), article e71693. Gs35.

[42] Falk-Krzesinski, H. J., & Tobin, S. C. (2015). How do I review thee? Let me count the ways: A comparison of research grant proposal review criteria across US federal funding agencies. *Journal of Research Administration, 46*(2), 79–94. Gs14.

3 Scientific Knowledge: Grant Review Features & Biases

article are: (1) the National Institutes of Health; (2) the National Science Foundation; (3) the Department of Veterans Affairs; (4) the Department of Education; (5) the Department of Defense; (6) the National Aeronautics and Space Administration; (7) the Department of Energy; (8) the US Department of Agriculture; (9) the National Endowment for the Humanities (NEH); and (10) the National Endowment for the Arts. From the perspective of grant review, we will highlight three points regarding grant review criteria.

First, the review uses table 3 in the article to show the seemingly **diverse grant review criteria** used by the ten federal funders. For example, the review lists criteria used by the NIH in 2015 (five core criteria: Significance, Innovation, Approach, Environment, and Investigator), the NSF in 2014 (two core criteria: Intellectual Merit, Broader Impact), and the NEH in 2014 (four core criteria: Humanities Significance, Quality of Innovation, Project Feasibility and Work Plan, and Project Staff Qualifications), with their own distinct set of rules and different terminology.

Second, the authors synthesize the diverse review criteria used in the ten US federal funding agencies into **eight fundamental questions** with relevant review criteria terms used by funding agencies. These right key questions with the actual review terms are: (1) Why does it matter? Significance, Importance. (2) How is it new? Innovation, Novelty, and Creativity. (3) How will it be done? Approach, Plan, Methodology, Objectives, and Aims. (4) In what context will it be done? Environment, Resources, Populations, and Facilities. (5) What is special about the people involved? Investigators, Organization, People, Researchers, Personnel, Partners, Collaborators, and Staff. (6) What is the return on investment? Impact, Value, and Relevance. (7) How effectively will the financial resources be managed? Budget. (8) How will success be determined? Evaluation, Assessment.

Last, the article has several **practical implications** for new grant writers. First, this review helps to demystify different grant review criteria used by federal funders. These criteria have similar underlying logic and share eight fundamental questions. This may help new grant writers to better understand these grant review criteria and better apply for federal funding. Second, given different funders use diverse criteria names and deliver subtle messages in a specific grant culture, it is important for new grant writers to learn and use original review criteria (e.g. intellectual merit and broader impact for NSF grants) to guide grant writing. Knowing different funders through their diverse grant review criteria will help diversify funding portfolios.

3.6 Hug & Aeschbach (2020): Review Criteria by Diverse Funders across the World

Criteria are an essential component of any procedure for assessing quality. After studying the ten US federal funding agencies, let us study a review article on twelve studies of grant review criteria used across the world.[43]

Overview
The article is titled: "Criteria for assessing grant applications: A systematic review." Here, the term "systematic review" refers to one type of review article that searches and synthesizes the existing literature rigorously and systematically. Both systematic review and meta-analysis are the two highly recommended methods of review research. It has been cited forty times as of 2023, according to Google Scholar.

The first author, Sven Hug, is a project manager at the Evaluation Office at the University of Zurich, His research areas are Research Evaluation, Bibliometrics, and Peer Review, and his h-index is 14. He has published multiple major papers on grant review.[44] Grantology researchers should follow his work as a promising emerging scholar, as well as the work of his mentor Lutz Bornmann at the Max Planck Society. The second author, Mirjam Aeschbach, is a Research and Teaching Assistant at the University of Zurich.

The article was published in *Humanities and Social Sciences Communications*, which is an open-access journal publishing scholarship from across all areas of the humanities, social, and behavioral sciences. The journal is published by Springer Nature. It had been operating under the title *Palgrave Communications* until 2020, And its impact factor was 3.5 in 2022.

Highlights
As a review article, it has six major sections: Introduction, Analytical framework, Mapping the research on criteria in grant peer review,

---

[43] Hug, S. E., & Aeschbach, M. (2020). Criteria for assessing grant applications: A systematic review. *Palgrave Communications, 6*(1), 1–15. Gs40.

[44] Hug, S. E. (2024). How do referees integrate evaluation criteria into their overall judgment? Evidence from grant peer review. *Scientometrics, 129*(2), 1–23. Gs1; Hug, S. E., & Ochsner, M. (2022). Do peers share the same criteria for assessing grant applications? *Research Evaluation, 31*(1), 104–17. Gs12; Hug, S. E. (2022). Towards theorizing peer review. *Quantitative Science Studies, 3*(3), 815–31. Gs13; Hug, S. E., Hołowiecki, M., Ma, L., Aeschbach, M., & Ochsner, M. (2020). Practices of peer review in the SSH I: A systematic review of peer review criteria. *Overview of Peer Review Practices, 14*, 61. Gs5.

3 Scientific Knowledge: Grant Review Features & Biases

Qualitative synthesis, Results, and Discussion and conclusion. From the perspective of grant review, especially grant review criteria, we highlight the following points.

First, in total, the review synthesizes **twelve published studies** on grant peer review criteria set by public and private funders in multiple countries, including Germany, France, Switzerland, the Netherlands, Finland, and the United States. Two-thirds of these studies examine criteria in the medical and health sciences, while studies in other fields are relatively scarce. Few studies compare criteria across different fields, and none focuses on criteria for interdisciplinary research.

Second, the authors introduced a **conceptual framework** that classifies what is generally referred to as "criterion" into an evaluated entity (i.e. the **object** of evaluation) and an evaluation criterion (i.e. the **dimension** along which an entity is evaluated).

Third, the review identified **four major evaluated entities** from the existing diverse grant review criteria in the world. Among them, 21 percent are on Applicant (e.g. generic qualification, past performance), 72 percent are on Project (e.g. topic, research question, research design, budget, project plan), 3 percent are on Environment (institutional resources, labs), and 3 percent are on Others (e.g. originality, reviewers). The review also identified **fifteen evaluation criteria** from the existing grant review criteria in the world, including Originality, Relevance, Appropriateness, Completeness, and Feasibility, as well as Quality, Rigor, Coherence, Clarity, Diversity, Motivation, and Traits.

Fourth, based on a network analysis, they further conceptualize all the evaluated entities and evaluation criteria used in the grant review within a **three-element model**: (1) The **aims** of a proposed project are assessed in terms of originality and relevance. (2) The **means** of a proposed project concern two core areas, research process and project resources. Specifically, the research process is evaluated both on content (quality, appropriateness, rigor, coherence) and on presentation (clarity, completeness). The project resources are evaluated in terms of feasibility with project resources and project plan, as well as applicants' abilities, achievements, and personality. (3) The **outcomes** of a proposed project are assessed in terms of originality and relevance, which is consistent with the project aims. This aim-means-outcome model can help us conceptually understand grant criteria from different funders.

Last, practical tips that can be gleaned from the article for new grant writers include: (1) It is important to understand the diversity of review criteria, appreciate various entities and criteria among different funders in the world with the three-element integrated model. (2) It is useful to use this review of existing grant review criteria to analyze and follow specific grant criteria of our target funders and to improve our grant writing.

3.7 Martin et al. (2010): Impacts of Panel Review Discussion

Overview

This article is titled: "An analysis of preliminary and post-discussion priority scores for grant applications peer reviewed by the Center for Scientific Review at the NIH."[45] It has several technical terms regarding the NIH review system. Briefly, *preliminary scores* (1 = exceptional; 9 = poor) are given to a proposal by individually assigned reviewers before the panel meeting; *post-discussion priority scores* (1 = exceptional; 9 = poor) are given to a proposal by each of the review panel members after the panel discussion, leading to a final priority/impact score (10 = exceptional; 90 = poor); the *Center for Scientific Review* (CSR) is an NIH unit designated for managing extramural grant reviews and coordinating the Scientific Review Group or the Study Sections.[46] This article is among the best in examining the impact of panel discussion meetings, and has been cited twenty-five times, according to Google Scholar.

Three authors contributed to the article. Michael Martin was the Development Manager of the NIH's Center for Scientific Review. Andrea Kopstein was Director of the NIH's Office of Program Analysis. Joy Janice is the Managing Director of Tunnell Government Services, a Life Sciences development firm.

The article was published in *PLoS One*, which is one of the earliest and largest open-access mega journals, published by the Public Library of Science (PLoS). It has published more than fifty important articles on grantology and thus researchers and students in grantology should closely follow it.

Highlights

The article presents an analysis of all R01 clinic application reviews by the CSR in the January 2009 review round. From the perspective of grant review, three interesting points of the article are highlighted below.

---

[45] Martin, M. R., Kopstein, A., & Janice, J. M. (2010). An analysis of preliminary and post-discussion priority scores for grant applications peer reviewed by the Center for Scientific Review at the NIH. *PLoS One*, 5(11), article e13526. Gs25.

[46] First level: Peer review, *NIH*, available at: https://grants.nih.gov/grants/peer-review.htm.

First, the article helps us understand the **specific impact** of panel discussion in the NIH. Expert review (generating preliminary priority scores by three reviewers) and panel review (generating the final priority scores by twenty to thirty-five members) are two key steps in the NIH review process. The results indicate that the preliminary scores are positively and significantly correlated with the final priority scores, while these two types of scores are also significantly different (the final scores are usually lower). As a result, the discussion at the panel meeting impacts percentile rankings and funding decisions for over 13 percent of the applications.

Second, the article helps us to see future mediations in the review procedure that the NIH will implement after 2010. The NIH has announced that they have modified the priority score scale used by reviewers to a single digit, rather than to a decimal. They have also announced a revision of the review criteria and the addition of a new class of applications, the Early Stage Investigators.[47] These modifications were implemented beginning with the October 2009 review round. There is also a recent major change in review criteria and scoring procedure.[48] The NIH, NSF, European Union, and many other funders are often modifying their procedures to improve grant review effectiveness and efficiency.[49]

Last, new grant writers can glean the following practical tips from reading the article: (1) Grant review is a complex and dynamic process. It is useful to know and understand the nature of this process in order to prepare better grant proposals. (2) NIH grant writers should understand two types of scores (preliminary vs. overall impact scores), two types of reviews (expert vs. panel review), and two types of funding decisions after the panel discussion (funded vs. not funded).

3.8   Tamblyn et al. (2018): Various Biases in Grant Review

Given that reviewer quality, review criteria, and review procedure are key elements for the grant review process, is the grant review effective and efficient in assessing the quality of grant applications? There is extensive literature on review bias in the grant review process, indicating review bias directly impacts outputs, outcomes, quality, effectiveness, and efficiency of

---

[47] Early stage investigator policies, *NIH*, available at: http://grants.nih.gov/grants/new_investigators.
[48] Enhancing peer review: The NIH announces new scoring procedures for evaluation of research applications received for potential FY2010 funding, *NIH*, available at: https://grants.nih.gov/grants/guide/notice-files/not-od-09-024.html.
[49] Changes coming to NIH applications and peer review in 2025, *NIH*, available at: https://grants.nih.gov/policy/changes-coming-jan-2025.

said process. Here, we will examine a strong empirical study.[50] Chapter 7, on grant decisions, will further address the impacts of review bias.

Overview

The article, titled "Assessment of potential bias in research grant peer review in Canada," focuses on identifying bias in the grant review process in the Canadian Institutes of Health Research, the Canadian version of the United States' NIH. Bias in review can be defined as grant review and funding decisions not being based on grant application quality, but rather on other non-quality factors related to reviewers (e.g. gender, race, inter-rate reliability), applicants (e.g. gender and race), criteria (e.g. unclear or biased criteria), or procedures (e.g. scores before and after panel discussion). The article has been cited 165 times, according to Google Scholar, and is one of the highest cited articles on review bias.

Five scholars from McGill University wrote the article. The first and corresponding author, Robyn Tamblyn, is a Professor of Medicine at McGill University. She is also the Scientific Director of the CIHR Institute of Health Services and Policy Research. She has published 337 articles, including a recent major article on grant review,[51] with 21,491 citations. Nadyne Girard and Christina Qian are researchers in Epidemiology. James Hanley is a Professor of Biostatistics with a h-index of 101.

Canadian Medical Association Journal is a **general medical journal** that publishes original research, commentaries, analyses and reviews, clinical practice updates, and thought-provoking editorials. Its publisher is the Canadian Medical Association, And its impact factor was 17.4 in 2023.

Highlights

This article is an empirical article, with a typical structure: Introduction, Methods, Results, and Interpretation. It collected 11,624 grant applications submitted to the CIHR between 2012 and 2014. It analyzed whether the characteristics of applications, principal applicants, and individual reviewers are related to the overall application score that was assessed after controlling the applicant's scientific productivity. From the grant review perspective, we highlight three key points.

---

[50] Tamblyn, R., Girard, N., Qian, C. J., & Hanley, J. (2018). Assessment of potential bias in research grant peer review in Canada. *Canadian Medical Association Journal, 190*(16), E489–E499. Gs165.

[51] Tamblyn, R., Girard, N., Hanley, J., Habib, B., Mota, A., Khan, K. M. et al. (2023). Ranking versus rating in peer review of research grant applications. *PLoS One, 18*(10), article e0292306.

First, the study identified **various biases** in the grant review process. The CIHR uses a review system similar to that of the NIH and MRC. The grant review was handled by the fifty-three standing committees, and each committee has ten to fifteen members. It has two steps. First, two members are assigned to independently review a proposal, rating it (1 = poor, 4.9 = excellent) and providing comments. Second, the standing committee uses mean scores and rankings of all the applications after discussing and scoring by each member. Only top-ranked applications are funded. For the CIHR's review system, it was found that: (1) significantly lower application scores were received by female applicants, especially those in applied science applications and who have higher past success rates; (2) significantly lower application scores were associated with both reviewers being female or the applications of both reviewers being outside of the scientific domain of the applicant; (3) significantly lower application scores were associated with applicants who were older or evaluated by female reviewers only; and (4) significantly higher scores were associated with past funding success and h-index, and reviewers with high expertise when reviewing applicants with higher past success rates. These systematic biases have substantial impacts on changing application scores from fundable to non-fundable. Thus, the study provides a window which shows that the effectiveness and efficiency of the grant reviews are unsatisfactory and calls for change in the review procedure and funding policies.

Second, the study systematically analyzed the **sources of systematic bias**. Specifically, the systematic bias is related to: (1) **application** characteristics (e.g. whether applications are in biomedical basic science or applied clinic science, and whether they are a new submission or a resubmission); (2) **reviewer** characteristics (e.g. their research expertise, grant experience, scientific domain, and past success at the CIHR); and (3) **applicant** characteristics in demographic aspects (e.g. their age, gender, affiliation) and in scientific productivity aspects (e.g. their previous CIHR funding success rate and publication h-index).

Third, the study motivates further research on review bias as an important research area in grantology. While there exists an extensive literature on review bias,[52] a wide consensus has not yet formed. We need robust

---

[52] Schmaling, K. B., & Gallo, S. A. (2023). Gender differences in peer reviewed grant applications, awards, and amounts: A systematic review and meta-analysis. *Research Integrity & Peer Review*, 8(1), 2. Gs813; Witteman, H. O., Hendricks, M., Straus, S., & Tannenbaum, C. (2019). Are gender gaps due to evaluations of the applicant or the science? A natural experiment at a national funding agency. *The Lancet*, 393(10171), 531–40. Gs510; Fang, F. C., Bowen, A., & Casadevall, A. (2016). NIH peer review percentile scores are poorly predictive of grant productivity. *Elife*, 5, article

evidence, innovative methods, and strong theories to advance the scientific understanding of review bias.

Last, the study has important implications for new grant writers. The modern grant review system is not perfect and various random or nonrandom factors play a part in the review process that are beyond our control. Thus, grant writers should not self-blame too much if their proposal is rejected. However, there are various factors that grant writers can control, for example, writing a grant proposal for two types of reviewers, considering reviewers within or across domains, being persistent in revisions and resubmissions, and, of course, being aware of certain systematic biases and possible coping strategies.

4 Grantology vs. Journalology: Grant Review and Manuscript Review

4.1 Comparing the History

As discussed in Chapter 2, the first grant system emerged in 1825. As a mechanism of selecting and awarding grant proposals, grant review emerged in 1853 when the Government Grant Committee in the United Kingdom appointed three multiple-member subcommittees to review each grant application.[53] In 1902, the Carnegie Institution of Washington in the United States set up eighteen advisory committees to review specific grant proposals. After this, with the Carnegie Institute and other private funders, the federal funders started the grant review procedure. In the 1910s, the Hygienic Laboratory (the antecedent of the NIH) used the National Advisory Health Council as a peer review group. In 1921, the American Association for the Advancement of Science used the Committee on Grants to make awards for scientific research.[54] In 1951, the NSF started

---

e13323. Gs122; Severin, A., Martins, J., Heyard, R., Delavy, F., Jorstad, A., & Egger, M. (2020). Gender and other potential biases in peer review: Cross-sectional analysis of 38,250 external peer review reports. *BMJ Open, 10*(8), article e035058. Gs42; Fogelholm, M., Leppinen, S., Auvinen, A., Raitanen, J., Nuutinen, A., & Väänänen, K. (2012). Panel discussion does not improve reliability of peer review for medical research grant proposals. *Journal of Clinical Epidemiology, 65*(1), 47–52. Gs90; Pier, E. L., Brauer, M., Filut, A., Kaatz, A., Raclaw, J., Nathan, M. J. *et al.* (2018). Low agreement among reviewers evaluating the same NIH grant applications. *Proceedings of the National Academy of Sciences, 115*(12), 2952–7. Gs178.

[53] MacLeod, R. M. (1971). VI. The Royal Society and the government grant: Notes on the administration of scientific research, 1849–1911. *Historical Journal, 14*(2), 323–58. Gs63.

[54] Burnham, J. C., Sauer, J. E., & Gibbs, R. D. (1987). Peer-reviewed grants in US Trade Association research. *Science, Technology, & Human Values, 12*(2), 42–51. Gs6.

4 Grantology vs. Journalology

to use expert review to make funding decisions.[55] Currently, after roughly 170 years, grant review is commonly used by public and private funders worldwide.

Around 166 years earlier than the first grant system, the first academic journal appeared in 1665. In 1752, the Royal Society took over the editorial responsibility from Henry Oldenburg and adopted a review procedure for publishing the Philosophical Transactions.[56] Throughout the nineteenth and into much of the twentieth century, external referee reports were considered an optional part of journal editing.[57] Institutionalization of the review process then took place, due to the increasing number of manuscripts submitted for publication and the increasing demands for expert authority and review objectivity.[58]

Historically, grant review has grown in the grant funding system independently, while manuscript review has grown on its own in the journal publication system. These two types of reviews, interestingly enough, did not influence each other.[59]

4.2 Comparing Similarities

Grant review and manuscript review share a few important similarities.

First, both grant and manuscript review are a process of **formal or professional assessment** before deciding on funding a proposal or accepting a manuscript. Both are conventional and professional strategies for quality control. Both have similar basic elements needed in the assessment system (e.g. reviewers, review criteria, review processes, and review outcomes). In the previous chapters, we have compared several pairs of terms used in grantology and journalology (e.g. grant vs. article, grantology vs. journalology, grant writer vs. article writer, grant writing vs. manuscript writing,

---

[55] Mazuzan, G. T. (1992). "Good science gets funded ..." The historical evolution of grant making at the National Science Foundation. *Knowledge*, *14*(1), 63–90. Gs16; Rothenberg, M. (2010). Making judgments about grant proposals: A brief history of the merit review criteria at the National Science Foundation. *Technology & Innovation*, *12*(3), 189–95. Gs34.

[56] Spier, R. (2002). The history of the peer-review process. *TRENDS in Biotechnology*, *20*(8), 357–8. Gs607; Kronick, D. A. (1990). Peer review in 18th century scientific journalism. *JAMA*, *263*(10), 1321–2.

[57] Baldwin, M. (2018). Scientific autonomy, public accountability, and the rise of "peer review" in the Cold War United States. *Isis*, *109*(3), 538–58. Gs173.

[58] Burnham, J. C. (1990). The evolution of editorial peer review. *JAMA*, *263*(10), 1323–9. Gs477; Campanario, J. M. (1998). Peer review for journals as it stands today – Part 1. *Science Communication*, *19*(3), 181–211. Gs305; Campanario, J. M. (1998). Peer review for journals as it stands today – Part 2. *Science Communication*, *19*(4), 277–306. Gs221.

[59] Burnham, J. C. (1990). The evolution of editorial peer review. *JAMA*, *263*(10), 1323–9. Gs477.

funder vs. journal, grant officer vs. journal editor), and we will do so for a few more pairs of terms (grant decision vs. editorial decision, grant management vs. publication management, and grant impacts vs. publication impacts). Comparing all of these aspects, grant and manuscript review appear to be the most similar. Even among diverse types of professional assessment across different sectors, grant and manuscript review are indeed the two closest siblings.

Second, grant review and manuscript review also share a few specific features. (1) Both are essentially **free** professional services provided by the reviewers, while a good review requires expertise and takes hours or days to complete. (2) Both are **imperfect** systems that have been receiving criticism for decades, but are still considered to be the best available systems and thus are still widely used. (3) Relevant to the point above, both still **keep improving** themselves with various innovative or experimental efforts that have been proposed or implemented,[60] although the grant funding system and the journal publication system have existed for decades (e.g. the first grant system emerged in 1825 and the first academic journal appeared in 1665). Both need further high-quality research[61] to find research-based innovative ways for grant review and manuscript review.

4.3 Comparing Differences

Despite several similarities, if we further examine grant review and journal review, we will find multiple important differences between these two forms of scientific review.

The first difference relates to documentation. One of the most obvious differences is that grant review needs to assess **multiple** different files in a submission package, such as a project proposal (focusing on scientific quality), biography of researchers (focusing on qualification of grantees), budget request, justification (focusing on financial aspects of a proposal), and institutional supportive letters (focusing on institutional supports). This way, multiple aspects of a proposal will be assessed. In contrast, a manuscript review assesses a **single** submitted manuscript to judge its scientific contributions to the literature.

---

[60] Chubin, D. E., & Hackett, E. J. (1990). *Peerless Science: Peer Review and US Science Policy*. State University of New York Press. Gs985; Burnham, J. C. (1990). The evolution of editorial peer review. *JAMA, 263*(10), 1323–9. Gs477.
[61] Burnham (1990), *ibid*.

The second difference relates to focus. Grant review focuses on assessing the **potential** of proposed projects, whereas journal review focuses on assessing the **outcome** of completed projects. The former could be considered as the beginning of a research project to obtain funding and plan a study, whereas the latter could be considered the end of a research project to disseminate the learned knowledge.

The third difference relates to process. Funding agencies such as the NIH and NSF typically conduct the grant review **collectively** (e.g. two to three individual reviewers read the proposal individually and then a study section or a review panel of ten to twenty reviewers meet to discuss proposals as a group). However, manuscript review is usually conducted by two to three reviewers **individually**, while editors might conduct initial editorial screening.

The fourth difference relates to criteria. Grant review generally has **specific** and **explicit** criteria, although different funding agencies may have different criteria. For instance, the NSF has explicit criteria on intellectual merit and broader impacts.[62] The NIH has five criteria before 2025 and will reduce the number to three after 2025.[63] These criteria are extremely transparent and widely publicized to everyone, including applicants, reviewers, program officers, mass media, and the general public. In contrast, manuscript review typically has **simple** and **general** criteria, while different journals certainly have different criteria for different types of articles. For example, *Nature* has its three criteria for publication: scientific papers must: report original rather than published scientific research; have outstanding scientific importance; and reach a conclusion of interest to an interdisciplinary readership.[64] Similarly, *Science*'s criteria for publication are both simple and general: "We seek to publish papers that are influential in their fields or across fields and that will substantially advance scientific understanding. Selected papers should present novel and broadly important data, syntheses, or concepts."[65] Note that in *Nature*, *Science*, and other highly selective journals, typically, their in-house professional editors play a critical role (e.g. declining most submissions without peer

---

[62] Overview of the NSF proposal and award process, *US National Science Foundation*, available at: www.nsf.gov/bfa/dias/policy/merit_review/.
[63] Review, *NIH*, available at: https://grants.nih.gov/grants-process/review.
[64] Editorial criteria and processes, *Nature*, available at: www.nature.com/nature/for-authors/editorial-criteria-and-processes.
[65] Mission and scope, *Science*, available at: www.science.org/content/page/mission-and-scope; Peer review at Science journals, *Science*, available at: www.science.org/content/page/peer-review-science-publications; Information for authors, *Science*, available at: www.science.org/content/page/science-information-authors.

review, primarily based on whether a manuscript has a broad readership across disciplines).

The fifth difference relates to selection. This is perhaps the most important difference between grant and manuscript review. Grant review is to select the best among all submitted proposals based on the review criteria (i.e. ratings), the strengths relevant to other proposals (i.e. ranking), and the budget availability. Thus, it is essentially a **norm-referenced** selection system. That is, the goal is to help identify the best proposals for limited funding slots. In contrast, manuscript review is to publish manuscripts that receive good peer reviews. Thus, it is essentially a **criteria-referenced** selection system to select manuscripts with high quality without a slot limitation (it can always be published in the next issue if needed), but with page limitation (although this is no longer common in digital publication). Thus, the critical message for new grant writers is that we need to write a proposal to stand out clearly among other competitive proposals rather than just meet the criteria. In this sense, grant review is much more competitive (funding the best) than manuscript review (publishing the qualified), very much like college admission vs. college graduation.

The sixth difference relates to output. This difference is also obvious. Grant review leads to a funding **recommendation** of funding or decline to program officers and funding agencies, whereas a manuscript review leads to a **recommendation** of acceptance, major or minor revision, or rejection to editors.

5 Action Suggestions: Reading and Writing Grant Reviews

5.1 Understanding Grant Review as a Complex Multifaceted Assessment System

As you might recall, the five intuitive responses demonstrate that, while these new grant writers have a certain knowledge of grant review, their knowledge is often inaccurate, incomplete, and unspecific, with partial misunderstandings, and with a large variation in knowledge levels, from quite limited to rather strong.

We have discussed eight real-life cases of grant review. Among them, the first and second cases mainly concern the issue of grant reviewers (the European Union's annual call for grant reviewers and the NIH's removing disqualified grant reviewers). The third and fourth cases concern the issue of review criteria (the NSF's broader impact criterion and the NIH's new review criteria). The fifth and sixth cases concern the issue of review processes (the MRC's normal grant review process and the NEA's abnormal move of changing decisions). The final two cases concern the issue of negative review outcomes (administrative burden and gender biases in grant review). These cases show that grant review involves not only multiple elements (e.g. reviewers, criteria, processes, and outcomes), but also large complexity (e.g. the NIH needs to remove disqualified reviewers and the NEA wants to overturn the scientific reviewer results).

After presenting the eight cases, we discussed eight research articles. The first and second articles focus on classic analyses of grant review as a complex process. The third and fourth focus on recent results of grant reviewers. The fifth and sixth focus on summarizing review criteria in various funders in the United States and around the world. The final two articles focus on the outputs and outcomes of grant reviews. These studies showcase the particularly extensive research on the topic of grant review.

In comparing grant review and manuscript review, while both are a process of formal or professional assessment and share a few similarities, six important differences exist in documentation, focus, process, criteria, selection, and output, especially in selection, namely, that grant review is to select the best among all submitted proposals based on the review criteria as a norm-referenced selection system, whereas manuscript review is to publish manuscripts that receive good peer reviews as a criteria-referenced selection system. This falsifies a common misconception among new grant writers that grant and manuscript review are basically the same.

5.2 Reading Many Grant Reviews and Writing Many Grant Reviews

First, it is always useful and practical for new grant writers to find and study at least five existing examples of grant reviews, along with grant proposals. We can search and find such examples from funding agencies. Published articles on grant review also provide examples, and we can ask our experienced colleagues. You can analyze the many grant reviews you have collected and use this analysis to guide your grant writing.

Second, it is also always interesting and helpful for new grant writers to write reviews for student organizations, internal competitions, professional conferences, academic journals, and eventually grant agencies. If there are review panel activities, apply for them and join the panels. Volunteer to review grant proposals for other researchers before their submission to the institutional grant office or funders. In addition, invite friends, classmates, mentors, advisors, or experienced colleagues to review your own proposals, especially before submission. Of course, it is always important for new grant writers to write reviews on their grant proposals using the required criteria of a funder and then compare these reviews with those written by grant reviewers after you submit a proposal and receive feedback from funders.

CHAPTER 7

Grant Decisions

Outline

1 Intuitive Knowledge: How Many Grant Proposals Are Funded? 230
  1.1 Responses from New Grant Reviewers 230
  1.2 Understand the Complexity of Grant Decisions 231
2 Real-Life Cases: From Funding Decisions
  to Tips after Rejection 233
  2.1 The ACS: How Was the Final Funding Decision Made? 233
  2.2 The NSF: Good Answers about Grant Decisions 235
  2.3 The NIH: Twenty-Two PIs Secured 222 Grants in a Year! 236
  2.4 The EPSRC: The Death of British Physical Sciences? 238
  2.5 The NIH: Declines in NIH R01 Grant Funding 238
  2.6 The NSF: Success Rates Moved Up in 2022 239
  2.7 NPR: Two Scientists Gave Up Their Academic Careers 240
  2.8 Drs. Finney and Wynne-Jones: Six Tips after Rejection 241
3 Scientific Knowledge: From Success Rates
  to Resubmission Strategies 242
  3.1 McCarthy (2017): Complexity in Estimating Success Rates 242
  3.2 Cushman *et al.* (2015): Complexity in Estimating Impacts
  of Success Rates 246
  3.3 Bromham, Dinnage, & Hua (2016): Grant Funding
  for Interdisciplinary Research 248
  3.4 Swenor, Munoz, & Meeks (2020): Grant Funding
  for Researchers with Disabilities 251
  3.5 Borgstrom *et al.* (2023): Grieving Grant Rejections 253
  3.6 Doyle *et al.* (2021): Success Rates between Resubmission
  and New Submission 255
  3.7 Boyington *et al.* (2016): Resubmission Rates
  among Young Researchers 257
  3.8 Lasinsky *et al.* (2024): A Comprehensive Picture
  of Resubmission 259
4 Grantology vs. Journalology: Grant Decisions and Article Decisions 261
  4.1 Grant Decisions 261
  4.2 Article Decisions 262

5   Action Suggestions: Understanding the Complexity of Grant Decisions
    and Learning to Resubmit a Rejected Proposal   264
    5.1   Understanding the Complexity of Grant Decisions   264
    5.2   Learning to Resubmit a Rejected Proposal   266

1   Intuitive Knowledge: How Many Grant Proposals Are Funded?

1.1   Responses from New Grant Reviewers

I asked a few individuals with little grant writing experience to quickly answer two short questions: On average, how many grant proposals are funded? What are the major features of funded projects? Below are some quick responses.

- Response 1: Maybe 5 percent. Not sure about the features of funded proposals.
- Response 2: I think there is no standardized answer to this, depending on the funder. Only one in ten proposals are funded by some funders. It is also possible that up to 30 percent of grant proposals can be funded by some grant organizations. I think the major reasons that they are funded, the major features would be significant and timely.
- Response 3: I am not sure of the specific number or percentage for how many grant proposals are funded on average, as this varies widely depending on the granting organization, the field, the type of project, and the available funding. Generally, I think that the success rate for grant proposals can range from as low as 5 percent to as high as 50 percent or more. It is essential to thoroughly research and understand the funding organization's requirements and priorities when crafting a grant proposal to receive funding.
- Response 4: For the first question, the success rate of grant proposals varies depending on the field of research, funding agency, and program, but generally, the funding rates range from less than 10 percent to over 30 percent. This answer is basically from ChatGPT since I am not sure of my guess. For the second question, a funded project should but is not limited to have: (1) a promising and valuable research contribution; (2) a clear research question/objective; (3) a solid and appropriate methodology; (4) strategic alignment with the funder's priorities; (5) well-planned budget; (6) feasible implementation plan.

1 Intuitive Knowledge: How Many Proposals Are Funded? 231

- Response 5: My guess is about 3 to 5 percent of the proposals will be funded. The major features of the funded projects are as follows: (1) the research proposal meets the requirements and needs of the funding provider; (2) the proposal has received several rounds of feedback from peers and even from the grant providers and has gone through revisions based on the feedback; (3) the research proposed is both innovative and valuable – that means it has unique contributions to the research field and social practice; (4) the research methods and research plan proposed are feasible; (5) the researchers of the proposals have expertise in the research fields and may even have received grants on relevant projects before.

1.2 Understand the Complexity of Grant Decisions

The above intuitive responses indicate a reasonable initial knowledge about grant decisions among these new grant writers. First, for grant success rates, while the fourth response was based on ChatGPT, these five responses did provide a range of intuitive estimations (i.e. about 5, 10–30, 5–50, 10–30, and 3–5 percent, respectively). Second, for features of a successful proposal, except for the first response without an answer, the other four responses provide brief or detailed descriptions of two to five features. Obviously, there exist many variations among them (e.g. the first response is rather rudimental, and the final response is more sophisticated).

However, these five responses share one common feature: these new grant writers have a limited understanding of the complexity of success rates, funding success, and various other issues regarding grant decisions. For instance, they might not be aware of the existence of other concepts besides success rates (e.g. submission rate, funding rates, award rates, resubmission rates, or resubmission success rates), let alone the different estimation methods of success rates.

Grant decisions, sometimes called grant funding or grant award, among other terms, are a critical step in the grant process and a complex topic in grantology. As shown in Figure 7.1, the process of grant decisions directly leads to the grant implementation process (for funded proposals) and the resubmission cycle (for unfunded proposals), and is indirectly related to the new submission and management cycles. Thus, it is in the intersection of multiple pathways (see the outlined parts in bold in Figure 7.1) and perhaps the most critical and most complex process in the entire grant procedure for both grant writers and grant funders.

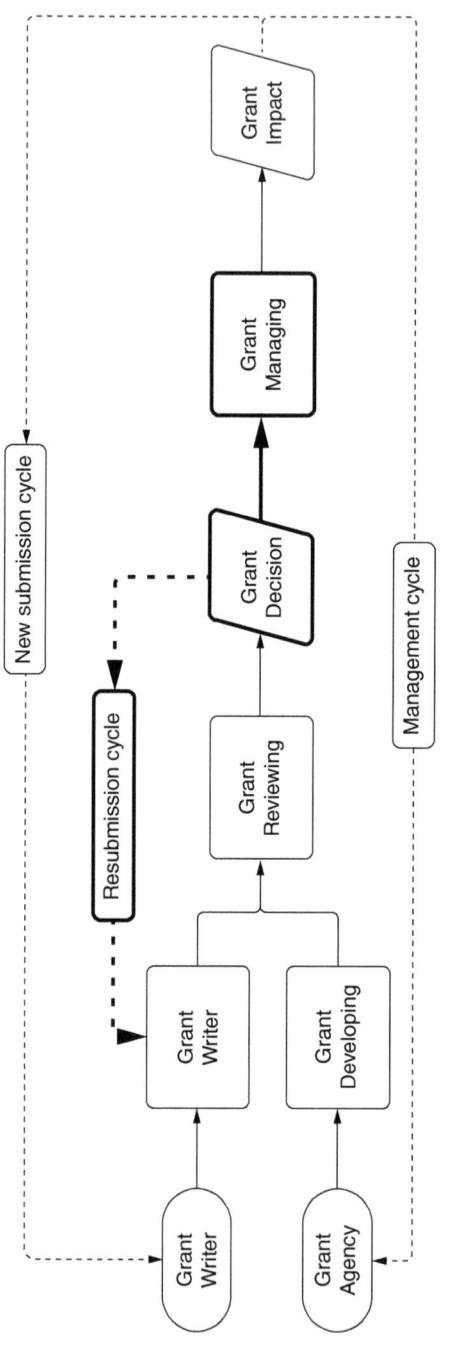

Figure 7.1　The importance of grant decisions in the grant process

The intellectual goal of this chapter is to develop a good understanding of the complexity of grant decisions by building on the intuitive knowledge of new grant writers and discussing real-life cases, research studies, comparisons between grant decisions and journal decisions, and action suggestions. Note that this chapter will focus on three major topics related to rejected proposals: success rates, rejection experiences, and especially resubmissions. We will discuss implementing successful proposals in Chapter 8.

2 Real-Life Cases: From Funding Decisions to Tips after Rejection

2.1 The ACS: How Was the Final Funding Decision Made?

In September 2010, Kendell Powell, a science writer, wrote a story for *Nature*[1] vividly documenting how a panel meeting made funding recommendations. This is a rare opportunity to gain some insight, since federal law prohibits the public from attending review panel meetings of federal funding agencies such as the NIH and NSF. Fortunately, as a private funder, the American Cancer Society (ACS) allowed a reporter from *Nature* to observe and report a review panel meeting, with the condition that the identities of the reviewers and the grant applicants were to be protected. Thus, we have a singular chance to examine and summarize the story below.

The ACS is the largest private non-profit funder of cancer research in the United States. It relies on private donors as its sole source of income. It makes research grants of $120 million a year. Its average success rate for grant applications has recently slipped to roughly 15 percent, largely due to fewer donations during the economic downturn. The ACS decides its success rate based on the available annual budget and the number of proposals recommended for funding from its twenty peer-review panels. For example, given that the budget this year is $120 million and one average grant is $800,000 for four years or $200,000 per year, if each of the twenty panels can only fund three grants and one panel has twenty submitted proposals, then the success rate will be 15 percent. The panel has fifteen panel members (thirteen biomedical scientists, one cancer survivor, and one oncology nurse); two of them also act as panel chair

---

[1] Powell, K. (2010). Making the cut: Careers are made and broken by grant-funding committees. So how are the key decisions really made? *Nature*, 467(7314), 383–6. Gs19.

and vice chair. An ACS program officer attends to monitor the meeting. The panel's job is to fund two Research Scholar Grants of $800,000 for four years to two applicants who are in the first six years of their independent careers from seventeen submitted applications, with a success rate of 11 percent. This success rate puts immense pressure on the grant review panels. Generally, when the success rate is around 30 percent or above, the review process works well at identifying the best science. But when success rates are less than 20 percent, the process starts to fall apart. Panel reviewers have to look for any excuse not to fund a project rather than focusing on its merits, and have to make impossible choices between equally worthy proposals.

Before the panel meeting, about six months prior, each panelist was assigned around six twenty-five-page grant applications to review. They then wrote comments and assigned a preliminary score for each application (outstanding = 1.0–1.5, excellent = 1.5–2.0, good = 2.0–2.5, fair = 2.5–3.0, or poor = 3.0–5.0). This can easily take up to two weeks twice a year, for four years, during their typical term as a reviewer for the ACS. Each reviewer is paid an honorarium of $250 for participating in a review panel.

One morning in June 2009, the panel first discussed six outstanding proposals based on preliminary scores. After a heated debate, they decided to keep four proposals still in the category of *outstanding* and moved two down to the category of *excellent*. After another heated debate, the panel divided all seventeen applications into three categories: four proposals are *outstanding*, six proposals are *non-competitive* but can be resubmitted in the next funding cycle, and seven proposals were rejected, with scores so poor that they may not win funding even on resubmission. In the afternoon, during an even more heated debate, the panel discussed the four most competitive proposals for two categories, recommending for funding and for the pay-if program, which will be funded only if there is an unexpected circumstance (e.g. budget surplus or a new significant donation). At the end of the discussion, the entire panel voted individually with a secret ballot to rank each of the top four proposals. After the meeting, only the program officer counted the votes, decided the ultimate order, and made a recommendation to his supervisor for further review and final approval.

After one month, in the last week of July 2009, two of the top applicants received an email from an ACS program officer, informing them of the grant decision: "I am pleased to inform you that the committee recommended your application be considered for funding."

2 Real-Life Cases

The other two top applicants also received an email, indicating the decision: "Unfortunately, due to budgetary constraints, the committee recommended your application be considered for the pay-if program." At the same time, the other fifteen applicants received rejection letters.

From this case, we can see how individual reviews and panel discussions led to funding decisions. Only exceptional applicants will have a chance to secure a grant from the ACS. In fact, nowadays, this kind of competitiveness is really similar to many public and private funders from many countries around the world.

2.2 The NSF: Good Answers about Grant Decisions

Besides eight doctorates, the NSF has five **offices**, one of which is the Office of Budget, Finance and Award Management. This office has six **divisions**, one of which is the Division of Institution and Award Support (DIAS). This division has six **units**, one of them being the Policy Office, responsible for developing, implementing, and issuing proposal and award policies for NSF programs, including the famous Proposal & Award Policies & Procedures Guide (PAPPG). Here, this three-level hierarchical organization is another example of how complex a funding agency like the NSF is and how complicated its mode of operating is.

Now different from official documents published by the NSF, surprisingly, the Policy Office once posted a page titled "Merit review facts."[2] In a rather humorous way, it listed seven facts with the NSF's brief discussions to present important facts about the NSF's merit review process. Here, we choose three topics most relevant to the present chapter on grant decisions and present them in a Q&A format.

Question 1: Do awarded proposals have to receive all "Excellents"?[3] The NSF's answer:

> It is not true that a proposal must receive all "Excellents" to be funded; in fact, most proposals that are awarded do not receive all "Excellents." Furthermore, even if you get all "Excellents," you may not be funded. See the annual reports to the National Science Board on the National Science Foundation's Merit Review Process for data about proposals and success rates, as well as further information and data concerning the merit review process.

---

[2] Merit review facts, available originally at: www.nsf.gov/bfa/dias/policy/merit_review/facts.jsp.
[3] Note that NSF reviewers typically rate a proposal on five levels: Excellent, Very Good, Good, Fair, and Poor, and also between two levels, such as E/VG or G/F.

Question 2: Do external reviewers make recommendations to fund or decline a proposal? The NSF's answer: "Reviewers do not make funding decisions. The analysis and evaluation of proposals by external reviewers provide information to NSF Program Officers in making their recommendations to award or decline a proposal. See Phase II: Proposal Review and Processing."[4]

Question 3: Do Principal Investigators submit on average about 2.3 proposals for every award they receive? The NSF's answer:

> A common misconception is that once declined, you will always be declined. However, the NSF statistics show that on average, Principal Investigators submit about 2.3 proposals for every award they receive. That is, many Principal Investigators who receive awards also have been declined. See Resubmission process (A declined proposal may be resubmitted after it has undergone substantial revision. See PAPPG Chapter IV.E. Resubmission). Another common misconception is that one cannot get funded on a first submission. NSF statistics show that, in 2020, 36 percent of new PIs received their first award on their first attempt.

These topics must be developed based on some of the most frequently asked questions received by the Office. While we should further study the NSF's recommended documents carefully to better understand the complexity of grant decisions, here we can gain three insights into the NSF grant decision process: Reviewers' ratings are quality assessments but not funding decisions; the funding decision is recommended by program officers and approved by division directors; and grant resubmissions are the norm rather than the exception. There are clearly some complete or partial misconceptions about the grant decision process and resubmission (we will discuss resubmission further in this chapter).

2.3 The NIH: Twenty-Two PIs Secured 222 Grants in a Year!

On March 20, 2008, Eric Hand with Meredith Wadman, both veteran reporters from *Nature*, published a News piece for *Nature*, titled "222 NIH grants: 22 researchers."[5] It reports the astonishing fact that in 2007, twenty-two researchers received 222 NIH grants, on average eleven grants per researcher, and one researcher even secured thirty-two grants.

---

[4] See also an overview of the three phases on the NSF website: www.nsf.gov/bfa/dias/policy/merit_review/.

[5] Hand, E., & Wadman, M. (2008). 222 NIH grants: 22 researchers. *Nature*, 452(7185), 258–9. Gs13.

While many funders' annual budget goes down and many researchers' proposals are rejected, it seems unbelievable that one researcher can secure nine, ten, eleven, or even thirty-one grants from the NIH in one year.

One obvious explanation is that established laboratories led by eminent researchers have for years produced streams of rich data with many grants, then design more new experiments and secure more new grants. This is the Matthew effect: the rich get richer while the poor get poorer. But for new researchers, do the poor have to get poorer, while the rich get richer?

One careful explanation is that many small grants were awarded to organize conferences or run training workshops. For example, Andrew Robertson received thirty-two small grants to organize conferences for Keystone Symposia on Molecular and Cellular Biology, a non-profit organization that convenes approximately fifty to sixty open, peer-reviewed conferences annually.

Another explanation is that the absolute number of grants is misleading. Sten Vermund, Director of the Institute for Global Health at Vanderbilt University (now the Dean of Yale School of Public Health), received eleven grants worth $24 million in 2007. However, most of that total was made up from one large $19 million grant for a global HIV prevention trial involving hundreds of researchers working on four continents at dozens of institutions. Seven of his grants were smaller, and were all for one international AIDS training program. Vermund did acknowledge that he learned how to "package" and "market" winning proposals when he oversaw a $50 million grant portfolio in AIDS research as a branch chief of the NIH. Former NIH Director Zerhouni's explanation is extremely interesting and inspirational. He indicated that the inequities between the haves and have-nots were first caused by a doubling of NIH funding between 1998 and 2003. As funding levels rose, many new PhD student positions were created. Then, established investigators were able to hire more new PhD students and submit more and better grant proposals by using research produced by these new PhD students. However, after 2003, when NIH funding dropped significantly, too many PhD students graduated and started to apply for grants that were too limited and thus repeatedly had their grant proposals rejected. Ironically, this is why NIH funds significantly more people over the age of 70 than under the age of 30.

This case suggests that grant funding is complex, diverse, and extremely impactful, with various surprises, while grant skills are extremely important.

2.4 The EPSRC: The Death of British Physical Sciences?

In 2012, *Nature* published an essay titled "Duel to the death" on research grants in the News column.[6] This news starts with a photo of six scientists and students of science in black suits marching for a macabre funeral in front of the Houses of Parliament in London.

It turned out that this was a mock funeral, signifying the death of British science. These scientists and students were protesting against the Engineering and Physical Sciences Research Council (EPSRC), the United Kingdom's major governmental funding agency for physical sciences, for its recent multiple changes in funding policy. These changes included: (1) researchers could no longer resubmit rejected grant proposals and (2) researchers with a record of rejections could not submit any further funding applications for twelve months. The EPSRC has developed a blacklist of grant applicants. With its budget declining for many years and an overwhelming number of proposal submissions, the EPSRC wanted to cut grant submissions and pull the success rate from 22 percent back up to 30–35 percent. Furthermore, the EPSRC planned to: (1) divide its research portfolio into over 100 fields, expanding funding in some areas, such as energy storage, and reducing funding in others, such as mathematical physics and (2) fund future postdocs and other fellowships only in priority areas (e.g. funding mathematics postdocs only in statistics and applied probability).

From this case, we can see that grant policies and grant decisions on success rates are critical and complex, generating significant negative impacts in addition to significant positive impacts as presented in the previous case on twenty-two NIH grant superstars.

2.5 The NIH: Declines in NIH R01 Grant Funding

In 2006 and 2008, two distinguished scholars, H. George Mandel at the George Washington University School of Medicine and Elliot S. Vesell at Pennsylvania State University College of Medicine, published their two letters in *Science* on declines in NIH R01 funding between 1999 and 2007.[7]

---

[6] Bhattacharya, A. (2012). Duel to the death. *Nature*, *487*(7409), 20. Gs11.
[7] Mandel, H. G., & Vesell, E. S. (2008). Declines in NIH R01 research grant funding. *Science*, *322*(5899), 189. Gs16; Mandel, H. G., & Vesell, E. S. (2006). Declines in funding of NIH R01 research grants. *Science*, *313*(5792), 1387–8. Gs17.

2 *Real-Life Cases* 239

According to their analyses, for example, among the new submissions of Type-1 grants between 1999 and 2007, the number the applications submitted increased from 8,957 to 112,021, the number of grants awarded decreased from 1,761 to 864, and success rates fell from 19.7 to 7.2 percent. Similarly, among the continuation (renewal) submission of Type-2 grants between 1999 and 2007, the number the applications submitted decreased from 3,214 to 360, the number of grants awarded decreased from 1,772 to 909, and success rates fell from 55.1 to 25.2 percent.

These two letters by Mandel and Vesell reveal that the important R01 federal program for unamended applications, both new and competing continuations, is in the midst of a perfect storm. While the number of submissions went up significantly and the number of grants awarded fell significantly, the success rate dropped to 50 percent.

2.6 *The NSF: Success Rates Moved Up in 2022*

On May 13, 2022, Jeffrey Mervis, Senior Correspondent at *Science*, wrote a short piece for *Science* titled "Odds for winning NSF grants improve as competition eases" in the "Funding" section.[8] He reported an unusual observation that, in 2022, the NSF's number of applications dropped significantly, its success rate increased considerably, and the number of grants awarded increased noticeably.

Jeffrey Mervis used the NSF's newly released data and outlined the general trend in the number of applications submitted, the number of grants awarded, and the success rates between 2011 and 2022. Specifically, the number of applications submitted to the NSF has dropped from 51,562 in 2011 to 42,723 in 2020. The number of grants awarded increased from 11,344 in 2011 to 11,962 in 2022. The success rates jumped from 22 percent in 2011 to 28 percent in 2020. It was concluded that the significant drop in the number of applications in 2022 led to a noticeable increase in the success rate in 2022. Different parties had different reactions to these statistics. On the one hand, the National Science Board worried that the decline in the number of applications would harm the nation's scientific innovation potential and planned to diagnose and halt the decline. But, on the other hand, researchers and institutional administrators welcomed the higher success rate because that would certainly encourage more investigators to apply.

[8] Mervis, J. (2022). Odds for winning NSF grants improve as competition eases. *Science*, *376*(6594), 684.

This short case can teach us about the importance of observing the general trend over a period, contributing factors and possible impacts in relation to the success rate, and even embracing the occasional good news rather than constantly struggling with the decline in funding as presented in the last case.

2.7 NPR: Two Scientists Gave Up Their Academic Careers

On September 9, 2014, Richard Harris, a veteran science correspondent of National Public Radio (NPR) for over thirty-eight years, reported a disappointing story about two biology scientists who gave up their science careers after grant proposals were rejected.[9]

The first scientist is Dr. Ian Glomski. He received his PhD in molecular and cell biology at the University of California at Berkeley and was an Assistant Professor at the University of Virginia running his microbiology lab. However, his repeated grant applications to the NIH were all fruitless. Funding is so competitive that reviewers shy away from ideas that might not pan out. Instead of helping society improve its defenses against deadly anthrax, he quit his academic career in microbiology and started a liquor distillery in Charlottesville, Virginia,[10] and is excited about the change in career.

The second scientist is Dr. Randen Patterson.[11] He received his PhD in biochemistry and molecular biology at the University of Maryland and completed postdoctoral training in Dr. Solomon Snyder's neuroscience laboratory at Johns Hopkins University. He was an Assistant Professor at Pennsylvania State University and then at the University of California, Davis. He has published his work in *Science, Nature, Cell, PNAS*, and other highly prestigious journals, and has a high h-index of 32. He also has multiple patents. However, he had struggled his entire career to secure grants to fund his research. Over the years, he has written a series of grant proposals and received repeated rejections, As the last of his funding dried up, he quit his academic job at UC Davis and now owns a grocery store in Guinda, California.

Harris concluded the sob story by stating: "There are no national statistics about how many people are giving up on academic science, but an NPR analysis of National Institutes of Health (NIH) data found that

---

[9] When scientists give up, *wbur*, available at: www.wbur.org/npr/345289127/when-scientists-give-up.
[10] Ian Glomski, *LinkedIn*, available at: www.linkedin.com/in/ian-glomski-aa147b/.
[11] Randen Patterson, *Google Scholar*, available at: https://scholar.google.com/citations?user=BNz7x4Y AAAAJ&hl=en&oi=ao.

3,400 scientists lost their sustaining grants between 2012 and 2013. Some will eventually get new funding, others will retire; but others, like Glomski and Patterson, will just give up."

This widely read story highlights the dark side of funding decisions and how scientists responded to this in real-life. Federal funding for biomedical research has declined by more than 20 percent over the past decade. There are simply far more scientists competing for grants than there is money to support them. What should and can we do?

2.8 Drs. Finney and Wynne-Jones: Six Tips after Rejection

In March 2024, Andrew Finney and Gwen Wynne-Jones, two experienced researchers from the School of Nursing and Midwifery at Keele University, United Kingdom, while acknowledging that having a grant proposal rejected can be disheartening, recommended ten action points to learn and recover from the experience.[12]

Their ten tips are as follows: (1) Calm down and start to reflect on your proposal to see where you have done it correctly or incorrectly. (2) Understand that it is about what the reviewers think and how much money is available in that funding call, no matter how good you think your proposal is. (3) Understand that while your proposal might be reviewed as good quality and important for funding, you might still be unsuccessful, if several other proposals were considered better than yours. (4) Understand that your discipline might be an underrepresented one and has only an 8–10 percent success rate, whereas other disciplines have a 40–50 percent success rate. (5) Understand that spending time on an unsuccessful grant is not a waste and resubmission is the norm professionally. Most successful proposals have been revised and resubmitted multiple times. (6) Take reviewers' feedback seriously and improve your proposal for the next submission. (7) Start with a research funding checklist. (8) Be proactive in completing various tasks for the resubmission. (9) Be aware that there are always new funding opportunities on the way, especially for new researchers. Be ready to apply. (10) Do not give up. If at first you do not succeed, try, try again.

These ten tips are by no means miraculous or exhaustive. But the message of this case is clear: rejection of grant submission is common, perhaps much more common than rejection of manuscript submission; grant

---

[12] Finney, A., & Wynne-Jones, G. (2024). How to deal with an unsuccessful research bid. *Nurse Researcher*, 32(1), 6–7. Gso.

resubmission is common, perhaps even more common than journal manuscript resubmission. The good news is that you can always follow the procedure and resubmit the proposal to the funder multiple times, unlike a rejection letter from a journal editor, which typically means we need to resubmit the article to other journals.

3 Scientific Knowledge: From Success Rates to Resubmission Strategies

After discussing eight real-life cases and gaining knowledge of grant decisions, let us now study eight journal articles and develop our scientific knowledge of grant decisions. While grant decisions typically lead to only two simple outcomes, namely, funding or rejection of a grant proposal, various important and complex issues are involved. Given the extensive literature in this area,[13] we will focus on three topics: success rates, grant rejection, and grant resubmission.

3.1 McCarthy (2017): Complexity in Estimating Success Rates

Overview

This article is titled "Success rates in Horizon 2020."[14] It is a short article, but it reveals the complexity of the success rate of grant applications. The term "Horizon 2020" refers to the European Union's funding programme

---

[13] Finney, A., & Wynne-Jones, G. (2024). How to deal with an unsuccessful research bid. *Nurse Researcher*, *32*(1), 6–7; Boyington, J. E., Antman, M. D., Patel, K. C., & Lauer, M. S. (2016). Toward independence: Resubmission rate of unfunded National Heart, Lung, and Blood Institute R01 research grant applications among early stage investigators. *Academic Medicine*, *91*(4), 556–62. Gs111; Pohlhaus, J. R., Jiang, H., Wagner, R. M., Schaffer, W. T., & Pinn, V. W. (2011). Sex differences in application, success, and funding rates for NIH extramural programs. *Academic Medicine*, *86*(6), 759–67. Gs250; Burns, K. E., Straus, S. E., Liu, K., Rizvi, L., & Guyatt, G. (2019). Gender differences in grant and personnel award funding rates at the Canadian Institutes of Health Research based on research content area: A retrospective analysis. *PLoS Medicine*, *16*(10), article e1002935. Gs97; Chen, C. Y., Kahanamoku, S. S., Tripati, A., Alegado, R. A., Morris, V. R., Andrade, K. et al. (2022). Systemic racial disparities in funding rates at the National Science Foundation. *Elife*, *11*, article e83071. Gs63; Bol, T., de Vaan, M., & Van de Rijt, A. (2022). Gender-equal funding rates conceal unequal evaluations. *Research Policy*, *51*(1), article 104399. Gs43; National Research Council (US) Committee on the Funding of Young Investigators in the Biological, & Biomedical Sciences (1994). *The Funding of Young Investigators in the Biological and Biomedical Sciences*, National Academies Press. Gs448; Bromham, L., Dinnage, R., & Hua, X. (2016). Interdisciplinary research has consistently lower funding success. *Nature*, *534*(7609), 684–7. Gs556; Rylance, R. (2015). Grant giving: Global funders to focus on interdisciplinarity. *Nature*, *525*(7569), 313–15. Gs137.
[14] McCarthy, S. (2017). Success rates in Horizon 2020. *Journal of Innovation Management*, *5*(4), 18–22. Gs7.

on research and innovation that ended in 2020. "Framework Programmes" are funding programmes created by the European Union to support and foster research in the European Research Area. The first Framework Programmes (FP1) operated from 1984 to 1987. Starting in 2014, the funding programmes were named Horizon. Horizon 2020 was the eighth framework programme (FP8) that operated from 2014 to 2020. The article used the data in its first three years (2014–16) to predict the success rate in 2017–20. Currently, FP9 is Horizon Europe (2021–7). Multiple studies examine Horizon 2020,[15] but this article is unique in presenting how to calculate success rates meticulously and has been cited seven times.

The author of the article is Dr. Seán McCarthy.[16] He is the founder and Managing Director of Hyperion, an Ireland-based company that provides grant training courses across Europe to help research organizations, grant administrators, and individual researchers design and implement their research strategy for Horizon Europe. He has provided training courses to seventy-four of the top 100 organizations in Horizon 2020. He has forty years of experience in all aspects of European research. The European Association of Research Managers and Administrators presented him with an award for outstanding contribution to the research management and administration profession.

The article was published in the *Journal of Innovation Management*, which is an open-access multidisciplinary journal on innovation and management, established in 2013.[17] The article was published under the category of Letter from Industry.

Highlights

This article can be considered a short concept or methodology paper because it focuses on the conceptualization and calculation of success rate. The article uses data from two reports: (1) the Annual Monitoring Report

---

[15] Other articles on the Horizon programme include: Enger, S. G., & Castellacci, F. (2016). Who gets Horizon 2020 research grants? Propensity to apply and probability to succeed in a two-step analysis. *Scientometrics*, *109*(3), 1611–38. Gs51; Ajdarpašić, S., & Qorraj, G. (2019). Does university performance matter for EU programmes in South East Europe: Case study Horizon 2020. *Management: Journal of Contemporary Management Issues*, *24*(2), 1–10. Gs14; Vidmar, U., & Vukasović, T. (2019). A model for a successful approach to applying for Horizon 2020. *International Journal of Value Chain Management*, *10*(1), 26–52. Gs1; Wanzenböck, I., Lata, R., & Ince, D. (2020). Proposal success in Horizon 2020: A study of the influence of consortium characteristics. *Quantitative Science Studies*, *1*(3), 1136–58. Gs14; Luby, Š., & Lubyová, M. (2016). Predictions of the success rate of EU new member states in receiving Horizon 2020 funding. *Informatologia*, *49*(1–2), 41–6. Gs3.
[16] Sean McCarthy, *Hyperion*, available at: www.hyperion.ie/seanmccarthy.htm.
[17] *Journal of Innovation Management* website, available at: https://journalsojs3.fe.up.pt/index.php/jim.

released in 2015 by the European Commission on the annual progress and (2) the Mid-Term Evaluation of Horizon 2020 released in 2017, reporting the progress of Horizon 2020 in the first three years (2014–16). It has five sections: Introduction, Evaluation process in Horizon 2020, Success rates in Horizon 2020 (2014–16), Success rate in Horizon 2020 (2015), and Conclusions. We will discuss a few of the article's highlights from the perspective of grant decisions.

First, the **grant decision process of Horizon 2020** is relatively common. It has a five-step funding decision process. (1) When a proposal arrives in Brussels, it is first reviewed by a Commission official who will check each proposal against **'eligibility'** criteria. 'Eligible' means that all the forms are filled in properly and all the basic requirements are met. Note that even a proposal based on a very weak scientific idea or method is classified as "eligible." Thus, a submitted proposal becomes an eligible proposal. (2) The eligible proposals are sent to independent scientific evaluators to be **assessed individually**. In some programs, the evaluators meet in a consensus meeting, and in other cases, they simply send their evaluation scores to the relevant grant administrator. A final score is given based on the evaluators' individual scores. (3) A **threshold** is set to define low-quality proposals. For example, if the maximum score is 15, a threshold can be set at 10. Any proposal scoring below 10 is considered low quality and automatically eliminated. If research organizations had effective quality control procedures, these proposals would never have been submitted in the first place. In the case of the ERC Programme, the maximum score is 8 and a threshold of 4 is set. (4) Following this evaluation, a list of **"high-quality proposals"** is compiled. (5) The **final selection** of successful proposals is based on these high-quality proposals.

Second, as specified in its title, the focus of the article is on **success rates** in Horizon 2020. The article presents two methods of calculating success rates used in 2014–16: the **reported success rate**, which is based on the ratio of funded proposals and eligible proposals; and the **real success rate**, which is a ratio of funded proposals and high-quality proposals. Specifically, Horizon 2020 received over 104,000 proposals. Eligible proposals totaled 102,076, since around 2,000 proposals did not complete the forms correctly and were removed from the pool. The 102,076 eligible proposals were then rated and split between two categories: 56,444 low-quality proposals below the funding threshold; and 45,632 high-quality proposals above the funding threshold. Finally, 11,108 proposals were funded. Thus, in 2014–16, based on the reported success rate calculated on the ratio of funded proposals and eligible proposals, it was only

10.88 percent (11,108/102,076). However, based on the real success rate calculated on the ratio of funded proposals and high-quality proposals, it was **24.34 percent** (11,108/45,632), about 14 percentage points higher. It was concluded that the real success rate is more reasonable to use, perhaps because it reflects the real chance of being funded if a proposal is of a high standard. Thus, when calculating the success rates, the number of eligible proposals is not the best denominator to use, whereas the number of high-quality proposals is a far better denominator to use.

Third, the article displays the complexity of success rate, perhaps only the tip of a huge iceberg, even though success rate seems to be such a simple, common, straightforward, and widely used concept. We have learned about the reported success rate and real success rate from the article. There exist different ways to estimate **success rates** and thus different programs and funders at different times may report different rates. For example, the article shows different aspects of complexity at the NIH. The NIH defines success rates as the percentage of reviewed grant applications that receive funding on a fiscal year basis.[18] Furthermore, the NIH has three types of rates: **success rates, award rates**, and **funding rates**.[19] Success rates are calculated by the number of awards made divided by the number of **new** applications reviewed in a fiscal year, excluding resubmission. This focuses on how many new applications are submitted. Award rates are calculated by the number of awards made divided by the **absolute** number of applications, including resubmissions, in a fiscal year. This focuses on how many applications are submitted. Funding rates are calculated by the number of **applicants** receiving any funding divided by the number of applicants for a fiscal year. This focuses on applicants. Funding rates are the highest, then success rates, and award rates are the lowest in indexing the "success" of NIH applicants, while each focuses on project, submission, or person.

Last, McCarthy's article has **important** practical **implications** for the European Commission, research organizations, and researchers. (1) The European Commission should not continue to quote success rates based on eligible proposals, but rather based on high-quality proposals. (2) Research organizations should have better quality control procedures in place to identify and improve low-quality proposals before submission. (3) For individual researchers, the taking-home message is that it

---

[18] NIH success rate definition, *NIH*, available at: https://report.nih.gov/sites/report/files/docs/NIH_Success_Rate_Definition.pdf; Success rates, *NIH*, available at: https://report.nih.gov/funding/nih-budget-and-spending-data-past-fiscal-years/success-rates.

[19] Comparing success rates, award rates, and funding rates, *NIH Office of Extramural Research*, available at: https://nexus.od.nih.gov/all/2014/03/05/comparing-success-award-funding-rates/.

is important to have a thorough understanding of the evaluation process and do your best to submit a high-quality proposal rather than an eligible or low-quality one.

3.2   Cushman et al. (2015): Complexity in Estimating Impacts of Success Rates

Let us now study a second article on success rates to further understand their complexity. This second article shows how success rates impact researchers' scientific productivity.

Overview

The article is titled "Impact of declining proposal success rates on scientific productivity."[20] It focuses on two key concepts: success rates and scientific productivity. It has been cited eight times – six being between 2020 and 2023.

Seven scientists contributed to the article. They are all distinguished scholars at major research universities and members of the Proposal Pressures Study Group of the Astronomy & Astrophysics Advisory Committee (AAAC). The first author, Priscilla Cushman, is the AAAC Chair and Professor of Physics and Astronomy at the University of Minnesota.[21]

The article is special for two reasons. First, it is a "discussion draft" completed on November 9, 2015 for the AAAC meeting on November 12–13, for the purpose of encouraging comments from the community before the meeting. Note that: (1) Astronomical Sciences are one of five divisions in the NSF's Directorate for Mathematical & Physical Sciences; (2) the AAAC advises the NSF, the National Aeronautics and Space Administration and the US Department of Energy on selected issues within the fields of astronomy and astrophysics; the term for a member is two years; and (3) the AAAC established the Proposal Pressures Study Group in 2014 to examine the effect of falling success rates in context.[22] Second, the article has not been published in a formal journal, but on the preprint server, arXiv, one of

---

[20] Cushman, P., Hoeksema, J. T., Kouveliotou, C., Lowenthal, J., Peterson, B., Stassun, K. G. *et al.* (2015). Impact of declining proposal success rates on scientific productivity. *arXiv*, available at: https://arxiv.org/abs/1510.01647.
[21] von Hippel, T., & von Hippel, C. (2015). To apply or not to apply: A survey analysis of grant writing costs and benefits. *PLoS One 10*(3), article e0118494. Gs69; Szell, M., & Sinatra, R. (2015). Research funding goes to rich clubs. *Proceedings of the National Academy of Sciences, 112*(48), 14749–50. Gs34.
[22] AAAC Proposal Pressures Study Group, Interim report, *US National Science Foundation*, available at: www.nsf.gov/attachments/134636/public/Cushman_AAAC_Nov13.pdf.

3 Scientific Knowledge

the earliest and largest open-access repositories of electronic preprints and postprints.[23] Both Dr. Cushman and Dr. von Hippel explained briefly why this group of distinguished scholars published this insightful study as a preprint on arXiv, but not an article in a peer-reviewed journal (personal communication, July 3, 2023, and June 17, 2024): (1) The group had planned to do a survey and follow up on some of the findings, but did not find time working on it. (2) The topic was never anyone's primary research and many of us cycled off the AAAC after the two-year term was over.

Highlights
The article has five sections: (1) Executive summary; (2) Introduction; (3) Proposal success rates and demographic trends; (4) What should be the minimum acceptable funding rate for meritorious science?; and (5) Conclusion. From the grant decision perspective, especially regarding the success rate, we highlight the following points.

First, the article analyzes the **significant decline** in grant success rates. Over the last decade or so, proposal success rates in the fundamental sciences across agencies have dropped significantly, from 30 to 15 percent. This significant decline does not result from any of the following: (1) a decline in proposal merit since the proportion of proposals receiving high rankings is largely unchanged; (2) a shift in proposer demographics because seniority, gender, and institutional affiliation have all remained unchanged; (3) an increase beyond inflation in the average requested funding per proposal; (4) an increase in the number of proposals per investigator in any one year. Rather, this decline is due to the following: (1) agency budgets for competitive research are flat or decreasing; (2) the overall population of investigators has grown; and (3) a larger proportion of these investigators are resubmitting meritorious but unfunded proposals, which is related to the decreased success rates.

Second, the article concludes that the **most desirable success rate** for scientific productivity is around 30–35 percent. The significantly increasing "proposal pressure" has been widely recognized since the 1980s.[24] As a strategic response, the authors used a model developed by one of them[25] to estimate the impact of different success rates on the probabilities of being

---

[23] ArXiv, *Wikipedia*, available at: https://en.wikipedia.org/wiki/ArXiv; List of preprint repositories, *Wikipedia*, available at: https://en.wikipedia.org/wiki/List_of_preprint_repositories.
[24] Proposal pressure in the 1980s: An indicator of stress on the federal research system, *Office of Technology Assessment Archive*, available at: https://ota.fas.org/reports/9036.pdf.
[25] von Hippel, T., & von Hippel, C. (2015). To apply or not to apply: A survey analysis of grant writing costs and benefits. *PLoS One, 10*(3), article e0118494. Gs69.

rejected after multiple resubmissions of an unfunded proposal. The model is: **Probability of rejection after n attempts = (1 − success rate)^n**. For example, if a funder has a success rate of 20 percent, for the first attempt of resubmission, the probability of rejection is 80 percent because P = (1−20 percent)^1 = 80 percent. For the second resubmission, the probability of rejection is 64 percent, because P = (1−20 percent)^2 = 64 percent. And for the third resubmission, the probability of rejection is 51 percent, because P = (1−20 percent)^3 = 51 percent, which means the luck of being funded after the three resubmissions is still at the random level. Clearly, the success rate of 20 percent makes multiple efforts of resubmissions essentially useless. In contrast, if a funder has a success rate of 35 percent, for the first attempt at resubmission, the probability of rejection is 65 percent, for the second attempt, the probability is 42 percent, and for the third attempt, the probability is 27 percent, which means the chance of being funded after the three resubmissions is really promising.

Third, the article further presents a core concept of **minimum benchmark** for scientific productivity. As we know, it takes time and energy to write grant proposals, resubmit unfunded proposals, publish articles, and generate patents. For a very high success rate, the time spent on writing funded proposals will increase scientific productivity (e.g. researchers can use the grant to collect more data and publish more papers). However, for a very low success rate, the time spent on resubmitting unfunded proposals will decrease scientific productivity (e.g. researchers waste their time on unsuccessful resubmissions and do not have time to publish papers). Thus, for both grantees and grantors, the minimum benchmark for scientific productivity is closely related to the most desirable success rate of 30–35 percent. If a success rate is lower than 20 percent, then the time that researchers (especially new researchers) spend on writing proposals would exceed the time spent on publishing research articles. This is not sustainable for the scientific community.

3.3 Bromham, Dinnage, & Hua (2016): Grant Funding for Interdisciplinary Research

After studying two articles on success rates in general, let us now discuss an article on one of the factors influencing funding decisions and funding results. There is extensive literature on differences in funding results (e.g. gender differences, race gaps, and age biases). We will examine a well-known empirical study on low funding success due to the interdisciplinary nature of proposals.

Overview

This article is titled "Interdisciplinary research has consistently lower funding success."[26] This title addresses a hot topic regarding grant funding and delivers a central argument that low funding success exists among interdisciplinary studies. The term "interdisciplinary" essentially concerns an approach to using multiple academic disciplines and has large variations – for example, multidisciplinary, pluridisciplinarity, cross-disciplinary, and transdisciplinary.[27] This is a highly cited article, having been cited 563 times according to Google Scholar.

The first author of the three authors, Lindell Bromham, is a Professor of Evolutionary Biology at Australian National University. The second author, Russell Dinnage, is a Research Assistant Professor at Florida International University, with expertise across evolutionary biology and computer science. The final author, Xia Hua, is a lecturer in the Mathematical Sciences Institute at Australian National University, with research areas in evolutionary biology and computational biology. This article is their first and only major publication on grantology.

The article was published under the category of Letter in *Nature*. In *Nature*, a letter is a type of article that discusses a new and important research result. Letters are less substantial than articles, but the findings should be general and important enough to interest people outside of the field. *Nature*'s impact factor was 50.5 in 2023.[28]

Highlights

This is an empirical study. It has four major sections: Background, Method, Results, and Discussion. From the perspective of grant decisions, we can highlight the following three points.

First, the study focuses on an **important and challenging question** in grant funding. Interdisciplinary research is widely recognized as an effective approach to innovations and breakthroughs in science. However, it is also widely perceived to be less likely to be funded than research with a narrower disciplinary focus. Furthermore, this commonly held belief has

---

[26] Bromham, L., Dinnage, R., & Hua, X. (2016). Interdisciplinary research has consistently lower funding success. *Nature*, *534*(7609), 684–7. Gs563.
[27] Frodeman, R., Klein, J. T., & Pacheco, R. C. D. S. (eds.) (2017). *The Oxford Handbook of Interdisciplinarity*, Oxford University Press. Gs1230.
[28] Wouters, P., Sugimoto, C. R., Larivière, V., McVeigh, M. E., Pulverer, B., de Rijcke, S. *et al.* (2019). Rethinking impact factors: Better ways to judge a journal. *Nature*, *569*(7758), 621–3. Gs100; Rylance (2015), note 13 above; Sun, Y., Livan, G., Ma, A., & Latora, V. (2021). Interdisciplinary researchers attain better long-term funding performance. *Communications Physics*, *4*(1), 263. Gs43.

been difficult to evaluate empirically, partly because of the lack of a quantitative measure of the degree of interdisciplinarity that can be applied to funding application data. The study addressed this methodological challenge and verified the common belief on low funding success in interdisciplinary research.

Second, the study generated **convincing evidence**, confirming the long-held belief that interdisciplinarity is significantly and negatively correlated with funding success (slope = –0.40, $p < 0.001$). Based on the article's figure 1, a proposal with the lowest interdisciplinarity has around a 24 percent success rate, whereas a proposal with the highest interdisciplinarity might have around a 17 percent success rate, which is roughly a 7 percent difference between the two. The study further confirms that this significant negative impact of interdisciplinarity is robust and consistent, regardless the number of collaborators (e.g. a large or small number of PIs collaborating across disciplines in a project), primary research field (e.g. the primary field being business, maths, or history), and type of institution (e.g. top universities with a high success rate may submit more interdisciplinary proposals). Why do interdisciplinary proposals have lower funding success rates? The study discussed the following specific reasons: (1) reviewers traditionally do not have interdisciplinary expertise to assess grant proposals; (2) the novelty of interdisciplinary is difficult to specify and justify; (3) the feasibility is easy to challenge since interdisciplinary collaborations demand a large amount of time, effort, and energy to build; and (4) outcome and impact are difficult to measure and make clear.

Third, the researchers in the study used **innovative methods** to generate the above major findings. (1) Conceptually, they adopt established concepts in evolutionary biology to account for relatedness between biological lineages to develop a hierarchical classification of research fields. (2) Methodologically, they invented a biodiversity metric or interdisciplinary distance metric to successfully compare the degree to which research proposals span disparate fields. (3) They used an appropriate dataset that includes all proposals submitted to the Australian Research Council's Discovery Programme between 2010 and 2014, which captures the relative representation of different fields and their degree of difference. The Programme is a single annual nationwide competitive grants scheme that covers fundamental research in all disciplines, including arts, humanities, and sciences. In total, the researchers analyzed 18,476 proposals submitted to the Programme over five consecutive years, including successful and unsuccessful applications.

Finally, extensive literature exists, examining **various factors** that influence funding decisions, funding success, or funding rates. These factors include: (1) grantee-related (e.g. gender, race, age, surgery, disability); (2) grantor-related (e.g. the NIH, the NSF, Horizon Europe, the Australian Research Council); and (3) grant-related (e.g. types, fields, sizes, interdisciplinary). This article clearly shows that the funding decision can be influenced by one factor: interdisciplinarity. It is one of the best on this topic. For researchers interested in this hot topic, the references included in the article include some major publications.[29]

3.4 Swenor, Munoz, & Meeks (2020): Grant Funding for Researchers with Disabilities

Overview

This article is titled "A decade of decline: Grant funding for researchers with disabilities 2008 to 2018."[30] It is the first major study on funding inequities among grantees with a disability, while extensive literature exists on funding inequities among groups of different gender, race, ages, and other characteristics. It was published in *PLoS One* and has been cited thirty-three times.

The first of the three authors, Bonnielin Swenor, is an Associate Professor at the Johns Hopkins University School of Nursing. As the founder and director of the Johns Hopkins Disability Health Research Center, her research career is motivated by her personal experience with vision impairment. Her h-index is 44, and she has published other articles on grantology.[31] The second author, Beatriz Munoz, is an expert in visual

---

[29] Rylance (2015), note 13 above; Lyall, C., Bruce, A., Marsden, W., & Meagher, L. (2013). The role of funding agencies in creating interdisciplinary knowledge. *Science & Public Policy*, *40*(1), 62–71. Gs201; Woelert, P., & Millar, V. (2013). The "paradox of interdisciplinarity" in Australian research governance. *Higher Education*, *66*(6), 755–67. Gs113; National Academy of Sciences, Committee on Science, Public Policy, & Committee on Facilitating Interdisciplinary Research (2005). *Facilitating Interdisciplinary Research*, National Academies Press. Gs64; Langfeldt, L. (2006). The policy challenges of peer review: Managing bias, conflict of interests and interdisciplinary assessments. *Research Evaluation*, *15*(1), 31–41. Gs235; Nichols, L. G. (2014). A topic model approach to measuring interdisciplinarity at the National Science Foundation. *Scientometrics*, *100*(3), 741–54. Gs144; Ma, A., Mondragón, R. J., & Latora, V. (2015). Anatomy of funded research in science. *Proceedings of the National Academy of Sciences*, *112*(48), 14760–5. Gs95; Porter, A. L., Garner, J., & Crowl, T. (2012). Research coordination networks: Evidence of the relationship between funded interdisciplinary networking and scholarly impact. *Bioscience*, *62*(3), 282–8. Gs40.
[30] Swenor, B. K., Munoz, B., & Meeks, L. M. (2020). A decade of decline: Grant funding for researchers with disabilities 2008 to 2018. *PLoS One*, *15*(3), article e0228686. Gs33.
[31] Castro, F., Stuart, E., Deal, J., Varadaraj, V., & Swenor, B. K. (2024). STEM doctorate recipients with disabilities experienced early in life earn lower salaries and are underrepresented among higher academic positions. *Nature Human Behaviour*, *8*(1), 72–81. Gs3.

impairment at Johns Hopkins University. The final author, Lasa Meeks, is an expert in disabilities in medical education at Michigan University.

Highlights

The article is an empirical study. The study aggregated and analyzed data on the self-reported disability status of NIH research grant applicants and awardees from 2008 to 2018. The four major disability categories include mobility, hearing, and visual disabilities, among others. It has five major sections: Introduction, Materials and Methods, Results, Discussions, and Conclusion. We will highlight two key points of the article.

First, comparing the number of NIH grant applicants with the number of applications reporting disabilities, the percentage of NIH grant applicants with a disability declined significantly, from 745 (1.9 percent) in 2008 to 617 (1.2 percent) in 2018. Likewise, the percentage of NIH grant awardees with a disability also dropped significantly, from 235 (1.9 percent) in 2008 to 191 (1.2 percent) in 2018. A declining trend is obvious.

Second, comparing different types of disabilities, across the ten years, the percentage of applications with PIs with visual disabilities (16.5 and 15.2 percent) were lower than the percentage reporting mobility (34.2 and 28.7 percent) or hearing disabilities (37.8 and 32.4 percent) in 2008 and 2018. Likewise, the percentage of awards to PIs with visual disabilities (19.6 and 16.8 percent) was also lower than the percentage reporting mobility (29.8 and 33 percent) or hearing disabilities (36.2 and 32.5 percent) in 2008 and 2018. Clearly, the percentages for visual disabilities are the lowest.

Third, comparing success rates among three groups, for average grant **success rates** in 2008–18, those reporting disability (27.2 percent) were significantly lower than those reporting no disability (29.7 percent), but with surprise, were significantly higher than those reporting unknown or withholding reporting (18.6 percent). Funding inequalities for those with disabilities are evident, but the unexpected finding for the unknown/withheld group is worth further research.

Last, the study has practical implications for new grant writers, especially those with various disabilities. Given the underrepresentation of grant applicants and grant awardees with disabilities and lower grant success rates among PIs with disabilities as reported in the study, this group of grant writers should develop an awareness of the potential challenges they might face and learn to use different strategies to meet the challenges, while funders and home institutions should develop policies and design interventions to remedy the inequities among the underrepresented groups, including the group with disabilities.

3 Scientific Knowledge 253

3.5 Borgstrom et al. (2023): Grieving Grant Rejections

Overview

This article is titled "Grieving academic grant rejections: Examining funding failure and experiences of loss."[32] It has been cited once since it was published in 2023. This is a unique study using qualitative data to document what individuals' grief experiences are like after the rejection of a grant proposal and discuss how to better conceptualize it for improved practice. It is an extremely insightful work.

The article has six authors, all of whom work in health-related areas, with five from the United Kingdom and one from Australia. The first author, Erica Borgstrom, is a Professor of Medical Anthropology at The Open University, with a specialist interest in end-of-life care and death studies. Her h-index is 19. The article is her only one on grantology.

The article was published in 2023 in *The Sociological Review*. Founded in 1908, *The Sociological Review* is the United Kingdom's oldest sociology journal and one of the world's foremost journals for sociological inquiry in all traditions, with over 100 years of publishing high-quality and innovative articles. The journal is published by SAGE on behalf of the Sociological Review Foundation's company, Sociological Review Publication Ltd. Its impact fact was 2.1 in 2023.

Highlights

The article is a qualitative empirical article. It has five major sections: Introduction, Background, Methods, Thinking and talking through grant loss and grief, and Conclusions. From the grant decision research perspective, we can highlight the following key points.

First, the article used a **unique method**, auto-ethnography, to document individuals' experiences after a grant proposal was rejected. (1) Starting in 2000, the six authors discussed virtually as a small international interdisciplinary research group on death, dying, and bereavement. (2) These six authors have all been actively involved in grant writing over the past few years. They have been successful in securing grant funding and at the same time received rejections of their grant applications. As a result, they shared their highs and lows of grant writing. (3) In discussing their grant failure and sharing their emotions, they found that notions of grief and loss were a common theme and began to think through their

---

[32] Borgstrom, E., Driessen, A., Krawczyk, M., Kirby, E., MacArtney, J., & Almack, K. (2024). Grieving academic grant rejections: Examining funding failure and experiences of loss. *Sociological Review*, 72(5), 998–1017. GsI.

experiences using a sociological framework of grief rather than a common framework of resilience, regrouping, repurposing, and recycling. (4) In the end, they decided to use autoethnography to document and analyze their own experiences of grant rejections, through an iterative and collective analytical writing process.

Second, the article documented how the authors **made sense** of the various losses and grief they experienced through grant failure in three layers: (1) The six authors had various emotional responses to the notification of unsuccessful grant applications: devastated, disappointed, angry, furious, hopeless, at a loss, self-pity, uncertainty about how to feel, and even feel relief for avoiding further rounds of proposal writing and rewriting. (2) The authors felt a strong normative expectation to "move on" rather than to dwell on emotional reactions when a grant was rejected. However, this standardized expectation was counter-productive because this made them feel disqualified from feelings of loss, disassociated from the emotional labor of managing that loss, and embarrassed when others expressed sympathy for that loss. The authors observed that "the labor and time invested into unsuccessful grants are often made invisible: in many instances, unsuccessful grants are neither listed, nor counted, nor acknowledged as a loss." (3) The authors finally experienced the ripple effects of funding failure, namely: unsuccessful grant applications generated even broader consequences, including the loss of time that could be spent elsewhere more productively (e.g. having less time for research article publication), the loss of relationships (e.g. feeling guilty for disappointing grant collaborators), and the loss of professional identities (e.g. failure to secure key career grants impacting job, tenure, or promotion).

Last, the **practical implications** for new grant writers are tremendous. Grant failure is extremely common for early-career researchers and seasoned grant writers. Emotional reactions after grant rejection are totally normal. However, we should handle our loss and grief of funding failure innovatively rather than conventionally, just as we handle our other forms of loss and grief. As suggested by the authors, we should see an unsuccessful grant more from the positive side, normalize the grant failure (e.g. creating CVs of failure or Walls of Rejection), and promote more collective and collaborative work. Next, we recommend another inspiring article on why and how academics continue their unfunded research.[33]

---

[33] Edwards, R. (2022). Why do academics do unfunded research? Resistance, compliance and identity in the UK neo-liberal university. *Studies in Higher Education*, 47(4), 904–14. Gs51.

3.6 Doyle et al. (2021): Success Rates between Resubmission and New Submission

Overview

This article is titled "Downstream funding success of early career researchers for resubmitted versus new applications: A matched cohort."[34] There are two technical terms in the title. First, upstream, midstream, and downstream commonly refer to the beginning, middle, or end sections of a process. In grantology, downstream funding is late-career funding, whereas upstream funding is early-career funding. However, the term "downstream funding success" used in the study refers to funding success within three to five years. Second, a matched cohort is a particular longitudinal design in that a cohort of participants is first matched on a control factor and then assessed over time – for example, a twin study where participants are matched in pairs to control confounding factors and then assess changes over time in parallel.[35] Essentially, the article attempted to answer a specific practical question: if a grant is rejected, should one resubmit the original proposal or submit a new one as a better strategy to secure funding? It has been cited three times since 2021.

Three authors contributed to the article. The first author, Jamie Mihoko Doyle, is from the NIH, and the two co-authors, Michael Baiocchi and Michael Kiernan, are from Stanford University. Kiernan and Baiocchi also published an applied statistical paper on grantology.[36]

The article was published in 2021 in *PLoS One*. As mentioned previously, *PLoS One* is one of the earliest and largest open-access mega journals. It has published hundreds of studies on grantology.

Highlights

This is an empirical article focusing on resubmission, with a data analysis that had a sophisticated design and was meticulously performed. It consists of four major sections: Introduction, Materials and Methods, Results, and Discussion. From the perspective of resubmission after a negative grant decision, we highlight the following points.

---

[34] Doyle, J. M., Baiocchi, M. T., & Kiernan, M. (2021). Downstream funding success of early career researchers for resubmitted versus new applications: A matched cohort. *PLoS One*, *16*(11), article e0257559. Gs3.

[35] Cummings, P., & McKnight, B. (2004). Analysis of matched cohort data. *Stata Journal*, *4*(3), 274–81. Gs99.

[36] Kiernan, M., & Baiocchi, M. T. (2022). Casting new light on statistical power: An illuminating analogy and strategies to avoid underpowered trials. *American Journal of Epidemiology*, *191*(8), 1500–7.

First, the study used **sound methods**. First-time applicants with US medical school academic faculty appointments who submitted an unfunded R01 application between 2000 and 2014 yielded 4,789 discussed and 7,019 not discussed applications. Comparable groups of first-time R01 applicants (resubmitted original R01 application or submitted new NIH applications) were created using optimal full matching that included applicant and application characteristics. Primary and subgroup analyses used generalized mixed models with obtaining any NIH R01 funding within three and five years as the two outcomes. A gamma sensitivity analysis was performed.

Second, the study generates **strong evidence**. It analyzed 11,809 first-time R01 applications during the period 2004–14 to determine whether they received any R01 grant within three to five years of their original unfunded R01 applications. The major findings were as follows: (1) Overall, first-time R01 applicants resubmitting their original, unfunded R01 application were more successful in obtaining R01 funding within three and five years than applicants submitting new applications.[37] (2) Specifically, for applications that were discussed by an NIH study section with priority scores and percentiles, the applicants resubmitting their original, unfunded R01 application were 4.17 and 3.33 times more successful in obtaining R01 funding within three and five years than applicants submitting new applications. Likewise, for applications that were not discussed by an NIH study section without priority scores and percentiles, the applicants resubmitting their original, unfunded R01 application were 2.81 and 2.47 times more successful in obtaining R01 funding within three and five years than applicants submitting new applications.

Last, the immediate practical implication for new grant writers is strikingly clear. For early-career researchers, resubmitting an R01 application is a much better strategy than submitting a new R01 application to receive the grant, regardless of whether the original application is discussed with priority scores and percentiles and not discussed without priority scores and percentiles. As the authors point out, this is consistent with an NIH working group's recommendations to develop interventions to encourage resubmission.[38]

---

[37] This is another submission cycle in addition to resubmission cycle in the diagram of the grant process.
[38] Frequently asked questions, *NIH*, available at: https://grants.nih.gov/faqs?a_htm=#/resubmission .htm; Revise and resubmit an application, *National Institute of Allergy and Infectious Diseases*, available at: www.niaid.nih.gov/grants-contracts/revise-resubmit-application.

3.7 Boyington et al. (2016): Resubmission Rates among Young Researchers

After studying different funding successes in new submission vs. resubmission, let us now discuss how often early-career researchers decide to resubmit (resubmission rates) and what factors encourage them to do so (influencing factors).

Overview
This article has a long title, "Towards independence: Resubmission rate of unfunded national heart, lung, and blood institute R01 research grant applications among early stage investigators."[39] It focuses on how early-stage investigators can secure the NIH's standard research grant R01 and become independent investigators. This is one of the first empirical studies thoroughly examining the resubmission issue. It has been cited eleven times according to Google Scholar.

Four NIH researchers contributed to this article. The first author, Josephine Boyington, is a health scientist administrator and a program director of the National Heart, Lung, and Blood Institute (NHLBI). The second author, Melissa Antman, is a health scientist administrator at the NHLBI. The third author, Katherine Patel, is a mathematical statistician at the NHLBI. The final author, Michael S. Lauer, was the Director of Division of Cardiovascular Sciences at the NHLBI and is currently the Deputy Director for Extramural Research at the NIH. There is a note at the end of the article specifying that the authors are NIH employees, this work was conducted as part of their work activities, and no extra funding was received. Note that there is a long outstanding tradition that NIH administrators and staff scientists have been studying and publishing their research in grantology since the Van Slyke 1946 seminal article (see Chapter 2).

The article was published in 2016 on *Academic Medicine*. It has been the official journal of the Association of American Medical Colleges since 1926. Its impact factor in 2023 was 5.3 and its publisher is Wolters Kluwer.

Highlights
The article is an empirical study, consisting of five major sections: Terms, consideration, and R01 review process, Method, Results, Discussion, and Conclusions. From the perspective of resubmission after a rejection

---

[39] Boyington, J. E., Antman, M. D., Patel, K. C., & Lauer, M. S. (2016). Towards independence: Resubmission rate of unfunded National Heart, Lung, and Blood Institute R01 research grant applications among early stage investigators. *Academic Medicine*, 91(4), 556–62. Gs11.

decision, we will highlight the following important points of the article. Note that it would be difficult to understand the results if we do not know various technical terms used by the NIH, such as ESI, payline, priority scores, overall scores, and percentile. However, we can always check the NIH's online Glossary[40] and find the exact meaning of an NIH term.

First, the major findings of the study are **clear, convincing, and interesting**, as summarized here. (1) Among the 4,587 NHLBI R01 applications, 833 (18.2 percent) were applications from early-stage investigators (ESI). The NIH defines ESI as investigators who have completed their terminal research degree within the past ten years, but have not yet competed successfully for an NIH independent research award. (2) Their overall R01 resubmission rate was 51.4 percent (422 of 821). (3) 382 of 821 (46.5 percent) were discussed and given a percentile score based on the good quality of proposals. (4) 294 of 821 (35.8 percent) scored less than 50, as a fundable indicator, and 82.3 percent (242 of 294) were resubmitted. (5) Out of 527 of 821 applications with a percentile score equal to or greater than 50, as an unfundable indicator, only 180 (34.2 percent) were resubmitted. (6) During FY 2010–12, the NHLBI funded 342 (new and resubmitted) ESI R01 applications. A total of 202 (59 percent) of these had percentile scores above but within ten points of the NHLBI R01 pay line (i.e. the fundable level) and were awarded funding based on the NHLBI's special funding consideration for ESIs.

Second, the method of data analysis is **sound and innovative**. (1) The authors extracted and de-identified all unfunded, competing, new R01 applications that had undergone peer review during FY 2010, 2011, and 2012. To analyze the collected data, they used the retrospective cohort design, namely, a longitudinal research design comparing retrospectively two cohorts of individuals who were either exposed to or not exposed to a factor to determine the factor's influence. (2) As potential predictors of resubmission, they considered grant-based factors (e.g. year of original submission and peer-review scores), applicant-based factors (e.g. demographics, training, prior funding), and institution-based factors (e.g. ranking in receipt of NIH funding, and type of institution). (3) They determined the frequency of variables with descriptive analyses, then used Random Forest methodology,[41] a machine-learning approach to studying a large number of predictors, to identify the most important predictors, and finally used

---

[40] Glossary, *NIH: Grants and Funding*, available at: https://grants.nih.gov/grants/glossary.htm.
[41] Breiman, L. (2001). Random forests. *Machine Learning*, 45, 5–32. Gs 128697; Biau, G. (2012). Analysis of a random forests model. *Journal of Machine Learning Research*, 13(1), 1063–95. Gs1861.

selected predictors to run logistic regression models. (4) They first analyzed the overall pool of applications and then the subset of applications that were discussed and percentiled.

Last, the study has practical **implications** for new grant writers who aim to become independent PIs. Given that the overall resubmission rate was only 51.4 percent (only 34.2 percent for the application with a lower percentile score), we should increase our resubmission efforts if an initial submission is rejected. Given that the only significant predictor of resubmission was the percentile score, which is one of the grant-based factors, efforts should be made to improve applicant-based factors (e.g. decision-making skills and motivations) and institution-based factors (mentoring and training). Given that over half of the ESI R01 applications with percentile scores above just ten points of the fundable level were funded by the NHLBI due to the special funding considerations for ESI, continuous policy efforts and personal efforts should be made.

3.8 Lasinsky et al. (2024): A Comprehensive Picture of Resubmission

After studying two empirical articles on resubmission, let us zoom out and obtain an expansive landscape of existing resubmission literature by studying a review article.

Overview

This article has a relatively long title: "If at first you don't succeed: Biomedical research grant resubmission rates, and factors related to success – a scoping review."[42] It has three elements: (1) It first adapts a famous line: "If at first you don't succeed try, try and try again." Robert the Bruce, King of Scotland, used this line to encourage his troops before they defeated the enemy in 1314.[43] (2) It then indicates that the article was to analyze the resubmission rate and contributing factors for success. (3) It finally indicates that the article is not an empirical study, but rather a scoping review – a special review that focuses on a quick and broad synthesis of the current knowledge on a topic. Since 2024, it has had one citation.

---

[42] Lasinsky, A., Wrightson, J., Khan, H., Moher, D., Kitchin, V., Khan, K. M. *et al.* (2024). If at first you don't succeed: Biomedical research grant resubmission rates, and factors related to success – a scoping review, *Social Science Research Network*, available at: https://papers.ssrn.com/sol3/papers.cfm?abstract_id=4803560. Gs1.

[43] Peck, T. (2010). Try try again works for Robert the Brice, 130 years late, *Independent*, January 14, available at: www.independent.co.uk/news/uk/this-britain/try-try-again-works-for-robert-the-bruce-ndash-130-years-late-1867261.html.

Seven authors wrote this article – a research team mainly from Canada and mainly in the field of sports medicine, mixed with senior and junior researchers. Among them, the first author, Anne Lasinsky, is an instructor at the School of Kinesiology at the University of British Columbia. Her research meets at the intersection of research and policy, involving the creation and evaluation of a provincial health initiative for children with obesity. She published at least three more preprints on grant resubmission.[44] One co-author, David Moher, is a well-known scholar in journalology and review methodology.

The article was published in 2024 in the *Social Science Research Network*. This journal is an open-access research platform for preprints[45] and has grown to become the **most** interdisciplinary service of its kind, covering applied sciences, health sciences, humanities, life sciences, physical sciences, and social sciences. The publisher is Elsevier.

Highlights

This article is a scoping review of forty articles on resubmission rates and impacting factors. It attempted to paint a big picture and provide an expansive landscape of resubmission. From the perspective of grant resubmission, we can highlight the following points.

First, the review attempted to achieve a **challenging goal**, demonstrating a large landscape of existing resubmission research. As a general trend, most first-time biomedical research grant applications are not funded, and resubmitting a grant application is a necessary and routine job for grant writers. Thus, identifying which factors influence their decision to resubmit and their success of resubmissions is useful and informative to funders and grant applicants. However, data on resubmissions are fragmented and underreported, which limits the resubmissions research.

---

[44] Wrightson, J. G., Lasinsky, A., Snell, R. R., Hogel, M., Mota, A., Khan, K. M. *et al.* (2024). What factors are important to the success of resubmitted grant applications in health research? A retrospective study of over 20,000 applications to the Canadian Institutes of Health Research, *medRxiv*, available at: www.medrxiv.org/content/10.1101/2024.05.29.24308137v1; Khan, S. J., Lasinsky, A., Giustini, D., Wrightson, J., Cobey, K., Moher, D. *et al.* (2023). Exploring sex and/or gender disparities in STEMM research grant funding – a scoping review protocol, *OSF Registries*, available at: https://osf.io/3vgq7/resources; Lasinsky, A., Ardern, C., Kitchin, V., Khan, H., Wrightson, J., Khan, K. *et al.* (2022). Grant resubmissions scoping review, *OSF Registries*, available at: https://osf.io/fxdz4/resources.

[45] Here is a general note about preprints since we have studied multiple preprints in the book. A preprint means: (1) this is an early but completed version of a manuscript that has been or is about to be submitted to a journal and (2) it has not gone through the peer-review process or been accepted by a journal. At present, the preprint offers immediate and free access to a worldwide readership; it has gained increased acceptance as the scholarly record, especially in some disciplines such as physics and mathematics; and there is a rapidly increasing number of preprint platforms to host preprints.

Second, the review has achieved its goal to some extent and showed a large landscape of **resubmission research**. Its general findings are as follows: (1) Based on forty identified studies, thirteen funding agencies in the world were studied for resubmission rates. The most common funders are from the United States, especially the NIH, and other funders are from Canada, the Netherlands, the United Kingdom, Australia, Switzerland, and the European Union. (2) Based on five studies, resubmission rates varied, ranging from 18 to 50 percent, with an average of 33 percent, which is shockingly low. (3) Based on eleven studies, the initial submission success rate on average is 24 percent, ranging from 6 to 44 percent. In contrast, the resubmission success rate on average is 36 percent, ranging from 16 to 82 percent. That is, on average, the resubmission success rate in a grant cycle was 12 percentage points higher than the original submission rate. This benefit of resubmissions is both important and useful to note. (4) Based on five studies, two types of factors are associated with the resubmission success rate. The applicant-related factors include career stages, time spent on the resubmission, successful grant writing history, frequency and percentage of resubmissions, and experience of completing a training program. The application-related factors include original submission discussed, favorable priority scares received, favorable percentage ranking received, total funds requested, types of studies proposed (e.g. human vs. animal studies), and the number of PIs included. Among all the factors, favorable priority scores and percentage ranking were more likely to be successful upon resubmission.

Last, **practical implications** of this review for grant writers include the following: (1) Given the low average resubmission rate of 33 percent, we should do our best to resubmit unsuccessful grants. (2) Given the high average resubmission success rate of 36 percent, we should consider the applicant-related and application-related factors to achieve resubmission success.

4 Grantology vs. Journalology: Grant Decisions and Article Decisions

4.1 Grant Decisions

One of the key topics of grant decisions is the success rate. Around the world, different funders have different funding budgets, grant programs, and calculations of success rates. For example, the NIH's success rates depend on different fiscal years, institutions, and grant mechanisms. Currently, the NIH defines success rates as the percentage of reviewed grant applications that receive funding. In 2023, the average success rate across institutions was approximately 20 percent (e.g. in the National Cancer Institute, in 2023, 8,618 proposals were reviewed, 1,369 proposals were awarded, and the success rate was therefore 15.9 percent).[46]

Another topic of grant decisions is grant rejection. Worldwide, the unsatisfactory response to the rejection of a grant proposal is perhaps quite universal to everyone. Nevertheless, there exists extensive literature on various funding biases, reporting and analyzing whether or how various grant rejections are biased against gender, age, race, and discipline, and other scientific and non-scientific factors.

The third topic is resubmission. Again, around the world, different funders have different policies and procedures for resubmission, formal or informal. For example, when an NSF program officer sends you an email regarding the funding decision of your submitted proposal, the email can either inform you that your proposal is funded, along with an instruction on the post-award procedure, or your proposal is rejected, along with the reviewers' comments and a panel discussion summary. For a rejected proposal, there is no explicit or implicit invitation about the possibility of future resubmission. Thus, experienced grant writers will study the review comments and panel summary and plan to revise and resubmit the proposal. However, for new grant writers with no experience, they might consider this to be the end of the process. However, the NSF does have specific policies and procedures in place on the resubmission process of rejected proposals in the NSF Proposal & Award Policies & Procedures Guide.[47]

4.2 Article Decisions

In the journalology literature, acceptance rate and rejection rate are usually used in terms of decisions. Worldwide, different publishers, journals, disciplines, editors, formats (e.g. subscription vs. open-access), and calculations (e.g. Björk, 2019[48]) have different reported or estimated

---

[46] Success rates, *NIH RePORT*, available at: https://report.nih.gov/funding/nih-budget-and-spending-data-past-fiscal-years/success-rates.

[47] NSF Proposal & Award Policies & Procedures Guide (PAPPG), *US National Science Foundation*, available at: https://new.nsf.gov/policies/pappg.

[48] Björk, B. C. (2019). Acceptance rates of scholarly peer-reviewed journals: A literature survey. *El profesional de la información*, 28(4), article e280407. Gs70.

4 Grantology vs. Journalology

acceptance rates or rejection rates.[49] For example, *Nature* itself (not *Nature* journals, *Nature Communications*, or scientific reports), around 8 percent of submitted manuscripts will be accepted for publication and around 80 percent of submissions are declined without being sent out for peer review.[50]

The editorial decision to reject a manuscript is always disappointing to authors. An extensive literature exists, reporting various existing biases, such as publication biases,[51] reason biases,[52] and desk rejection biases.[53] Clearly, the journal publication practice, especially the rejection behavior, should be further improved.

Typically, after peer reviews are received, an editor will send an editorial letter to an author, indicating whether a new manuscript is rejected without revision or is invited for major or minor revisions. Then after a revised manuscript is resubmitted and further reviews are received, the editor will inform the author whether the revised manuscript is accepted, needs further revisions, or is rejected due to unsatisfactory revisions. While various journals set up specific resubmission policies and procedures,[54] skills for effective revision and resubmission, including

---

[49] Sugimoto, C. R., Larivière, V., Ni, C., & Cronin, B. (2013). Journal acceptance rates: a cross-disciplinary analysis of variability and relationships with journal measures. *Journal of Informetrics*, 7(4), 897–906. Gs119; Björk (2019), *ibid.*; Hargens, L. L. (1988). Scholarly consensus and journal rejection rates. *American Sociological Review*, 53(1), 139–51. Gs365.

[50] Editorial criteria and processes, *Nature*, available at: www.nature.com/nature/for-authors/editorial-criteria-and-processes.

[51] Franco, A., Malhotra, N., & Simonovits, G. (2014). Publication bias in the social sciences: Unlocking the file drawer. *Science*, 345(6203), 1502–5. Gs1661; Okike, K., Kocher, M. S., Mehlman, C. T., Heckman, J. D., & Bhandari, M. (2008). Publication bias in orthopaedic research: An analysis of scientific factors associated with publication in the Journal of Bone and Joint Surgery (American Volume). *Journal of Bone & Joint Surgery*, 90(3), 595–601. Gs108.

[52] Shalvi, S., Baas, M., Handgraaf, M. J., & De Dreu, C. K. (2010). Write when hot – submit when not: Seasonal bias in peer review or acceptance? *Learned Publishing*, 23(2), 117–23. Gs27; Ausloos, M., Nedič, O., & Dekanski, A. (2019). Correlations between submission and acceptance of papers in peer review journals. *Scientometrics*, 119(1), 279–302. Gs7.

[53] Dwivedi, Y. K., Hughes, L., Cheung, C. M., Conboy, K., Duan, Y., Dubey, R. *et al.* (2022). How to develop a quality research article and avoid a journal desk rejection. *International Journal of Information Management*, 62, article 102426. Gs54; Hassell, H. J. (2021). Desk rejects widen inequalities within academia. *PS: Political Science & Politics*, 54(4), 699–702. Gs3; Moustafa, K. (2015). Blind manuscript submission to reduce rejection bias? *Science & Engineering Ethics*, 21(2), 535–9. Gs116; Mueller, J., & Yin, Y. (2021). Unraveling the bias against novelty: Guiding the study of our tendency to desire but reject the new. In J. Zhou & E. D. Rouse (eds.), *Handbook of Research on Creativity and Innovation* (pp. 267–89). Edward Elgar. Gs13.

[54] Introducing the Journal of the Medical Library Association's manuscript resubmission deadlines: Creating accountability structures for our authors, *Journal of the Medical Library Association*, available at: https://jmla.pitt.edu/ojs/jmla/article/view/1902; Information for authors, *Clarivate*, available at: https://clarivate-scholarone-prod-us-west-2-s1m-public.s3.amazonaws.com/wwwRoot/prod1/societyimages/tip-ieee/tip-infoauth-2228318-x.pdf.

skills for writing an effective cover letter, have been widely recognized as being one of the most critical journal publication competencies and have been frequently discussed in various journals.[55]

In summary, comparing grant decisions and article decisions, there are various similarities and differences in success rate/acceptance rate, decision biases, and resubmission policies and procedures. One interesting similarity is that before the review process starts, a funder often uses various screening strategies (e.g. using triage and excluding from panel discussion), while journals use different editorial screening strategies (e.g. editor's desktop rejection and in-house staff review). One key difference relates to the resubmission procedure: the grant resubmission procedure is implicit and less known, whereas the article resubmission procedure is explicit and widely known. Passing the initial screening and completing resubmission are fundamental and critical as the very first step for new grant writers and new article writers to receive funding or publish an article.

5 Action Suggestions: Understanding the Complexity of Grant Decisions and Learning to Resubmit a Rejected Proposal

5.1 Understanding the Complexity of Grant Decisions

Grant decisions are critical to everyone. As shown in Figure 7.1, the process of grant decisions is at the intersection of multiple pathways. It directly leads to the grant implementation process (for funded proposals) and the resubmission cycle (for unfunded proposals), and is indirectly related to the new submission cycle and the management cycle. Thus, it is perhaps the most critical and most complex step in the entire grant procedure. In this chapter, we chose to focus on understanding (1) the complexity of success rates, (2) rejection as the norm rather than the exception, and (3) the importance of resubmission.

---

[55] Calcagno, V., Demoinet, E., Gollner, K., Guidi, L., Ruths, D., & de Mazancourt, C. (2012). Flows of research manuscripts among scientific journals reveal hidden submission patterns. *Science*, *338*(6110), 1065–9. Gs145; Lusher, A. D. (2015). Peer review process, editorial decisions, and manuscript resubmission: A reference for novice researchers. *Journal of Osteopathic Medicine*, *115*(9), 566–9. Gs5; Hardré, P. (2013). The power and strategic art of revise-and-resubmit: Maintaining balance in academic publishing. *Journal of Faculty Development*, *27*(1), 13–19. Gs5; Langhan, M. L., & Tiyyagura, G. (2022). Revise and resubmit. *Academic Pediatrics*, *22*(5), 711–12. Gs0; Romero, V. (2002). Getting published: Revise and resubmit. *APS Observer*, *15*. Gs0.

5 Action Suggestions

In the section on Intuitive Knowledge, the intuitive responses indicate a reasonable initial knowledge about grant decisions among these new grant writers. First, for grant success rates, while the fourth response was based on ChatGPT, overall the five responses did provide a range of intuitive estimations (i.e. around 5, 10–30, 5–50, 10–30, and 3–5 percent). Second, for features of a successful proposal, except for the first response without an answer, the other four responses provide brief or detailed descriptions of two to five features. Obviously, there exist many variations among them (e.g. the first response is rudimentary, whereas the last response is more sophisticated). However, these five responses share one common feature: these new grant writers have a limited understanding of the complexity of success rates, funding success, and various other issues regarding grant decisions.

In the section on Real-Life Cases, we discussed eight grant decision cases. We have seen how the final funding decision was made, how the NSF's Policy Office addressed important facts about the NSF's merit review results, how the NIH's twenty-two PIs secured 222 grants in a year, how the EPSRC allegedly caused the death of British physical sciences, how the NIH's NIH R01 grant funding has declined, how the NSF's success rates increased in 2022, how two scientists gave up their academic careers after proposal rejections, and how Drs. Finney and Wynne-Jones shared their six tips after rejection. Studying these real-life cases should improve our understanding of the complexity of grant decisions.

In the section on Scientific Knowledge, we have studied McCarthy (2017) in terms of complexity in estimating success rates; Cushman *et al.* (2015) in terms of complexity in estimating impacts of success rates; Bromham, Dinnage, and Hua (2016) in terms of grant funding for interdisciplinary research; Swenor, Munoz, and Meeks (2020) in terms of grant funding for researchers with disabilities; Borgstrom *et al.* (2023) in terms of grieving grant rejections; Doyle *et al.* (2021) in terms of success rates between resubmission and new submission; Boyington *et al.* (2016) in terms of resubmission rates among young researchers; and Lasinsky *et al.* (2024) in terms of a comprehensive picture of resubmission.

In the section comparing grant decisions and article decisions, we have studied various similarities and differences in success rate/acceptance rate, decision biases, and resubmission policies and procedures. We ended with one interesting similarity and one key difference, suggesting passing the initial screening and completing resubmission are fundamental and critical for new grant writers and new article writers to receive funding or publish an article.

5.2 Learning to Resubmit a Rejected Proposal

Based on the above discussion on grant decisions, we can formulate the following simple suggestions for taking action: First, choose one of your target funders and try to learn its success rates in recent years. Second, find and study one of the rejected grant proposals, either by you or by other grant writers, and highlight the salient points from the reviewer comments and the general summary. Last, develop a resubmission plan after you revisit the reviews, discuss with your mentors, and consult with the program office.

CHAPTER 8

Grant Management

Outline

1 Intuitive Knowledge: What Should We Do after Receiving a Grant? 268
   1.1 Responses from New Grant Writers 268
   1.2 Understand the Importance and Complexity
of Grant Management 268
2 Real-Life Cases: From Four Sentences to Misconduct 270
   2.1 The Only Thing Worse than Not Being Funded
Is Being Funded 270
   2.2 Pre-Award Management: Postdocs vs. Graduate Assistants 271
   2.3 Post-Award Management: No-Cost Extension
during COVID-19 272
   2.4 Eric Poehlman: The First Criminal Case of Research Misconduct 273
3 Scientific Knowledge: From Management Skills
to Misconduct Management 274
   3.1 Ingersoll & Eberhard (1999): Grant Management
as a Complex Process 274
   3.2 Duffy (2010): Grant Management by a Scientist 276
   3.3 Smaglik (2013): Grant Management by a Grant Administrator 278
   3.4 Selby-Harrington *et al.* (1993): Grant Managing
by Grantees and Grant Managers 279
   3.5 Wedekind & Philbin (2018): Grant Management by a Project
Management Office 281
   3.6 The NSF (2023): Grant Management by a Grant Agency 283
   3.7 Almond *et al.* (2021): Scientific Misconduct Management 286
4 Grantology: Grant Management and Article Production 289
   4.1 Grant Management 289
   4.2 Article Production 289
5 Action Suggestions: Understanding and Drafting
a Grant Management Plan 291
   5.1 Understanding the Importance and Complexity
of Grant Management 291
   5.2 Studying Grant Management Plans and Drawing
a Management Flowchart 292

268   8 Grant Management

1   Intuitive Knowledge: What Should We Do after
    Receiving a Grant?

1.1   Responses from New Grant Writers

- Response 1: Just imagining that makes me feel good. If my grant proposal is funded, I will take the next steps as follows: (1) Review the award letter and any attached materials. (2) Develop a detailed plan of how you will use the funds, following the guidelines and requirements outlined in the award letter. (3) Do research and follow the plan. (4) Acknowledge the funder's support in related activities (i.e. publication).
- Response 2: This question is very difficult for me because I lack this kind of experience. But from my perspective, the first thing must be to open some champagne. Then, I might be able to buy research equipment or hire some necessary researchers to support my project, as described in the grant proposal. We should have a good plan for the budget. Furthermore, we should also guarantee our progress to keep up with the estimated schedule stated in the grant proposal.
- Response 3: I have very limited knowledge or even imagination regarding what to do after funding. Here is my guess besides appreciating the provider and having a big celebration: (1) inform the university that the project is funded, (2) check if there are any new requirements from the funding provider, (3) contact the relevant departments to find out how we can use the money (e.g. do we need to create a new bank account? Do we need to make applications and keep records regarding how the money will be spent?), and (4) update the research plan and start to work.
- Response 4: If our proposal is funded, we should (1) move on with the project more efficiently, such as recruiting research assistants and participants or buying any essential experimental apparatus; (2) reach out to the institution that the principal investigator (PI) is currently in for how to use that funding; (3) keep in touch with the founders termly in terms of research progress, budget and spending, and/or any other miscellaneous matters.

*1.2   Understand the Importance and Complexity
       of Grant Management*

The above four responses suggest that these new grant writers had limited knowledge about grant management. (1) The post-award grant management involves three processes by three parties: research management by the grantee, grant administration by the grantee's institution, and grant management by the grantor. The first two responders mentioned only the first party, whereas the last two did mention the three parties briefly. (2) The post-award grant management concerns three basic aspects: science management (e.g. how to complete a funded project scientifically), finance management (e.g. how to open, use, and close a grant account), and personnel management (e.g. how to hire a lab manager and research assistants). The four responders all emphasized the science aspect, while the first and third responders also mentioned the finance aspect, and the second and fourth responders were aware of the finance and personnel aspects. (3) The second and third responders explicitly indicated that "I lack this kind of knowledge" or "I have very limited knowledge and even imagination." It is uncommon for them to feel really challenged in answering such a basic question related to grant management. This indicates that grant management knowledge may be the weakest link in their intuitive knowledge of grantology, in comparison to their decent intuitive knowledge about grant writers, grant review, and grant decisions.

Intriguingly, grant management research is also the weakest area in grantology research.[1] For instance, the number of journal articles on this topic is limited; published studies are scattered over various small disciplines (e.g. management research and research integrity rather than sociology and economics); and it is difficult to find empirical studies, especially high-quality and high-impact ones.

Grant management is critical because it concerns whether a funded project can be completed and generate strong impacts successfully. Grant management is also complex because it involves knowledge in various disciplines, such as law, finance, methodology, human resources, management, and administration. However, it has not received adequate professional attention and has long been neglected in grant research and grant practice. Given the limited knowledge shown by the new grant writers and the limited literature on grant management, in this chapter, we will use: (1) "grant management" as an umbrella term to refer to research management by researchers, grant administration by institutions, and grant management by funders[2] and (2) various types of available materials

---

[1] Selby-Harrington, M. L., Donat, P. L., & Hibbard, H. D. (1993). Guidance for managing a research grant. *Nursing Research*, *42*(1), 54–61. Gs9.
[2] Learmonth, M. (2005). Doing things with words: The case of "management" and "administration." *Public Administration*, *83*(3), 617–37. Gs141.

270   8 Grant Management

(e.g. funders' documents and practical guidelines) along with typical published empirical articles to discuss grant management. We will also set up a realistic intellectual goal for this chapter, namely, to better understand the importance and complexity of grant management.

2   Real-Life Cases: From Four Sentences to Misconduct

2.1   *The Only Thing Worse than Not Being Funded Is Being Funded*

Several years ago, I asked a few graduate students what they would like to do after their paper is accepted for publication. One of them told me: "I want to open a big bottle of champagne to celebrate!"

Last year, I asked a few graduate students what they would like to do after their grant proposal is funded. One of them told me: "The first thing to me must be to open champagne to celebrate!"

Felix Dennis (1947–2014) is an English publisher and philanthropist. As a publishing mogul, he founded his company *Dennis Publishing*, pioneered computer hobbyist magazines (e.g. *Personal Computer World* and *MacUser*), wrote one of his best-sellers titled *How to Make Money*, and became a self-made multi-millionaire (an estimated net worth of £750 million). As a philanthropist, he gave £175 million to the Heart of England Forest, a charity primarily supporting the planting and conservation of trees. He once said: "The only thing worse than not having money is having it and not being able to manage it."[3]

Gail Ingersoll (1949–2011) and Julia Eleanor, two experts in grant writing and grant administration, wrote one of the best practical summaries of the grant management process (we will examine this in Section 3.1 of this chapter). Reflecting on their decades-long experiences and observations as veteran grant writers and grant managers, they opened their article with the sentence: "There is a saying among proposal writers that the only thing worse than not being funded, is being funded."[4]

In a sense, we might say that these four sentences from the five individuals represent two different views before and after a success. The first two sentences about celebrating are a little naive, but entirely understandable. The final two sentences are extremely wise and based on years of successful and unsuccessful experience. These two sentences reveal much about

---

[3] Nigerian Seminars and Trainings website, available at: www.nigerianseminarsandtrainings.com/.
[4] Ingersoll, G. L., & Eberhard, D. (1999). Grants management skills keep funded projects on target. *Nursing Economics*, *17*(3), 131–41. Gs6.

pre- and post-award grant management, especially the challenges in post-award management.

2.2 Pre-Award Management: Postdocs vs. Graduate Assistants

When I started to apply for grants, I routinely always requested a budget for graduate assistants to help my research, and never thought I should request a budget for postdocs. My assumption was that a postdoc would be much more expensive than a graduate assistant. One day, I learned a colleague of mine received a grant and she was recruiting a postdoc. So I congratulated her and then asked her a naive question: Is a postdoc more expensive than a graduate assistant?

My further learning and study of various materials indicate: (1) In general, expertise in budgeting is needed to answer this seemingly simple but in reality rather complicated question professionally. It might take a full course of Budget 101 to learn it well. (2) In general, it is true that the annual salary of a postdoc is much higher than that of a graduate assistant. For instance, at the National Institutes of Health (NIH), postdocs will now be paid at least $61,008, and in contrast, graduate students will be paid at least $28,224.[5] (3) In general, the total relevant budget covers three major items: stipend, benefits, and tuition. Because a graduate assistantship usually includes the tuition (about $30,000 per year), but a postdoc does not need to, the difference in total budget between a graduate assistant and a postdoc could be much smaller than initially estimated. (4) In general, postdocs will be more skillful and productive in conducting research, publishing articles, and submitting grants in a short period of time, whereas predocs will still require research training, and will probably still be studying the required courses for their degrees. Thus, for a faculty member with limited grants, hiring a postdoc rather than a predoc could be a very reasonable option.

The above suggests a few brief important lessons about pre-award grant management: (1) It should start as early as possible. (2) It is as important, if not more important, than post-award grant management. (3) Budgeting and hiring concerns finance management and personnel management, and these are two important and technical tasks of pre-award and post-award grant management.

---

[5] NSF 101: Graduate and postdoctoral researcher funding opportunities, *US National Science Foundation*, available at: https://new.nsf.gov/science-matters/nsf-101-graduate-postdoctoral-researcher-funding; Langin, K., NIH boosts pay for postdocs and graduate students, *Science*, available at: www.science.org/content/article/nih-boosts-pay-postdocs-and-graduate-students.

2.3 Post-Award Management: No-Cost Extension during COVID-19

In 2020, like all other people in the United States and across the world, I was facing an unprecedented challenge in my life and work. We were required to avoid public interactions. We were required to teach and learn online. At that time, I was working on an ongoing NSF-funded three-year project. However, given the unprecedented circumstances of COVID-19, the award periods would end before the data collection and data analysis were completed. I wondered what should I do and how the National Science Foundation (NSF) could help me.

It turned out that it is not uncommon to modify the award period due to various unforeseen circumstances. The NSF's Proposal and Award Policy and Procedure Guide outlines its post-award management procedure called "No-Cost Extension" (NCE). Specifically, there are three types of NCEs. (1) **Grantee-Approved Extension**. Grantees themselves may authorize a one-time extension of the grant end date of up to twelve months, under two requirements: the extension is to assure adequate completion of the original scope of work (i.e. "extension"); and the remaining funds are sufficient to achieve this (i.e. "no-cost"). The recipient must notify the NSF, providing supporting reasons for the extension and the revised period of performance, at least ten calendar days before the end date specified in the grant. (2) **NSF-Approved Extension**. If additional time beyond the extension provided by the grantee is required and exceptional circumstances warrant, a formal request must be signed and submitted by the Authorized Organizational Representative in an institution. The request should be submitted to the NSF at least forty-five days before the grant end date. The request must explain the need for the extension and include an estimate of the remaining funds and a plan for their use. The first NCE request will be considered for approval by the NSF Program Officer. The second or any subsequent NCE request will be subject to the approval of an NSF Grants and Agreements Officer. (3) **Two-Year Extensions for Special Creativity**. A Program Officer may initiate and recommend the extension of funding for certain research grants beyond the initial period. This is to offer the most creative investigators an extended opportunity to tackle pioneering, "high-risk" opportunities.[6]

---

[6] Proposal & Award Policies & Procedures Guide (PAPPG), *US National Science Foundation*, available at: https://new.nsf.gov/policies/pappg.

2 Real-Life Cases: From Four Sentences to Misconduct 273

Besides the above standard procedure, during the COVID-19 pandemic, the NSF also established a special procedure to manage COVID-related circumstances. This was in addition to the receipt of funds from two major relief Acts: $75 million under the Coronavirus Aid, Relief, and Economic Security Act of 2020; and $600 million under the American Rescue Plan Act of 2021.

In 2020, I followed the NCE procedure, seamlessly extended my project twice, and completed my project successfully. During the process, my university's grant administrator and the NSF's program office provided invaluable assistance, which enabled me to have a unique and uncomplicated post-award grant management experience.

This case suggests that post-award grant management involves various planned and unexpected issues and NCE is only one of the most common procedures.

2.4 Eric Poehlman: The First Criminal Case of Research Misconduct

In 1987, Eric Poehlman graduated with a PhD in physiology at the University of Vermont. His dissertation is titled *Aging, Physical Activity, and Energy Expenditure*. In the same year, he became an Assistant Professor in the College of Medicine at the University of Vermont. In 1992, he became an Associate Professor at the University of Maryland, Baltimore. In 1995, he became a full Professor at the University of Vermont. As one of the leading authorities on metabolism and aging, his research was well-funded and influential in his field. He has published over 200 journal articles and received sixty grants for around $8 million from 1988 to 2000 from the NIH alone.

However, in 2000, Walter DeNino, a student researcher working in his lab at the University of Vermont, was shocked to find that Poehlman altered the research data and later filed a report against Poehlman to the University. The University initiated an investigation in 2001. The Office of Research Integrity of the Department of Health and Human Services launched a further investigation. Ultimately, Poehlman acknowledged falsifying seventeen grant applications to the NIH for nearly $3 million, and fabricating data in ten published articles. Poehlman has been barred for life from receiving US grants. This became one of the largest research misconduct cases on record and he became the first academic in the United States to be jailed for falsifying data in a grant application.[7]

---

[7] Dalton, R. (2005). Obesity expert owns up to million-dollar crime. *Nature, 434*(7032), 424–5. Gs26.

This case is one of many instances of scientific misconduct,[8] which is part of the work that grant management needs to handle professionally.

3 Scientific Knowledge: From Management Skills to Misconduct Management

3.1 Ingersoll & Eberhard (1999): Grant Management as a Complex Process

Overview

The article is titled "Grants management skills keep funded projects on target."[9] It focuses on the steps and strategies of grant management as a multi-phase process in detail. It has been cited six times as of 2023, according to Google Scholar.

The first author of the article, Gail Ingersoll (1949–2011),[10] is Julia Eleanor Chenault Professor of Nursing and Associate Dean for Research at Vanderbilt University School of Nursing. This is her only paper on grantology. She passed away in 2011 after a battle with cancer. Ingersoll is remembered as a pioneer in the field of nursing research, a prolific grant writer, and a catalyst for improving family-centered care. The second author, Dianne Eberhard, is a Grants Administrator at Vanderbilt University School of Nursing.

The article was published in 1999 in *Nursing Economic$*.[11] The journal publishes current and emerging best practices in healthcare management, economics, and policymaking. Its impact factor in 2022 is 1.2. The publisher is Anthony Jannetti through Wolters Kluwer.

Highlights

This article is one of the best practical summaries of the grant management process. It has four major sections: The grants management process; Pre-funding activities (including budget planning and development);

---

[8] Case summaries, *The Office of Research Integrity*, available at: https://ori.hhs.gov/content/case_summary; List of scientific misconduct incidents, *Wikipedia*, available at: https://en.wikipedia.org/wiki/List_of_scientific_misconduct_incidents#cite_ref-3.
[9] Ingersoll, G. L., & Eberhard, D. (1999). Grants management skills keep funded projects on target. *Nursing Economic$, 17*(3), 131–41. Gs6.
[10] Nursing professor and researcher Gail Ingersoll dies at age 62, *University of Rochester Medical Center*, available at: www.urmc.rochester.edu/news/story/nursing-professor-and-researcher-gail-ingersoll-dies-at-age-62.
[11] Nursing Economic$, *Wolters Kluwer*, available at: www.wolterskluwer.com/en/solutions/ovid/nursing-economic-1862.

Post-funding activities (including project oversight); and Summary. From the perspective of grant management, we highlight the following comments and insights for grantology research and practice.

First, the article opens with: "There is a saying among proposal writers that the only thing worse than not being funded, is being funded." This could be counterintuitive for many of us. This interesting saying also conflicts with the common focus on obtaining grants. It stresses the challenging nature of grant management, especially after securing one. It no doubt reflects the two authors' years of experience and observations as veteran grant writers and grant managers. They specifically recommend taking several critical steps during the proposal development phase and in the early post-funding period. These steps serve to identify the activities required to achieve project goals and to guarantee sufficient funds available to cover the time and resources needed.

Second, it is also important and interesting to learn from the authors that "the grants management process **begins as soon as** the first steps are taken toward developing a project proposal." This is also counterintuitive to many of us. Research methodology skills and grant management skills should be used in parallel rather than in sequence. The authors further thoughtfully discuss the grant management process in two phases: the pre-funding phase and the post-funding phase.

Third, for **pre-funding** activities of grant management, the authors discuss a long list of tasks, specifically focusing on: (1) how to plan and develop a budget, including how to budget personnel, equipment, travel, and direct and indirect costs; (2) how to plan program activities with program planning software and a grant management planning table; and (3) how to handle administrative review and approval.

Fourth, for **post-funding activities** of grant management, the authors elaborated on eight key elements: (1) overseeing the start of the project and enhancing project team productivity; (2) setting up various mechanisms using a grant management flowchart; (3) communicating with the sponsored research officer; (4) setting up an account; (5) scheduling team meetings; (6) managing budget; (7) writing interim and final reports using the meeting minutes and decision logs; and (8) communicating with funders for modifications (e.g. discussing re-budget items, requesting extra funding, using unspent money, extending the time frame, and asking for an NCE).

Last, the **practical implication** for new grant writers is straightforward and important. We must develop knowledge and skills of grant management, a practically critical but often neglected area in the grant process, in addition to developing grant writing knowledge and skills. For those who would like to study grant management skills further, two books are recommended.[12]

3.2 Duffy (2010): Grant Management by a Scientist

Usually, grant efforts focus on securing grants, including writing, submitting, and revising proposals. Furthermore, research training focuses on conducting research, including research design, data collection, data analysis, and writing up for knowledge dissemination (e.g. conference presentation and article publication). However, grant management skills are often left out, but should be an integral part of pursuing grants and conducting research to complete a funded project and generate broad impacts. Let us study researchers' grant management by examining a short article.

Overview

The article is a short essay, titled "Grant management skills are critical for young scientists."[13] This title suggests three key ideas: (1) grant management demands various important professional skills; (2) these skills are crucial rather trivial; and (3) it is even more critical for young scientists. The article is thought-provoking, although it has been cited only twice as of 2023, according to Google Scholar.

The author, Brion Duffy (1967–2021),[14] was a senior researcher in Environmental Genomics and Systems Biology at Zurich University of Applied Sciences. His major research areas are bacteriology, pathogen ecology, epidemiology, and population genomics. His h-index is 60. This article is his only grant-related publication. He passed away unexpectedly

---

[12] Hall, J. L. (2009). *Grant Management: Funding for Public and Nonprofit Programs*, Jones & Bartlett Publishers. Gs14; Kerridge, S., Poli, S., & Yang-Yoshihara, M. (eds.) (2023). *The Emerald Handbook of Research Management and Administration around the World*, Emerald Publishing. Gs3.

[13] Duffy, B. (2010). Grant management skills are critical for young scientists. *Nature Biotechnology*, 28(11), 1152–3. Gs2; Brion Duffy, *Google Scholar*, available at: https://scholar.google.com/citations?user=bYTFCD0AAAAJ&hl=en&scioq=Singhvi,+A.+%26+Sachdev,+P.+Nat.+Biotechnol.+28,+378%E2%80%93379+(2010).&oi=sra.

[14] On June 9, 2023, I sent Dr. Duffy a short email and asked him why he wrote the paper as a bacteriology expert, how editors of *Nature Biotechnology* viewed his piece, whether there would be major differences in grant management between Europe and North America, and who could be the leading experts in grant management research. However, I never received a reply. Dr. Fabio Rezzonico, a member of his research group of Environmental Genomics and Systems Biology, was kind enough to tell me that Dr. Duffy passed away suddenly in January 2021, and said that "Brion was critical for my career development and is sorely missed as mentor, scientist and friend."

in 2021 from COVID-19,[15] and his colleagues admired him for being both creative and innovative in the field of bacteriology and being extraordinarily successful in grantsmanship with diverse EU research grants.

The article was published under the category of Correspondence in 2010 in *Nature Biotechnology*, which publishes significant studies on technologies and methodologies relevant to the biological, biomedical, agricultural, and environmental sciences. It also covers the commercial, political, ethical, legal, and societal aspects of biotechnology.[16] Its impact factor was 68.164 in 2021. In *Nature Biotechnology*, Correspondence is one type of non-primary research article (e.g. Reviews, Perspectives, Comments, News & Views, Book Reviews, Patent Articles, Careers and Recruitment). These types of writing do not include original or previously unpublished results or data and contain only minimal new supporting findings.[17] The Correspondence section provides a forum for comment on relevant issues and may be peer-reviewed at the editors' discretion.

Highlights

This article is a letter to the editor as Correspondence regarding a previously published comment on research skills needed for young scientists. It is only 1.5 pages – short, but rich in detail. It has six paragraphs: (1) specifying the importance of skills in grant management, especially financial management and collaboration management; (2) pinpointing a narrow view that obtaining grants is considered the difficult part and managing grants comes naturally (a recipe for disaster), followed by a discussion of accountability as a core concept in modern funding programs in Europe and the United States; (3) discussing the details of accounting and financial management skills; (4) detailing the legal aspects of accountability; (5) elaborating on collaboration skills in management; and (6) suggesting scientists should master grant management skills early on for the long term because their management duties will increase over time. Thus, grant agencies and research institutions should support improving and simplifying grant management. From the perspective of grant management by researchers, we highlight a few key points from the letter.

First, as shown in the title, grant management skills are **critical** for young scientists. This central judgment is based on the author's experience both

---

[15] Liao, Y.-Y., García-Rodríguez, R., and da Silva, K., When early-career professionals understand what they need during a pandemic, *Phytopathology News*, available at: www.apsnet.org/members/community/phytopathology-news/2021/march/Documents/PhytoNews_V55_N3_March_2021.pdf.
[16] Aims & scope, *Nature Biotechnology*, available at: www.nature.com/nbt/aims.
[17] Content types, *Nature Biotechnology*, available at: www.nature.com/nbt/content.

as a well-accomplished scientist for his grant success in Environmental Genomics and Systems Biology and as the Head of the Research Group at Zurich University of Applied Sciences for his grant administration experiences. He explicitly explains why grant management skills are critical from the perspectives of finance, law, and collaboration.

Second, as one of the first to specify grant management skills in the grantology literature, he discusses **accountability** as a key concept in modern grant programs. Scientists assume accountability not only for managing typical scientific performance (e.g. completing funded projects, administering staff and facility, reporting to granting agencies, and publishing results), but also for managing various non-scientific work (e.g. maintaining transparent bookkeeping records for future audits).

Third, for the first time, he raised issues of **mismanagement** that will damage researchers' careers. Some brief examples include failure to pass subsequent audits, allowing institutions to squeeze grant overhead, and avoiding legal responsibility for scientist mismanagement.

Last, this article has **important implications** for new grant writers. While the early-career grant training has been on the pre-award process, it is now time to develop the post-award knowledge, especially the knowledge of accountability. While, traditionally, the focus of research training is on research methodology skills, it is now time to develop various research management skills.

3.3 Smaglik (2013): Grant Management by a Grant Administrator

This article is titled "Administration: A watchful eye on grant funding,"[18] suggesting one of the functions of grant administration is to monitor grant funding. It vividly describes multiple cases of scientific administrators in terms of how they manage and administer grants and other scientific and research activities. It has only one citation as of 2023.

Paul Smaglik is the author of the article. He is a seasoned writer, journalist, and editor, with approximately thirty years of journalistic leadership and writing experience in the science, technology, and medical publication sectors. He began his career in newspapers, but switched to scientific magazines. His work has appeared in publications including *Science News*, *Science*, *Nature*, and *Scientific American*.

The article was published in 2013 in the Career Section of *Nature*.

---

[18] Smaglik, P. (2013). Administration: A watchful eye on grant funding. *Nature*, *501*(7466), 269–71. GsI.

Highlights
The article is featured as a non-research piece in *Nature*. While it has only three pages, it is full of interesting and inspiring points regarding grant management by scientific administrators. Below are three highlights from the article.

First, there are **different types** of grant management. It can be performed at three levels: grant, program, and policy. Grant-level administrators assign or manage grants given to individual investigators. Program-level administrators supervise multiple investigators or projects. And policy-level administrators oversee grants for an entire department, an institution, a university, or even university systems. Grant management can also be accomplished in three types of organizations: universities, federal agencies, and foundations. Grant management often takes place among multiple parties. For example, a grant administrator at a university can work with the investigator, the granting agency, and other parts of the university.

Second, grant management can also be achieved at **different stages of careers**, for example, awarding grants at a small foundation as a grant administrator in the early career phase, managing various grant programs as a program officer at the NIH in mid-career, working with twenty-eight investigators and three postdocs at twelve institutions toward the end of mid-career, and administering ten research universities and five medical centers as a senior administrator in the late career phase, as described in a case by Smaglik.

Third, grant management might fulfill **various types of tasks**, for example, working for non-profit accounting, checking grant compliance, evaluating investigators' needs and setting their priorities, being a liaison with different parties, being a head of logistics, being a scientific review officer, becoming a grant operations manager, monitoring the review committee, updating different forms, revising deadlines, monitoring implementation process, dealing with deadlines, attention to detail, selecting and reviewing new investigators, running multiple scientific meetings each year, building and evaluating budgets, managing financial and personnel systems, and having concrete goals and keeping a broad perspective of the big picture.

3.4 Selby-Harrington et al. (1993): Grant Managing by Grantees and Grant Managers

Careful readers might have already noticed that researchers in the discipline of nursing are particularly active in not only pursuing grants, but also conducting grant research. Here, we will study another article by scholars in nursing.

8 Grant Management

Overview

This article is titled "Guidance for managing a research grant."[19] It provides detailed practical instructions on grant management and has nine citations as of 2023.

Three authors wrote the article. The first, Maija Selby-Harrington, is Associate Professor and Director of Research in the School of Nursing at the University of North Carolina at Greensboro. The second author, Patricia Donat, is a Research Associate working with Selby-Harrington in the same school. The third author, Heddy Hibbard, is a health science administrator of the Center for Medical Effectiveness Research of the US Public Health Service. They have published another two articles on grant management together.[20]

The article was published in 1993, over thirty years ago, in the journal *Nursing Research*. This is an academic journal celebrating over sixty years as the most sought-after nursing resource. As the official journal of the Eastern Nursing Research Society and the Western Institute of Nursing, it publishes the latest research techniques, quantitative and qualitative studies, and new state-of-the-art methodological strategies. Its 2023 impact factor is 2.364.

Highlights

This is a "methods paper" published in the Methodology Corner section of the journal. According to the journal, "methods papers" in the Methodology Corner are articles that describe applications of advancing methodologies in nursing research or present advances in methodology motivated by challenges of nursing research. The article has an introduction and ten sections covering the entire process of grant management, from the waiting period after grant submission to preparing for future grants. Below are two highlights.

First, from the **perspective of the grantees**, the three authors listed major post-award activities and tasks at every major step in detail.[21] These

---

[19] Selby-Harrington, M. L., Donat, P. L., & Hibbard, H. D. (1993). Guidance for managing a research grant. *Nursing Research*, 42(1), 54–61. Gs9.

[20] Selby-Harrington, M. L., Donat, P. L., & Hibbard, H. D. (1994). Research grant implementation: Staff development as a tool to accomplish research activities. *Applied Nursing Research*, 7(1), 38–46. Gs3; Selby, M. L., Riportella-Muller, R., & Farel, A. (1992). Building administrative support for your research: A neglected key for turning a research plan into a funded project. *Nursing Outlook*, 40(2), 73–7. Gs5.

[21] For the details of grant management right after submission, see the following useful and informative article: Bergstrom, N., & Baun, M. M. (1994). The proposal-reality gap: The mechanics of implementing a funded research proposal. *Nursing Outlook*, 42(6), 272–8. Gs3.

steps include: the waiting period, responding to the scientific review, planning for implementation, finance management, personnel management, additional measures for quality control, adhering to a timeline, authorship, the continuation application, and preparing for future grants. These three authors have worked with grantees for years and the instructions provided in the article are particularly practical and hands-on.

Second, from the **perspective of grant managers**, the authors specified in detail that grant managers must work with five different parties for grant management and administration: (1) program officers of funders for grant management; (2) the budget officer in the home institution for financial management; (3) the personnel office in the home institution for personnel management; (4) the Institutional Review Board for recruitment management; and (5) other offices in the home institution for quality management and communication management.

3.5 Wedekind & Philbin (2018): Grant Management by a Project Management Office

Overview
This article is titled "Research and grant management: The role of the Project Management Office (PMO) in a European research consortium context."[22] Note that a unit for professional project management has different names: the Project Management Office, the Programme Management Office, and the Portfolio Management Office. These names share the same acronym PMO and are closely related as a management unit within an organization. Similar names also include the Research Administration Office and the Office of Sponsored Programs in the university setting. This article focuses on the PMO on grant management that moves from traditional academic research projects to research and innovation consortium projects at a college in the European Union. The article has thirty-nine citations as of 2023.

The first author of the article is Gerben Wedekind. He is a partner in Grants and Incentives at the Innovation Group of Ernest & Young Global and previously worked as a project manager in the Programme Management Office at Imperial College London. The second author, Simon Philbin, is a Professor at Kingston University London, with major research areas in Engineering Management. His h-index is 24.

---

[22] Wedekind, G. K., & Philbin, S. P. (2018). Research and grant management: The role of the Project Management Office (PMO) in a European research consortium context. *Journal of Research Administration, 49*(1), 43–62. Gs39.

The article was published in 2018 in the *Journal of Research Administration*. Again, as mentioned in previous chapters, it is the official journal of the Society of Research Administrators International.

Highlights

The article is a case study. It has five major sections: Background on the project management office (PMO); Exploring the PMO role in EU-funded research and innovation grants; Case study: The EDEN2020 project; Conclusion; and Future work. From the perspective of grant management at the institutional level, two insights from the article are highlighted below.

First, the article classifies three types of grant management by the PMO. The first type of management is **supportive**. It advises on calls for proposals and grant requirements, shares best project management practices, facilitates set-up of the research team and networking with potential consortium partners, and provides training on consortium management where required. It has a low degree of control. The second type of management is **controlling**. It involves preparing and submitting grant applications to the funding agency, ensuring the adoption of best project management practices, ensuring usage of standardization forms and templates, and providing input in project decisions. It has a moderate degree of control. The third type of management is **directive**. It directs the preparation and submission of grant applications, manages the research project according to project management standards, ensures the project is implemented according to budget, schedule, and specification criteria, conducts risk management throughout the project, engages in non-research-related project tasks (such as consortium management, innovation management, and research commercialization), leads on reporting to the grant authority, and manages project closure. It has a high degree of control.

Second, it presents a **real-life case** to illustrate the three types of grant management at the five steps of a grant cycle at the PMO of Imperial College London. The supportive role of the PMO involved all five steps: ideation, proposal preparation and submission, grant preparation and negotiation, project implementation, and closure. The controlling role involved two steps: proposal preparation and submission, and project implementation. The directive role involved only the step of project implementation. This is inspirational for us to see how grant managers effectively and efficiently integrate different management types into daily grant management.

3 Scientific Knowledge

3.6 The NSF (2023): Grant Management by a Grant Agency

It is always useful to learn and understand a set of strong and detailed policies and procedures to manage grants at program, organizational, national, and international levels. Public and private funders usually have their grant management policies and procedures available in print and/or online. This kind of document is enormously important for grant management research because most are carefully written and revised to reflect funders' accumulated experience and knowledge of grant management over the years. Here, we will study an exemplary document produced by the NSF.

Overview

The document is titled "Proposal & Award Policies & Procedures Guide (PAPPG)."[23] To understand and remember this long title and its acronym, we could consider that the title has three elements: (1) It is the NSF's official guide (G); (2) it covers the NSF's policies and procedures (PP); and (3) it consists of two major parts, proposal submission and award administration (PA). The NSF consolidated its various separate guides into a single document, the PAPPG, in 2000 and has revised and released it annually. Because its contents are authoritative and comprehensive, it is sometimes called the bible for NSF grants. Note that, different from the NSF's PAPPG, the NIH's Grants Policy Statement (NIHGPS)[24] summarizes important policy requirements that serve as the terms and conditions of NIH grant awards, but the NIHGPS has to be consulted in conjunction with the NIH Guide for Grants and Contracts, which is the NIH's official publication of notices of grant policies, guidelines, and funding opportunities, updated daily and weekly. In other words, the NIHGPS is relatively similar to but less comprehensive than the NSF's PAPPG.

Highlights

The PAPPG, after a brief introduction, has two major parts. The first covers proposal preparation and submission guidelines. It includes five chapters: pre-submission information, proposal preparation instructions, processing and review, non-award decisions and transactions, and renewal proposals. The second part covers awards, administrating and monitoring of awards. It consists of seven chapters: awards, award administration,

---

[23] PAPPG, above note 6.
[24] NIH Grants Policy Statement, *NIH Grants & Funding*, available at: https://grants.nih.gov/policy-and-compliance/nihgps.

284   8 Grant Management

financial requirements and payments, recipient standards, allowable coasts, other post-award requirements and considerations, and award administration disputes and misconduct. From the perspective of grant management for PIs, grant administrators, and program officers, several important management-related matters will be highlighted below.

First, the PAPPG is **authoritative** legally. (1) In the United States, the **Code of Federal Regulations** (CFR) is the codification of the general and permanent rules published in the Federal Register by the departments and agencies of the Federal Government. It is divided into fifty titles representing broad areas subject to federal regulation. (2) **Title 2** concerns Grants and Agreements. It has two chapters: Chapter I on Office of Management and Budget Government-wide Guidance for Grants and Agreements; and Chapter II on Office of Management and Budget Guidance. (3) **Part 200** within Title 2 concerns uniform administrative requirements, cost principles, and audit requirements for federal awards. It has six subparts, including Subpart C on pre-federal award requirements and contents of federal awards and Subpart D on post-award requirements, with twelve appendices. (4) Based on the NSF, the **PAPPG** essentially serves as the NSF's formal implementation of "2 CFR §200" (i.e. Title 2 of CFR, Part 200) on uniform administrative requirements, cost principles, and audit requirements for federal awards. In addition, the PAPPG also implements other relevant public laws (e.g. the NSF Act), executive orders, and other directives.

Second, the PAPPG is **comprehensive** content-wise. It is more than 200 print pages long. Its coverage provides the NSF's guidance for its grant process from the pre-award phase to the post-award phase, especially proposal submission and award administration. The PAPPG has been designed for use by both the NSF's proposer and recipient community and the NSF's own leaders and staff members.

Third, during the **Pre-Award** stage, various management issues are involved. (1) During the pre-submission stage, management issues might include categories of funding opportunities, types of submissions, applicant eligibilities, submission deadlines, and submission procedure. (2) During the proposal preparation stage, many management issues include requests for reasonable accommodations, authorization to deviate from NSF proposal preparation requirements, proposals involving live vertebrate animals, proposals involving human subjects, seeking and obtaining indigenous nation approval, managing special types of proposals (e.g. rapid response research, RAPID, or early-concept grants for exploratory research, EAGER), and potentially disqualifying conflicts of interest. (3) During the

3 Scientific Knowledge 285

proposal review stage, important management issues might include selection of reviewers, funding recommendation, the NSF's decision to award or decline proposals, review information provided to PIs, and release of recipient proposal information, non-award decisions and transactions, proposal withdrawal, proposal not accepted or returned without review, declinations, reconsideration, resubmission, and renewal proposals.

Fourth, during the **Post-Award** stage, further management issues are involved. (1) For the award offer, management issues might include award acceptance, award periods, and additional funding support. (2) For award administration, various management issues may include monitoring project performance, changes in project direction or management, reporting requirements (annual and final annual project reports, project outcomes report for the general public, foreign financial disclosure report, award closeout), and record retention and audit. (3) For financial management, various issues are involved: payment requirements, cash refunds and credits to the NSF, award financial reporting requirements and final disbursements, post-award financial monitoring notifications, property management, and direct and indirect costs. (4) For personnel management, various issues include conflicts of interest, and responsible and ethical conduct of research. (5) For legal issues, management might involve post-award requirements and considerations, non-discrimination statutes and regulations, protection of living organisms, intellectual property, national security, and scientific integrity. (6) For award administration disputes and misconduct, management issues might include suspension and termination procedures, informal resolution of award administration disputes, and research misconduct (NSF policies and responsibilities, the role of recipients, reporting possible misconduct).

Last, the PAPPG has **important practice implications** for grant writers and grant administrators. Clearly, the PAPPG is a rich and invaluable source to study and follow, and to learn from, and that is one of the reasons why more than 100 management issues are listed in the PAPPG. While the PAPPG is only for the NSF community, we can still learn various general lessons about grant management from this guide. These lessons might include that grant management is: (1) complex (e.g. concerning laws, regulations, guidelines, standards, requirements, and professional codes); (2) comprehensive (e.g. involving science management, finance management, and personnel management); (3) ubiquitous (e.g. managing from the beginning to the end of the grant process rather than just one step or one task); and even (4) challenging (e.g. dealing with disputes and misconducts).

286   8 Grant Management

3.7 Almond et al. (2021): Scientific Misconduct Management

After gaining a broad picture of grant management and administration for funders like the NSF, let us now study a specific topic on scientific misconduct management.

Overview

The article in question is titled "A scoping review of the literature featuring research ethics and research integrity cases."[25] The title suggests two unique features of the article: (1) it is a special type of review that **scopes** or scans a large topic initially and quickly rather than a systematic review that **synthesizes** a given topic comprehensively and thoroughly and (2) it reviews published research misconduct **cases** as the basic unit of analysis, while a typical review synthesizes empirical **studies** as the basic unit of analysis. This is one of the first carefully written reviews on research ethics and research integrity. It has been cited sixty times as of 2023.

The authors of the article are seven established researchers of medical ethics from Hungary, the United Kingdom, Ireland, and Norway. They are all members of a consortium called Mapping Normative Frameworks for Ethics and Integrity of Research, with twelve institutions from multiple countries in Europe. The first author, Anna Catharina Vieira Armond, is from the Department of Behavioural Sciences at the University of Debrecen, Hungary. Currently, she is a postdoctoral fellow at the Ottawa Hospital Research Institute. She has published several articles on research integrity.[26]

The article was published in 2021 in *BMC Medical Ethics*, which is an open-access journal that publishes original research articles on the ethical aspects of biomedical research and clinical practice. Its 2023 impact factor was 3.0. *BMC Medical Ethics* is one of 250 scientific journals from the BioMed Central (BMC), which is a UK-based scientific open-access platform. The publisher is Springer Nature.

---

[25] Armond, A. C. V., Gordijn, B., Lewis, J., Hosseini, M., Bodnár, J. K., Holm, S. *et al.* (2021). A scoping review of the literature featuring research ethics and research integrity cases. *BMC Medical Ethics*, 22(1), 50. Gs55.
[26] Armond, A. C. V., & Kakuk, P. (2022). Perceptions of research integrity climate in Hungarian universities: Results from a survey among academic researchers. *Science & Engineering Ethics*, 28(4), article 30; Armond, A. C. V., & Kakuk, P. (2023). Research integrity guidelines and safeguards in Brazil. *Accountability in Research*, 30(3), 133–49; Armond, A. C. V., & Kakuk, P. (2023). Perceptions of publication pressure among Hungarian researchers: Differences across career stage, gender, and scientific field. *Accountability in Research*, 30(8), 766–75; Goddiksen, M. P., Allard, A., Armond, A. C. V., Clavien, C., Loor, H., Schöpfer, C. *et al.* (2024). Integrity games: An online teaching tool on academic integrity for undergraduate students. *International Journal for Educational Integrity*, 20(1), article 7.

Highlights
While this is a review article, it is organized like an empirical article in five major sections: Background, Methods, Results, Discussion, and Conclusion. As a scoping review, the article searched cases involving misbehavior, poor judgment, or detrimental research practice in PubMed, Web of Science, SCOPUS, JSTOR, Ovid, and Science Direct in 2018, without language or publication year restriction. Data relating to the articles and the cases were extracted from case descriptions. Before being published, the article went through multiple rounds of revisions in an open peer-review process.[27]

From the perspective of grant management related to research misconduct, six important points of the article can be highlighted.

First, the review scopes a **particularly broad** literature. Among a total of 10,566 articles identified, it covers three broad and rapidly evolving areas: research ethics, research integrity, and scientific misconduct. It is closely related to all aspects of the grant process (e.g. application, review, decision, implementation, and impact). In fact, handling issues of research ethics, research integrity, and scientific misconduct is one of the most important, complex, and challenging tasks in grant management.

Second, the review focuses on **published cases** that are unique, appropriate, and thorough. It reviews published scientific misconduct cases rather than published empirical studies as the basic unit of analysis. This is because research misconducts have been disclosed publicly largely via published cases (especially highly publicized cases) rather than via published empirical studies (especially randomized controlled experiments). To locate the published cases, the authors searched ten sections of scientific journals and newspapers: News, Editorial, Commentary, Misconduct notice, Retraction notice, Review, Letter, Book review, Case analysis, and Educational (e.g. a case description was incorporated in a training program to illustrate guidelines and policies).

Third, this scoping review provides the **first and best case-based general picture** of scientific misconduct.[28] Through the search and screening,

---

[27] Peer review reports, *Springer Nature Link*, available at: https://link.springer.com/article/10.1186/s12910-021-00620-8/peer-review; Ross-Hellauer, T. (2017). What is open peer review? A systematic review. *F1000Research*, 6; Ford, E. (2013). Defining and characterizing open peer review: A review of the literature. *Journal of Scholarly Publishing*, 44(4), 311–26. Gs221; van Rooyen, S., Godlee, F., Evans, S., Black, N., & Smith, R. (1999). Effect of open peer review on quality of reviews and on reviewers' recommendations: A randomised trial. *British Medical Journal*, 318(7175), 23–7.
[28] Another fine analysis is Dubois, J. M., Anderson, E. E., Chibnall, J., Carroll, K., Gibb, T., Ogbuka, C. *et al*. (2013). Understanding research misconduct: A comparative analysis of 120 cases of professional wrongdoing. *Accountability in Research*, 20(5–6), 320–38. Gs89.

the authors studied 10,556 published articles in multiple languages and identified 238 unique cases of various types of scientific misconduct from 388 articles with sufficient case descriptions. This offers a basic sense of the extent of the existing published literature. Note that not all scientific misconduct cases were detected, reported, investigated, sanctioned, and published. Obviously, the published cases represent only part of scientific misconduct in the real world. As the article noted, "the published cases are not representative of all instances of misconduct, since most of them are never discovered, and when discovered, not all are fully investigated or have their findings published with sufficient information."

Fourth, the review generates **important findings**. (1) Among all 238 cases of scientific misconduct, falsification and fabrication were the most frequently identified violations (44.9 percent). The lack of informed consent and research ethics committee approval was the second most frequently tagged violation (15.7 percent), followed by patient safety issues (11.1 percent) and plagiarism (6.9 percent). (2) Across different scientific fields, 80.8 percent of cases were dominantly from the Medical and Health Sciences, 11.5 percent from the Natural Sciences, 4.3 percent from Social Sciences, 2.1 percent from Engineering and Technology, and 1.3 percent from Humanities. (3) Regarding the geographical distribution, the 307 articles that include geographical information originated from twenty-six countries. Most of the articles emanated from the United States (61.9 percent) and the United Kingdom (14.3 percent), followed by Canada (4.9 percent), Australia (3.3 percent), China (1.6 percent), Japan (1.6 percent), Korea (1.3 percent), and New Zealand (1.3 percent). (4) The most discussed cases include the Imanishi-Kari, Gallo, and Schön cases (the United States), the Fisher/Poisson and Olivieri cases (Canada), the Wakefield and CNEP trial cases (the United Kingdom), the Hwang case (South Korea), and the RIKEN case (Japan). (5) Regarding sanctions imposed by funding agencies, journals, and institutions, eleven types of sanctions were reported: paper retraction, exclusion of fund applications, exclusion from service, fired or suspended, paper correction, resignation, manuscript rejection, study termination, fines, legal trials, and prison sentences. Among the 238 cases, 141 cases (59 percent) were reported as single or multiple sanctions, while ninety-seven cases did not include this information. Paper retraction (45.4 percent) and exclusion from funding applications (35.5 percent) were the most prevalent sanctions.

Fifth, there exist thirty-nine types of major and minor misconducts related to **almost all aspects of grant management** directly and indirectly. Examples explicitly related to the Pre-Award and Post-Award process are extensive: deleting data selectively, modifying and fabricating data, modifying results or conclusions due to pressure of a sponsor, presenting misleading information in a grant application, failing to disclose a sponsor of the study, unfair review of grant applications or promotion cases, and submitting or resubmitting papers or grant applications without consent from all authors.

Last, there is an **important practical implication** for new grant writers. Given that misconducts are related to almost all aspects of grant management and that fabrication and falsification are the two most common research misconducts, we should do our best to prevent these from taking place in grant writing and grant management.

4 Grantology: Grant Management and Article Production

4.1 Grant Management

Grant management, as we studied so far in this chapter, includes research/project management by grantees, grant administration by institutions, and grant management by grantors. It is **critical** because it is the only way to complete a funded project, generate impacts, and realize the goals of a funded project, which will be discussed in Chapter 9. It is also **complex** because it involves multiple parties (e.g. grantees, grantors, and home institutions), multiple phases (e.g. the pre-award phase and the post-award phase), and multiple dimensions (e.g. science, finance, personnel, and ethics). It is an area of knowledge that is not very familiar among researchers and has received little attention in both grant research and grant practice. Compared with the extensive research on grant writing, grant review, and grant impacts, research in grant management is extremely limited in its quantity and quality. Thus, researchers in grantology should conduct more studies to advance the scientific knowledge of grant management.

4.2 Article Production

The grant process is generally considered as the beginning of a research process, whereas article publication is considered as the end point of a research process. Thus, after a proposal is funded, there are various important tasks to complete, whereas after a manuscript is accepted, it seems that there is not much more to do. There is essentially no article management phase in both journal publication practice and the journalology literature. Perhaps what article writers need is knowledge management.[29] The only relevant step after an article is published is the journal production phase, mainly undertaken by the publisher (e.g. checking proofs, submitting high-quality images), and the post-publication phase, in which authors' participation is perhaps very limited (e.g. media communication, social media dissemination, article citations). Perhaps this is one of the reasons why researchers are not well prepared for grant management: they might use their journal publication experience to guide their grant management practice.

Technically, after manuscripts are accepted, the publisher team is actually busy with the journal **production** process. Based on the production process at *Nature*,[30] this might involve six steps: (1) Preparation: The accepted manuscript and associated files are exported to the production system and assigned a Digital Object Identifier (DOI); the manuscript text is converted into structured XML and the images are resized to fit the standard journal styles; a subject specialist will copyedit the article for clarity, readability, consistency, accuracy, and adherence to the journal style. (2) License to Publish and Open Access payment: The author will be contacted by the Author Service team, who will help create the relevant license to publish the article; the author will be able to choose to either pay an Article Publication Charge or check if an authors' institute is covered under an existing transformative agreement. (3) Proofing: An electronic proof is sent to the corresponding author for review. (4) Finalization: A copyediting specialist reviews any e-proof amendments; all content changes and final production quality checks are completed. (5) Scheduling: The article is assigned a publication date and the *Nature* Press Office is notified. Research articles are typically published as Advance Online Publications ahead of the journal issue. (6) Publication: The article is sent to *Nature*'s central data repository, which coordinates the final stages of publication; metadata feeds to third-party repositories are completed.

Besides the article production stage, authors should consider how a published article can generate scientific and societal impacts, which is similar to a funded project (grant impacts include article publication as one of

---

[29] Alavi, M., & Leidner, D. E. (2001). Knowledge management and knowledge management systems: Conceptual foundations and research issues. *MIS Quarterly*, 25(1), 107–36. Gs17572; Wiig, K. M. (1997). Knowledge management: An introduction and perspective. *Journal of Knowledge Management*, 1(1), 6–14. Gs1467; Mårtensson, M. (2000). A critical review of knowledge management as a management tool. *Journal of Knowledge Management*, 4(3), 204–16. Gs1185.
[30] Production process, *Nature Biotechnology*, available at: www.nature.com/nbt/submission-guidelines/production-process.

the key impacts). There might be several tasks after an article is in press in order to generate impacts. For example, authors might have to deal with media releases, publication embargoes, social media, article usage, article citations, and journal impact factors.

In summary, it seems that, up until this point, numerous parallels can be drawn between grantology and journalology, but in relation to the grant management phase covered in this chapter, this comparison effort suddenly becomes an awkward metaphor. Clearly, in both the pre-award and post-award phases, grant management is a critical and complex step in the entire grant process to complete funded projects and generate grant impacts, although not everyone truly realizes it. In contrast, before and after acceptance, article management may not even be an existing phase in journal article publication for article writers. It seems that minimum efforts are needed for an author to go through the publication process and generate impacts. Thus, at this moment, we might state that the differences in management between the grant funding process and the article publication process are much larger than their similarities. Thus, the most important implication is that we as article writers could open champagne to celebrate because the publisher will take care of the rest; on the contrary, we as grant writers should work even harder with various parties to complete projects and generate impacts.

5 Action Suggestions: Understanding and Drafting a Grant Management Plan

5.1 Understanding the Importance and Complexity of Grant Management

In the section on intuitive knowledge, we have seen that these new grant writers had limited knowledge about grant management. (1) The post-award grant management involves three processes by three parties: research management by the grantee, grant administration by the grantee's institution, and grant management by the grantor. The first two responders mentioned only the grantee, whereas the last two did briefly mention the three parties. (2) The post-award grant management concerns three basic aspects: science management, finance management, and personnel management. The four responders all emphasized the science aspect, while the first and third responders also mentioned the finance aspect, and the second and fourth responders were only briefly aware of the finance and personnel aspects. (3) The second and third responders explicitly indicated that "I lack this kind of knowledge" or "I have very limited knowledge and even imagination." This indicates that grant management knowledge may be the weakest link in their intuitive knowledge of grantology.

In the section on real-life cases, we examined four grant management cases, namely: (1) the high level of difficulty of grant management specified by experienced grant managers; (2) budgeting postdocs vs. research assistants in pre-award management; (3) a project extension in post-award management; and (4) misconduct management.

In the section on science knowledge, we have seven studies, examining seven aspects of grant management: (1) as a complex process; (2) by a scientist; (3) by a grant administrator; (4) by grantees and grant managers; (5) by a Project Management Office; (6) by a grant agency; and (7) in relation to scientific misconduct management.

In the section comparing grantology and journalology, we have learned there is significant divergence between grant management and article production. In both the pre-award and post-award phases, grant management is a critical and complex step in the entire grant process. However, before and after acceptance, article management may not even be an existing phase in journal article publication for article writers. Thus, we as article writers could celebrate the acceptance of an article and let the publisher take care of the rest, but we grant writers should work even harder to complete projects and generate impacts.

5.2 Studying Grant Management Plans and Drawing a Management Flowchart

Based on our improved understanding of the importance and complexity of grant management, two action-based suggestions are detailed below.

First, find and study a few research management cases. We might find two to three articles, including the ones discussed in this chapter, focus on tables, diagrams, and forms included in these articles, and study how grant management should take place in the real world.

Second, draw a management flow diagram. This diagram should consider multiple parties (e.g. research management by grantees, grant administration by institutions, and grant management by grantors), multiple phases (e.g. the pre-award phase and the post-award phase), and multiple dimensions (e.g. science, finance, personnel, and ethics). This should prove useful in guiding us throughout the entire grant cycle.

CHAPTER 9

Grant Impacts

Outline

1	Intuitive Knowledge: What Are the Impacts of a Grant?	294
	1.1 Responses from New Grant Writers	294
	1.2 Understand the Importance and Complexity of Grant Impacts	294
2	Real-Life Cases: From Required Impact Statement to National Impacts	295
	2.1 European Union: Required Impact Statement in Horizon 2020 and Horizon Europe	295
	2.2 Nobel Prize: Significant Impacts of NIH Grants	297
	2.3 Career Impacts: More Grants or More Articles to Achieve Tenure?	299
	2.4 The NSB: National Impacts of Scientific and Engineering Investment	300
3	Scientific Knowledge: From Small Scientific Impacts to Negative Impacts	301
	3.1 Jacob & Lefgren (2011): Small Scientific Impacts	301
	3.2 Sattari et al. (2022): Influential Training Impacts	304
	3.3 Bloch et al. (2014): Positive Career Impacts	307
	3.4 Payne & Siow (2003): Complex Institutional Impacts	310
	3.5 King (2004): Diverse National Impacts	311
	3.6 Salter & Martin (2001): Substantial Economic Impacts	313
	3.7 Bornmann (2013): Increasingly Important Societal Impacts	315
	3.8 Thyer (2011): Negative Impacts	318
4	Grantology vs. Journalology: Grant Impacts and Article Impacts	320
	4.1 Grant Impacts	320
	4.2 Article Impacts	320
5	Action Suggestions: Understanding and Learning about Grant Impacts	321
	5.1 Understanding the Importance and Complexity of Grant Impacts	321
	5.2 Learning about Impact Policies, Impact Statements, and Impact Sections	322

293

9 Grant Impacts

1 Intuitive Knowledge: What Are the Impacts of a Grant?

1.1 Responses from New Grant Writers

Below are three responses from three new grant writers to the question: What are the impacts of a grant?

- Response 1: I think the impact of a research grant is to provide financial support to researchers and promote good-quality research.
- Response 2: From my understanding, the impacts of a research grant are the guarantee of conducting meaningful and valuable research and generating scientific achievements that make great contributions to society.
- Response 3: Research grants can (1) motivate and support more people who are passionate about a field to join, (2) support the career development of researchers, (3) support the building and development of academic organizations, such as the department and the university, (4) promote the development of human knowledge, (5) benefit the world (especially the funded practical research).

1.2 Understand the Importance and Complexity of Grant Impacts

The above three responses show three levels of understanding regarding the impacts of grants. The first response suggests a conceptual confusion about grant goals (aims and purposes, the beginning of the grant process) vs. grant impacts (i.e. outputs and outcomes, the end of the grant process).[1] In addition to the conceptual misunderstanding, the focus was clearly on scientific research. The second response reveals a two-dimensional understanding of grant impacts: "generating scientific achievements that make great contributions to society" – that is, the direct and primary impacts are scientific impacts; the indirect and secondary impacts are societal impacts. The third

---

[1] Stannard-Stockton, S. (2010). Getting results: Outputs, outcomes and impact, *Stanford Social Innovation Review*, available at: https://ssir.org/articles/entry/getting_results_outputs_outcomes_impact; Weiss, A. P. (2007). Measuring the impact of medical research: Moving from outputs to outcomes. *American Journal of Psychiatry*, *164*(2), 206–14. GS136; Cruz Rivera, S., Kyte, D. G., Aiyegbusi, O. L., Keeley, T. J., & Calvert, M. J. (2017). Assessing the impact of healthcare research: A systematic review of methodological frameworks. *PLoS Medicine*, *14*(8), article e1002370. GS173; Ozanne, J. L., Davis, B., Murray, J. B., Grier, S., Benmecheddal, A., Downey, H. *et al.* (2017). Assessing the societal impact of research: The relational engagement approach. *Journal of Public Policy & Marketing*, *36*(1), 1–14. GS150; Summerfelt, W. T., & Meltzer, H. Y. (1998). Efficacy vs. effectiveness in psychiatric research. *Psychiatric Services*, *49*(6), 834–5. GS39; Mills-Scofield, D. (2012); It's not just semantics: Managing outcomes vs. outputs, *Harvard Business Review*, available at: https://hbr.org/2012/11/its-not-just-semantics-managing-outcomes.

response demonstrates a five-dimensional broad understanding of grant impacts, mentioning people, careers, institutions, knowledge, and the world.

However, grant impacts are much more complex than what these new grant writers considered. In general, we can consider grant impacts as a set of nested circles that share a common center of the completed project with funding, like tree trunks and pond ripples. As a tree grows, it forms a series of rings around its center, each representing one year of growth. When a stone is thrown into a pond, it creates a disturbance that radiates outward in all directions, forming a series of concentric circles. After a funded project is completed, it is expected to generate different circles of impacts, such as scientific (e.g. publications and patents), individual (e.g. tenure promotions and career development), institutional (e.g. department reputation, school influence/attraction), economic (e.g. university revenues), societal (e.g. community development), and national impacts (e.g. contributing to R&D and GDP). In addition, different impacts will be related to different indicators, further increasing the complexity of grant impacts.

As discussed in Chapter 1, a grant is essentially an investment and thus should maximize its returns and minimize its risks. However, the potential returns or potential impacts of a funded project are complex, with multiple types, dimensions, and levels. For instance, there are direct vs. indirect impacts (e.g. the spillover effect, the ripple effect, the Matthew effect), major vs. minor impacts, and intended vs. unintended impacts. These make grant impacts a complex system. At the beginning of the grant process, we need to consider the funders' mission, grant program purposes, grant objectives, or grantees' motivations for a proposed project. At the end of the process, we need to consider project outputs and outcomes, and eventually grant impacts for a funded project.

Thus, the intellectual goal of this chapter is to understand the **importance** and **complexity** of grant impacts and to develop a systematical understanding of grant impacts so that we can use this to guide our professional grant practice.

2 Real-Life Cases: From Required Impact Statement to National Impacts

2.1 *European Union: Required Impact Statement in Horizon 2020 and Horizon Europe*

Starting in 2014, Horizon 2020 (2014–20), the European Union's research and innovation (R&I) funding program and the world's largest R&I

funding program, required an impact statement in grant proposals to describe how the proposed project would generate scientific, economic, social, and environmental impacts. Horizon Europe (2021–7), the successor to Horizon 2020, continues this requirement with a strong emphasis on detailing the expected impacts of R&I projects as a critical part of external review and funding decisions.

Based on Horizon 2020 and Horizon Europe, grant impacts are neither the original motivation to carry out the proposed project nor the anticipated immediate results of their project. Grant impacts are much broader than research motivations or immediate results, answering a question about how significant benefits are from a proposed project. Specifically, there are three Key Impact Pathways (KIPs): (1) Scientific Impact: creating high-quality new knowledge, strengthening human capital in R&I, and fostering diffusion of knowledge and open source; (2) Societal Impact: addressing EU policy priorities and global challenges through R&I, delivering benefits and impact through R&I missions, and strengthening the uptake of R&I in society; and (3) Economic/Technological Impact: generating innovation-based growth, creating more and better jobs, and leveraging investments in R&I.

The impact section in the Horizon Europe proposals consists of three sub-sections: (1) Project's pathways toward impact; (2) Measures to maximize impact; and (3) Summary canvas.[2] The project's pathways toward impact consist of the following three elements: (1) Results: the immediate, short-term outputs of the project; (2) Outcomes: expected medium-term effects of funded projects under a given topic; and (3) Impacts: wider, long-term effects on society, economy, and science. They generally occur some time after the end of the project. Impacts should refer to the specific contribution of the project to the European Union's expected impacts.

This case reveals a worldwide impact-driven trend that demands higher impacts of funded projects. Many public and private funders require the impact statement as a mandated part of a grant proposal and conduct both the ex-ante review and the ex-post evaluation. Thus, it is more important than ever for grant writers to consider, design, generate, deliver, and assess grant impacts, especially to write a strong impact statement in a grant proposal.

---

[2] How to approach the Horizon Europe impact section for collaborative projects, *Enspire*, available at: https://enspire.science/how-to-approach-the-horizon-europe-impact-section-for-collaborative-projects/.

2 Real-Life Cases: Impact Statement & National Impacts

2.2 Nobel Prize: Significant Impacts of NIH Grants

In October 2023, the Nobel Committee[3] announced that Katalin Karikó and Drew Weissman were awarded the Nobel Prize in Physiology or Medicine "for their discoveries concerning nucleoside base modifications that enabled the development of effective mRNA vaccines against COVID-19." Soon, Lawrence Tabak, then Acting Director of the National Institutes of Health (NIH), posted a blog,[4] congratulating them on their Award, and indicating that the NIH has supported their seminal research as cited by the Nobel Assembly as key publications. The NIH funding support includes grants from two institutes to Katalin Karikó – the National Heart, Lung, and Blood Institute (NHLBI) and the National Institute of Neurological Disorders and Stroke (NINDS), and grants from three institutes to Drew Weissman – the National Institute of Allergy and Infectious Diseases (NIAID), the National Institute of Dental and Craniofacial Research, and the NHLBI.

Specifically, the grant acknowledgment of the three articles cited by the Nobel Committee explicitly specified the NIH grants that support the research. For one article,[5] this work was supported by three NIH grants, NIAID AI060505, AI50484, and DE14825.

For another article,[6] this work was supported by four NIH grants – NIAID AI-050484, NHLBI HL87688, and NINDS NS-29331, as well as the NIH's Ruth L. Kirschstein National Research Service Awards to the second author Hiromi Muramatsu.

For the third article,[7] the work was supported by seven NIH grants: R01AI50484, R21DE019059, T32GM07229, T32DK07748, T32RR007063, R42HL87688, and R01GM058709.

---

[3] The Nobel Assembly, consisting of fifty professors at Karolinska Institutet, awards the Nobel Prize in Physiology or Medicine. Its Nobel Committee evaluates the nominations. Since 1901, the Nobel Prize has been awarded to scientists who have made the most important discoveries for the benefit of humankind.

[4] Tabak, L. (2023). Persistence pays off: Recognizing Katalin Karikó and Drew Weissman, the 2023 Nobel Prize winners in physiology or medicine, *NIH Director's Blog*, available at: https://directorsblog.nih.gov/2023/10/12/persistence-pays-off-recognizing-katalin-kariko-and-drew-weissman-the-2023-nobel-prize-winners-in-physiology-or-medicine/.

[5] Karikó, K., Buckstein, M., Ni, H., & Weissman, D. (2005). Suppression of RNA recognition by Toll-like receptors: The impact of nucleoside modification and the evolutionary origin of RNA. *Immunity*, 23(2), 165–75. Gs2743.

[6] Karikó, K., Muramatsu, H., Welsh, F. A., Ludwig, J., Kato, H., Akira, S. *et al.* (2008). Incorporation of pseudouridine into mRNA yields superior nonimmunogenic vector with increased translational capacity and biological stability. *Molecular Therapy*, 16(11), 1833–40. Gs1883.

[7] Anderson, B. R., Muramatsu, H., Nallagatla, S. R., Bevilacqua, P. C., Sansing, L. H., Weissman, D. *et al.* (2010). Incorporation of pseudouridine into mRNA enhances translation by diminishing PKR activation. *Nucleic Acids Research*, 38(17), 5884–92. Gs675.

Historically, based on the NIH, 169 scientists either at the NIH as NIH staff scientists or whose research is supported by NIH funds have been the sole or shared recipients of 101 Nobel Prizes since 1939.[8] The Nobel Prize is awarded for "the greatest benefit to humankind." Between 1901 and 2023, Nobel Prizes were awarded 621 times to 1,000 people and organizations.

This recent real-life story is a perfect example of grant impacts, especially the scientific impacts of grants. Katalin Karikó and Drew Weissman have received multiple grants from the NIH to support their projects. The major impacts of these grants include scientific impacts, societal impacts, and economic impacts.

Specifically, for the scientific impacts: (1) these funded projects generated new important knowledge of mRNA and led to their three major articles[9] cited by the Nobel Committee for awarding the Prize; (2) these three major articles alone have received 2743, 1,883, and 675 citations respectively; (3) their research on mRNA technology has received multiple patents, including modified mRNA patents, a patent for mRNA vaccine platforms, and a patent for the mRNA delivery system.

In terms of societal impacts, their fundamental discoveries are critical to advancing the use of mRNA-based vaccines and therapies. Amid the breakout of the global COVID-19 pandemic, Karikó and Weissman's decades of work along with the tireless efforts of many academic, industry, and government scientists, enabled the world to rapidly develop lifesaving vaccines. Now, researchers are exploring how mRNA could be used in vaccines for other infectious diseases and in cancer vaccines.

In terms of economic impacts, both Pfizer/BioNTech vaccines and Moderna vaccines use these licensed patents from the University of Pennsylvania. As a result of these patent licensing activities, the University of Pennsylvania, Karikó, and Weissman have received significant financial benefits based on the sale of these products. In 2022, Karikó and Weissman founded another small biotech company, Viral Vector Bio, which is focused on advancing mRNA technology for a range of applications, including vaccines and therapeutics. The company receives funding from the NIH to explore the use of nucleoside-modified mRNA for gene therapy. In addition, since 2013, Weissman has worked

---

[8] Nobel Laureates, *NIH*, available at: www.nih.gov/about-nih/what-we-do/nih-almanac/nobel-laureates.
[9] Karikó *et al.* (2005), note 5 above; Karikó *et al.* (2008), note 8 above; Anderson *et al.* (2010), note 7 above.

2 Real-Life Cases: Impact Statement & National Impacts

with Biopharmaceutical New Technologies (BioNTech), a Germany-based company,[10] by collaborating with the BioNTech teams and publishing together.[11]

2.3 Career Impacts: More Grants or More Articles to Achieve Tenure?

A few years ago, I received a call from a very good friend of mine. We used to be close colleagues in a national institution of educational research, but had not seen each other for years and thus we had a long phone conversation about almost everything. At one point, even though we both achieved tenure years ago, we briefly talked about our experiences and observations of achieving tenure. He then told me a surprising story about a young colleague at his university.

My friend's young colleague was a newly hired tenure-track assistant professor. One of the reasons the university decided to hire him several years ago was that he had secured multiple external grants. Over the next few years, he continued to receive more and more grants and developed a very impressive grant portfolio. However, while he spent a significant amount of time writing, receiving, and implementing grants, surprisingly, he had very few journal publications under his belt. In the end, unfortunately, his tenure case was denied.

Generally, at a research university in the United States, tenure applications are evaluated on several criteria, such as publications, citations, grant money, teaching evaluations, student advisement, university services, professional services, and external reviewers' assessment. Among them, for a tenure-track assistant professor, securing external grants (especially competitive and prestigious ones), securing internal grants, and even unsuccessful grant applications are often viewed really positively as a sign of excellent scholarship. The existing literature indicates that securing grants increases the chance of achieving tenure.[12] Tenure failure is not uncommon, the reasons generally being major or complex

---

[10] Statement on Katalin Karikó and Drew Weissman awarded the Nobel Prize in Medicine 2023, *BioNTech*, available at: https://investors.biontech.de/node/15551/pdf.
[11] Sahin, U., Karikó, K., & Türeci, Ö. (2014). mRNA-based therapeutics – developing a new class of drugs. *Nature Reviews Drug Discovery*, *13*(10), 759–80. Gs2218.
[12] Bloch, C., Graversen, E. K., & Pedersen, H. S. (2014). Competitive research grants and their impact on career performance. *Minerva*, *52*(1), 77–96. Gs124; Bozeman, B., & Gaughan, M. (2007). Impacts of grants and contracts on academic researchers' interactions with industry. *Research Policy*, *36*(5), 694–707. Gs512.

(e.g. inadequate research or unfit for the institution),[13] but this was the first time I'd heard about such a rare case where securing too many grants led to tenure denial.

This rare case delivers a common message regarding grant impacts on careers. That is, securing grants generally significantly helps tenure promotion; however, this is not always the case.

2.4 The NSB: National Impacts of Scientific and Engineering Investment

In March 2024, the National Science Board (NSB) released the biennial Science and Engineering Indicators report, *The State of U.S. Science and Engineering 2024*.[14] This carefully crafted important report has drawn extensive nationwide and worldwide attention.

The report analyzes US scientific and engineering investment.:(1) The United States is the largest performer of research and development (R&D), with $806 billion in gross domestic expenditures on R&D in 2021. Other top R&D-performing countries include China ($668 billion), Japan ($177 billion), Germany ($154 billion), and South Korea ($120 billion). (2) The absolute amount of federally funded R&D increased from 2011 to 2021; however, due to significant growth in R&D funded by businesses, the share of total US R&D funded by the federal government decreased from 30 percent in 2011 to 19 percent in 2021. The business sector now funds 36 percent of basic research, close to the 40 percent share of basic research funded by the federal government. The federal government is the largest supporter of academic R&D, funding 52 percent of all R&D performed by higher education institutions and supporting 15 percent of full-time scientific and engineering graduate students in 2021.

The report also analyzes the impacts of US scientific and engineering investment. (1) The United States is also among the world's most R&D-intensive economies, with R&D expenditures equaling 3.5 percent of its **gross domestic product** in 2021. (2) Science and engineering research

---

[13] Kaminski, D., & Geisler, C. (2012). Survival analysis of faculty retention in science and engineering by gender. *Science, 335*(6070), 864–6. Gs231; Feder, T. (2023). When tenure fails. *Physics Today, 76*(10), 44–51. Gs3; Wapman, K. H., Zhang, S., Clauset, A., & Larremore, D. B. (2022). Quantifying hierarchy and dynamics in US faculty hiring and retention. *Nature, 610*(7930), 120–7. Gs157.

[14] NSB & National Science Foundation (2024). *Science and Engineering Indicators 2024: The State of U.S. Science and Engineering*. NSB-2024-3. Alexandria, VA, available at: https://ncses.nsf.gov/pubs/nsb20243.

3 Scientific Knowledge: Impacts 301

publications, **patenting**, and knowledge- and technology-intensive industry **output** are concentrated in the United States, East and Southeast Asia, and Europe. Over the past decade, China has significantly increased its share of global science, technology, and innovation capabilities. China is the top overall producer of scientific and engineering (S&E) **publications** and international **patents** and has the greatest knowledge, technology, and innovation (KTI) manufacturing **output**. The United States, which has a greater share of its publications among the most highly cited S&E research, is the world leader in KTI services.

This case is a fine example of the national impact of grants. It shows that different R&D investments will generate different impacts on more highly cited articles and patents at a country level. The NSB's report reveals dramatic changes in the science and engineering landscape and calls for new US strategies to secure US leadership and deliver the benefits of scientific and technological progress to all Americans.

3 Scientific Knowledge: From Small Scientific Impacts to Negative Impacts

3.1 Jacob & Lefgren (2011): Small Scientific Impacts

Let us first study whether grants can impact scientific research and improve scientific productivity.

Overview
The article we will study is titled "The impact of research grant funding on scientific productivity." We might immediately wonder what kinds of specific grants are discussed and how scientific productivity was defined in the article. This article focuses on the NIH's standard research grants G01 and three types of scientific productivity: article publication, article citation, and future grant success. The article has been cited 680 times as of 2023, a particularly high citation in the field of grantology.

The first author, Brian Jacob, has been the Walter Annenberg Professor of Education Policy, Economics, and Education at the Ford School of Public Policy at the University of Michigan since 2007. He is also a Research Associate and Faculty Research Fellow at the National Bureau of Economic Research. His primary fields of interest are labor economics and economics of education. His h-index is 58. His grant portfolio is extensive, receiving forty-three grants from public and private funders. Together with Lefgren, he published two articles on grant impacts,[15] so it is recommended that researchers and students in grantology should follow his work. The second author, Lars Lefgren, is Professor of Economics at Brigham Young University. His specialism is the economics of education and applied microeconomics, and his h-index is 27.

The article was published in 2011, well over a decade ago, in the *Journal of Public Economics*. This is a monthly peer-reviewed academic journal covering public economics, with particular emphasis on the application of modern economic theory and methods of quantitative analysis. It is published by Elsevier and had an impact factor of 4.8 in 2023.

Highlights
This is an empirical article in economics with a major strength in thorough quantitative analysis. This article and another were based on the results of one NBER study[16] written by the two authors in question. Basically, the authors attempted to use a quasi-experiment design to estimate the impact of receiving an NIH grant on subsequent article publications and article citations of individual investigators. They compared 15,477 unsuccessful applications with 39,294 successful applications (not applicants!) to the NIH from 1980 to 2000 for standard research grants (R01s), and examined if differences exist in journal publication, article citation, and future grant success. They found strong evidence to conclude that the scientific impact of NIH grants is small rather than moderate or large.

The article has eight main sections: Introduction, Prior literature, Institutional background, Data, Methodology (regression, below cut, normalization in detail), Findings (small effect and sensitivity analysis in detail), Discussion (displacement hypothesis, conclusion), and Conclusions. From the grant impacts perspective, we highlight several points regarding grant impacts on scientific research outcomes.

First, one major finding of the article is rather surprising or perhaps quite disappointing. For individual investigators, the successful applications of an NIH standard research grant (the average G01 grant size is

---

[15] Jacob, B. A., & Lefgren, L. (2011). The impact of research grant funding on scientific productivity. *Journal of Public Economics*, 95(9–10), 1168–77. Gs680; Jacob, B. and Lefgren, L. (2011). The impact of NIH postdoctoral training grants on scientific productivity. *Research Policy*. 40(6): 864–74. Gs138; Goldring, T., Jacob, B., Kreisman, D., & Ricks, M. (2024). *Loopholes and the Incidence of Public Services: Evidence from Funding Career & Technical Education* (No. w32390). National Bureau of Economic Research. Gso.

[16] Jacob, B., & Lefgren, L. J. (2007). The impact of research grant funding on scientific productivity, NBER Working Paper No. 13519.

around $1.7 million over three years) increase **only 1.2 more publications** over the next five years than the unsuccessful application, just a 7 percent increase. The finding is robust because it was estimated after controlling for a series of variables, including priority scores, institutional features, years of award, applicant characteristics, prior publications, and prior funding. This result suggests that NIH research grants do not have a substantial impact on article publications.

The authors developed a **displacement hypothesis** as a major reason to explain this small effect. That is, the loss of an NIH grant simply causes unsuccessful researchers to shift to another source of NIH or non-NIH funding, to collaborate often with successful grant receivers, and to displace the initial unsuccessful application to alternative successful grant applications (e.g. from smaller funders and home institutions) to conduct or continue their research.

Second, in addition to the journal publication, the study also found that receiving the G01 funding leads to: (1) **forty-nine more citations** within the next one to five years following grant application and (2) **$251,000 more NIH funding** within the next six to ten years. However, it is not clear why these two results have not been discussed in detail in the discussion and conclusion, unlike the extensive discussion on article publication, given that all three results indicate a small effect. Third, further research is needed to estimate **how these findings could be generalized**. While the study thoughtfully used the quasi-experiences to estimate a small scientific impact of successful and unsuccessful applicants for one grant submission cycle, we should consider that the study focused on NIH rather than diverse public and private funders, on one grant program of R01 rather than various other grant programs, on the grants on biomedical science rather than other research fields, and the twenty years between 1980 and 2000 rather than more recent years, and, most importantly, on the scientific impacts on three proxies, publication, citation, and future funding, rather than other indicators of scientific productivities to examine scientific impacts.

Fourth, there is a **large literature** on research funding on scientific outputs and outcomes. Some major studies have been cited and reviewed in the article.[17] For instance, Payne and Siow also reported a small scientific

---

[17] See e.g. Fortin, J. M., & Currie, D. J. (2013). Big science vs. little science: How scientific impact scales with funding. *PLoS One, 8*(6), article e65263. Gs223; Payne, A. A., & Siow, A. (1999). *Does Federal Research Funding Increase University Research Output?* Institute of Government and Public Affairs, University of Illinois. Gs285; Hottenrott, H., & Thorwarth, S. (2011). Industry funding of

impact, an increase of $1 million in federal research funding to a university resulted in eleven to eighteen more articles.[18] Other studies also examined the scientific impacts of funding on patents.[19] For instance, Azoulay and his collaborators found that a $10 million increase in NIH funding leads to a net increase of 2.7 private-sector patents.[20]

Last, **practical implications** for new grant writers include the following: (1) We should care not only about how to secure grants, but also about how to generate impacts. (2) Grant impacts are a complex topic and challenging practice. (3) Scientific impacts of grants on publications and patents are rather small. (4) We should better understand the mechanism of how grants generate impacts to improve the effectiveness of grants and productivities of researchers.

3.2 Sattari et al. (2022): Influential Training Impacts

Both the National Science Foundation (NSF) and the NIH, like various other funders, emphasize both scientific discoveries and scientific developments. Here, we will study one article related to grant impacts on scientist training.

Overview

The article is titled "The ripple effects of funding on researchers and output."[21] A ripple effect occurs when an initial disturbance spreads outward to a larger portion of a system, like an object being dropped into a pond and ripples expanding across the water.[22] The article attempts to examine

---

university research and scientific productivity. *Kyklos, 64*(4), 534–55. Gs165; Goldfarb, B. (2008). The effect of government contracting on academic research: Does the source of funding affect scientific output? *Research Policy, 37*(1), 41–58. Gs247; Hottenrott, H., & Lawson, C. (2014). Research grants, sources of ideas and the effects on academic research. *Economics of Innovation & New Technology, 23*(2), 109–33. Gs85; Heyard, R., & Hottenrott, H. (2021). The value of research funding for knowledge creation and dissemination: A study of SNSF research grants. *Humanities & Social Sciences Communications, 8*(1), 1–16. Gs31.

[18] Payne & Siow (1999), *ibid*.
[19] See e.g. Azoulay, P., Graff Zivin, J. S., Li, D., & Sampat, B. N. (2019). Public R&D investments and private-sector patenting: Evidence from NIH funding rules. *Review of Economic Studies, 86*(1), 117–52. Gs306; Li, D., Azoulay, P., & Sampat, B. N. (2017). The applied value of public investments in biomedical research. *Science, 356*(6333), 78–81. Gs163; Payne & Siow (1999), above note 17; Jaffe, A. B., Trajtenberg, M., & Henderson, R. (1993). Geographic localization of knowledge spillovers as evidenced by patent citations. *Quarterly Journal of Economics, 108*(3), 577–98. Gs11473.
[20] Azoulay *et al.* (2019), *ibid*.
[21] Sattari, R., Bae, J., Berkes, E., & Weinberg, B. A. (2022). The ripple effects of funding on researchers and output. *Science Advances, 8*(16), article eabb7348. Gs11.
[22] Ripple effect, *Wikipedia*, available at: https://en.wikipedia.org/wiki/Ripple_effect#:-:text=In%20sociology%2C%20the%20ripple%20effect,community%20to%20broaden%20its%20impact.

the ripple effect of funding on a special group of researchers and their publication output. It took two full years for this article to be published, as shown in a publication history note at the end of the article. It has been cited eleven times as of 2023.

A team of four authors contributed to the article. Reza Sattari is a Senior Specialist at Canada Mortgage and Housing Corporation. Jung Bae is a Manager at KPMG Economic Services. Enrico Berkes is Pausch Endowed Assistant Professor of Economics at the University of Maryland Baltimore County, with a main research area in innovation and urban Growth. Bruce Weinberg is Eric Byron Fix-Monda Endowed Professor at Ohio State University, with expertise in labor economics and innovation. His h-index is 41. He and his collaborators have published multiple articles on grantology.[23]

The article was published fairly recently in *Science Advances*, which is an open-access multidisciplinary journal published by the American Association for the Advancement of Science, like *Proceedings of the National Academy of Sciences of the United States of America*. It publishes impactful research papers and reviews in all areas of science, in both disciplinary-specific and broad, interdisciplinary areas. Its impact factor was 14.14 in 2023.

Highlights
This article is an empirical paper and has a rather typical structure with a slightly different order from those published in *Science* or *Nature*. The major sections include: Introduction, Results, Discussion, Materials and Methods (data, regression). Using unique *matched* UMETRICS data on people employed on research projects and strong data on biomedical publications, this article shows that NIH funding stimulates research by supporting the teams that conducted it. The scientific productivity of both principal investigators (PIs) and other faculty members is heavily affected by funding, similarly for trainees and staff. The authors found that the largest effects of funding on research output are ripple effects on publications that do not include PIs. From the grant impact perspective, this article offers several insights.

---

[23] Weinberg, B. A., Owen-Smith, J., Rosen, R. F., Schwarz, L., Allen, B. M., Weiss, R. E. *et al.* (2014). Science funding and short-term economic activity. *Science*, *344*(6179), 41–3; Chang, W. Y., Cheng, W., Lane, J., & Weinberg, B. (2019). Federal funding of doctoral recipients: What can be learned from linked data. *Research Policy*, *48*(6), 1487–92; Goldschlag, N., Bianchini, S., Lane, J., Sola, J., & Weinberg, B. A. (2016). Research funding and regional economies. US Census Bureau Center for Economic Studies Paper No. CES-WP-16–32.

First, the impacts of grant funding are often through diverse effects (e.g. the Matthew effect, the spillover effect, and the displacement effect).[24] The article shows that grant impacts can be through another effect, the **ripple effect**. Compared with various other typical grant impacts (e.g. scientific, societal, and economic impacts), the article examined the unique training effect of funding on trainees and staff involved in grants rather than PIs, Co-PIs, senior personnel, and postdocs. Furthermore, extensive studies examined the impacts of training grants on early-career investigators and postdocs.[25] However, the study empirically demonstrates that the largest effects of funding on research output are ripple effects on publications by **trainees and staff** employed on funded projects rather than by PIs and Co-PIs. These are the unique contributions of the article to the grant impacts literature.

Second, the study generated **convincing evidence** of the ripple effect with a thoughtful design. (1) To address what science funding supports, the analysis breaks down the direct costs of a grant into three components: employees of all types, sub-awards to other institutions, and spending on purchased inputs from vendors (e.g. materials, supplies, and travel). They found that spending on employees is the largest cost, around 68 percent of the total direct cost, and the sub-award is the second largest, around 10 percent of the total direct cost. (2) To address what science funding produces, the analysis focused on post-award publications as the target science output. Specifically, they used the independent variable, being total NIH funding in the seven years, and the dependent variable, being the number of unique publications in a year by personnel employed on a PI's grant. It was found that, overall, there are around **0.80 additional publications per $100,000** in funding. (3) To address who science funding supports, the article divided grant personnel into six types: faculty (PIs and other faculty), postdocs, graduate students, undergraduate students, research staff, and other staff (e.g. technical support, clinical staff, and instructional staff). Among these six types of personnel, the faculty understandably generated

---

[24] Merton, R. K. (1968). The Matthew effect in science: The reward and communication systems of science are considered. *Science, 159*(3810), 56–63. Gs11477; Myers, K. R., & Lanahan, L. (2022). Estimating spillovers from publicly funded R&D: Evidence from the US Department of Energy. *American Economic Review, 112*(7), 2393–423. Gs77; Jacob & Lefgren (2011), The impact of research grant funding, note 15 above.

[25] Jacob & Lefgren (2011), The impact of NIH postdoctoral training grants, note 15 above; Tham, W. Y., Staudt, J., Perlman, E. R., & Cheng, S. D. (2024). Scientific talent leaks out of funding gaps. *arXiv preprint arXiv:2402.07235*. Gs2; Guo, L., Wang, Y., & Li, M. (2024). Exploration, exploitation and funding success: Evidence from junior scientists supported by the Chinese Young Scientists Fund. *Journal of Informetrics, 18*(2), article 101492.

the largest effect, with around **0.25 additional publications per $100,000**. However, the effects on publications by graduate students, undergraduates, research staff, and non-research staff together are around **0.26 additional publications per $100,000**. Here, we can see the ripple effect on publications that were generated by the graduate students, undergraduates, research staff, and non-research staff through a funded project.

Last, the most obvious practical implication of the study to new grant writers is that we should participate in various types of grant projects, even with minor or marginal roles (e.g. volunteer helpers, non-paid assistants, or lab administrators). Being PIs or Co-PIs is, of course, important and impactful. However, through the ripple effects, we can benefit tremendously in our own conference presentations, journal publications, small internal grants, and many other research outcomes. As for the implications for funders, they should consider how funding ripples through a wide range of people, including trainees and staff, who work on various funded projects.

3.3 Bloch et al. (2014): Positive Career Impacts

Overview

The next article[26] we will study is titled "Competitive research grants and their impact on career performance." Clearly, we know now that the article will examine the relationship between grant funding and career performance, and without doubt we need to know later on how the authors defined competitive grants and career performance and how they analyzed how competitive grants are related to career performance. The article has been cited 124 times as of 2023.

Three Danish authors wrote the article. The first author, Carter Bloch, is a Professor of Political Science at Aarhus University of Demark. He has published multiple articles in grantology[27] and his h-index is 34.

---

[26] Bloch, C., Graversen, E. K., & Pedersen, H. S. (2014). Competitive research grants and their impact on career performance. *Minerva*, 52(1), 77–96. Gs124.

[27] Bloch, C., Sørensen, M. P., Graversen, E. K., Schneider, J. W., Schmidt, E. K., Aagaard, K., *et al.* (2014). Developing a methodology to assess the impact of research grant funding: A mixed methods approach. *Evaluation & Program Planning, 43*, 105–17; Bloch, C., & Sørensen, M. P. (2015). The size of research funding: Trends and implications. *Science & Public Policy, 42*(1), 30–43; Bloch, C., & Schneider, J. W. (2016). Performance-based funding models and researcher behavior: An analysis of the influence of the Norwegian Publication Indicator at the individual level. *Research Evaluation, 25*(4), 371–82; Schneider, J. W., Aagaard, K., & Bloch, C. W. (2016). What happens when national research funding is linked to differentiated publication counts? A comparison of the Australian and Norwegian publication-based funding models. *Research Evaluation, 25*(3), 244–56; Aagaard, K.,

The second author, Ebbe Graversen, is an Associate Professor at Aarhus University of Demark, with an h-index of 14. He co-authors with Carter Block several articles in grantology.[28] The final author, Heidi Pedersen, is also from Aarhus University.

The article was published in 2014, over a decade ago, in *Minerva*. Literarily, Minerva is the ancient Roman goddess of wisdom and justice. As a journal, *Minerva* has the full title, *Minerva: A Review of Science, Learning and Policy*. It has covered the sociological study of scientific knowledge and research since 1962. It has published the study of ideas, traditions, cultures, and institutions in science, higher education, and research, including tens of articles related to grantology. Its impact factor was 3.1 in 2023 and its publisher is Springer Nature.

Highlights
The article is an empirical study with a mixed method, combining quantitative econometric analysis with in-depth qualitative interviews. It has six major sections: Introduction, Literature review, Quantitative and qualitative methodology, Data, Analysis, and Conclusion.

From the grant impact perspective, we have the following highlights.

First, the major quantitative finding on the **career effects of grants** is inspiring. It was found that research grants have important positive effects on academic faculty's career advancement (e.g. from postdoc to assistant professor, from assistant professor to tenure, and from associate professor to full professor). Specifically, it used the grant award data from the Danish Council for Independent Research in the period 2001–7. It used Propensity Score Matching to develop a matched sample of the 582 grant recipients vs. 369 rejected applicants to determine the unbiased true effect of grants on academic careers. In general, the probability for career advancement three years after the grant application is 23 percent for grant recipients and 15 percent for rejected applicants. Specifically, the probability of obtaining a full professorship three years after the grant application is 16 percent for grant recipients and 9 percent for rejected applicants.

Second, the major qualitative finding on the **academic benefits of grants** is interesting. Based on the semi-structured interviews with a

---

Bloch, C., & Schneider, J. W. (2015). Impacts of performance-based research funding systems: The case of the Norwegian Publication Indicator. *Research Evaluation*, 24(2), 106–17.

[28] Bloch, C., & Graversen, E. K. (2012). Additionality of public R&D funding for business R&D – A dynamic panel data analysis. *World Review of Science, Technology & Sustainable Development*, 9(2–4), 204–20; Bloch, C., & Graversen, E. K. (2008). Additionality of public R&D funding in business R&D. Danish Centre for Studies in Research and Research Policy, University of Aurhus.

random sample of twenty grant recipients, they found that, besides the scientific impacts of grants (e.g. an increase in publications, research management experience, collaboration opportunities, and internationalization scope), grants do impact their academic careers through heightened status, increased recognition, expanded networking, securing more grants, and even experiencing a "snowball effect," namely, following funding, researchers have experienced an increased demand to participate in conferences, give presentations of their research, and act as peer reviewers.

Third, there is an **extensive literature** on the impacts of funding on researchers in their early careers, suggesting the importance of grants during this career phase.[29] However, there is a line of studies that have examined the eminent scholars in their later careers, indicating exceptional work was often unfunded.[30]

Last, based on quantitative and qualitative evidence rather than personal experience and subjective intuition, there exist positive effects of securing grants at different career stages. For new grant writers in the early stage of their careers, this study **motivates** us to plan our career development and pursue our research grants.

---

[29] Connelly, M. T., Sullivan, A. M., Chinchilla, M., Dale, M. L., Emans, S. J., Nadelson, C. C. et al. (2017). The impact of a junior faculty fellowship award on academic advancement and retention. *Academic Medicine*, *92*(8), 1160–7. Gs18; McGroarty, E., Jimenez, T. R., Linley, J., Li, Y., Granberry-Russell, P., & Williams, K. P. (2014). External funding: Impact on promotion and retention of STEM assistant professors. *Journal of Academic & Business Ethics*, *8*, 1–16. Gs2; Saygitov, R. T. (2014). The impact of funding through the RF president's grants for young scientists (the field–medicine) on research productivity: A quasi-experimental study and a brief systematic review. *PLoS One*, *9*(1), article e86969. Gs12; Scott Van Epps, J., & Younger, J. G. (2011). Early career academic productivity among emergency physicians with R01 grant funding. *Academic Emergency Medicine*, *18*(7), 759–62. Gs11; van den Besselaar, P., & Sandström, U. (2015). Early career grants, performance, and careers: A study on predictive validity of grant decisions. *Journal of Informetrics*, *9*(4), 826–38. Gs217; Hussinger, K., & Carvalho, J. N. (2022). The long-term effect of research grants on the scientific output of university professors. *Industry & Innovation*, *29*(4), 463–87. Gs7.

[30] Tatsioni, A., Vavva, E., & Ioannidis, J. P. (2010). Sources of funding for Nobel Prize-winning work: Public or private? *FASEB Journal*, *24*(5), 1335–9; Elliott, T. R. (2016). External funding and competing visions for academic counseling psychology. *The Counseling Psychologist*, *44*(4), 525–35; Nicholson, J. M., & Ioannidis, J. P. (2012). Conform and be funded. *Nature*, *492*(7427), 34–6. Gs215; Patsopoulos, N. A., Ioannidis, J. P., & Analatos, A. A. (2006). Origin and funding of the most frequently cited papers in medicine: Database analysis. *British Medical Journal*, *332*(7549), 1061–4. Gs2; Stavropoulou, C., Somai, M., & Ioannidis, J. P. (2019). Most UK scientists who publish extremely highly-cited papers do not secure funding from major public and charity funders: A descriptive analysis. *PLoS One*, *14*(2), article e0211460. Gs16; Lilienfeld, S. O., Bowes, S. M., Strother, A. N., Liu, C. J., Costello, T. H., Norton, K. A. et al. (2022). On the association between grants and scholarly achievement among the world's most eminent psychologists. *Current Psychology*, *42*(6), 1–12. Gs0.

3.4 Payne & Siow (2003): Complex Institutional Impacts

Overview

This article is titled "Does federal research funding increase university research output?"[31] Clearly, it essentially assesses the institutional impact of grants from the scientific research perspective. It has been cited 289 times as of 2023, among the highest on the specific topic.[32]

The first author of the article is A. Abigail Payne, currently the Ronald Henderson Professor at the University of Melbourne and Director of Melbourne Institute: Applied Economic & Social Research. Her major research areas are in public economics and economics of education and her h-index is 26. She has published multiple articles on grants and thus researchers in grantology should follow her work. The second author is Aloysius Siow, Professor of Economics at the University of Toronto. Her main research areas are economics of the family and labor economics and her h-index is 27.

The article was published in 2003 in *Advanced in Economic Analysis & Policy*. The journal publishes studies that use microeconomics to analyze issues in business, consumer behavior, and public policy, with practical implications for areas such as antitrust policy, pollution, health, education, trade, taxation, labor, and growth. It had an impact factor of 4.444 in 2023, and was published by Berkeley Electronic Press.

Highlights

This article is an economic analysis. It has five major sections: Empirical framework, Congress and Federal R&D Funding of Universities, Other data, Results (Effect of Funding on Articles Published, Effect of Federal Funding on Citations to Articles Published, Effect of Federal Funding on Patents, Effect of Federal Funding on Faculty Salary), and Conclusion.

From the perspective of grant impacts, especially institutional impacts, we can highlight two key points.

First, the article has **thoughtful methods** for data collection and data analysis. The study aimed to examine the impacts of federal R&D funding as the

---

[31] Payne, A. A., & Siow, A. (2003). Does federal research funding increase university research output? *Advances in Economic Analysis & Policy*, 3(1), 1–24. Gs289.
[32] Byrne, M. M., Losso, I. S., & Koniaris, L. G. (2010). What is the institutional financial impact of an MD-PhD program without extramural funding? *Teaching & Learning in Medicine*, 22(1), 56–9. Gs5; Himanen, L., Auranen, O., Puuska, H. M., & Nieminen, M. (2009). Influence of research funding and science policy on university research performance: A comparison of five countries. *Science & Public Policy*, 36(6), 419–30. Gs81; Auranen, O., & Nieminen, M. (2010). University research funding and publication performance – an international comparison. *Research Policy*, 39(6), 822–34. Gs673.

3 Scientific Knowledge: Impacts

key independent variable on the US research university's research output as the key dependent variable. The studies chose seventy-one public and private research universities in the United States, such as UC Berkeley, University of Michigan, Harvard University, and Princeton University. They used two innovative methods. First, given the large diversity in research capabilities among universities, an estimated correlation between funding and research output will be primarily dominated by differences in research capabilities across universities themselves (e.g. $1 million of funding might generate significant research outputs at a university, but could be mainly due to the existing excellent research capacity of that university), rather than a true relation between funding and research output. To control for this university diversity effect, the study used alumni affiliation on the US congressional appropriations committees as a measure of federal R&D funding. Second, instead of analyzing the funding-output relations at a given year cross-sectionally, the study used longitudinal panel data to estimate the causal effect of change in funding on change in research output over multiple years.

Second, the article presents interesting evidence showing a **complex picture** of the institutional impacts of federal grants on research universities' scientific achievements in the United States. It was found that: (1) the impact on article publications and faculty salaries is strong: an increase of $1 million in federal research funding results in eleven to eighteen more articles and $353,000 more in faculty salaries at a research university; (2) the impact on citations as a measure of quality of the published papers has two slightly different results using two methods: federal funding reduces the quality of research or federal funding does not produce higher quality research; and (3) the impact on patents is either no impact or a slightly positive impact from an increase in federal funding, while multiple issues (e.g. non-patentable research also receives funding, by Congress, federally funded patents could not be issued to universities before the Bayh-Dole Act of 1980) exist in the analysis.

3.5 King (2004): Diverse National Impacts

Overview

This article is titled "The scientific impact of nations: What different countries get for their research spending."[33] It is one of the most cited international studies on the scientific impact of research funding. As a classic paper in grantology, it has been cited 1,807 times as of 2023.

---

[33] King, D. A. (2004). The scientific impact of nations: What different countries get for their research spending *Nature, 430*(6997), 311–16. Gs1807.

The author of the article is Sir David King.[34] He was previously the United Kingdom's Chief Scientific Advisor from 2000 to 2007. He was Head of the Department of Chemistry at Cambridge University from 1993 to 2000. Sir David King has published over 500 papers on science and policy, for which he has received numerous awards and holds twenty-two Honorary Degrees from universities around the world. He became a Fellow of the Royal Society in 1991 and a Foreign Fellow of the American Academy of Arts and Sciences in 2002. He was knighted in 2003.

Highlights
The article was published in 2004 as a featured article in *Nature*. It is seven print pages long (a long article for *Nature*) and has seven major sections: Introduction, The premier league, Dividing disciplines, Bang for the buck, Fuelling economic growth, An unequal world, and Top of the class. From the perspective of national impacts of grant funding, we can highlight the following key points of the article.

First, right in the first paragraph, the author specifies that his article was substantially influenced by May's 1997 classic paper.[35] We have discussed May's paper in Chapter 1. Both May and King have made extraordinary contributions to the grant impact literature by **pioneering a rigorous international study paradigm** of comparing different countries on the impacts of their scientific investment on article publications and article citations. This should be the most important value of this article.

Second, the article used a **particularly large dataset**. It studied thirty-one countries that accounted for more than 98 percent of the world's highly cited papers in 2004, whereas the world's remaining 162 countries contributed less than 2 percent in total. The citation data include all fields of science and engineering from more than 8,000 journals in thirty-six languages between 1993 and 2002.

Third, the study **adapted a series of metrics** for scientific investment input and scientific outputs to study funding impacts. Specifically, it examined: (1) how private sector R&D spending is related to the output of PhDs and researchers; (2) how the national GDP as the function of the national wealth intensity is related to national science citation intensity as measured by the ratio of the citations to all papers; and (3) how the

---

[34] David King (chemist), *Wikipedia*, available at: https://en.wikipedia.org/wiki/David_King_(chemist).
[35] May, R. M. (1997). The scientific wealth of nations. *Science*, 275(5301), 793–6. Gs887; May, R. M. (1998). The scientific investments of nations. *Science*, 281(5373), 49–51. Gs94; Macilwain, C. (2010). Science economics: What science is really worth. *Nature*, 465(7299), 682–4. Gs154.

percentage of GDP spent on publicly funded R&D and the percentage of GDP spent on higher education R&D are related to Citations per unit GDP, Publications per researcher, Citations per researcher, and Citations per unit Higher Education R&D. With these metrics, different scientific investments of different countries were found to impact scientific outputs, but through various pathways.

Fourth, the article pointed out **three important issues** for future study of funding impacts. Future research should examine: (1) lag effects between changes in research funding and outputs (publications) and between outputs and their impact; (2) the complex relations between the input and the output using multivariate models; and (3) international spillover effects that raising one country's expenditure may increase output in other countries through direct collaboration across counties.

3.6 Salter & Martin (2001): Substantial Economic Impacts

Overview

The article is titled "The economic benefits of publicly funded basic research: A critical review."[36] The title indicates that it examines economic impacts; it focuses on basic research supported by public funders; and it is a review. It is one of the highest cited articles on the economic effects of grants, with a citation of 2,074 as of 2023.

The article was written by two distinguished scholars, at that time working in the well-known Science Policy Research Unit (SPRU)[37] at the University of Sussex. The first author is Ammon Salter, now a Professor of Technology and Innovation Management at the University of Warwick. His main research area is innovation studies and his h-index is 63. He and his collaborators have published multiple articles on grantology.[38] He is a

---

[36] Salter, A. J., & Martin, B. R. (2001). The economic benefits of publicly funded basic research: A critical review. *Research Policy*, 30(3), 509–32. Gs2074.
[37] Schot, J., & Steinmueller, W. E. (2019). Transformative change: What role for science, technology and innovation policy? An introduction to the 50th Anniversary of the Science Policy Research Unit (SPRU) Special Issue. *Research Policy*, 48(4), 843–8. Gs29; Soete, L. (2019). Science, technology and innovation studies at a crossroad: SPRU as case study. *Research Policy*, 48(4), 849–57. Gs65; Nelson, R. R. (1959). The simple economics of basic scientific research. *Journal of Political Economy*, 67(3), 297–306. Gs5255; Science Policy Research Unit, *Wikipedia*, available at: https://en.wikipedia.org/wiki/Science_Policy_Research_Unit.
[38] Martin, B., Salter, A., & Hicks, D. (1996). *The Relationship between Publicly Funded Basic Research and Economic Performance*, University of Sussex, Science Policy Research Unit. Gs112; Martin, B. R., Hicks, D., & Salter, A. (1996). *The Relationship between Publicly Funded Basic Research and Economic Performance: A SPRU Review*, Science Policy Research Unit, University of Sussex. Gs107; Salter, A., D'Este, P., Pavitt, K., Scott, A., Martin, B., Geuna, A. et al. (2000). Talent,

co-editor of *Research Policy*. He has also been a PI or Co-PI on several million pounds of external research funding, from the Economic and Social Research Council, Engineering and Physical Sciences Research Council, and European Commission. The second author, Ben Martin, is now a Professor of Science and Technology Policy Studies at the University of Sussex Business School. His h-index is 60. He has co-published another well-cited article on grantology.[39]

The article was published in 2001 in *Research Policy*, which is a leading journal that publishes studies on policy, management, and economic studies of science, technology, and innovation. Its impact factor was 7.2 in 2022 and the publisher is Elsevier. It has published articles on grantology.

Highlights
This is a **review** article, a type of article that *Research Policy* does not often publish. It has six major sections: Introduction, Definition and scope, Conceptual and methodological overview, Relationship between publicly funded research and economic growth (this is the core of the article, discussing return rates and spillovers and localization), The main types of benefits (knowledge, graduates, instruments, networks, technologic solutions, and new firms), and Conclusion. From the perspective of economic impacts of grants, we can highlight several key points.

First, the article is one of the **most-cited** review articles or a citation classic on the economic impacts of grants. It is a standalone good example of the intellectual impacts of a journal article. Even though it was published in 2001, twenty-two years ago, this article is still well-cited at present (e.g. in the last five years, there have been about 100 new citations per year).

Second, the economic impact of grants is a complex and critical topic in grantology. As suggested by the article title, the review **wisely specifies its focus**, namely, concentrating on the positive economic impacts of grants but not negative economic impacts, on public grants but not private grants, on basic research but not applied research, and on critical review rather than a narrative or systematical review.

Third, its review of the economic benefits of public grants on basic research is **particularly thorough and comprehensive**. The authors conceptually link economic benefits with broad concepts of information, knowledge, innovation, research, and technology. The two major findings

not technology: The impact of publicly funded research on innovation in the UK. Science Policy Research Unit, University of Sussex, UK.
[39] Geuna, A., & Martin, B. R. (2003). University research evaluation and funding: An international comparison. *Minerva*, *41*(4), 277–304. Gs996.

of the review include the following: (1) Based on the econometric research literature, the economic benefits are particularly substantial. For instance, the **private rate of return** to private investment of basic research from research projects to organizations ranged between 10 and 43 percent, and the **social rate of return** to private investment of basic research from research projects to the whole society ranged between 10 and 160 percent. Similarly, for public investment in basic research, the **rate of return** ranged between 20 and 67 percent, suggesting that publicly funded basic research has a large positive return, although it is relatively smaller than privately funded basic research. Furthermore, econometric studies also suggest the spillover effect. The spillover effect occurs when governmental funding to research centers spreads its benefits to local industrial firms or other sectors (e.g. increasing collaborations, increasing citations, and increasing patents). (2) Based on the literature using surveys and case studies, there are six types of benefits from publicly funded research to economic growth: increasing the stock of useful knowledge; training skilled graduates; creating new scientific instrumentation and methodologies; forming networks and stimulating social interaction; increasing the capacity for scientific and technological problem-solving; and creating new firms. Thus, the economic benefits of public grants for basic research take a variety of forms rather than follow a simple model.

Fifth, the authors insightfully reviewed the work of **Paul Romer**, the University Professor in Economics at New York University. Seventeen years later, Paul Romer won the 2018 Nobel Prize in Economic Sciences for his work on the role of knowledge, innovative ideas, and technologies in economic growth. Here, we can see evidence again that grantology is an interdisciplinary field, and economics, like sociology, plays a critical role.

3.7 Bornmann (2013): Increasingly Important Societal Impacts

After studying a review article on the economic impacts of grants, let us now discuss another review article, this time on societal impacts.

Overview

This article is titled "What is societal impact of research and how can it be assessed? A literature survey."[40] The title delivers two messages about the article: It will review two topics, what the societal impact of research is and

---

[40] Bornmann, L. (2013). What is societal impact of research and how can it be assessed? A literature survey. *Journal of the American Society for Information Science & Technology*, 64(2), 217–33. Gs763.

how to assess societal impact; and it is a common narrative review. Societal impacts are complex, perhaps even more complex than economic impacts, so this thoughtful review provides useful insights into this topic.

The author, Lutz Bornmann, is a sociologist of science in the Administrative Headquarters of the Max Planck Society. His main research areas are quantitative science studies and quantitative research evaluation. For his outstanding contributions to the fields of quantitative studies of science, he received the Derek de Solla Price Memorial Medal in 2019. His h-index is 87, indicating he is a highly productive researcher. He has published more than thirty articles on grantology (e.g. societal impacts and gender differences in grant review).[41] Students and researchers in grantology should therefore closely follow his research.

The article was published in 2013, over a decade ago, in the *Journal of the American Society for Information Science & Technology* (JASIST). It was published on behalf of the Association for Information Science and Technology. For more than half a century, JASIST has provided intellectual leadership by publishing original research that focuses on the production, discovery, recording, storage, representation, retrieval, presentation, manipulation, dissemination, use, and evaluation of information. Its impact factor was 2.8 in 2023. Its publisher is Wiley, one of the three largest academic publishers, along with Elsevier and Springer Nature.

Highlights
The article is a long and comprehensive review. It has three major sections: Introduction, Societal impact assessment in research and application, and

---

[41] Bornmann, L. (2012). Measuring the societal impact of research: Research is less and less assessed on scientific impact alone – we should aim to quantify the increasingly important contributions of science to society. *EMBO Reports, 13*(8), 673–6. Gs385; Bornmann, L. (2014). Validity of altmetrics data for measuring societal impact: A study using data from Altmetric and F1000Prime. *Journal of Informetrics, 8*(4), 935–50. Gs202; Bornmann, L., Haunschild, R., & Marx, W. (2016). Policy documents as sources for measuring societal impact: How often is climate change research mentioned in policy-related documents? *Scientometrics, 109*(3), 1477–95. Gs140; Bornmann, L., & Marx, W. (2014). How should the societal impact of research be generated and measured? A proposal for a simple and practicable approach to allow interdisciplinary comparisons. *Scientometrics, 98*, 211–19. Gs121; Bornmann, L., & Haunschild, R. (2017). Does evaluative scientometrics lose its main focus on scientific quality by the new orientation towards societal impact? *Scientometrics, 110*(2), 937–43. Gs99; Bornmann, L., Mutz, R., & Daniel, H. D. (2007). Gender differences in grant peer review: A meta-analysis. *Journal of Informetrics, 1*(3), 226–38. Gs418; Marsh, H. W., Bornmann, L., Mutz, R., Daniel, H. D., & O'Mara, A. (2009). Gender effects in the peer reviews of grant proposals: A comprehensive meta-analysis comparing traditional and multilevel approaches. *Review of Educational Research, 79*(3), 1290–326. Gs205; Bornmann, L., Mutz, R., & Daniel, H. D. (2009). The influence of the applicants' gender on the modeling of a peer review process by using latent Markov models. *Scientometrics, 81*(2), 407–11. Gs17.

Discussion. Its second section is the main body of the article and includes four sub-sections: National evaluation systems, Criteria used in the grant peer-review processes, Studies which assess societal impact, and Projects to find possible societal impact indication. From the perspective of grant impacts, we can highlight several key points.

First, the article outlines **major changes** in research investment impacts. Before the 1980s, research investment was automatically assumed to have inherent positive impacts. In the late 1980s, research investment was demanded to assess scientific impacts specifically (labeled as Model 1). Since the 1990s, research investment was tasked with broadly demonstrating societal impacts (labeled Model 2).

Second, the article explains that the concept of societal impacts of research is **particularly complex**. A fairly long list of different terms has been introduced to refer to the societal impact, for example, third-stream activities, societal benefits, societal quality, usefulness, public values, knowledge transfer, and societal relevance. These diverse terms essentially concern four types of societal impact from scientific investment: social (e.g. stimulating new approaches to various social issues), cultural (e.g. contributing to cultural preservation), environmental (e.g. reducing pollution), and economic (e.g. improving productivity). Given the conceptual complexity of societal impacts, there exist various challenges to examining them, for example: distinguishing different types of societal impacts conceptually and practically, assessing the causality of the impact, identifying impacting factors, considering its long-term impact, and determining its global dimension, choosing diverse models, and assessing both positive and negative impacts. These challenges render the assessment of societal impacts difficult.

Third, the article reviews the existing policy documents and research literature on **assessing societal impacts**. (1) Multiple countries assess the societal impact through national evaluation systems. For example, the Netherlands includes social, economic, and cultural impacts of research as grant assessment criteria; the United Kingdom's Research Excellence Framework includes social, economic, and cultural benefits as impact elements. (2) Funding agencies assess applications with the societal impact criteria. For example, the NSF is the first grant agency to use the broad impact criteria in the 1990s. Other funding agencies include the NIH, the National Sciences and Engineering Research Council of Canada, the Dutch Technology Foundation, and the European Commission Framework Programme. (3) The economic literature and survey literature quantitatively estimate the rate of social benefits, reporting that the rate of return of public and private research investment to social benefit ranged between 10 and 67 percent. (4) The indicator literature shows multiple methods have been used to identify, assess, and compare societal impacts. For example, universities identified and developed different types of major indicators of societal impacts, including technology commercialization (e.g. patenting activities), entrepreneurial activities (e.g. joint ventures, spin-offs, start-ups, and incubators), and advisory work (e.g. presenting to funders or attending advisory meetings). (5) An initial typology of societal impacts was proposed, with eleven dimensions: science (e.g. research activities), technology (e.g. services), economy (e.g. investments), culture (e.g. attitudes), society (e.g. welfare), policy (e.g. national security), organization (e.g. planning), health (e.g. health system), environment (e.g. climate and meteorology), symbolic (e.g. notoriety), and training (e.g. pedagogical tools).

Last, there are **practical implications** for new grant writers. We should understand the current trend to emphasize societal impacts by funders, know the importance and challenge of generating societal impacts, and plan societal impacts well in our grant proposals.

3.8 Thyer (2011): Negative Impacts

Overview

The article is titled "Harmful effects of federal research grants."[42] It has been cited twenty-three times and is one of the highest-cited articles on the topic of the negative effects of grants.[43]

The author of the article is Bruce Thyer, a Distinguished Research Professor at Florida State University. His main research areas include research methods, social work, psychology, mental health, and evidence-based practice. His h-index is 56.

The article was published in 2011 in *Social Work Research*, which is an official journal of the National Association of Social Workers. It publishes exemplary research on social work practice. Its publisher is Oxford University Press and its impact factor was 1.20 in 2023.

---

[42] Thyer, B. A. (2011). Harmful effects of federal research grants. *Social Work Research*, *35*(1), 3–7. Gs23.
[43] Martin, J. J. (2020). Grants: The good, the bad, the ugly, and the puzzling. *Kinesiology Review*, *10*(1), 18–28. Gs4; Thelwall, M., Kousha, K., Abdoli, M., Stuart, E., Makita, M., Font-Julián, C. I. *et al.* (2023). Is research funding always beneficial? A cross-disciplinary analysis of UK research 2014–20. *Quantitative Science Studies*, *4*(2), 501–34. Gs10; Howard, M. O. (2011). Harmful effects of federal research grants: A rejoinder. *Social Work Research*, *35*(1), 3–7. Gs6; Corvo, K., Chen, W. Y., & Selmi, P. (2011). Federal funding of social work research: High hopes or sour grapes? *Social Work*, *56*(3), 225–33. Gs7.

Highlights

This is a guest **editorial** along with a rejoinder.[44] It has only five pages, but is well-written. From the perspective of negative impacts of grants, we can highlight several key points.

First, the author thoughtfully pointed out that writing, revising, receiving, and executing grants do not always have positive effects, but instead are **often really harmful**. This point is thought-provoking, but might not be widely considered. For example, as shown in the opening section of this chapter, the three initial responses from the new grant writers did not mention a single negative impact of grants, while multiple positive impacts were specified, suggesting positive impacts should be automatically assumed.

Second, the author specified **six harmful effects** of federal research grants: (1) writing grants wastes resources, especially writing unsuccessful grants; (2) federal grant priorities often mismatch our original true passions for research; (3) institutional demands to secure grants distort the quality of teaching, service, and administration; (4) many funded studies have few short- and long-term effects in daily practice; (5) the current national high deficit spending does not justify federal fundings; and (6) the grant review process has major flaws. From the grant impact perspective, these six harmful effects are actually related to negative scientific impacts (2 and 6), negative career impacts (1 and 3), negative economic impacts (5), and negative societal impacts (#4).

Third, this article is primarily based on the author's **observation and experience** in one discipline (i.e. social work), on one type of grant (i.e. federal research grants), and within a university setting (mainly Florida State University). Thus, further research evidence is needed to understand and quantify the negative effects of grants.

Fourth, along with this short editorial, the journal also published a **short rejoinder** by Matthew Howard, the Frank A. Daniels Distinguished Professor of the School of Social Work at the University of North Carolina, Chapel Hill. Howard agreed with Thyer's major points presented in the editorial by choosing to use "costs" rather than "harmful effects" (e.g. various key costs are associated with federal grants), while pointing out several benefits of securing grants (e.g. focusing on large randomized controlled trials, often conducting high-quality peer review, and enhancing social work research).

---

[44] Howard (2011), *ibid.*

Last, the direct **practical implication** for new grant writers is that we should not automatically assume grant activities always have positive impacts, we should be aware of possible negative impacts, and we should make every effort to maximize positive impacts and minimize negative ones.

4 Grantology vs. Journalology: Grant Impacts and Article Impacts

4.1 Grant Impacts

As the defining feature, grant funding is a scientific investment to advance scientific knowledge and improve human life. A good investment must maximize the return and minimize the risk. If we use the input-process-output model[45] to analyze the grant impacts, the input is the number of grants to invest in a project, the process is the pre-award, during-award, and post-award process, and the output is the grant impacts. As discussed in the previous section of this chapter, grant impacts include seven major types: scientific, training, personal career, institutional, national, economic, and social. Each major impact can be divided into smaller subtypes (e.g. scientific impacts usually include the number of publications, the number of citations, and the number of patents). In the real world, we can also distinguish positive grant impacts from negative grant impacts, as well as short-term impacts from long-term impacts. We can also rate the degree of grant impacts, from no impacts, to low, moderate, high, and significantly high.

4.2 Article Impacts

As the defining feature, article publication is to disseminate knowledge. In a sense, article impacts are part of the scientific impacts of grant funding. Thus, grant impacts are much broader and more complex than article impacts. Using the input-process-output model to analyze the article impacts, we can consider the input as the work on writing a manuscript to summarize a completed project, the process is the journal article publication process, and the output is the impacts generated by a published article. In the real world, we can see positive and negative scientific and social impacts generated by articles after publication. We can also observe

---

[45] McGrath, J. E. (1964). *Social Psychology: A Brief Introduction*. Rinehart & Winston. Gs1639.

different degrees of impact that articles can generate, usually indexed quantitatively by the number of citations, as well as the number of views or downloads. Furthermore, citation counts as one of the article-level metrics that can link with author-level indexes (e.g. h-index) and journal-level metrics (e.g. impact factors). Multiple studies have been conducted to examine what makes an article influential.[46]

In summary, comparing grant impacts and article impacts has various important practical implications for new grant writers. (1) Article impacts are relatively simple (e.g. the number of citations), whereas grant impacts are much more complicated (e.g. scientific, personal, institutional, societal, national, economic, and social impacts). (2) Article impacts are not mandatory by a journal or a publisher and almost occur naturally, whereas the impact statement is often required to be included in a grant proposal to be judged for the possibility of funding. To a grant proposal, grant impacts are central rather than marginal. (3) Article impact is relatively straightforward to predict and generate because the research projects have been completed and the only remaining step is to disseminate the findings, whereas grant impacts are difficult to predict since it takes a long scientific exploratory process to complete a funded project and generate various impacts. (4) Article impacts have been studied extensively in bibliometrics, informetrics, webometrics, altmetrics, and scientometrics; however, a series of qualitative indicators of grant impacts have not been developed in grantology, except for economic impacts.

5 Action Suggestions: Understanding and Learning about Grant Impacts

5.1 Understanding the Importance and Complexity of Grant Impacts

In the section on intuitive knowledge, we observed three levels of understanding of the impacts of grants among new grant writers: a low level of understanding, with conceptual confusion about grant goals vs. grant

---

[46] Sternberg, R. J., & Gordeeva, T. (1996). The anatomy of impact: What makes an article influential? *Psychological Science, 7*(2), 69–75. Gs176; Haslam, N., Ban, L., Kaufmann, L., Loughnan, S., Peters, K., Whelan, J. *et al.* (2008). What makes an article influential? Predicting impact in social and personality psychology. *Scientometrics, 76*(1), 169–85; Sternberg, R. J. (1992). Psychological Bulletin's top 10 "hit parade." *Psychological Bulletin, 112*(3), 387–8. Gs76; Baumgartner, H., & Pieters, R. (2000). *The Influence of Marketing Journals: A Citation Analysis of the Discipline and Its Sub-Areas* (No. 2000-123). Gs35.

impacts; a higher level of understanding, with two dimensions of grant impacts, namely, scientific and societal impacts; and the highest level of understanding, with five dimensions of grant impacts, namely, individual, career, institutional, scientific, and societal impacts.

In the section on real-life cases, we learned about four instances: the European Union's requirement of the impact statement, the scientific impacts of NIH grants on the Nobel Prize, a negative career impact on a tenure case, and newly reported national impacts of scientific and engineering investment. These cases demonstrate a few recent grant impact trends in the real world.

In the section on scientific knowledge, we discussed seven articles on seven types of grant impacts: (1) surprisingly small scientific impacts generated by grants; (2) influential training impacts; (3) positive career impacts; (4) complex national impacts on publication and citation; (5) increasingly important societal impacts; (6) substantial economic impacts; and (7) negative impacts. From these articles, we can further see the importance and complexity of grant impacts.

In the section on grantology vs. journalology, we compared grant impacts with article impacts and learned four differences between them: (1) Article impacts are relatively simple, whereas grant impacts are much more complicated. (2) Article impacts are not mandatory by a journal or a publisher and almost occur naturally, whereas the impact statement is often required to be included in a grant proposal. (3) Article impact is relatively straightforward to predict and generate because the research projects have been completed and the only remaining step is to disseminate the results, whereas grant impacts are difficult to predict since it takes a long scientific exploratory process to complete a funded project and generate various impacts. (4) Article impacts have been studied extensively in bibliometrics, informetrics, webometrics, altmetric, and scientometrics; however, a series of qualitative indicators of grant impacts have not yet been developed in grantology, except for economic impacts.

5.2 Learning about Impact Policies, Impact Statements, and Impact Sections

Given the importance and complexity of grant impact, we have the following two action-based suggestions for new grant writers.

First, locate and read two to three impact policies from public and/or private funders to study how funders stress the importance of grant impacts and develop relevant policies and procedures.

Second, locate and read the impact statement section of two to three grant proposals to learn how to design and write an effective impact statement.

Third, draw a mind-map or develop an outline of the potential impacts of your proposals in order to develop a strong impact section.

PART III
Conclusion

CHAPTER 10

Pursuing Grants in the Future

Outline

1 Intuitive Knowledge — 328
  1.1 How Long Will It Take to Become a Successful Grant Writer? — 328
  1.2 What Kinds of Careers Will Grant Professionals Have? — 329
  1.3 What Will Be the Future of Grantology in the Next Ten Years? — 330
2 Real-Life Cases: From Grant Writers and Grant Professionals, to Grant Scholars — 331
  2.1 Growth of Grant Writers: Four Examples — 331
  2.2 Careers of Grant Professionals: Five Examples — 333
  2.3 The Future of Grant Scholarship: Two Examples — 335
3 Scientific Knowledge: From Three Stages of Growth to Two Options for Distributing Grants — 337
  3.1 Lauer *et al.* (2017): Three Stages of Development of Grant Writers — 337
  3.2 Kulage *et al.* (2020): Developing Early-Career Grant Writers — 339
  3.3 Goodman (2019): Fifty Years of Grant Professionals as a Career — 341
  3.4 Vidal *et al.* (2015): Impacts of Specialized Support by Grant Managers — 343
  3.5 Ioannidis (2011): Fund Researchers rather than Projects — 345
  3.6 Aagaard, Kladakis, & Nielsen (2020): Concentrating or Dispersing Research Funding — 347
4 Grantology vs. Journalology: Comparing the Future in Growth, Career, and Scholarship — 350
  4.1 Growth: Grant Writers vs. Article Writers — 350
  4.2 Career: Grant Professionals vs. Journalists — 351
  4.3 Scholarship: Journalology vs. Grantology — 351
5 Action Suggestions: Understanding and Planning the Future as Grant Writers, Grant Professionals, and Grant Scholars — 352
  5.1 Understanding the Future as Grant Writers, Grant Professionals, and Grant Scholars — 352
  5.2 Planning the Future as Grant Writers, Grant Professionals, and Grant Scholars — 353

10 Pursuing Grants in the Future

This final chapter, different from the previous chapters, is primarily future-oriented. It discusses three ways of pursuing grants in the future, namely, as a grant writer, as a grant professional, and as a grantology scholar. The book will have to end here, but we can then better foresee and plan our future in the real world.

1 Intuitive Knowledge

As always, I asked relevant questions to several new grant writers. Below are my three questions and their initial responses.

1.1 How Long Will It Take to Become a Successful Grant Writer?

- Response 1: Three years.
- Response 2: I think there is no exact answer. The time spent can vary depending on many factors. If an individual has good writing ability and sufficient publication experience, I think he/she will be a good grant writer very soon. However, if a novice lacks research experience, it may take a few years to become proficient in grant writing.
- Response 3: I would say it depends. People have different educational backgrounds and life experiences. It may take months to years to learn and practice to become a successful grant writer. Or maybe never.
- Response 4: I think that it is different by the person. That's because the time it takes for a novice to become a successful grant writer depends on various factors, such as their prior writing experience, knowledge of the grant-making process, ability to identify funding sources, understanding of the specific requirements of the grants they are applying for, and even mentors (e.g. advisors or senior colleagues).
- Response 5: It would depend on the degree of a new researcher's experience. This degree could be realized in terms of: (1) how many grants the novice received before; (2) how much experience in participating in grant applications; (3) to what degree the novice has enough research experience in leading, conducting, and manipulating research projects, etc. From my point of view, this might take a couple of years, which also considers the period of **completing** a project that might take a few years, for example, a longitudinal study.
- Response 6: I feel that depends on how we define "successful." Suppose it means becoming professional in grant writing. In that

1 Intuitive Knowledge 329

case, I think after a person formally completes the whole process of grant writing and application (including getting feedback and revising the grant proposal) for two or three grant proposals, that person would already be experienced in grant writing. Suppose it means getting a grant successfully, it depends on many other factors, such as the budget and whether the application is competitive.

As we can see from the above responses, most of these new grant writers used the phrase "it depends on ..." to answer the question, "How long will it take to become a successful grant writer?" A few said it might take a few months to a few years. The first response is three years as the most straightforward and the final response seems to be the most sophisticated because it concerns two groups of people, successful grant professionals and successful grant writers.

1.2 What Kinds of Careers Will Grant Professionals Have?

- Response 1: Professors and academic administration.
- Response 2: I think grant professionals can be faculty in a university or researchers in institutions. Some employees from private companies can also be grant professionals.
- Response 3: They can study specific research fields and also get grants more easily to support their research with their knowledge of getting grants; be the experts who teach people how to apply for and even assist people in regulating their grants; and work as professionals who review grant applications or regulate the grant system.
- Response 4: The grant professionals could work for educational institutions, healthcare facilities, non-profit organizations, or governments.
- Response 5: If I understand correctly, grant professionals could be grant writers, grant managers, grant researchers, and grant developmental directors.
- Response 6: Grant professionals can work in a variety of careers and job roles, such as grant writers, grant managers, program officers, development directors, and fundraising consultants.

The above responses show that these new grant writers have different levels of knowledge about grant professionals. The first three responses are partially incorrect because a professor or a researcher at a university is usually a grant writer, but not a full-time grant professional. The fourth response only pointed out four general areas in which grant professionals may find their jobs, but did not say what kind of jobs or careers they may have. The final two responses are the most knowledgeable, specifying multiple types of careers that grant professionals could have.

1.3 What Will Be the Future of Grantology in the Next Ten Years?

- Response 1: The future of grant writing could become more and more challenging with the increasing number of grant applications. And I also think the diversity and interdisciplinary programs and projects would be prioritized.
- Response 2: It should be more explicitly introduced to the current graduate education system. There should be courses targeting grant writing similar to courses we normally have, such as scholarly writing.
- Response 3: The university may provide some courses to teach students how to apply for grants and be good grant writers. This would be very helpful and fascinating.
- Response 4: The future of grantology, or the study and practice of grant-making and grant-seeking, is likely to be influenced by several factors: changes in the political landscape, economic trends, shifts in people's priorities trends, or even uncontrollable situations (e.g. COVID-19 emergency).
- Response 5: To be honest, I am not sure about the answers to this question since I am not a professional and experienced grant writer, and the future of grantology is subject to many factors such as changes in economic trends, social development and needs, especially under the influence of AI technology. Do you think AI technology, for example, ChatGPT, has an effect on grant applications?
- Response 6: Artificial intelligence will be used in the evaluation of grants in ten years.

Compared with the first two questions, understandably, the last question received the most divergent answers, given that grantology is an emerging field. The first response is off point, mainly addressing grant writing rather than grant research or grantology. The second and third responses both hoped to have formal courses in grantology. Both the fourth and fifth responses thoughtfully pointed out the difficulty in predicting the future of grantology. And the fifth and sixth responses both pointed out the use of AI in the future, either in grant writing or in grant review.

2 Real-Life Cases: Writers, Professionals, & Scholars

Now, using the above intuitive knowledge of the three questions as the baseline, the intellectual objective of this chapter is to improve our knowledge of being a grant writer, a grant professional, and a grant scholar. We will present multiple real-life cases, discuss multiple journal articles, compare the future of grantology and journalology, and offer a few actionable suggestions to conclude our intellectual journey throughout reading this book.

2 Real-Life Cases: From Grant Writers and Grant Professionals, to Grant Scholars

2.1 Growth of Grant Writers: Four Examples

Kendall Powell and Emily Sohn are both excellent freelance journalists in Minneapolis and Lafayette respectively. In 2017, Kendall Powell published a short but well-written essay in *Nature*, titled "The best-kept secrets to winning grants."[1] In 2020, Emily Sohn also published a short but well-written essay in *Nature*, titled "Secrets to writing a winning grant."[2] In these two articles, they vividly described three types of grant writers in the early career, middle career, and late career and provided real-life information on the development of grant writers. Below are four examples from these two articles.

A grant writer in the very early career stage is Aerin Jacob.[3] In 2013, she began her master's program in environmental science at the University of Toronto. As the first grant effort, she applied for a grant from the Natural Sciences and Engineering Research Council of Canada (NSERC). However, it was rejected. She contacted NSERC for feedback and learned that one of the major reasons was her relatively weak undergraduate transcript at the University of Guelph. She decided to strengthen her application by increasing her research experiences, publishing research articles, and obtaining strong letters of recommendation. After two years, on her third try, she finally received the grant from NSERC. This two-year grant writing experience helped her grow in her very early career. Now she is Director of Science and Research at Nature Conservancy of Canada after receiving her PhD at McGill University, completing her postdoc at the University of Victory, and working as a conservation scientist at Yellowstone to Yukon Conservation Initiative.

---

[1] Powell, K. (2017). The best-kept secrets to winning grants. *Nature, 545*(7655), 399–402. Gs10.
[2] Sohn, E. (2020). Secrets to writing a winning grant. *Nature, 577*(7788), 133–5. Gs41.
[3] Aerin Jacob, *LinkedIn*, available at: www.linkedin.com/in/aerinj/details/experience/.

A grant writer in the early-career stage is Peter Negele. He is currently Professor of Anesthesia and Critical Care at the University of Chicago and the editor of *Anesthesiology*.[4] In 2007, he had already earned two early career grants for his lab at Washington University School of Medicine in St. Louis, and one of them was a Clinical Research Curriculum Award (K30) from the National Institutes of Health (NIH). However, when he applied for two major research grants (G01) from the NIH for the first time, both were rejected. He learned that the first proposal for a 10,000-patient clinical trial was too large in scope to be eligible and the second one was not a priority area. In 2015, eight years after the two rejections, he submitted another G01 proposal. Before submitting, he solicited feedback from colleagues, talked with an NIH program officer, added experienced co-investigators, and enhanced the significance and feasibility of the research. This time, on his third attempt, his proposal for a smaller clinical trial was finally funded. It took eight years for him to be an independent investigator with the first G01 grant.

A grant writer in the middle-to-late-career stage is Kylie Ball.[5] She is currently an Emeritus Professor in the School of Exercise and Nutrition Sciences at Deakin University in Melbourne, with a research area in behavioral nutrition and physical activity. Kylie Ball completed her PhD in Public Health at the University of Queensland in 2002. After graduation, she became a Lecturer in Public Health at the University of Queensland in 2002. She received one of the first grants in 2004 and received around two to four grants per year for two decades. She has had more than sixty competitive grants funded for more than $25 million in total and also published around 600 articles with a high h-index of 101. In reflecting on the funding successes and failures that she has experienced in her early and middle career, she said that she had more than 120 proposals rejected. But she did learn very much from these rejected proposals, which led to more successful grants.

A grant writer in the late-career stage is Carol Greider.[6] Carol Greider is the Distinguished Professor of Molecular, Cellular, and Developmental Biology at UC Santa Cruz. She won the Nobel Prize in Physiology or

---

[4] Peter Nagele, MD, MSc, *LinkedIn*, available at: www.linkedin.com/in/peter-nagele-md-msc-05b8021/details/education/; Peter Nagele, *University of Chicago*, available at: https://profiles.uchicago.edu/profiles/display/13396569.

[5] Kylie Ball, *Deakin University*, available at: https://experts.deakin.edu.au/132-kylie-ball/grants; Kylie Ball, *Nature Master Classes*, available at: https://masterclasses.nature.com/kylie--ball/19719134.

[6] Carol Greider, *Nobel Prize*, available at: www.nobelprize.org/womenwhochangedscience/stories/carol-greider.

2 Real-Life Cases: Writers, Professionals, & Scholars 333

Medicine in 2009, with Elizabeth Blackburn and Jack Szostak, "for the discovery of how chromosomes are protected by telomeres and the enzyme telomerase." As a superstar in securing research grants, she has secured about eighty-three grants from the NIH, with a total of $28 million since 1989 after she completed her PhD in molecular biology in 1987 at Berkeley. In total, there are forty-eight R01 grants, twenty-one R37 grants, seven R37 grants, and four T32 grants. However, being a renowned scientist does not always ensure success in grant applications. On the same day that Carol Greider won a Nobel Prize in 2009, she learned that her recently submitted grant proposal was rejected or more precisely was "triaged," that is, it was deemed not worthy even for the panel discussion. She used this anecdote to advise the graduating students to expect both ups and downs in their research careers, but never to be discouraged.

2.2   Careers of Grant Professionals: Five Examples

A career in a federal agency. Jon Lorschis is the Director at the National Institute of General Medical Sciences (NIGMS).[7] He received a BA in Chemistry with Honors in 1990 from Swarthmore College, received a PhD in Biochemistry in 1995 from Harvard University, and completed the Post-doctoral Fellow training in 1999 at Stanford University. From 1999 to 2013, he was first Assistant Professor, then Associate Professor, and finally Professor in the Department of Biophysics and Biophysical Chemistry at Johns Hopkins University School of Medicine. Since 2013, he has been the Director of the NIGMS, overseeing the Institute's budget of $3.2 billion (in FY 2023) and supporting basic research that increases understanding of biological processes for diagnosis, treatment, and prevention of diseases. The NIGMS supported more than 4,800 investigators and more than 5,500 research grants in FY 2023.

A career in a private foundation. Amanda Stanley[8] received a BS in Wildlife Biology from the University of Montana in 1996 and received her PhD in Ecology from the University of Washington in 2005. She was an Ecologist in the Institute for Applied Ecology from 2005 to 2011. For six years, between 2011 and 2017, she was the Program Officer of Conservation Science at Wilburforce Foundation, a private philanthropic organization that supports land, water, and wildlife conservation efforts.

---

[7] NIGMS Director, *National Institute of General Medical Sciences*, available at: www.nigms.nih.gov/about/director.
[8] Amanda Stanley, *LinkedIn*, available at: www.linkedin.com/in/amanda-stanley-64167211/.

As a Program Officer, she used grants to support diverse ways for science to more effectively inform conservation. She partnered with COMPASS to create the Wilburforce Leaders in Conservation Science program and supported eighty leaders from four cohorts through this transformative program. Since 2017, She became the Executive Director of COMPASS, a Seattle-based company that supports and connects diverse science leaders to improve the wellbeing of people and nature.

A career in a research institute. Cheryl Smythe[9] received a BA in Biochemistry from Trinity College Dublin in 1992, received her PhD in Clinical Biochemistry from the University of Cambridge in 1997, and completed a Postdoc at Imperial College London in 2004. Between 2004 and 2022. she worked at Babraham Institute, a UK-based innovative life science research institute, starting as coordinator of the European Science Foundation Research Network on Functional Genomics, then as International Funding Support Officer, and finally as Head of Strategic Research Development. Since 2022, she has been the Head of Scientific Engagement at Altos Labs, a private biotechnology company in California (United States) and Cambridge (United Kingdom).

A career as a grant workshop professional. Like Kylie Ball who moved from being a successful grant writer to a popular grant workshop owner, as discussed in the previous section, John Robertson[10] is currently the managing member and owner of a company, Grant Writers' Seminars and Workshops, LLC (GWSW),[11] a widely known grant-writing company committing to young scientists since 1994 and having more than 250 academic institutions and research institutes as their clients. He graduated with a PhD in Pharmacology and Toxicology at the University of Texas, Austin, in 1999 and completed his postdoc in Toxicology and Cell Biology at Karolinska Institutet of Sweden in 2003. Starting in 2004, he was an Assistant Professor at the University of Kansas Medical Center. After seven years in academia, he moved to become an Associate Member of GWSW for fourteen years and became the Managing Member in 2017. He has won competitive extramural funding from both the NIH and non-federal sources, has served in grant review panels, and was a good mentor for junior faculty grant applicants before he was recruited to GWSW. In addition, he enjoyed playing tennis competitively. Based on the National

---

[9] Cheryl Smythe, *LinkedIn*, available at: www.linkedin.com/in/cherylsmythe/?originalSubdomain=uk.
[10] John Robertson, *LinkedIn*, available at: www.linkedin.com/in/john-robertson-2734638/.
[11] John D. Robertson, *Grant Writers' Seminars & Workshops, LLC*, available at: www.grantcentral.com/about-us/professional-staff/john-d-robertson/.

Tennis Rating Program's classification system that rates tennis players from 1.0 (beginner) to 7.0 (touring pro), his NTRP rating is 4.5!

A career as a grant writer in the non-profit field. Mary Brown[12] graduated from the University of Missouri-Kansas City. As a senior grant writer, she has been running her grant-writing business, MB GrantWriters, since 2001.[13] She has also been working as a freelance grant writer with long-term contracts for TDC Learning Centers, Kansas City Autism Training, Bach Aria Soloists, Unicorn Theatre, and Integrated Behavioral Technologies. In 2016, she moved to a leadership role and started working with associate grant writers to mentor new professionals entering the not-for-profit world. She has spent her entire professional career in the non-profit field. Note that there exists a good job market in the United States for freelance grant writers like Mary Brown.

Generally speaking, the careers of grant professionals are quite diverse, but can be divided into two areas for careers: the grantor-side professionals and the grantee-side professionals. The first three examples in this section showcase various careers working in public and private funders as grantor-side professionals. The last two examples present different career options of having independent or private practice as grantee-side grant professionals. These grant professionals almost always have advanced degrees, accumulate many years of experience, make significant professional contributions, and often transfer from other professions into the grant profession.

2.3 The Future of Grant Scholarship: Two Examples

Future grantology research could be considered in different ways, for example, advancing theories, using true experiment methods, starting a professional association, establishing a journal on grantology, and offering graduate programs. However, as in the previous two sections on grant writers and grant professionals, in this section, we will use two examples to illustrate potential directions of grantology research rather than providing exhaustive but poorly grounded predictions.

One way to study the future of grantology is to explore the current work of excellent research centers on grantology. Here, we can examine the National Bureau of Economic Research's Science of Science Funding

---

[12] Mary Brown, *LinkedIn*, available at: www.linkedin.com/in/mary-brown-69b56127/. Note that there is another Mary Brown who is also a grant writer (www.linkedin.com/in/mary-brown-81665870/).
[13] Again, there is another similar grant writing company, *MB Professional Writing* (www.mbprofessionalwriting.com/), run by Michal Fagan.

initiative, one of the **excellent centers in grantology** in the world.[14] The initiative has been operating since 2019. After five years of annual meetings/institute on the science of science funding, the first meeting in 2024 focused on investments in **early-career scientists**. Around 100 researchers gathered in April and discussed various topics on how to support early-career researchers, including international postdocs, students entering industry careers, female doctoral students, and graduate students. There exists an extensive literature on funding early-career researchers, but the theme in 2024 suggested it should and will be an important research area for future research in grantology. Developing innovative projects and developing promising researchers are essentially the two major missions of many public and private funders.

Another way of considering the future of grantology is to examine the current work of **distinguished scholars** in grantology in the world.[15] Here, we focus on Pierre Azoulay,[16] Professor of Innovation, Entrepreneurship, and Strategic Management at MIT Sloan School. He was introduced in Chapter 1 and now we will attempt to study his current research directions. While his major research focus is on the impact of different funding systems on scientific progress, his two recent papers reveal his most recent research directions. One of his latest research papers is on the complex relationship between **risk and return** in scientific research.[17] This research topic is significant, as it

---

[14] Other excellent centers in grantology in the world include the Technological Innovation, Entrepreneurship, and Strategic Management Group of MIT, the Center for Science of Science and Innovation of Northwestern University, the Danish Centre for Studies in Research and Research Policy of Aarhus University, the Science and Technology Policy Unit of the University of Sussex, the National Science Foundation's National Center for Science and Engineering Statistics, and the NIH's Office of Extramural Research.

[15] Other distinguished scholars in grantology include Danielle Li at MIT, Robert May at Cambridge University, David King at Cambridge University, Cassius James Van Slyke at the NIH, Robert Merton at Columbia University, Arnout van de Rijt at European University Institute, Grit Laudel at Berlin University of Technology, Kristine Kulage at Columbia University, Dashun Wang at Northwestern University, Yang Wang at Xi'an Jiaotong University, Donna Ginther at the University of Kansas, Walter Schaffer at the NIH, Paula Stephon at Georgia State University, Ernest Mason Allen at the NIH, David Markowitz at Michigan State University, Hillary Shulman at Ohio State University, Ulla Connor at Indiana University-Purdue University Indianapolis, Anne Marie Weber-Main at the University of Minnesota, Stephen Cole at State University of New York Stony Brook, Jonathan Cole at Columbia University, Sven Hug at the University of Zurich, Robyn Tamblyn at McGill University, Michael Lauer at the NIH, Brian Jacob at the University of Michigan, Bruce Weinberg Ohio State University, Carter Bloch at Aarhus University of Demark, A. Abigail Payne at the University of Melbourne, Ammon Salter at the University of Warwick, Ben Martin at the University of Sussex, and Lutz Bornmann at the Max Planck Society.

[16] Pierre Azoulay, *MIT Management*, available at: https://mitsloan.mit.edu/faculty/directory/pierre-azoulay.

[17] Greenblatt, W., Maity, S. K., Levy, R. P., & Azoulay, P. 2022. Does grant peer review penalize scientific risk taking? Evidence from the NIH. Working Paper, MIT.

touches on two of the most fundamental concepts of grant funding as scientific investment: risk and return. High-risk scientific projects may be more likely to lead to unexpected breakthroughs and disruptive innovations, but often involve the risks of failure, and they also face challenges in winning necessary support and critical recognition. He and his collaborators found that risky grants are renewed at markedly lower rates than "safer" ones. Another of his latest papers is related to **AI technology**.[18] The paper applies innovation economics to examine how the competitive environment shapes generative AI advances. Although it might not be directly related to grantology, it does send a strong signal that AI technology should and will very likely become a promising area in grantology in the next five to ten years.

3   Scientific Knowledge: From Three Stages of Growth to Two Options for Distributing Grants

3.1   Lauer et al. (2017): Three Stages of Development of Grant Writers

Here, we begin by examining two articles about the development of grant writers. The first is a policy piece, and the second is an empirical study. We will study these two articles in order to gain scientific knowledge of the future of grant writers.

Overview
The first article is titled "The next generation researchers initiative at NIH."[19] It is an Opinion piece introducing the new initiative launched by the NIH in 2017 to develop the young generation of biomedical researchers. This initiative aims to address longstanding challenges faced by researchers trying to embark upon and sustain independent research careers, and to take steps to promote the growth, stability and diversity of the biomedical research workforce.

The three authors of the article are all NIH senior leaders. **Michael Lauer** has been the Director of the Office of Extramural Research and then Deputy Director for Extramural Research at the NIH since 2015.[20]

---

[18]   Azoulay, P., Krieger, J. L., & Nagaraj, A. (2024). Old moats for new models: Openness, control, and competition in generative AI (No. w32474). National Bureau of Economic Research. Gs28.
[19]   Lauer, M., Tabak, L., & Collins, F. (2017). The next generation researchers at NIH. *Proceedings of the National Academy of Sciences*, 114(45), 11801–3. Gs25.
[20]   About us, *NIH Grants & Funding*, available at: https://grants.nih.gov/aboutoer/intro2oer.htm; Immediate Office of the Director (IMOD), *NIH Grants & Funding*, available at: https://grants.nih.gov/aboutoer/oer_offices/imod.htm.

He has two lines of research: cardiology epidemiology in his early medical career; and grant funding, peer review and clinical research in his later administrative career. Lauer won an Arthur S. Flemming Award for exceptional federal service. He has a signature smile as a public face of the NIH in sending letters and news on behalf of the organization. He has published multiple important articles on grants and should thus be considered a leading scholar in grantology. His h-index is 107. **Lawrence Tabak** is a US dentist and biomedical scientist serving as the acting Director of the NIH. He is the principal Deputy Director of the NIH. His research area is glycobiology and science policy, and his h-index 63. He has published several important grant policy papers.[21] **Francis Sellers Collins** is a US physician-geneticist who discovered the genes associated with several diseases and led the Human Genome Project. He was Director of the NIH for twelve years, from 2009 to 2021, serving under three presidents. In February 2022, he joined the Cabinet of Joe Biden as Acting Science Advisor to the President. He published over 500 peer-reviewed articles, including multiple articles in *Science* on grant policy. Students and researchers in grantology should closely follow and carefully study these three authors, especially Michael Lauer.

The article was published in 2017 when the NIH launched the initiative in the *Proceedings of the National Academy of Sciences*. Again, *PNAS* is a journal of the National Academy of Sciences, publishing high-impact original research in natural and social sciences. Its impact factor was 9.4 in 2023.

Highlights
This is a unique and short **Opinion** piece. It has four sections: (1) Introduction; (2) Finding remedies; (3) A new approach; and (4) Funding sources. Obviously, it is a grant policy piece, announcing the Next Generation Researchers Initiatives by NIH senior leaders and presenting the background, the previous efforts, and the specific policy considerations. It is an important article for grantology research in general and grant writer development in particular. From the grant writer development perspective, we can highlight the following two insights.

First, the article formally defines **three stages** of development of grant writers from the perspective of the NIH. The first is early-stage

---

[21] Collins, F. S., & Tabak, L. A. (2014). Policy: NIH plans to enhance reproducibility. *Nature*, 505(7485), 612–13. Gs1256; Bernard, M. A., Johnson, A. C., Hopkins-Laboy, T., & Tabak, L. A. (2021). The US National Institutes of Health approach to inclusive excellence. *Nature Medicine*, 27(11), 1861–4. Gs14.

investigators (ESIs), who are within ten years of the terminal degree or clinical training. The second is early-established investigators (EEIs), who are within ten years of first achieving research independence and planning to sustain the funding. The third is later-career independent investigators, who can successfully and consistently receive a greater proportion of research funding. Each stage takes roughly ten years, covering around thirty years of career development. While empirical evidence is not fully available for this typology, it is based on the NIH's extensive practical experiences and everyday observations and thus is limited to biomedical research that funded by the NIH. We can use this typology as the first benchmark or initial landmark to describe the three-stage development of grant writers' careers. Now, for the first time, we might say that it takes about ten years to become an early-established grant writer in basic biomedical research. This might be the major contribution of the article to grantology.

Second, the article re-emphasizes the importance of **early-career development** of researchers as the NIH's new initiative. For twenty years from 1997 to 2017, the NIH designed and implemented a series of strategies, such as the New Investigator Research Awards (R23), the Early Stage Investigator Policy, the Early Independence Award (DP5), the Pathway to Independence Award program (K99/R00), New Innovator Awards (DP2), and the Next Generation Researchers Initiative.[22] Both advancing science and training scientists have been equally critical for the NIH to achieve its mission. Through this initiative, the NIH explicitly prioritizes ESIs and EEIs as a particularly critical area with regard to the training of scientists. In 2021, Michael Lauer and Deepshikha Roychowdhury analyzed the effectiveness of the initiative and reported that career-stage trends have stabilized, with equivalent proportions of early-, mid-, and late-career investigators funded from 2017 to 2020.[23]

3.2 Kulage et al. (2020): Developing Early-Career Grant Writers

After studying the policy article above, it is now useful to study an empirical article on how to develop an early-career grant writer.

---

[22] History of NIH support for early career investigators, *NIH Grants & Funding*, available at: https://grants.nih.gov/policy/early-stage/history.

[23] Lauer, M. S., & Roychowdhury, D. (2021). Inequalities in the distribution of National Institutes of Health research project grant funding. *elife*, *10*, article e71712. Gs54.

Overview

Overview

This article is titled "A 10-year examination of a one-on-one grant writing partnership for nursing pre- and post-doctoral trainees."[24] The title is relatively long, but it delivers two basic messages. This is an evaluation study of the effects of a grant writing program that ran annually for ten years (2011–20). The program focused on grant skill development for pre- and post-doctoral trainees. It has been cited only once as of 2023.

Nine authors contributed to this paper. They are mainly from the School of Nursing at Columbia University. The first author, Kristine Kulage, introduced in Chapter 3, is Director of Research and Scholarly Development at the School of Nursing at Columbia University and led a highly successful research grant program.

The article was published in 2022 in *Nursing Outlook*. As mentioned in Chapter 3, *Nursing Outlook* is the official journal of the American Academy of Nursing.

Highlights

This is an empirical study that has six major sections: (1) Genesis of the partnership; (2) Fit with the school mission; (3) Review of literature; (4) Methods; (5) Findings; and (6) Discussion. From the grant writer development perspective, we can highlight several key points of the article.

First, the article provided a **detailed description** of this one-on-one grant training partnership program. Usually, predocs or postdocs work with their faculty mentors and develop **mentorship** to secure external grant funding. This program focuses on **partnerships** between the predocs or postdocs and a facilitator who has grant submission and grant management experiences to facilitate project development and grant writing. The partnership facilitator will review all files of the grant application, including providing writing and editing support. While faculty mentors provide a scientific review, the support provided by the partnership facilitator includes a review of documents by focusing on clarity, organization, meaning, understanding, and flow in writing. Specifically, this one-on-one partnership program includes four features. First, regular one-on-one partnership **meetings** are held between a trainee and a facilitator to support the grant-writing process step by step, while a faculty advisor of the trainee will still offer scientific mentorship. Second, a timeline for weekly

---

[24] Kulage, K. M., Corwin, E. J., Liu, J., Schnall, R., Smaldone, A., Soled, K. R. *et al.* (2022). A 10-year examination of a one-on-one grant writing partnership for nursing pre- and post-doctoral trainees. *Nursing Outlook*, *70*(3), 465–77. GS1.

activities is followed with major **milestones** by the trainee and the facilitator until the final grant submission. One of the key elements is to work one-on-one to write the specific objective and aims section. Third, one-on-one writing and editing **support** is provided by the facilitator, while a faculty advisor reviews the scientific contents. Fourth, working one-on-one between the trainee and the facilitator to produce high-quality **administrative** documents (e.g. the facilities and other resource file, the protecting human subjects file).

Second, the article reported the **positive effects** of the program. From 2011 to 2020, the school had submitted forty applications by thirty applicants, with twenty-one applications in the program and nineteen not in the program. Among the program participants, 81 percent (17/21) received funding, in contrast, for those who did not participate, 42 percent (8/19) received funding, indicating significant differences in the funding rate between the two groups.

Third, the article reviews **various programs** for grant writing. After a careful search of the existing literature on numerous grant-writing workshops, the authors identified and reviewed twenty-four recently published grant training programs. These programs had different initiatives (e.g. mentorship programs, grantsmanship workshops, intense boot camps), targeted different populations (e.g. junior faculty, postdocs, predocs, or underrepresented minorities), and covered different disciplines (e.g. medicine, nursing, psychiatry, STEM, and social sciences). This information is very useful to help and guide individuals and institutions to choose and develop their own programs.

Last, the article also has important implications for the research and practice of the development of new grant writers. While it might normally take about ten years to become an independent principal investigator of the NIH G01 grant, individuals and institutions can and should **design, develop, and implement** strong innovative training programs, like the one-on-one partnership program presented in the article, to improve the development process of grant writers in the early-career stage.

3.3 Goodman (2019): Fifty Years of Grant Professionals as a Career

We will now discuss two articles related to grant professionals. One is a reflection piece and another is an empirical article. Each shows different aspects of grant professionals as a career.

10 Pursuing Grants in the Future

Overview

The first article we will study is titled "Remembering 50 years in research administration."[25] It is a reflection on the author's fifty years of experience as a research administrator. It has been cited five times as of 2023.

The author, Ian Goodman, has been an experienced research administrator in higher education since 1968. He was the Director of Research Administration at New York University, overseeing the administration of research funding, ensuring compliance with regulations and policies, and providing support and guidance to researchers and faculty at the University. He was then Director of Research Administration in the Office of Research Affairs at the University of California, administrating research projects, grants, and compliance within the university. He considers the profession of research administration a perfect match for him. Except for the article, his professional information is extremely limited.

The article was published in 2019 in the *Journal of Research Administration*. This journal, as mentioned previously, is the official journal of the Society of Research Administrators International.

Highlights

The paper is a retrospective essay rather than an empirical article. It consists of three major sections: (1) The regulatory landscape; (2) The technology transforms research administration; and (3) Research administration hits its stride as a profession. These three sections show how research administration as a professional career has evolved in three major aspects, namely, regulations, technology, and professional practice. From the perspective of a career as a grant administrator, we can highlight the following key points.

First, the article provides a detailed account of how **federal regulatory policy and procedure** have been substantially changed. In the 1960s, the flow of federal regulations had just started. Over five decades, a series of regulations have been introduced, such as the CFR Part 200, the Patent and Trademark Law Amendments Act, 45 CFR 74.34 on equipment management, 21 CFR 11 on food and drugs, 45 CFR 46 on the Institutional Review Board, and the Laboratory Animal Welfare Act. Thus, research administrators face increasing challenges in complying with and implementing new federal regulations.

Second, the article briefly summarizes the **impact of technologies** on research administration. In the 1960s, common technologies were

[25] Goodman, I. S. (2019). Remembering 50 years in research administration. *Journal of Research Administration*, 50(1), 13–20. Gs5.

calculators, word processors, telephones, fax machines, and IBM/Apple computers. Grant applications were all paper-based and grant submissions were by mail or in person. Nowadays, however, grant applications, grant reviews, and grant award communications are all digital, saving significant time, money, and staff costs of pre- and post-award grant management. New digital technologies have made grant administration much more efficient.

Third, the article outlined **tremendous changes** in research administration as a profession. In the 1960s, this profession did not exist and there was no formal job title for research administrators. Instead, people worked as department administrators, department coordinators, program managers, executive assistants, administrative assistants, grant and contract specialists, fund managers, grant accountants, and grant analysts. Nowadays, however, research administration is a highly specialized profession due to the increasing need to comply with complex federal regulations. It contains multiple special skills, such as research compliance, research risks, research ethics, research finance, and pre- and post-award administration. This profession attracts individuals from a wide variety of professional backgrounds, such as science, engineering, ethics, law, accounting, and finance. It requires advanced degrees. There are certificate programs and graduate degrees in research administration, as well as various on-site training. It has a career ladder from a junior position to a senior position, serving a specialized leadership role at universities and not-for-profits. Gradually, professional organizations emerged, such as the Grant Professionals Association, the National Association of College and University Business Officers, the National Council of University Research Administrators, the National Grants Management Association, and the Society of Research Administrators International.

3.4 Vidal et al. (2015): Impacts of Specialized Support by Grant Managers

Overview

The title of the next article is "Assessing the impact of grant managers on the success of grant applications."[26] Clearly, the title indicates that this article focuses on how much a grant manager will influence the success of a grant proposal. It has been cited sixteen times as of 2023.

---

[26] Vidal, S., Laureano, R., & Trindade, M. (2015). Assessing the impact of grant managers on the success of grant applications. *Perspectives: Policy & Practice in Higher Education, 19*(3), 84–91. Gs16.

Three Portuguese researchers wrote the article. Sheila Vidal and Margarida Trindade are veteran research funding administrators and Raul Laureano is an expert in statistics.

The article was published in 2015 in *Perspectives: Policy & Practice in Higher Education*. The journal provides higher education managers and administrators with innovative research that analyzes and informs their practice of management. It is affiliated with the United Kingdom's Association of University Administrators, and the publisher is Taylor & Francis Online.

Highlights
This is an empirical article. It consists of four major sections: (1) Understand of the role of grant managers; (2) A study of two Portuguese research-intensive institutions; (3) Using statistics to determine if grant managers help secure grants; and (4) Looking ahead for extended roles in grant management. From the perspective of a grant professional in terms of career, we can highlight several important points.

First, the study had a **thoughtful design** to assess the impact of grant managers. The data were collected from two Grant Offices of two Portuguese biomedical research institutions from 2008 to 2011. The study focused on the Marie Curie grants or formally the Marie Skłodowska-Curie Actions.[27] The grants are the European Union's flagship funding programme for doctoral education and postdoctoral training of researchers. Named after the renowned physicist and chemist Marie Curie, the grants are among Europe's most competitive and prestigious research and innovation fellowships. The data analysis was performed to compare the success rates of funding applications in two groups. One is the advanced support group who received specialized input into their grant proposals from grant managers and another is the group with less support, who received limited input from grant managers. Specifically, the group with less support received either basic administrative support (e.g. providing information on funding applications and offering online resources) or intermediate administrative support (e.g. suggesting application strategy, providing budget review). The advanced support group received detailed writing support on proposal contents (e.g. commenting on text coherence, logical flow of ideas, language style, clarity of objectives and work plan, alignment with the goals of the funder and evaluation criteria, completeness), in addition to administrative support.

---

[27] Marie Skłodowska-Curie Actions, *European Commission*, available at: https://marie-sklodowska-curie-actions.ec.europa.eu/about-msca.

3 Scientific Knowledge

Second, the study generated **good evidence** of the impact of grant managers. Among seventy-eight Marie Curie grant submissions between 2008 and 2011 from the two offices, the success rate of the advanced support group was 61 percent, with twenty-five funded projects of forty-one submissions, which is significantly higher than the success rate of 19 percent of the group with less support, with seven funded projects of thirty-seven submissions. The results suggest that grant managers' specialized support rather than administrative support is essential for winning highly competitive grant proposals like the Marie Curie grants. This is one of the first published articles that empirically assesses the impacts of different types of support offered by grant managers.

3.5 Ioannidis (2011): Fund Researchers rather than Projects

We will now study two articles related to the future of grant scholars. The first is an opinion piece and the second is an empirical article. These two articles can shed some light on the future scholars of grantology. Note that the future of grantology is not about the future of funding trends, but rather the future directions of research in grantology. It answers a question: How can scholars advance the field of grantology in the future?

Overview
The first article is titled "Fund people not projects."[28] It tells us that the central theme of this article is that the funding priority should focus on excellent investigators rather than excellent projects. Traditionally, whether investigators are strong has been one of the criteria in proposal review and funding decisions. What the author attempted to emphasize in his article is that reviewers and funders should have a paradigm shift and whether investigators are strong should be the only or the most important criterion for funding. Among funders across the world, Howard Hughes Medical Institute is known for funding excellent investigators generously. The article has been cited 193 times as of 2023, showing its good impact.

The author is John Ioannidis. He is a Professor of Medicine and Biomedical Data Science at Stanford University. His major research areas include meta-research, clinical epidemiology evidence-based medicine research methods, and meta-analysis. His h-index is 259, one of the highest in the scientific community, indicating his extremely high productivity.

---

[28] Ioannidis, J. P. (2011). Fund people not projects. *Nature*, *477*(7366), 529–31. Gs193.

He has published multiple major articles on funding.[29] Thus, we should follow him closely as a leading scholar in grantology.

The article was published in 2011 in *Nature*. As mentioned previously, *Nature* is one of the most prestigious science journals in the world.

Highlights

This article is short, only three pages in total, and was published under the category of Comment.[30] Note that, in addition to original research articles, *Nature* published other types of materials (e.g. News or Comment) that may only contain minimal new supporting research findings. For grantology research, this line of materials is particularly valuable and informative, demonstrated by the article we are studying here. The article has five sub-headings: Fund everyone (or a lucky few); Fund according to merit; State broad goals; Ignore grant portfolios in promotion; and What we can do now. From the perspective of future scholarship in grantology, we can highlight several important points.

First, the article offers the **strongest criticism** of the current funding system. It starts with one bold statement to reveal a brutal reality that almost all scientists recognize: "The research funding system is broken." Three research examples are provided to support this statement: (1) scientists now spend all of their time writing grants and no longer have time for science; (2) the funding requirement on scientific and social impacts leads to predictable but not innovative outcomes; and (3) 30 percent of the pivotal papers from Nobel laureates were written without direct funding.

Second, the article reviewed **six innovative proposals** to change the current funding system. These proposals are: (1) funding everybody (e.g. sharing small grants with all eligible researchers); (2) funding at random (e.g. using lottery to award small grants);[31] (3) funding based on peer assessment of creativity and promise of scientists (e.g. funding twenty to thirty MacArthur fellows); (4) funding based on automated impact indices (e.g. using average citations); (5) funding based on good scientific citizenship

---

[29] Tatsioni, A., Vavva, E., & Ioannidis, J. P. (2010). Sources of funding for Nobel Prize-winning work: Public or private? *FASEB Journal, 24*(5), 1335–9. Gs44; Patsopoulos, N. A., Ioannidis, J. P., & Analatos, A. A. (2006). Origin and funding of the most frequently cited papers in medicine: Database analysis. *British Medical Journal, 332*(7549), 1061–4. Gs177; Nicholson, J. M., & Ioannidis, J. P. (2012). Conform and be funded. *Nature, 492*(7427), 34–6. Gs215; Chalmers, I., Bracken, M. B., Djulbegovic, B., Garattini, S., Grant, J., Gülmezoglu, A. M. *et al.* (2014). How to increase value and reduce waste when research priorities are set. *The Lancet, 383*(9912), 156–65. Gs1311.
[30] Other types of submissions, *Nature*, available at: www.nature.com/nature/for-authors/other-subs.
[31] Shaw, J. (2023). Peer review in funding-by-lottery: A systematic overview and expansion. *Research Evaluation, 32*(1), 86–100. Gs14.

3 Scientific Knowledge 347

practices (e.g. data sharing, open collaboration); and (6) funding projects with broad goals (e.g. submitting a broad goal statement rather than a lengthy proposal). In addition, the article proposed not to use the size of grant portfolios for tenure and promotion.

Third, the article suggested **four strategies** to test and implement these proposals. These strategies are: (1) take either small progressive steps or large extensive renovations through pilot programs as a desirable approach; (2) consider large diversity among various funding programs to decide the best options because some programs are good for funding numerous scientists and others are useful for elite researchers; (3) use strengths and avoid weaknesses of prospective and retrospective assessment methods; and (4) focus on achieving the long-term goal of science to advance knowledge and yield useful applications.

Fourth, the article raises a fundamental question to researchers in grantology and voices one of the strongest criticisms of current grant practice: "**it is a scandal** that billions of dollars are spent on research without knowing the best way to distribute that money." Practically, it is senseless to demand scientists to spend most of their time writing grants rather than conducting innovative research. Future research in grantology should address this challenging problem effectively and efficiently.

3.6 Aagaard, Kladakis, & Nielsen (2020): Concentrating or Dispersing Research Funding

After examining a thought-provoking Comment paper, let us now study an empirical article on one topic related to future research in grant scholarship.

Overview
This article is titled "Concentration or dispersal of research funding?"[32] It examines a challenge: given limited funding, to maximize the effectiveness of funding, should funding be focused on a few major projects or distributed to a large number of small projects? It addressed a specific trend of grant funding: the size of funding or the distribution of funding.

The first of the three authors, Kaare Aagaard, is a research leader of VIA University College of Denmark, the third largest educational institution in the country after Copenhagen University and Aarhus University.[33]

---

[32] Aagaard, K., Kladakis, A., & Nielsen, M. W. (2020). Concentration or dispersal of research funding? *Quantitative Science Studies*, *1*(1), 117–49. Gs93.
[33] VIA University College, *Wikipedia*, available at: https://en.wikipedia.org/wiki/VIA_University_College.

His research areas include research policy research funding, open science, research assessment, and science indicators. His h-index is 18. He has published multiple articles on grants and is an established researcher in grantology.[34] The second author, Alexander Kladakis, has contributed a chapter in the *Handbook of Public Funding of Research*, which is a reputable and useful handbook on public funding. The third author, Mathias Nielsen, is an Associate Professor of Sociology at the University of Copenhagen. His research interest is in the sociology of science, and his h-index is 24. Note that the first two authors are from the Danish Centre for Studies in Research and Research Policy, which is part of the Department of Political Science at Aarhus University of Denmark. The Director of the center is Carter Bloch, who has published multiple major articles on the impacts of funding.[35] The Center can be considered one of the most excellent research centers on grantology in the world, similar to the ones at MIT's Technological Innovation, Entrepreneurship, and Strategic Management Group and Northwestern University's Center for Science of Science and Innovation. The article was published in *Quantitative Science Studies*, the official journal of the International Society for Scientometrics and Informetrics. This is an important journal related to grantology. The founding editor is Ludo Waltman, an established scholar in grantology from Leiden University. Its publisher is MIT.

Highlights
The article is a long literature review, totaling thirty-two printed pages. It is the first narrative review on grant size, a timely and important topic. It has six major sections: (1) Introduction; (2) Materials and methods; (3) Descriptive analysis; (4) Key arguments in the literature (based on opinion-based grey literature) in favor of concentration and dispersion on efficiency (not effective, epistemic, organization, and peer review and allocation problems); (5) Empirical evidence on effect of funding size on research performance; and (6) Discussion and conclusions. From the

---

[34] Kaare Aagaard, *Google Scholar*, available at: https://scholar.google.com/citations?user=VkSHvpMAAAAJ&hl=en&oi=ao; Alexander Kladakis, *ORCID*, available at: https://orcid.org/0000-0002-0668-6379; Alexander Kladakis, *Google Scholar*, available at: https://orcid.org/0000-0002-0668-6379; Mathias Wullum Nielsen, *Google Scholar*, available at: https://scholar.google.com/citations?user=XbdUGEsAAAAJ&hl=en&oi=sra; The Danish Centre for Studies in Research and Research Policy, *School of Business and Social Sciences, Aarhus Universitet*, available at: https://ps.au.dk/en/research/research-centres/the-danish-centre-for-studies-in-research-and-research-policy.
[35] Prosecon, *School of Business and Social Sciences, Aarhus Universitet*, available at: https://ps.au.dk/forskning/forskningscentre/dansk-center-for-forskningsanalyse/research-projects/prosecon/.

3 Scientific Knowledge

perspective of future research in grant scholarship, we can focus on several key highlights.

First, based on the identified ninety-two relevant articles, the authors carefully reviewed **key arguments** in favor of concentration or dispersal respectively. Documented key arguments in favor of concentration include three types: (1) improve research efficiency (e.g. increasing economies of scale and reducing administrative burden); (2) improve research quality (e.g. achieving scientific excellence and focusing on merit-based funding system); and (3) improve organizational conditions (e.g. offering stable funding, generating spillover effects, providing critical research infrastructure and equipment). On the other hand, documented key arguments in favor of dispersal include four types: (1) improve research efficiency (e.g. producing more productive small-sized research groups); (2) improve research quality (e.g. diversifying risk, increasing chances of innovative breakthroughs, and embracing greater research breadth); (3) improve organizational conditions (e.g. engaging more researchers and students, developing early- and middle-career investigators, reducing the Matthew effect); and (4) improve the grant review and grant decision processes (e.g. releasing pressure for selecting only a few safe projects, increasing success rates, encouraging more meritorious proposals from more unfunded investigators).

Second, based on twenty-four empirical articles focusing on the relationship between grant size and research performance (mainly article publications and article citations), the authors summarized **one major surprising finding**: seventeen of the twenty-four articles demonstrate either a negative association or diminishing returns to investment for grant sizes above a certain threshold. For instance, an analysis of 2,938 grants from the US National Institute of General Medical Sciences shows that the journal publications and publication citations per lab decrease with funding above $750,000, while funding between $250,000 and $300,000 is associated with a modest increase in research performance. An analysis of 1,755 R01 projects funded by the US National Institute of Mental Health suggests that basic research with grant sizes above $4.5 million exhibits diminishing returns to investment. To some extent, the review demonstrates a strong inclination toward arguments in favor of increased dispersal.

Last, the size of funding is not only a hot topic in current grantology research, but it is also a promising area for **future grantology research**. In fact, in the next ten years or so, together with rapid development and implementation of new innovative grant practices, researchers in grantology will need to understand a wide range of topics regarding diverse grant sizes, grantors, grantees, and grant purposes, and use a wide variety of methods regarding data collection (e.g. big data) and data analysis (e.g. AI technologies).

4 Grantology vs. Journalology: Comparing the Future in Growth, Career, and Scholarship

In this section, we will briefly compare growth as grant writers and article authors, compare careers as grant professionals and publishing professionals, and compare scholarships in grantology and journalology.

4.1 Growth: Grant Writers vs. Article Writers

As revealed in the previous sections, there is a large variation in professional growth from a new novice grant writer to an independent mature grant writer due to a wide variety of factors (e.g. experience, training, mentorship, and institutional support). Based on the NIH,[36] it takes ten years to grow from an ESI to an EEI in basic biomedical research. In other words, it usually takes ten years from having the first PhD to winning an NIH standard research grant as an independent grant writer.

How long does it take to grow from a new novice journal article writer to a successful, skillful article writer? So far, there is no explicit answer to this question. Of course, there are various factors involved (e.g. publishing a research article in *Nature* differs significantly from publishing a short research report in a third-tier journal). There is an extensive literature on challenges in writing and publishing scientific papers[37] and on training programs for improvement of writing and publishing scientific papers.[38] These two lines of study suggest that it is not easy to write and publish scientific papers professionally and thus it might take a relatively long time to develop, unlike the six to twelve months generally needed to become a successful freelance writer.

---

[36] Lauer *et al.* (2017), note 19 above.
[37] Iskander, J. K., Wolicki, S. B., Leeb, R. T., & Siegel, P. Z. (2018). Successful scientific writing and publishing: A step-by-step approach. *Preventing Chronic Disease, 15*(6), article 180085. Gs61; Pittman, J., Stahre, M., Tomedi, L., & Wurster, J. (2017). Barriers and facilitators to scientific writing among applied epidemiologists. *Journal of Public Health Management & Practice, 23*(3), 291–4. Gs17.
[38] Galipeau, J., Moher, D., Campbell, C., Hendry, P., Cameron, D. W., Palepu, A. *et al.* (2015). A systematic review highlights a knowledge gap regarding the effectiveness of health-related training programs in journalology. *Journal of Clinical Epidemiology, 68*(3), 257–65. Gs58; Galipeau, J., Moher, D., Skidmore, B., Campbell, C., Hendry, P., Cameron, D. W. *et al.* (2013). Systematic review of the effectiveness of training programs in writing for scholarly publication, journal editing, and manuscript peer review (protocol). *Systematic Reviews, 2*(1), 1–7. Gs21.

4 Grantology vs. Journalology: Comparing the Future

4.2 Career: Grant Professionals vs. Journalists

As discussed in the previous sections, while the careers of grant professionals are diverse, we can specify two general areas: the grantor-side professionals working in public and private funders (e.g. program officers and grant managers); and the grantee-side professionals having independent or private practice (e.g. grant-writing workshop organizers and freelance grant writers).

Likewise, there are a wide variety of careers for writing professionals. We can also see two general areas here: the journalist-related side and the publishing-related side. For a journalist-related career, the choices include reporters, correspondents, journalists, editors, editorial writers, columnists, and photojournalists. For example, in *The New York Times*, some jobs under the journalism category include assistant editor, finance editor, journalism education editor, lead writer, open-source reporter, reporter on courts, reporter on weather, senior editor, senior staff editor, video journalist, and video reporter.

For a publishing-related career, for example, in Wiley, one of the largest academic publishers in the world, there are ten categories of jobs: corporate, customer support, distribution, editorial, operations, marketing, project management, sales, student services, and technology. Jobs in the editorial line include editorial assistant, assistant editor, associate acquisitions editor, commercial editor, editor-in-chief, managing editor, senior copy editor, associate publisher, and publisher.

4.3 Scholarship: Journalology vs. Grantology

The worldwide grant-funding enterprise might not see dramatic changes over the next ten to twenty years. Overall, the available funding will continue to be more limited, grant applications will continue to increase, grant decisions will continue to be more competitive, funding biases will continue to exist rather than be eliminated, and grant impacts will continue to be largely unpredictable and elusive. Consequently, the grantology research in the next couple of decades is very likely to be within the existing paradigm rather than embrace a new one. Despite all of this, it would be very exciting if researchers in grantology throughout the world would work together to accomplish two tasks in the next five years: (1) starting a professional association of grantology and (2) establishing a journal on grantology.

In contrast, the journal publication enterprise in the next ten to twenty years will continue experiencing two major paradigm shifts: the shift from paper publication to digital publication, which started in the early 1980s with the emergence of the digital revolution; and the shift from the subscription model to the open access model, which began in 2002 when the Budapest Open Access Initiative was launched. Consequently, journalology will see major opportunities and challenges simultaneously over the next couple of decades.

Specifically, one way to study the current and future trending topics in journalology is to study the Eighth World Conference on Research Integrity held in June 2024 in Greece,[39] given that the Ninth International Congress on Peer Review and Scientific Publication completed in September 2022 and the Tenth International Congress on Peer Review and Scientific Publication will be held in September 2025.

In the broad context of the two paradigm shifts in journal publication, it is not surprising to see that the theme of the conference is research integrity and research ethics. Various symposiums, plenaries, presentations, and posters have addressed four major topics: (1) research integrity, innovation integrity, publication integrity, and policy-making integrity; (2) open science and research integrity; (3) generative artificial intelligence and research integrity; and (4) reproducibility and research integrity.

5 Action Suggestions: Understanding and Planning the Future as Grant Writers, Grant Professionals, and Grant Scholars

The present book is titled *Introductory Grantology: A Guide for Pursuing Competitive Grants*. In this final chapter, we will discuss three ways to pursue competitive grants: growing professionally in order to become an independent grant writer, being a competent grant professional, and becoming a successful grant scholar.

5.1 Understanding the Future as Grant Writers, Grant Professionals, and Grant Scholars

First, it is interesting to see intuitive knowledge of the future as grant writers, grant professionals, and grant scholars among new grant writers. For the question, "How long will it take to become a successful grant writer?",

---

[39] International Congress on Peer Review and Scientific Publication website, available at: https://peerreviewcongress.org/.

5 Action Suggestions: Understanding the Future 353

most of the new grant writers answered in general terms, while a few said it might take a few months to a few years. For the question, "What kinds of careers will grant professionals have?", the new grant writers have different levels of knowledge about grant professionals, from incorrectly considering professors or researchers at universities to be the full-time grant professionals, to generally pointing out some areas to find jobs, and to knowledgeably specifying multiple types of careers for grant professionals. For the question, "What will be the future of grantology in the next ten years?", this received the most divergent mix of answers, given that grantology is an emerging field. They suggested, among other developments, formal courses in grantology and using AI in grant writing and grant review.

Second, from the presentation of real-life cases, we can learn the following. (1) Different grant writers are at different stages of their careers. It might take years of work to advance from early career, to middle career, to late career. (2) The careers of grant professionals are diverse, but can be divided into two areas: the grantor-side professionals working in public and private funders; and the grantee-side professionals having independent or private practice. (3) The risk-return challenge and AI influences are among the future directions of grantology.

Third, from the discussion of the existing research literature, we have learned that: (1) it may take ten years to become an independent skillful grant writer for highly competitive grants, but there exist extensive innovative programs to train early-career grant writers; (2) grant professionals as a career has changed significantly over the past fifty years and has now become a highly specialized and impactful profession in the grant enterprise; and (3) future research in grantology needs to navigate various challenges and numerous opportunities in order to make this subject area a strong science and to promote the research-based practice of making and seeking grants.

Fourth, from the brief comparison of grant writer development vs. article writer development, grant professionals' careers vs. publishing professionals' careers, and grant scholars vs. publication scholars, we can immediately see major divergences rather than parallels, especially between the "quiet steam" in grantology and the "perfect storm" in journalology.

5.2 Planning the Future as Grant Writers, Grant Professionals, and Grant Scholars

Below are four suggestions to conclude this final chapter and the book as a whole.

First, take time to prepare for sufficient failure (writing and submitting ten grants), really develop your grant skills, and become an elite researcher with abundant grant funding.

Second, consider various career options, such as rotated NSF program officers, grant administrators, grant managers, foundation professionals, or freelance grant writers, with your existing professional training and expertise in nature and social science.

Third, pay attention to the latest developments in grantology to guide your grant success, make meaningful contributions to grantology, and generate important research questions.

Last, choose one out of the above three options, and draft and justify a five-year or ten-year plan for your future development as a grant writer, grant professional, and/or grant scholar.

The intellectual journey of learning how to pursue grants through this book has now come to an end. But our professional journey of advancing human knowledge and improving human life is only just starting. Remember: there are different ways to advance knowledge and improve life, with or without grants, with large or small grants, with public or private grants, and with research or non-research grants. The key is to be a responsible and creative scientist and a responsible and creative citizen.

Appendix

This review paper was submitted as a preprint on January 30, 2023 at https://osf.io/preprints/osf/ynepm. It has been viewed fifty-five times and downloaded seventy-four times as of October 2024. It is included in the book as a historical record of a research effort on grantology.

The Science of Research Grants: A Scoping Review of Journal Articles in Grantology Published in 1970–2020

Zheng Yan[a] Panpan Yang[a] Qingyang Liu[a] Joan J. Erickson[a]
zyan@albany.edu pyang2@albany.edu qliu@albany.edu
ericksjj@delhi.edu

[a]The University at Albany, State University of New York, USA

Author Note

Correspondence concerning this article should be addressed to Zheng Yan, Department of Educational and Counseling Psychology, School of Education, The University at Albany, State University of New York, 1400 Washington Avenue, Albany, NY 12222, USA. Email: zyan@albany.edu.

We would like to thank Yaosheng Lou for assembling references and Briana Benwell for proofreading the manuscript.

Abstract

Research grants are a critical means for research policy, research management, and research administration to generate scientific breakthroughs, technical innovations, and social impacts. Currently, the exponential growth of the research literature on research grants has been scattered across diverse outlets and disciplines. The present paper is the first scoping review to generate an overall coherent picture of the science of research grants or grantology by focusing on the basic literature published from 1970 to 2020. Based on both a process-based conceptual framework and 275 identified important research articles, we synthesize the current knowledge in seven key areas, i.e., grant writers, grant writing, grant agents, grant review, grant projects, grant management, and grant impacts. Our review indicates that three major topics, grant writing practices, grant review, and scientific impacts, have dominated the existing literature. Future research should examine four key topics, development of grant writers, grant resubmission, grant professionals, and grant use, to further advance the science of research grants. Limitations and implications of the study are discussed.

Keywords: research grant; scoping review; grant writers; grant agents; grant projects; grant impacts; grantology

1. Introduction

Grantology as the Science of Research Grants

Research grants are a critical means for research policy, research management, and research administration to generate scientific breakthroughs, technical innovations, and social impacts (e.g., Alberts, Kirschner, Tilghman, Varmus, 2014; Chapman & McCauley, 1993; Gulbrandsen & Smeby, 2005; Jacob & Lefgren, 2011; Merton, 1968; Salter & Martin, 2000; Walden & Bryan, 2010). Research grants could be defined broadly as any type of money spent to *create*, *diffuse*, and *apply* scientific knowledge, such as research investment, industrial funding, research and development funding, grants awarded by governments and foundations, or various other forms of scientific investments. However, research grants could also be defined narrowly as "a sum of money given by public and private organizations to support innovative scientific research" (Grants .gov Program Management Office, n.d.). Based on this definition, a research grant involves three basic elements: grant size (*a sum of money*), grant agencies (*public and private organizations*), and grant purpose (*to support innovative scientific research*). The narrowly defined term could have different variations, such as research awards, research funding, external grants, or grantsmanship, but its defining feature is to support innovative scientific research to create scientific knowledge rather than for other purposes (e.g., to diffuse and apply scientific knowledge). This study mainly focused on the narrowly defined research grants, while acknowledging that various forms of broadly defined research grants

Appendix: The Science of Research Grants   357

often are interconnected with each other and are embedded in each other. Generally, seeking research grants involves at least three types of human behavior: giving and receiving money as an *economic* behavior, developing and administering grant agencies as a *managerial* behavior, and supporting and conducting research as a *scientific* behavior. Thus, even based on the narrow definition, research grants are a multifaceted, multilayered, and multidisciplinary complex scientific enterprise in both the real world and the research literature (e.g., just considering the complex typology of grant mechanisms of NIH).

Journal Articles Published in 1970–2020

Although scientific research as a fundamental human behavior has an about 4,000-year history, modern scientific research supported by research grants occurred just about 200 years ago (e.g., NIH and NSF were founded in 1887 and 1950 respectively). And the history of studying research grants is even shorter. Van Slyke (1946) and Endicott and Allen (1953) can be considered the two earliest journal articles on research grants. The literature on the science of research grants or grantology did not emerge clearly until the 1970s. Figure A.1 shows an exponential growth of the publications on research grants in 80 years. On the basis of an initial search of key words "research grant*" on the Web of Science, starting in 1977, on average, 10 articles per year have been published; starting in 1992, the number of published articles went up to 100 per year; and starting in 2014, the published articles increased to 500 per year.

During the past 80-year exponential growth of the science of research grants, leading scholars have emerged and are widely recognized by the scientific community for their important scientific contributions to the field. Among them are two intellectual giants, Robert Merton, a late sociologist at Columbia University and best known for his study on the Matthew effect, and Jorge Hirsch, a physicist at the University of California at San Diego and best known for his invention of the h-index. Their seminal work on the effects of research rewards (Merton, 1968) or evaluation of research output (Hirsch, 2005), each with over 10,000 citations as the highest in the field, concerns the central issues of the science of research grants. Based on highly cited publications in Web of Science, multiple leading scholars have made significant theoretical, methodological, empirical, and/or practical contributions in six major areas: (1) grant writers (e.g., Ley & Hamilton, 2008; Pohlhaus et al., 2011; Walden & Bryan, 2010), (2) grant writing (e.g., Bordage & Dawson, 2003), (3) grant review (e.g., Ginther, Schaffer,

358 Appendix: The Science of Research Grants

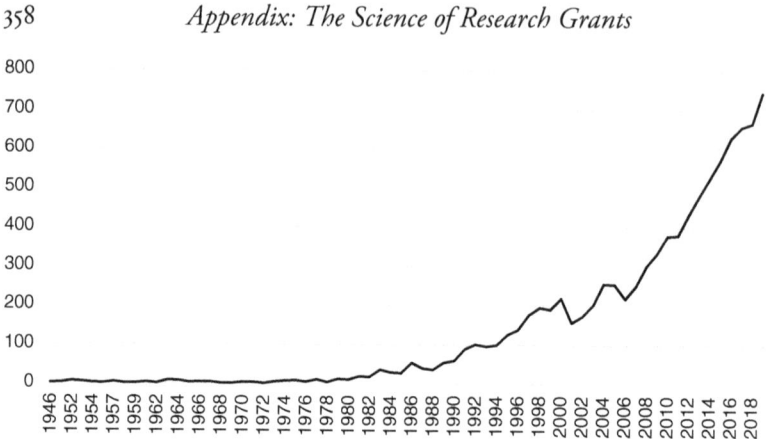

Figure A.1 Growth of the number of journal articles on research grants published in 1946–2019

& Schnell, 2011; Jayasinghe, Marsh, & Bond, 2003; Kotchen, Lindquist, Malik, & Ehrenfeld, 2004), (4) grant projects (e.g., Arora, David, & Gambardella, 1997), (5) researcher productivity (e.g., Gulbrandsen & Smeby, 2005; Pagel & Hudetz, 2011; Benway, Kalidas, & Cabello, 2009; Rad, Brinjikji, Cloft, & Kallmes, 2010), and (6) grant impacts (e.g., Jacob & Lefgren, 2011; Alberts, Kirschner, Tilghman, & Varmus, 2014).

Scoping Review

The study of research grants has encountered multiple challenges despite its exponential growth. These challenges include: (1) *unbalanced research*, i.e., the three topics of grant review, grant writing, and grant impacts have dominated the literature, while other important topics (e.g., grant use) need timely adequate attention; (2) *widely-spread publications*, i.e., all the publications have been scattered across nearly 200 journals, making it extremely difficult to locate them; (3) *practice orientations*, i.e., nearly 50 books on research grants and a large number of journal articles have been published, but their primary focus is on practical knowledge about how to seek research grants. While developing and promoting research grants toolkits are useful and important practically, empirical research is needed to fully understand the social and psychological process of getting research grants scientifically rather than merely practically; and (4) *bottom-up patterns*, i.e., the current literature has been focusing on a wide variety of specific topics, generally following a bottom-up approach. A *top-down* approach is needed to consider research grants as a research field to develop a bird's-eye view of the existing knowledge of the entire field. In addition, it is particularly important to use the top-down approach to examine the science of research grants as a subject matter. This follows not only the tradition of the philosophy and history of science (Kuhn, 2012: Popper, 2005) but also the emerging spirit of metascientific studies (Price, 1963), the science of science (Fortunato et al., 2018), and metascience (Zeng et al., 2017). Since the exploration of the complexity and dynamic structure of science helps the development of methods and policies to accelerate science, the study of the complex and dynamic structure of the science of research grants as a field did, does, and will inform research grant practices and research grant policies.

To overcome the existing challenges faced by the researchers and further advance the science of research grants, one of the first basic steps is to synthesize the existing scientific knowledge of research grants. As of 2020, at least 20 literature reviews on research grants have been published in various journals, such as *Research Policy, Research Evaluation, Journal of the Society of Research Administrators, Research Management Review, Journal of Informetrics, Review of Educational Research, Implementation Science,* and *PLoS One*. Specifically, these reviews have focused on three important topics: (1) *grant writers* (e.g., Harris, 1984; Preuss, 2015), (2) *grant review* (e.g., Bornmann et al., 2007; Marsh et al., 2009; Tricco et al., 2017), and (3) *grant impacts* (e.g., Canon et al., 2002; Salter & Martin, 2000; Smits & Denis, 2014; Saygitov, 2014). Each of these reviews has made valuable contributions in synthesizing various specific aspects of the science of research grants. It has also suggested an urgent need for a review that covers the *entire* scientific process involving research grants, from its beginning (e.g., becoming a grant writer) to its end (e.g., generating scientific impacts). Such a review, by providing an overall picture of a field, will not only contribute to a better understanding of various aspects of research grants scientific but also help improve research decision-making and research management practices effectively and efficiently.

To achieve this goal, a scoping review becomes the method of choice (Arksey & O'Malley, 2005; Armstrong et al., 2011; Munn et al., 2018). A scoping review is used to provide a *broad* overview of the existing literature without describing findings in great detail to determine the scope or coverage of a body of the existing literature (Arksey & O'Malley, 2005; Armstrong et al., 2011; Munn et al., 2018). It is particularly useful for examining emerging information that has not been comprehensively reviewed or a topic that is complex and diverse (Peters et al., 2015). Since the 2010s, a rapidly increasing number of scoping reviews have been published (Tricco et al., 2016). Building on a scoping review, more specific questions can be posed and addressed by a more precise and in-depth systematic review (Armstrong et al., 2011).

The present paper is a scoping review of the science of research grants or grantology. It aims to provide a broad overview of existing scientific knowledge on research grants by focusing on the *basic* process of seeking research grants and the *basic* literature on this topic. It is not intended to pursue an exhausted literature search and offer a systematic review for the various reasons discussed above. In this scoping review, the key research question to be addressed is: What is the scope of the current scientific knowledge about research grants? In the text that follows, after presenting methods of literature search and literature review, we will overview the current literature in seven areas: grant writers, grant writing, grant agents, grant review, grant projects, grant management, and grant impacts.

2. Method

2.1 Literature Search

Figure A.2 outlines the major steps of the literature search process. Given the complex nature of the field as an emerging interdisciplinary study, the literature search has undergone two rounds of search to overcome specific challenges in locating literature and maximizing the search coverage.

The initial round of literature search has three major steps. First, three researchers of the research team independently searched major databases, including Web of Science, Google Scholar, PubMed, and PsychINFO. The keywords used for the search consisted of "external grants", "external research funding", "external grant funding", "external funding", and "extramural funding". Second, the three researchers manually checked the references of the identified literature to obtain relevant studies in research grants. Last, the three researchers searched the relevant books (e.g., Hollenbach, 2018; Nicholson-Crotty, 2015; Orlich & Shrope, 2012) to further identify relevant journal articles that were cited in the books.

To check the initial search results, two different researchers of the research team conducted the second round of search on the Web of Science using a series of keywords again, including "research funding", "research grant", "external grant", "extramural funding", "grantsmanship", "research award", "extramural grant", "outside funding", and "outside grant". These two rounds of search yielded 2075 records.

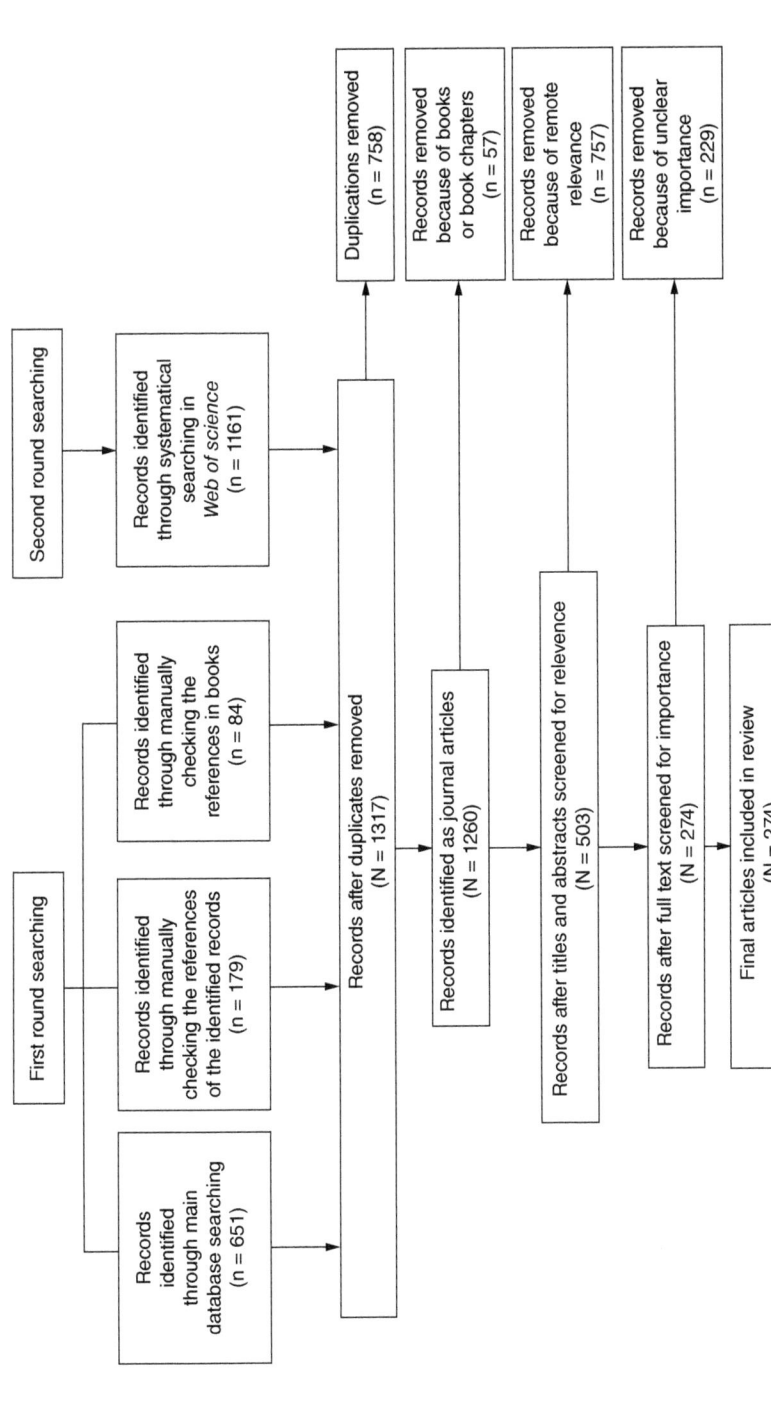

Figure A.2 The flowchart of the literature search process

With the initial search results, we removed non-English records, deleted duplications, excluded books or book chapters, screened for relevance based on titles and abstracts, and reviewed the full text of identified articles for importance. Specifically, one type of article was excluded due to remote relevance to the science of research grants. For instance, Álvarez-Bornstein, Morillo, and Bordons (2017) examined the completeness and accuracy of funding acknowledgments in the Web of Science. It is certainly an interesting study but indirectly and remotely related to the science of research grants and thus was not included in the current review. We also excluded another type of article that is clearly relevant but not highly important. For example, Anderson (1999) introduced NIH and NSF funding mechanisms applicable to interventional radiology. This article is certainly useful in guiding researchers to apply for federal funding, but might not be essential in contributing to the core knowledge of research grants. Through the screening and selecting process, a total of 275 journal articles were identified and included in the scoping review of the study.

2.2   *Literature Review*

We develop a process-based framework to synthesize the literature (see Figure A.3). This framework displays that a basic process of seeking research grants consists of four basic components (grant writers, grant agencies, grant projects, and grant impacts) that are connected with three basic steps (grant writing, grant reviewing, and grant managing). Specifically, this basic process might go as follows: (1) grant writers initiate the process of seeking research grants; (2) they go through the grant writing process and submit their grant proposals to grant agencies; (3) program officers of grant agencies organized review panels to assess the quality of research proposals and make recommendations; (4) program officers make decisions to fund selected research proposals; (5) program officers manage funded research projects, while selected researchers conduct funded research projects; and (6) researchers complete the funded project and generate impacts on science and society. Note that this basic

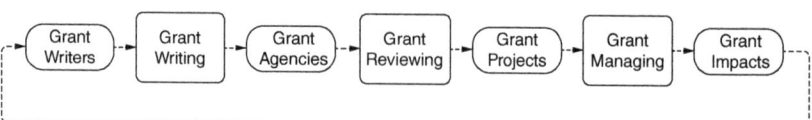

Figure A.3   Conceptual framework of seeking research grants as a scientific research process

Appendix: The Science of Research Grants 363

process can and should have a feedback loop, as indicated in the connection line in dot from Grant Impacts to Grant Writers, to inspire and motivate new grant activities.

To review the current basic literature on and develop a general picture of the science of research grants, the 275 selected articles were classified based on the basic process framework and reviewed under the following seven sections: grant writers, grant writing, grant agents, grant review, grant projects, grant management, and grant impacts. In each of these seven sections, we presented the results of the scoping review of each area using three commonly used strategies for scoping review: (1) presenting a summary table to specify the scope of the literature, (2) offering a short list of leading researchers with their highly cited work, given that leading scholars play a vital role in both scientific evolutions and scientific revolutions (e.g., Kuhn, 2012; Simonton, 1994; Sternberg & Gordeeva, 1996), and (3) presenting selected examples to provide some descriptive details for the scoping review within the limited space.

3. Grant Writers

Grant writers, including researchers, research collaborators, grant professionals, and large research teams, essentially initiate the entire research grant process. There exists relatively extensive literature, a total of 36 journal articles, examining grant writers applying for research grants. These articles have contributed to the scientific knowledge about grant writers in three main areas (see Table A.1): (1) psychological characteristics related to grant writers (n = 21, 58%), (2) sociological characteristics related to grant writers (n = 8, 22%), and (3) educational characteristics of academic training and tools that are beneficial for grant writers (n = 6, 17%). The most cited scholars in this area are (1) Grit Laudel at the Australian National University (2006), (2) Timothy Ley at Washington University Medical School (2008), (3) Jennifer Reineke Pohlhaus at Ripple Effect Communications, Inc, formerly at National Institutes of Health (2011), and (4) Susan Waisbren at Boston Children's Hospital (2008).

3.1 Psychological Characteristics Related to Grant Writers

3.1.1 Demographical Characteristics of Grant Writers
Extensive literature indicates that female faculty across disciplines submitted fewer proposals and secured fewer grants than male faculty (e.g., Jagsi, Motomura, Griffith, Rangarajan, & Ubel, 2009; Hechtman,

Table A.1 *An overview of existing studies on grant writers (N = 36)*

Major Area	Minor Area	Study Example
Psychological characteristics (n = 21)	1. Demographical characteristics (n = 8) 2. Motivators and barriers (n = 10) 3. Collaboration (n = 4) 4. Past grant-seeking experience (n = 3)	Waisbren et al., 2008 Boyer & Cockriel, 2001 Haller & Welch, 2014 Pinto & Huizinga, 2018
Institutional characteristics (n = 10)	Institutional contexts (n = 10)	Chval & Nossaman, 2014
Educational characteristics of training and tools for grant writers (n = 8)	1. Useful tools (n = 3) 2. Academic training (n = 5)	Boyer & Cockriel, 2001 Moore et al., 2016

Moore, Schulkey, Miklos, Calcagno; Aragon, & Greenberg, 2018; Ley & Hamilton, 2008; Witteman, Hendricks, Straus, & Tannenbaum, 2019). Factors that lead to lower application rates for females include female under-representation in senior jobs and tenured positions, and higher rates of part-time employment and career breaks due to family commitments (Keenihan, 2001). Waisbren et al. (2008) further investigated the influence of faculty academic rank on gender differences among grant writers at eight Harvard Medical School-affiliated institutions in 2001–3. Academic rank in this study was operationalized as four levels, instructor, assistant professor, associate professor, and full professor. Interestingly, they found that, after controlling for academic rank, *grant success rates* were not significantly different between males and females, while *grant submission rates* of females were still significantly lower at the lowest faculty rank than males.

3.1.2 Motivators and Barriers of Grant Writers

Multiple studies focused on exploring the motivators and barriers that grant writers have faced and generated similar findings. For instance, Boyer and Cockriel (2001) investigated the motivators and barriers that junior faculty have in the pursuit of grants. They found that the top three motivators for junior faculty to seek grants were "opportunity to probe or research new information", "consideration in tenure or promotion decisions", and "building [their] professional reputation as a capable researcher" (p. 21). The top three barriers that junior faculty have encountered were "heavy teaching loads", "inadequate support to submit in a timely manner", and "too many

Appendix: The Science of Research Grants 365

committee assignments" (p. 22). For tenured/tenure track faculty, Pinto and Huizinga (2018) found that faculty workload, retention, tenure, and promotion are key factors that can impact the faculty's grant-seeking behavior. Additionally, a few studies exclusively focused on ethnic minority grant writers. Shavers et al. (2005) investigated the barriers that racial minority researchers have in the application for NIH research funding. Nine clusters of barriers were identified, namely, (1) inadequate research infrastructure, training, and development, (2) obstacles to develop as independent researchers, (3) inadequate mentoring, (4) insensitivity, misperceptions, and miscommunications, (5) institutional bias in NIH policies (e.g., bias, prejudice, racism, and discrimination in peer-review groups), (6) unfair competitive environment, (7) limited support to certain research topics and methods, (8) social, cultural and environmental barriers, and (9) lack of institutional support.

3.1.3   Collaborations among Grant Writers

The existing studies have documented the importance of collaboration among researchers in grant applications. For example, Haller and Welch (2014) investigated three aspects of collaboration (i.e., collaboration network size, collaboration network tie strength, and collaboration network capability) in the association with grant applications and awards. They found that large collaboration network size and strong collaboration network tie strength might provide more resources, enhance confidential explorations, and develop more new ideas, and thus increase grant applications and received awards.

3.1.4   Past Grant-Seeking Experience

The existing research (Bogler, 1994; Laudel, 2006; Pinto & Huizinga, 2018) has indicated that past successful experience with a funding source has a strong impact on one's preference of seeking that funding source again and is closely associated with a higher chance of securing grants.

3.2   Institutional Characteristics Related to Grant Writers

To facilitate university faculty seeking external grants, Chval and Nossaman (2014) argued that university administrators should consider three essential components in the university support system. These components are to develop faculty's knowledge and skills related to seeking external grants, to enhance faculty's motivation, values, and self-concept, and to provide effective research grant tools. Specifically, these research grant tools include three major types: (1) grant writing manuals that outline college and university policies, procedures, and resources; (2) samples of proposal narratives, budgets, budget justifications, letters of support, and project timelines; and (3) supportive procedures offering effective and efficient application processes to save faculty's time and to give faculty emotional support. Empirical evidence suggests that enhancing these three components to support faculty significantly increases both grant proposal submission rates and grant success rates (Chval & Nossaman, 2014). Pinto and Huizinga (2018) have further examined both institutional support strategies and institutional barriers to grant-seeking activity through in-depth interviews with tenured or tenure-track faculty. They found three institutional support strategies, including hiring grant writers and offering administrative help for faculty, setting up pre-award research liaison to faculty, and offering internal seed awards to encourage faculty to do research, can increase faculty grant-seeking. In contrast, four institutional barriers, i.e., research administration changes, decentralization of pre-award and post-ward offices, lack of post-award support (e.g., submitting annual reports or paying contractors on time), and broken institutional promises (e.g., course releases) significantly decrease faculty grant-seeking intentions and attempts.

Recent search also indicates that faculty has experienced increasing pressure to seek external grants from universities and administrators (Anderson & Slade, 2016). For example, Musambira et al. (2012) conducted a national survey of 136 communications majors in the USA, examining whether the level of emphasis that the university places on external funding or the amount of research support provided at the university level predicted the amount of external funding faculty successfully obtained. The findings indicate that, while increasing the pressure on faculty, these universities do not increase the support for seeking grants. As a result, the success rate for obtaining external funding has not increased.

3.3 Educational Characteristics of Tools and Training for Grant Writers

3.3.1 Useful Tools for Grant Writers

To help researchers apply and obtain external grants, Moore et al. (2016), for example, presented the Funding Opportunities Database developed at a large southeastern university. As an innovative approach to professional development for faculty, this database identifies grant opportunities consistent with faculty research interests, provides faculty easy access to other grant-related support, and helps them gain the expertise required to succeed in securing funding for their research. The empirical evidence generated by the study indicates that most faculty liked the database and their grant activity has significantly increased after using it.

3.3.2 Academic Training on Grant Writers

Boyer and Cockriel (1997) found that only 51% of faculty who participated in a survey study received preparation in grant proposal writing from either their graduate institution or post-doctoral programs and called for graduate schools to institute training programs in proposal writing. Researchers (e.g., Boyer, 2007; Boyer & Cockriel, 2001) also found that faculty development workshops were useful to assist junior faculty in the grant-seeking process. However, much to our surprise, Shuman (2019) compared the formal training with the informal training in grant proposal preparation among all full-time, grant-seeking faculty members and discovered that informal training (i.e., "learn as you go" and "trial and error") tends to be more successful in the number of grant attainment and the total dollars attained.

4. Grant Writing

Writing a grant, including drafting a proposal, developing a budget, and submitting the application, is an important step in the research grant process. There is extensive literature on how to write a grant proposal, reflecting both perceived needs for grant writing training and accumulated experience in grant writing. In the area of grant writing, 60 studies have been identified (see Table A.2), addressing two major topics: key characteristics of rejected and successful grant writing (n = 8, 13%) and a wide variety of practical tips for grant writing in different fields for different targeted grant writers (e.g., graduate students, new faculty, tenured professors) (n = 52, 87%). The most cited scholars in this area are (1) Ulla Connor (1999) at Indiana University–Purdue University at Indianapolis, (2) Ernest Allen (1960) at the National Institutes of Health,[1] (3) Georges Bordage (2003) at the University of Illinois at Chicago, (4) Sharon Inouye

---

[1] Dr. Ernest Allen was the Chief of the Division of Research Grants during the earlier years of NIH and is a true pioneer in the science of research grant (e.g., Allen, 1960; Endicott & Allen, 1953; Lindsay & Allen, 1961). His 1960 paper is out of the coverage of this review in 1970–2020, but it is one of the most important and most cited articles in the area of grant writing. Thus, it is included in this review as the only exception.

Table A.2 *An overview of existing research on grant writing (N = 60)*

Major Area	Minor Area	Study Example
Characteristics of rejected and successful grant writing (*n* = 8)	1. Characteristics of rejected grant writing and application (*n* = 3)	Allen, 1960
	2. Characteristics of successful grant writing and application (*n* = 5)	Kanji, 2015
Tips on grant writing (*n* = 52)	1. General tips on grant writing in different fields (*n* = 45)	Madden & Wiles, 2003
	2. Academic writing vs. grant writing (*n* = 3)	Porter, 2017
	3. Factors related to resubmission (*n* = 2)	Boyington et al., 2016
	4. Tips on budget preparation (*n* = 4)	Bhatti et al., 2013
	5. Writing skills (*n* = 2)	Stenglin & Cléirigh, 2020

(2005) at Yale University School of Medicine, and (5) Kevin Chung (2008) at University of Michigan Health System.

4.1 Characteristics of Rejected and Successful Grant Writing

4.1.1 Characteristics of Rejected Grant Writing

Several studies analyzed and summarized the characteristics related to rejected grant writing and applications. Conducting one of the earliest and best analyses of grant applications, Allen (1960) investigated 605 rejected NIH grant applications and summarized four types of shortcomings of these rejected grant applications, including (1) *problem* that proposed research plans to answer (e.g., the importance of the proposed topic or timeliness is not sufficient to obtain the NIH grants), (2) *approach* that proposed research uses to answer the problem (e.g., the method on proposed research cannot generate sufficiently useful data), (3) *competence* that researchers have to pursue the grants (e.g., researchers do not have adequate experience or training for research), and (4) *logistic issues* (e.g., the requirements on personnel and/or equipment are unrealistic). The findings showed that 73% of rejected applications have shortcomings in *approach*, 58% of rejected applications have shortcomings in *problem*, 55% have a weakness in *competence*, and 16% have weaknesses in *others*.

4.1.2 Characteristics of Successful Grant Writing

Multiple studies have examined factors related to successful grant writing and preparation. Kanji (2015) suggested that a strong interest in the research topic is the most important thing if investigators are to be successful at grantsmanship and project completion. The careful preparation and planning before an actual grant application and specific efforts to align the goals of a project with the objectives of a funding agency are the most important factors to make a grant application successful. Koppelman and Holloway (2012) have found empirically that setting up long-term research goals and having experienced mentors, colleagues, and collaborators to improve grant proposals are crucial for successful grant preparation.

4.2 Tips for Grant Writing

4.2.1 General Tips on Grant Writing in Different Fields

More than 80% of the studies in this area discussed various tips in grant writing related to different fields for different targeted people. These studies (1) offered specific strategies on grant writing from the program officer's point of view; (2) discussed tips for grant writing in the medical field; (3) provided tips to young and novice researchers; (4) presented grant writing skills for graduate students in the Humanities and Social Sciences domain; and (5) suggested grant-writing strategies for counseling psychologists.

4.2.2 Academic Writing and Grant Writing

Multiple articles have been published to specify key differences between academic writing with grant writing. Porter (2017) argued that academic writing focuses on a scholarly pursuit and is past-oriented, theme-centered, expository rhetoric, impersonally toned, individualistic, has few length constraints, and uses specialized terminology. Grant writing focuses on sponsor goals and is future-oriented, project-centered, persuasive rhetoric, has a personal tone, is team-focused, has strict length constraints, and uses accessible language. Thus, the core problem in a failed grant proposal may lie in mistakenly using skills suitable for academic writing to write the grant proposal. Grant writing should use a strong, persuasive style (Porter, 2017; Connor & Mauranen, 1999). The emphasis of grant writing is to highlight the importance of the proposed research, to show the problem or gap in the field, and to discuss how the proposed research will fill the gap (Connor & Mauranen, 1999).

4.2.3 Factors Related to Resubmission

Revisions and resubmissions of a grant application are found to have a larger chance of being successful if researchers are willing to learn from peer reviewers' feedback (Madden & Wiles, 2003). This observation has been further confirmed by an empirical study that used a retrospective cohort study design to examine the resubmission rate as well as predictors of resubmission (Boyington et al., 2016). It was found that 54% of 821 unfunded NIH grant applications were resubmitted and that two significant predictors of resubmission are percentile scores and criterion scores rather than various demographics and institutional factors. Percentile score refers to the relative rank of an application compared to others reviewed by a particular study section, and the criterion score reflects reviewers' judgment of a PI's competence to execute a proposed project.

4.2.4 Tips on Budget Preparation

Several studies investigated how to make a successful budget plan. Careful preparation of the budget is essential (Madden & Wiles, 2003). Bhatti et al. (2013) provided suggestions for new investigators on how to write the proposed budget for health research funding agencies in Pakistan. A budget plan generally includes five subsections, personnel, materials, travel expenses, equipment, and indirect costs. To understand the allowed expenses, restrictions, and conditions of expenses, they recommended that researchers should seek professional advice from dedicated research officers who review grant budgets and from research managers who are involved in both research institutions and funding agencies.

4.2.5 Writing Skills in Grant Writing

A handful of studies explicitly focus on writing skills in grant writing. Stenglin and Cléirigh (2020), for instance, applied Halliday's Systemic Functional Linguistic Theory (Halliday & Matthiessen, 2014) and conducted a linguistic analysis of 18 grant applications. They found that the writers in three career stages have demonstrated three types of thematic patterning. For both mid-career researchers and senior established investigators, it is evolutionary (i.e., anchoring the project aims in past research while simultaneously addressing feasibility as it reflects the next logical step of their research) and revolutionary (i.e., going back to the fundaments and taking a radical approach to initiate a whole new approach and revolutionarily shift current paradigms). For an early-career researcher, it

Appendix: The Science of Research Grants 371

is a combination of these two prior thematic patterns aiming to propel a young investigator into a Principal Investigator career.

5. Grant Agencies

Grant agencies are professional institutions that provide and manage research grants, such as providing funding opportunities, organizing application reviews, making award decisions and notifications, handling post-award tasks such as grant distribution, progress reporting, and closeout. There is relatively limited literature on the grant agencies ($N = 37$), which can be summarized in three main areas (see Table A.3): (1) well-known public grant agencies ($n = 6$, 16%), (2) well-known private grant agencies ($n = 4$, 11%), (3) other related topics ($n = 30$, 81%). The most cited scholars in this area are (1) David King (2004) at the Office of Science and Technology, (2) Bruce Alberts (2014) at the University of California, San Francisco, (3) Lawrence Green (2001) at the National Center for Chronic Disease Prevention and Health Promotion, Centers for Disease Control and Prevention, Atlanta, (4) E. Ray Dorsey (2010) at University of Rochester Medical Center, and (5) Jacqueline Tetroe (2008) at the Canadian Institutes of Health Research.

5.1 Public Grant Agencies

Public agencies refer to agencies at the federal, centralized, or internationally collaborative funding bodies where budgetary decisions and spending statistics are made public (Dorsey et al., 2010; Viergever & Hendriks, 2016). We have found six studies discussing general information about public grant agencies. Although few in quantity, these studies provide relevant and useful comparisons of the annual grant amounts and various fields of research that were funded by public grant agencies. Particularly,

Table A.3 *An overview of literature on grant agencies (N = 36)*

Major Area	Minor Area	Study Example
Public grant agencies ($n = 6$)	Public grant agencies ($n = 6$)	Viergever & Hendriks, 2016
Private agencies ($n = 4$)	Philanthropic foundations ($n = 4$)	Birn, 2014
Grant agency policies ($n = 30$)	1. Grant policy improvement ($n = 17$)	Best, 2012
	2. Grant agency coordination ($n = 13$)	Kleer, 2010

in public health research, the grant agencies are ranked by their annual grant amounts throughout European, Asian, Australian, and Northern and Southern American nations (Bonetta, 2008; King, 2004; Viergever & Hendriks, 2016). For instance, Viergever and Hendriks (2016) indicate that NIH in the US was the largest public funder in 2013 worldwide. European Commission (EC), Medical Research Council (MRC) in the UK, Institute national de la santé et de la recherche médicale and Centre National de la Recherche Scientifique (CNRS) of France, and Department of Defense in the US are among other largest pubic funders. Other significant public funding agencies such as the Canadian Institutes of Health Research (CIHR), Australian National Health and Medical Research Council (NHMRC), Deutsche Forschungsgemeinschaft/German Research Foundation (DFG), and Japan Society for Promotion of Science (JSPS) also provide funding designated to health research.

5.2 Private Funding Agencies

Private agencies are non-government funding agencies based on individual donations, corporate gifts, industrial contracts, or non-profit foundation grants (Badelt, 2020; Reckhow & Snyder, 2014; Viergever & Hendriks, 2016). Several studies examined the largest private funding agencies around the world. Viergever and Hendriks (2016), for example, calculated about 40% of global health research spending that was supported by the 10 largest funders in the world, including the Wellcome Trust (UK) and the Howard Hughes Medical Institute (US) as two private funding agencies. The most profound discoveries regarding philanthropic foundations revolve around the potential threat of hidden objectives of philanthropic funders (Birn, 2014; Reckhow & Snyder, 2014). Birn (2014) points out that philanthropic funders such as the Rockefeller Foundation and the Bill & Melinda Gates Foundation (BMGF) might have embedded their long-term agenda for making other gains.

Although private agencies use their funding efforts to generate new knowledge on global health concerns, a philanthropic-capitalism dynamic is noted regarding the political and financial motives behind their funding practices (e.g., Birn, 2014; Viergever & Hendriks, 2016). Overall, private funders provide considerable practical contributions to the research community (Badelt, 2020; Viergever & Hendriks, 2016). Only certain well-known philanthropic funding agencies in the top funder chart have drawn sharp criticisms for their speculated funding motives.

Appendix: The Science of Research Grants 373

5.3 Grant Agency Policies

5.3.1 Grant Policy Improvement

Several studies have examined specific strategies for grant policy improvement. Viergever and Hendriks (2016) point out the importance of transparency in funding decisions across the public and philanthropic funders for the sake of better-integrated collaboration in health research. In the last four decades, NSF has been making changes to meet the large demands on proposal reviewing and decision making. NSF former program director Wilson (1975) penned multiple suggestions such as doling grants to include instrumentation purchases in university research proposals and separating proposal review panels from clerical staffing. To improve gender inequality in grantmaking, several studies made suggestions (Duchesne et al., 2017; Alvarez et al., 2019), such as allocating resources for evaluation of gender equality in review processes and using non-gendered terms in grant solicitations and reviewer guidelines.

Focusing on the improvement of policy makers, several studies investigated how to gauge funding agencies' efforts in transitioning research findings into actionable policies. Although typical promotional activities such as Push (i.e., using media), Pull (i.e., informing and influencing decision-making), and Linkage/Exchange (i.e., collaborating with other partners) are carried out (Tetroe et al., 2008; Cordero et al., 2008), few grant agencies sufficiently applied all three in research (McLean et al., 2018; Best, 2012). However, the spreading of knowledge does help policymakers adjust public research funding and implement systematic changes (Best, 2012; Smits & Denis, 2014). Further, grant agencies who are not professionals in a research field but work in positions such as legislative decision-making may need a different user-specific model to understand and help disseminate new knowledge in society (Green & Mercer, 2001). In European and North American countries, funding agencies help with the knowledge translation and ultimately influence the policymakers by asking the research community to publish the findings and share information on how to implement changes (Tetroe et al., 2008).

5.3.2 Grant Agency Coordination

A body of studies provides an initial understanding of how and where public and corporate funding agencies together to make a positive impact on innovative pursuits. For example, Kleer (2010) pointed out that public and corporate funders alike around the world have noticed how funding stimulates advancement in virtually every area of the sciences. China, Japan, South Korea, and Germany have all experienced positive growth in innovative technology through government research funds (Hong et al., 2016). Collectively speaking, government funding has been found to lead to a favorable outcome in patent production, which serves as an indicator for industry investors to follow suit in providing sponsorship (Azoulay et al., 2019; Kleer, 2010; Jensen et al., 2010). On the other hand, when universities allow industrial and corporate funding to enter academic research, the funder's agenda may have a coercive impact on research outcomes (Pachter et al., 2007).

6. Grant Review

A great review is a process of assessing the quality of submitted applications and making funding decisions. It has dominated the research literature in research grants over the last three decades. We found 54 journal articles (see Table A.4), addressing four major issues: (1) grant reviewers (n = 3, 6%); (2) grant review's criteria (n = 10, 19%); (3) grant assessment bias (n = 36, 67%), and (4) grant review improvement (n = 7, 13%). The most cited scholars in this area are (1) Christine Wenneras (1997) at Goteborg University, (2) Herbert Marsh (2008) at the University of Oxford, (3) Donna K. Ginther (2011) at the University of Kansas, (4) Domenic Cicchetti (2011) at Veterans Affairs Medical Center, and (5) Lutz Bornmann (2007) at the Swiss Federal Institute of Technology in Zurich.

Table A.4 *An overview of existing studies on grant review (N = 54)*

Major Area	Minor Area	Study Example
Grant reviewers (n = 3)	1. Characteristics of grant reviewers (n = 2)	Mutz et al., 2012
	2. Impact to grant reviewers (n = 1)	Gallo et al., 2019
Grant review's criteria (n = 10)	Grant review's criteria (n = 10)	Abdoul et al., 2012
Grant assessment bias (n = 36)	1. Decision-making bias (n = 20)	van den Besselaar & Leydesdorff, 2009
	2. Gender bias (n = 14)	Waisbren et al., 2008
	3. Race bias (n = 4)	Ginther et al., 2016
Grant review improvement (n = 7)	Suggestions to improve grant review (n = 7)	Shepherd et al., 2018

Appendix: The Science of Research Grants

6.1 Grant Reviewers

6.1.1 Characteristics of Grant Reviewers

Two studies explored characteristics of grant reviewers and found that female grant reviewers have a higher passing rate in grant proposals (Mutz et al., 2012) and selfish or negligent grant reviewers reduce the effectiveness of submitting more grant proposals while having less impact on funding declines (Roebber & Schultz, 2011).

6.1.2 Impact on Grant Reviewers

Only one research (Gallo et al., 2019) examined the impact of grant review experiences on reviewers and they found that peer reviewers can increase their grant-applying ability and inspire more new ideas by reviewing others' grant proposals.

6.2 Grant Review's Criteria

Abdoul et al. (2012) revealed that, among specific review criteria used by internal and external reviewers, the originality of a proposed study is considered the most crucial, methodological rigor is the second most crucial, and scientific relevance is the third crucial. While study feasibility, financial budget, proposal writing quality, and ethics are the least to be considered by the reviewers.

In addition, the measurement bias in the grant review has been documented by several studies (e.g., Sattler et al., 2015), including a lack of inter-rater reliability among reviewers and low reliability across countries and fields. Researchers have also examined potential solutions for increasing measurement reliability, including offering systematic training and increasing the number of reviewers. For example, Sattler et al. (2015) found that a brief training video can improve inter-rater reliability, rating scale, and time allocation to read grant criteria, based on the data of 75 public health professors as novice or experienced reviewers across different research universities in the United States.

6.3 Grant Assessment Bias

6.3.1 Grant Decision-Making Bias

The majority of the literature in this area uncovered that grant decision-making (1) overestimates or underestimates the grant applicants' long-term scientific performance, (2) gives fewer chances for the small universities to secure funding, and (3) is based on the applicants' published journal ranking. For example, the study by van den Besselaar and Leydesdorff (2009) investigated the grant applicants' success rates in the Netherlands Research Council. Their findings indicated that researchers whose grant proposals were rejected showed significantly higher success in their publications and citations than those whose proposals were funded suggesting that the grant selection process might not always be able to identify the "best" grant applicants.

In addition, researchers investigated institutional and individual factors that explicitly or implicitly influenced grant decisions. For example, Lepori et al. (2015) found a close association existed between university reputation and the number of applications for EU grants, and Enger and Castellacci (2016) further discovered that the scientific reputation of the applicant organization is strongly related to the EU's grant succeed rates. Individually, Martin et al. (2010) indicated that applicants' previous academic rating is closely related to final grant decisions, while Ernat et al. (2020) discovered that, in the orthopedics surgery field, the grant applicants' self-citation rates have minimal impacts on the success rate of grants.

6.3.2 Gender Bias

The majority of literature demonstrates that males have a higher chance to receive research funding than females across different medical fields, different countries, and different higher education institutions (e.g., Waisbren et al., 2008). However, some studies found that gender bias differs in scientific disciplines, suggesting that, in some certain areas such as life sciences, females received more grant funding than males (e.g., Rani & Luthra, 2011). There also exists some research that did not find gender bias in grant peer-review selection (e.g., Marsh et al., 2009). To reduce the gender bias in grant decision-making, researchers (e.g., Tricco et al., 2017) have provided the intervention and potential resolution for gender bias, proposing to decrease the gender information disclosure in the grant proposal references, recommendation letters, and review committee selection.

6.3.3 Race Bias

Researchers have reported that minority grant applicants had less chance to secure grants in the United States. For instance, Ginther et al. (2016) investigated the effects of gender and race on the probability of receiving the R01 grant from the National Institutes of Health (NIH). Based on a total of 47,424 grant applicants with 97,877 grant applications in 2000–2006 from different United States institutions, Asians and Blacks grant applicants had significantly less chance of receiving funding than Whites.

6.4 Grant Review Improvement

Regarding existing grant assessment bias, some of the existing research discussed reliable and approachable methods for grant review improvement, such as offering assistance to the young scholar, shortening grant application paperwork, and simplifying the complicated grant-review process. For instance, Shepherd et al. (2018) and Turner et al. (2018) indicated that simplifying grant proposal paperwork can increase effectiveness and efficiency in grant review decisions.

7. Grant Projects

Grant projects or funded projects are proposed research studies that have successfully received funding. Relatively extensive literature discussed funded projects ($N = 48$), mainly focusing on three areas (see Table A.5): (1) comparing grant projects in different disciplines ($n = 12$, 25%), (2) comparing grant projects by countries ($n = 6$, 13%), and (3) various trends in funded projects ($n = 32$, 67%). The most cited scholars in this area are (1) Cary Gross (1999) at Yale University School of Medicine, (2) Ingo Liefner (2003) at the University of Hannover, (3) Elizabeth Pellicano (2014) at the University of London, (4) Hamilton Moses (2015) at Johns Hopkins School of Medicine, and (5) Leslie Gillum (2011) at the University of California, San Francisco.

Table A.5 *An overview of studies on grant projects ($N = 47$)*

Major area	Minor area	Study example
Grant projects within disciplines ($n = 12$)	Discipline-specific funding projects ($n = 12$)	Gillum et al., 2011
Grant projects by countries ($n = 6$)	Strengths and weaknesses of grant projects by countries ($n = 6$)	King, 2004
Trends in grant projects ($n = 32$)	1. Worldwide change of grant projects ($n = 14$)	Bloch & Sørenson, 2015
	2. Grant projects change to reflect equity ($n = 19$)	Arora & Gambardella, 2005

378   Appendix: The Science of Research Grants

7.1 Comparing Grant Projects in Different Disciplines

Several studies analyzed funded projects in different disciplines, predominantly in medicine (e.g., Berger, 2005; Hume et al., 2015). Gross et al. (1999), for example, indicated that the most significant feature of NIH disease research funding was DALYs (disability-adjusted life-years, such as diabetes and AIDS as the diseases with the highest DALYs). Ten years later, similar results were echoed by Gillum et al. (2011) that the highest-funded projects by NIH were ADIS, diabetes, and perinatal conditions.

7.2 Comparing Grant Projects by Different Countries

Several studies provided an overview of the strengths and weaknesses of grant projects by countries. King (2004), for instance, divided 68 disciplinary units into seven fields (e.g., engineering, environment, mathematics, and health) and measured the funding amounts and publication citation rates across more than 190 countries. Looking across all the seven fields, Russia is strong in physical sciences and engineering but weak in life sciences; Japan is strong in physical sciences and engineering; France is strong in mathematics. Such comparison gives valuable insight into these countries' research strengths in a particular field. However, Huang and Huang (2018) reported that life science has the largest proportion of funded research output in countries such as Canada, China, France, and Germany, whereas China, Japan, Germany, and the US encourage nanotechnology research. Additionally, Russia and China tend to direct their public funding domestically, while NSF and NIH of the US are known to provide funding to non-domestic researchers (Huang and Huang, 2018).

7.3 Trends in Grant Projects

7.3.1 Worldwide Changes in Funding Size

A new trend was discovered that public funding programs worldwide are moving towards awarding a larger amount to research groups or research centers instead of individually (Bloch & Sørenson, 2015; Hong et al., 2016). The rationale is that such changes will create the critical mass needed for increasing scientific excellence. University research groups or research centers are more likely to initiate multi-disciplinary and university–industry collaborations. Increases in funding sizes are observed in multiple industrialized nations. For instance, Bloch and Sørenson (2015) found that Denmark's Council for Independent Research awarded 65% of its projects to small grants ($170,000) and 19% to grants larger than $260,000 in 2001. In 2009, however, the award distribution was flipped, with only 16% awarded on small-grant projects and 70% awarded on projects that called for $260,000 or more. Upward shifts in funding sizes also took place in the Norwegian Research Council that increased the average funding amount from $500,000 to $930,000 but lowered the funding rate from 19% to 11%. EU has also upped the project fund size in the hopes of establishing more coherent research collaborations with clear scientific priorities. DFG in Germany, NSF in the US, ARC in Australia, and JSPS in Japan have all placed noticeable increases in project funding amounts. Empirical evidence suggests that this change has generated strong effects on the development of science and innovation in China and Japan (Bonetta, 2008; Hong et al., 2016) as well as in the US and European Commission (see Gurwitz et al., 2014).

7.3.2 Various Changes in Funding Patterns

More than 20 articles examined how the changes in grant projects in funding patterns have affected research investigators' objectives. For instance, Dickler et al. (2007) found a significant difference in first-time NIH R01 application funding rates between MDs and PhDs where MD investigators were funded at a lower rate than PhD ones. Another NIH funding pattern was that award rates were disproportionately lower for surgeon scientists in the R01 surgical research (Hu et al., 2015). Besides funding patterns, it was found that both NIH and the Melinda and Bill Gates Foundation predominantly focused on predelivery research while a disproportionately meager amount of funding went to technology utilization that could also have effectively prevented children's deaths (Leroy et al., 2007). However, in the past, an increase in funding amounts has been also observed in some research areas, e.g., environmental science by EPA (Reichhardt, 1994) and bioengineering by NIH (Hendee et al., 2002).

8. Grant Management

Grant management typically concerns the post-award administration and implementation of funded projects. While it is an important step in the research grant process, the research literature is scarce. Only six journal articles were identified. However, five out of these six studies essentially discussed more about how to apply for research grants rather than how to manage grants after receiving them. The study by Abrahamson (1996) exclusively explored grant management and is the most cited one. Specifically, Abrahamson (1996) focused on how medical faculty managed an NIH grant after they received it. For faculty members, they need to obtain grants strategically and should allocate a portion of grants to support their salaries with another portion of grants to support school or institution revenue; for institutions, they need to consider increasing the administrative personnel staff positions to better utilize grants efficiently and reasonably.

9. Grant Impacts

As the final step of the research grant process, grant impacts refer to both direct scientific outcomes that the funded projects might produce and various impacts on individual researchers, research institutions, and the entire society as a whole. A total of 49 articles were identified that focus on grant impacts (see Table A.6), mainly addressing positive grant impacts (n = 39, 80%) and negative grant impacts (n = 10, 20%). The most cited scholars in this area are (1) Magnus Gulbrandsen (2005) at the University of Oslo,[2] (2) Otto Auranen (2010) at the Institute for Social Research of Academy of Finland,[3] (3) Bruce Alberts (2014) at the University of California at

Table A.6 *An overview of existing studies on grant impacts (N = 49)*

Major Area	Minor Area	Study Example
Positive impact (n = 39)	1. Positive impact on institutions (n = 20)	Dickson et al., 2019
	2. Positive impact on faculty (n = 15)	Van Epps & Younger, 2011
	3. Positive impact on graduate students (n = 4)	Byrne et al., 2010
Negative impact (n = 10)	Negative impact on productivity (n = 10)	Mongeon et al., 2016

---

[2] Yes, https://scholar.google.com/citations?hl=en&user=OWBAjtUAAAAJ&view_op=list_works&sortby=pubdate, innovation, entrepreneurial university.
[3] Yes, https://scholar.google.com/citations?hl=en&user=PEIjDNEAAAAJ&view_op=list_works&sortby=pubdate; university research performance.

Appendix: The Science of Research Grants

San Francisco,[4] (4) Brian Jacob (2011) at the University of Michigan,[5] (5) Barry Bozeman (2007) at the University of Georgia,[6] and (6) Abigail Payne (2003) at McMaster University.[7]

9.1 Positive Impact

9.1.1 Positive Impact on Institutions

The extensive literature (e.g., Dickson et al., 2019) has revealed that receiving grants can increase an institution's research outcomes, higher h – index, increase international connections, better policy and practice across different disciplines, and better scientific creativity. Dickson et al. (2019), for example, analyzed the effect of the grant funding on physical therapists' long-term research outcomes in 2008–2016 and found that receiving funding was related to higher research productivity.

9.1.2 Positive Impact on Faculty

The majority of the existing literature (e.g., Van Epps and Younger, 2011) revealed that receiving grants made various positive contributions to grant recipients' development. These positive contributions include (1) stronger career development across different medical research fields, (2) higher scholar citations in the field across various science disciplines, and (3) longer retention and salary increments among faculty after awarding grants. For instance, Van Epps and Younger (2011) analyzed 18 grant applicants' curricula vitae after receiving a prestigious medical grant. They found that successful grant recipients displayed better career development later on, with more publications and more external grants.

9.1.3 Positive Impact on Graduate Students

Several studies found that grants had a positive impact on graduate students' development. One study found that recipients of NSF graduate fellowships finished their doctoral program earlier (Chapman & McCauley, 1993). Other studies found that faculty receiving external grants provided

---

[4] X biomedical research enterprise,.
[5] X student achievement, teacher education.
[6] Yes, Transfer, job, https://scholar.google.com/scholar?hl=en&as_sdt=0%2C22&q=Barry+Bozeman+%282007%29+at+the+University+of+Georgia&btnG=.
[7] https://scholar.google.com/citations?hl=en&user=-6vVxUoAAAAJ&view_op=list_works&sortby=pubdate, crowd out, finance, STEM.

better opportunities to train graduate students and improve their graduate program (e.g., Byrne et al., 2010; Steinmetz, 2007).

9.2 Negative Impact on Productivity

Strong evidence suggests that receiving a grant was not always associated with higher scientific outputs, high-quality productivity, or better publications (e.g., Mongeon et al., 2016). For instance, Mongeon et al. (2016) assessed the relationship between the amount of funding allocated to 12,720 researchers in Quebec of Canada from 1998 to 2012 and their scientific output and impact from 2000 to 2014. They found that the most founded researchers who received 27 times, 40 times, and 32 times more funding than the rest of the researchers in health sciences, natural sciences, and social sciences published only six, five, and 19 times more than their average colleagues. Conversely, less funded researchers with higher publications were also identified. The research indicates that receiving more funding does not necessarily result in higher output and better impact. One possible explanation is related to time management. Researchers may spend much more time focusing on writing grant proposals to secure higher amounts of funding, leaving them less time performing research. It is also possible that researchers obtaining more funding may lead to larger projects that may require more coordination efforts and time. Consequently, less time may be left to focus on research.

10. Future Directions

This review developed a process-based conceptual framework, chose a Scoping Review approach, and generated a general picture of grantology as the science of research grants for the first time. Based on the conceptual framework mapping the science of research grants displayed in Figure A.3 and the existing literature reviewed in the seven areas, we can conclude that substantial research efforts have been accumulated in four areas of research, i.e., grant writing, grant reviewing (especially gender biases), grant projects, and grant impacts (see the four boxes in bold of Figure A.4). To further advance the science of research grants and develop evidence-based practice, we would point out four important research directions, development of grant writers, characteristics of grant professionals, processes of grant resubmission, and use and management of grants (see the four boxes in dot lines of Figure A.4).

Appendix: The Science of Research Grants 383

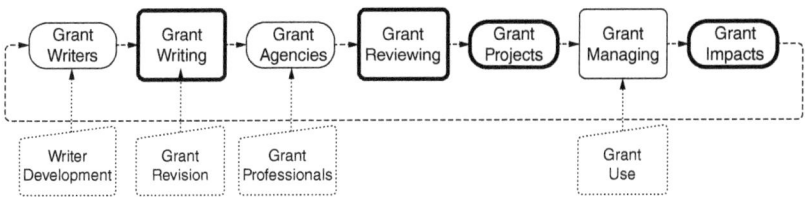

Figure A.4   Well-studied areas and much-needed areas in grantology as the science of research grants
Note. The four boxes in bold are well-studied research areas. The four boxes in dotted lines are much-needed research areas.

10.1   Development of Grant Writers

Journal publication, as studied in the science of scientific publications or *"journalology"*, and grant acquisition, as studied in the science of research grants or *"grantology"*, are two core professional skills for modern researchers (Yan, 2021). However, the grant application is more challenging than journal publication, especially for a junior researcher. The extensive literature exists, documented the characteristics of grant writers, individual and institutional factors that impact grant writers, and academic tools to enhance grant writers' capability. However, little is known about the developmental process of grant writers from a novice grant writer to a well-established grant writer. Answering this question will significantly advance the current knowledge about how to develop grantsmanship as a highly sophisticated and highly demanded professional skill. It will also have tremendous practical implications for training and supporting grant writers at different levels. Longitudinal studies are urgently needed to accumulate empirical evidence and design developmental programs.

10.2   Grant Revisions

Grant writing is one of the four most studied areas in the science of research grants. Most of the existing literature essentially has focused on practice-oriented descriptive and explorative research, and thus rigorous empirical studies are needed to generate robust evidence on how to prepare, write, and submit competitive grants. More importantly, given that most funded grant proposals normally go through iterations of revisions and resubmissions (Boyington et al., 2016; Madden & Wiles, 2003) but the literature on resubmission is still extremely limited, empirical research is urgently needed to synthesize and promote the current best practice of revisions and resubmission and to reveal the underlying processes and contributing factors of successful and unsuccessful resubmissions.

10.3 Grant Professionals

Given the importance of getting research grants, the increasingly competitive nature of getting grants, and the sophistication of the research grant enterprise, research is needed to further develop a deep and comprehensive knowledge of a wide variety of grant professionals. These grant professionals might include foundation senior executives, chief grant officers (CGOs), program directors, program officers, Institutional Review Board (IRB) officers, budget officers, grant managers, grant firm consultants, grant writing trainers, and professional grant writers. Grant professionals are actually involved in every step of the entire grant process, from the very beginning to the very end rather than just in one or two steps. It is no longer sufficient to study only grant writers or peer reviewers in the expanding large professional research grant community. It is time to study and understand the entire community, including the typology and the diversity of grant professionals, so that the knowledge of research grant professionals will be added or updated substantially for their increasingly important roles and increasingly lasting impacts on research grants.

10.4 Grant Use

Grant management and grant implementation are two critical tasks going in parallel after program officers make funding decisions and before researchers generate grant impacts. However, little is known scientifically about the details of this post-award process. Now it could be the weakest link in the grant research and grant practice. For grant *professionals*, including program officers and research managers, they will involve multiple aspects of research management, including equipment purchasing, accounting, project reporting and monitoring, protect termination, extension, or transfer, and program assessment and priority adjustment. For research *scientists*, receiving grants successfully is not only the ending point of the grant application process but also the starting point of the important and challenging process of using grants and conducting studies well to complete the funded projects so that they can make significant scientific contributions and generate broad social impacts. They might face various challenges in using the funding to complete the funded project effectively

Appendix: The Science of Research Grants 385

and efficiently. Thus, research efforts should be made to understand how the process takes place after a researcher finally receives the funding notice, who are the critical players involved in this process, what risk and protective factors are involved, and how to best use and manage grants to generate research impacts effectively and efficiently.

This review has limitations that should be overcome in future work. First, as an initial effort, the research question of the present review focused merely on the development of a genera picture of the science of research grants. Research grants are a complex and diverse topic, and have been examined on multiple aspects (e.g., philosophic, psychological, political, managerial, economic, and methodological aspects), at multiple levels (e.g., at individual, group, institutional, societal, and global levels), and in multiple scales (e.g., micro, meso, and micro scales). Future work should ask a wide variety of research questions to synthesize further the science of research grants. Second, the major method used in the study is a scoping review to address the current big-picture-oriented research question. Future work should expand from the current scoping review to the systematic review or meta-analysis to synthesize the literature more effectively and efficiently. Third, the present scoping review mainly focuses on empirical journal articles, especially highly cited ones. While this selection strategy is necessary and justifiable, future work should cover various types of literature (e.g., major handbooks, books, and book chapters; reports from governments, foundations, and think tanks; dissertations and theses; conference proceedings; and major case studies). Fourth, the conceptual framework used in the present review is a basic model that focuses on basic elements and basic steps of research grant activities. Built on this basic model, advanced and comprehensive models can and should be advanced to match closely the complex nature of research grant activities in the real-life world. While the present review has useful implications for both understanding the science of research grants (e.g., having a bird's-eye view of the entire field) and informing evidence-based policy decisions (e.g., enhancing ubiquitous roles of research professionals played in every aspect of the basic process of research grants), overcoming the limitations presented above will help advance knowledge of research grants and improve research grant practices.

Compliance with Ethical Standards

Funding: No funding was received for this study.
Ethical approval: This article does not contain any studies with human participants or animals performed by any of the authors.

References

Note: References indicate that studies are cited in this scoping review, while texts in the bibliography indicate that studies have been synthesized but not cited due to page limits.

Arora, A., & Gambardella, A. (2005). The impact of NSF support for basic research in economics. *Annales d'Economie et de Statistique, 79/80*, 91–117.

Abdoul, H., Perrey, C., Amiel, P., Tubach, F., Gottot, S., Durand-Zaleski, I., & Alberti, C. (2012). Peer review of grant applications: Criteria used and qualitative study of reviewer practices. *PLoS One, 7*(9), e46054.

Abrahamson, S. (1996). Time to return medical schools to their primary purpose: education. *Academic Medicine: Journal of the Association of American Medical Colleges, 71*(4), 343–347.

Alberts, B., Kirschner, M. W., Tilghman, S., & Varmus, H. (2014). Rescuing US biomedical research from its systemic flaws. *Proceedings of the National Academy of Sciences, 111*(16), 5773–5777.

Allen, E. M. (1960). Why are research grant applications disapproved? *Science, 132*(3439), 1532–1534.

Álvarez-Bornstein, B., Morillo, F., & Bordons, M. (2017). Funding acknowledgments in the Web of Science: completeness and accuracy of collected data. *Scientometrics, 112*(3), 1793–1812.

Anderson, D. M., & Slade, C. P. (2016). Managing institutional research advancement: Implications from a university faculty time allocation study. *Research in Higher Education, 57*(1), 99–121.

Anderson, J. H. (1999). NIH and NSF funding mechanisms applicable to interventional radiology. *Journal of Vascular and Interventional Radiology, 10*(1), 1–8.

Arora, A., David, P., & Gambardella, A. (1997). *Reputation and competence in publicly funded science*. Mimeo.

Auranen, O., & Nieminen, M. (2010). University research funding and publication performance – An international comparison. *Research Policy, 39*(6), 822–834.

Azoulay, P., Graff Zivin, J., Li, D., & Sampat, B. (2019). Public R&D investments and private-sector patenting: Evidence from NIH funding rules. *The Review of Economic Studies, 86*(1), 117–152.

Badelt, C. (2020). Private external funding of universities: Blind alley or new opening?. *Review of Managerial Science*, 1–12.

Benway, B. M., Kalidas, P., Cabello, J. M., & Bhayani, S. B. (2009). Does citation analysis reveal association between h-index and academic rank in urology? *Urology, 74*(1), 30–33.

Berger D. H. (2005). An introduction to obtaining extramural funding. *The Journal of Surgical Research, 128*(2), 226–231.

Best, R. K. (2012). Disease politics and medical research funding: Three ways advocacy shapes policy. *American Sociological Review, 77*(5), 780–803.

Bhatti, J. A., Akhtar, U., Butt, B. A., & Janjua, N. Z. (2013). Presenting budget in a research grant application. *Journal of Pakistan Medical Association, 63*(6), 793–796.

Birn, A. E. (2014). Philanthrocapitalism, past and present: The Rockefeller Foundation, the Gates Foundation, and the setting(s) of the international/global health agenda. *Hypothesis, 12*(1), e8.

Bloch, C., & Sørensen, M. (2015). The size of research funding: Trends and implications. *Science and Public Policy, 42*(1), 30–43.

Bonetta, L. (2008). Enhancing NIH grant peer review: A broader perspective. *Cell, 135*(2), 201–204.

Bordage, G., & Dawson, B. (2003). Experimental study design and grant writing in eight steps and 28 questions. *Medical Education, 37*(4), 376–385.

Boyer, P. G. (2007). Who's securing grants?: Demographics of full-time faculty at two-year institutions. *Community College Journal of Research and Practice, 31*(5), 409–420.

Boyer, P. G., & Cockriel, I. (2001). Grant performance of junior faculty across disciplines: Motivators and barriers. *Journal of Research Administration, 2*(1), 19–24.

Boyer, P., & Cockriel, I. (1997). Factors influencing grant writing: Perceptions of tenured and nontenured faculty. *SRA Journal, 29*(3/4), 61–68.

Boyington, J. E., Antman, M. D., Patel, K. C., & Lauer, M. S. (2016). Towards independence: Resubmission rate of unfunded national heart, lung, and blood institute R01 research grant applications among early stage investigators. *Academic Medicine: Journal of the Association of American Medical Colleges, 91*(4), 556–562.

Byrne, M. M., Losso, I. S., & Koniaris, L. G. (2010). What is the institutional financial impact of an MD-PhD program without extramural funding? *Teaching and Learning in Medicine, 22*(1), 56–59.

Chapman, G. B., & McCauley, C. (1993). Early career achievements of National Science Foundation (NSF) graduate applicants: Looking for Pygmalion and Galatea effects on NSF winners. *Journal of Applied Psychology, 78*(5), 815–820.

Chval, K., & Nossaman, L. (2014). Raising the bar on external research funding: Infrastructure and strategies for enhancing faculty productivity. *The Journal of Faculty Development, 28*(1), 41–48.

Connor, U., & Mauranen, A. (1999). Linguistic analysis of grant proposals: European Union research grants. *English for Specific Purposes, 18*(1), 47–62.

Cordero, C., Delino, R., Jeyaseelan, Lansang, M., Lozano, J., Kumar, S., Moreno, S., Pietersen, M., Quirino, J., Thamlikitkul, V., Welch, V., Tetroe, J., ter Kuile, A., Graham, I., Grimshaw, J., Neufeld, V., Wells, G., & Tugwell, P. (2008). Funding agencies in low- and middle-income countries: Support for knowledge translation. *Bulletin of the World Health Organization, 86*(7), 524–534.

Dickler, H., Fang, D., Heinig, S., Johnson, E., & Korn, D. (2007). New physician-investigators receiving national institutes of health research project grants: A historical perspective on the "endangered species." *JAMA, 297*(22), 2496–2501.

Dickson, T., Chen, P. D., & Taylor, B. (2019). Impact of funding allocation on physical therapist research productivity and DPT student graduates:

An analysis using panel data. *Advances in Health Sciences Education*, 24(2), 269–285.
Dorsey, E., de Roulet, J., Thompson, J., Reminick, J., Thai, A., White-Stellato, Z., Beck, C., George, B., & Moses, H. (2010). Funding of US biomedical research, 2003–2008. *JAMA*, 303(2), 137–143.
Endicott, K. M., & Allen, E. M. (1953). The growth of medical research 1941–1953 and the role of Public Health Service research grants. *Science*, 118(3065), 337–343.
Enger, S. G., & Castellacci, F. (2016). Who gets Horizon 2020 research grants? Propensity to apply and probability to succeed in a two-step analysis. *Scientometrics*, 109(3), 1611–1638.
Ernat, J. J., Yheulon, C. G., Lopez, A. J., & Warth, L. C. (2020). Does the h-index and self-citation affect external funding of orthopedic surgery research? An analysis of fellowship directors and their subspecialties. *Journal of Orthopaedics*, 20, 92–96.
Gallo, S. A., Thompson, L. A., Schmaling, K. B., & Glisson, S. R. (2019). The participation and motivations of grant peer reviewers: A comprehensive survey. *Science and Engineering Ethics*, 1–22.
Gillum, L., Gouveia, C., Dorsey, E., Pletcher, M., Mathers, C., McCulloch, C., & Johnston, S. (2011). NIH disease funding levels and burden of disease. *PLoS One*, 6(2), e16837.
Ginther, D. K., Kahn, S., & Schaffer, W. T. (2016). Gender, race/ethnicity, and National Institutes of Health R01 research awards: Is there evidence of a double bind for women of color? *Academic Medicine: Journal of the Association of American Medical Colleges*, 91(8), 1098–1107.
Green, L. W., & Mercer, S. L. (2001). Can public health researchers and agencies reconcile the push from funding bodies and the pull from communities? *American Journal of Public Health*, 91(12), 1926–1929.
Gross, C. P., Anderson, G. F., & Powe, N. R. (1999). The relation between funding by the National Institutes of Health and the burden of disease. *New England Journal of Medicine*, 340(24), 1881–1887.
Gulbrandsen, M. & Smeby, J. C. (2005) Industry funding and university professors' research performance. *Research Policy*, 34(6), 932–950.
Gurwitz, D., Milanesi, E., & Koenig, T. (2014). Grant application review: The case of transparency. *PLoS Biology*, 12(12), e1002010.
Haller, M. K., & Welch, E. W. (2014). Entrepreneurial behavior of academic scientists: Network and cognitive determinants of commitment to grant submissions and award outcomes. *Entrepreneurship Theory and Practice*, 38(4), 807–831.
Hechtman, L. A., Moore, N. P., Schulkey, C. E., Miklos, A. C., Calcagno, A. M., Aragon, R., & Greenberg, J. H. (2018). NIH funding longevity by gender. *Proceedings of the National Academy of Sciences*, 115(31), 7943–7948.
Hendee, W. R., Chien, S., Maynard, C. D., & Dean, D. J. (2002). The national institute of biomedical imaging and bioengineering: History, status, and potential impact. *Annals of Biomedical Engineering*, 30(1), 2–10.

Hollenbach, A. D. (2018). *A Practical Guide to Writing a Ruth L. Kirschstein NRSA Grant*. Academic Press.
Hong, J., Feng, B., Wu, Y., & Wang, L. (2016). Do government grants promote innovation efficiency in China's high-tech industries? *Technovation, 57–58*, 4–13.
Hu, Y., Edwards, B., Brooks, K., Newhook, T., & Slingluff, C. (2015). Recent trends in National Institutes of Health funding for surgery: 2003 to 2013. *The American Journal of Surgery, 209*(6), 1083–1089.
Huang, M. H., & Huang, M. J. (2018). An analysis of global research funding from subject field and funding agencies perspectives in the G9 countries. *Scientometrics, 115*(2), 833–847.
Hume, K. M., Giladi, A. M., & Chung, K. C. (2015). Factors impacting successfully competing for research funding: An analysis of applications submitted to the Plastic Surgery Foundation. *Plastic and Reconstructive Surgery, 135*(2), 429e.
Jagsi, R., Motomura, A. R., Griffith, K. A., Rangarajan, S., & Ubel, P. A. (2009). Sex differences in attainment of independent funding by career development awardees. *Annals of Internal Medicine, 151*(11), 804–811.
Jayasinghe, U. W., Marsh, H. W., & Bond, N. (2003). A multilevel cross-classified modelling approach to peer review of grant proposals: The effects of assessor and researcher attributes on assessor ratings. *Journal of the Royal Statistical Society: Series A (Statistics in Society), 166*(3), 279–300.
Jensen, R., Thursby, J., & Thursby, M. C. (2010). University-industry spillovers, government funding, and industrial consulting. *National Bureau of Economic Research*. Retrieved from www.nber.org/system/files/working_papers/w15732/w15732.pdf
Kanji, S. (2015). Turning your research idea into a proposal worth funding. *The Canadian Journal of Hospital Pharmacy, 68*(6), 458–464.
Keenihan, S. H. (2001). Gender bias in grant application rates. *Trends in Parasitology, 17*(4), 165.
King, D. (2004). The scientific impact of nations. *Nature* (London), *430*(6997), 311–316.
Kleer, R. (2010). Government R&D subsidies as a signal for private investors. *Research Policy, 39*(10), 1361–1374.
Koppelman, G. H., & Holloway, J. W. (2012). Successful grant writing. *Paediatric Respiratory Reviews, 13*(1), 63–66.
Laudel, G. (2006). The art of getting funded: How scientists adapt to their funding conditions. *Science and Public Policy, 33*(7), 489–504.
Lepori, B., Veglio, V., Heller-Schuh, B., Scherngell, T., & Barber, M. (2015). Participations to European Framework Programs of higher education institutions and their association with organizational characteristics. *Scientometrics, 105*(3), 2149–2178.
Leroy, J., Habicht, J., Pelto, G., & Bertozzi, S. (2007). Current priorities in health research funding and lack of impact on the number of child deaths per year. *American Journal of Public Health, 97*(2), 219–223.
Ley, T. J., & Hamilton, B. H. (2008). The gender gap in NIH grant applications. *Science, 322*(5907), 1472–1474.

Lindsay, D. R., & Allen, E. M. (1961). Medical research: Past support, future directions. *Science, 134*(3495), 2017–2024.

Madden, S., & Wiles, R. (2003). Developing a successful application for research funding. *Physiotherapy, 89*(9), 518–522.

Marsh, H. W., Bornmann, L., Mutz, R., Daniel, H. D., & O'Mara, A. (2009). Gender effects in the peer reviews of grant proposals: A comprehensive meta-analysis comparing traditional and multilevel approaches. *Review of Educational Research, 79*(3), 1290–1326.

Marsh, H. W., Jayasinghe, U. W., & Bond, N. W. (2008). Improving the peer-review process for grant applications: Reliability, validity, bias, and generalizability. *American Psychologist, 63*(3), 160–168.

Martin, M. R., Kopstein, A., & Janice, J. M. (2010). An analysis of preliminary and post-discussion priority scores for grant applications peer reviewed by the Center for Scientific Review at the NIH. *PLoS One, 5*(11), e13526.

McLean, R., Graham, I., Tetroe, J., & Volmink, J. (2018). Translating research into action: An international study of the role of research funders. *Health Research Policy and Systems, 16*(1), 44.

Mongeon, P., Brodeur, C., Beaudry, C., & Larivière, V. (2016). Concentration of research funding leads to decreasing marginal returns. *Research Evaluation, 25*(4), 396–404.

Moore, A. L., Reiser, R. A., Bradley, T. W., & Zhao, W. (2016). Faculty professional development focused on identifying funding opportunities: An interactive tool. *The Journal of Faculty Development, 30*(3), 5–14.

Moses, H., Matheson, D., Cairns-Smith, S., George, B., Palisch, C., & Dorsey, E. (2015). The anatomy of medical research: US and international comparisons. *JAMA, 313*(2), 174–189.

Musambira, G., Collins, S., Brown, T., & Voss, K. (2012). From "publish or perish" to "grant or perish" examining grantsmanship in communication and the pressures on communication faculty to procure external funding for research. *Journalism & Mass Communication Educator, 67*(3), 234–251.

Mutz, R., Bornmann, L., & Daniel, H. D. (2012). Does gender matter in grant peer review? An empirical investigation using the example of the Austrian science fund. *Zeitschrift für Psychologie, 220*(2), 121–129.

Nicholson-Crotty, S. (2015). *Governors, grants, and elections: Fiscal federalism in the American states*. JHU Press.

Orlich, D., & Shrope, N. (2012). *Developing a winning grant proposal*. Routledge.

Pachter, W., Fox, R., Zimbardo, P., & Antonuccio, D. (2007). Corporate funding and conflicts of interest: A primer for psychologists. *The American Psychologist, 62*(9), 1005–1015.

Pinto, K. M., & Huizinga, D. (2018). Institutional barriers and faculty persistence: Understanding faculty grant-seeking at a predominantly undergraduate institution. *The Journal of Faculty Development, 32*(1), 65–72.

Popper, K. (2005). *The logic of scientific discovery*. Routledge.

Porter, R. (2017). Reprint 2007: Why academics have a hard time writing good grants proposals. *Journal of Research Administration, 48*(1), 15–25.

Rani, K., & Luthra, R. (2011). Are research grants free from gender bias: An overview of funding pattern of CSIR extramural research projects in life sciences. *Current Science*, 38–42.
Reckhow, S., & Snyder, J. W. (2014). The expanding role of philanthropy in education politics. *Educational Researcher, 43*(4), 186–195.
Reichhardt, T. (1994). EPA reveals plans to double external grants. *Nature, 372*(6507), 583.
Salter, A. J., & Martin, B. R. (2000). The economic benefits of publicly funded basic research: A critical review. *Research Policy, 30*(3), 509–532.
Sattler, D. N., McKnight, P. E., Naney, L., & Mathis, R. (2015). Grant peer review: Improving inter-rater reliability with training. *PLoS One, 10*(6), e0130450.
Scott Van Epps, J., & Younger, J. G. (2011). Early career academic productivity among emergency physicians with R01 grant funding. *Academic Emergency Medicine, 18*(7), 759–762.
Shavers, V. L., Fagan, P., Lawrence, D., McCaskill-Stevens, W., McDonald, P., Browne, D., ... & Trimble, E. (2005). Barriers to racial/ethnic minority application and competition for NIH research funding. *Journal of the National Medical Association, 97*(8), 1063–1077.
Shepherd, J., Frampton, G. K., Pickett, K., & Wyatt, J. C. (2018). Peer review of health research funding proposals: A systematic map and systematic review of innovations for effectiveness and efficiency. *PLoS One, 13*(5), e0196914.
Shuman, K. M. (2019). Grant proposal preparation readiness: A glimpse at the education level of higher education faculty. *Journal of Research Administration, 50*(1), 89–107.
Smits, P., & Denis, J. (2014). How research funding agencies support science integration into policy and practice: An international overview. *Implementation Science: IS, 9*(1), 28.
Steinmetz, J. (2007). The importance of external grant support for a public college of arts and science. *Merrill Series on The Research Mission of Public Universities*, 28–31.
Stenglin, M., & Cléirigh, C. (2020). Scientific grant application writing: Re/packaging text to enhance its impact. *Journal of English for Academic Purposes, 44*, 100823.
Tetroe, J. M., Graham, I. D., Foy, R., Robinson, N., Eccles, M. P., Wensing, M., ... & Ward, J. E. (2008). Health research funding agencies' support and promotion of knowledge translation: An international study. *The Milbank Quarterly, 86*(1), 125–155.
Tricco, A. C., Thomas, S. M., Antony, J., Rios, P., Robson, R., Pattani, R., ... & Straus, S. E. (2017). Strategies to prevent or reduce gender bias in peer review of research grants: A rapid scoping review. *PLoS One, 12*(1), e0169718.
Turner, S., Bull, A., Chinnery, F., Hinks, J., Mcardle, N., Moran, R., ... & Wyatt, J. C. (2018). Evaluation of stakeholder views on peer review of NIHR applications for funding: A qualitative study. *BMJ Open, 8*(12), e022548.
van den Besselaar, P., & Leydesdorff, L. (2009). Past performance, peer review and project selection: A case study in the social and behavioral sciences. *Research Evaluation, 18*(4), 273–288.

Van Slyke, C. J. (1946). New horizons in medical research. *Science*, *104*(2711), 559–567.
Viergever, R., & Hendriks, T. (2016). The 10 largest public and philanthropic funders of health research in the world: What they fund and how they distribute their funds. *Health Research Policy and Systems*, *14*(1), 1–15.
Waisbren, S. E., Bowles, H., Hasan, T., Zou, K. H., Emans, S. J., Goldberg, C., ... & Longtine, J. (2008). Gender differences in research grant applications and funding outcomes for medical school faculty. *Journal of Women's Health*, *17*(2), 207–214.
Wilson, M. K. (1975). The top twenty and the rest: Big chemistry and little funding. *Annual Review of Physical Chemistry*, *26*(1), 1–17.
Witteman, H. O., Hendricks, M., Straus, S., & Tannenbaum, C. (2019). Are gender gaps due to evaluations of the applicant or the science? A natural experiment at a national funding agency. *The Lancet*, *393*(10171), 531–540.

Bibliography

Adair, J. G. (1986). Research resources in Canadian university psychology departments. *Canadian Psychology/Psychologie Canadienne*, *27*(4), 342–356.
Ali, M. M., Bhattacharyya, P., & Olejniczak, A. J. (2010). The effects of scholarly productivity and institutional characteristics on the distribution of federal research grants. *The Journal of Higher Education*, *81*(2), 164–178.
Al-Shukaili, A., & Al-Maniri, A. (2017). Writing a research proposal to the Research Council of Oman. *Oman Medical Journal*, *32*(3), 180–188.
Alvarez, S. N. E., Jagsi, R., Abbuhl, S. B., Lee, C. J., & Myers, E. R. (2019). Promoting gender equity in grant making: What can a funder do? *The Lancet*, *393*(10171), e9–e11.
Amiri, A. R., Kanesalingam, K., Cro, S., & Casey, A. T. (2014). Does source of funding and conflict of interest influence the outcome and quality of spinal research? *The Spine Journal*, *14*(2), 308–314.
Ardehali, H. (2014). How to write a successful grant application and research paper. *Circulation Research*, *114*(8), 1231–1234.
Arksey, H., & O'Malley, L. (2005). Scoping studies: Towards a methodological framework. *International Journal of Social Research Methodology*, *8*(1), 19–32.
Armstrong, R., Hall, B. J., Doyle, J., & Waters, E. (2011). 'Scoping the scope' of a Cochrane review. *Journal of Public Health*, *33*(1), 147–150.
Arora, A., & Gambardella, A. (2005). The impact of NSF support for basic research in economics. *Annales d'Economie et de Statistique*, 91–117.
Arthurs, O. J. (2014). Think it through first: Questions to consider in writing a successful grant application. *Pediatric Radiology*, *44*(12), 1507–1511.
Banta, M., Brewer, R., Hansen, A., & Heng-Yu, K. (2004). An innovative program for cultivating grant writing skills in new faculty members. *Journal of Research Administration*, *35*(1), 17–24.
Beaudry, C., & Allaoui, S. (2012). Impact of public and private research funding on scientific production. The case of nanotechnology. *Research Policy*, *41*(9), 1589–1606.

Bedi, G., Van Dam, N. T., & Munafo, M. (2012). Gender inequality in awarded research grants. *The Lancet, 380*(9840), 474.
Berg, K. M., Gill, T. M., Brown, A. F., Zerzan, J., Elmore, J. G., & Wilson, I. B. (2007). Demystifying the NIH grant application process. *Journal of General Internal Medicine, 22*(11), 1587–1595.
Berger, A. M., & Moore, T. A. (2011). Effective grant writing. *Journal of Infusion Nursing, 34*(3), 167–171.
Birkhahn, R. H., Van Deusen, S. K., Okpara, O. I., Datillo, P. A., Briggs, W. M., & Gaeta, T. J. (2006). Funding and publishing trends of original research by emergency medicine investigators over the past decade. *Academic Emergency Medicine, 13*(1), 95–101.
Blanco, M. A., & Lee, M. Y. (2012). Twelve tips for writing educational research grant proposals. *Medical Teacher, 34*(6), 450–453.
Blanco, M. A., Gruppen, L. D., Artino Jr, A. R., Uijtdehaage, S., Szauter, K., & Durning, S. J. (2016). How to write an educational research grant: AMEE Guide No. 101. *Medical Teacher, 38*(2), 113–122.
Bloch, C., Graversen, E. K., & Pedersen, H. S. (2014). Competitive research grants and their impact on career performance. *Minerva, 52*(1), 77–96.
Boardman, P. C., & Ponomariov, B. L. (2007). Reward systems and NSF university research centers: The impact of tenure on university scientists' valuation of applied and commercially relevant research. *The Journal of Higher Education, 78*(1), 51–70.
Bogler, R. (1994). The impact of past experience on people's preference: The case of university researchers' dependency on funding sources. *Higher Education, 28*(2), 169–187.
Bornmann, L., Leydesdorff, L., & Van den Besselaar, P. (2010). A meta-evaluation of scientific research proposals: Different ways of comparing rejected to awarded applications. *Journal of Informetrics, 4*(3), 211–220.
Bornmann, L., Mutz, R., & Daniel, H. D. (2007). Gender differences in grant peer review: A meta-analysis. *Journal of Informetrics, 1*(3), 226–238.
Bornmann, L., Wallon, G., & Ledin, A. (2008). Does the committee peer review select the best applicants for funding? An investigation of the selection process for two European molecular biology organization programmes. *PLoS One, 3*(10), e3480.
Bozeman, B., & Gaughan, M. (2007). Impacts of grants and contracts on academic researchers' interactions with industry. *Research Policy, 36*(5), 694–707.
Braun, D. (1998). The role of funding agencies in the cognitive development of science. *Research Policy, 27*(8), 807–821.
Brock, M. V., & Bouvet, M. (2010). Writing a successful NIH mentored career development grant (K award): Hints for the junior faculty surgeon. *Annals of Surgery, 251*(6), 1013–1017.
Brooks, D. (2004). How to write grants: The best kept secret in the school business. *The Journal, 31*(10), 30–34.
Brownson, R. C., Colditz, G. A., Dobbins, M., Emmons, K. M., Kerner, J. F., Padek, M., ... & Stange, K. C. (2015). Concocting that magic elixir: Successful grant application writing in dissemination and implementation research. *Clinical and Translational Science, 8*(6), 710–716.

Burrow-Sánchez, J. J., Martin, J. L., & Imel, Z. E. (2016). Applying for grant funding as a counseling psychologist: From thought to action. *The Counseling Psychologist, 44*(4), 479–524.

Campbell, E. G., Louis, K. S., & Blumenthal, D. (1998). Looking a gift horse in the mouth: Corporate gifts supporting life sciences research. *JAMA, 279*(13), 995–999.

Canon, B. C., Gabel, M., & Patton, D. J. (2002). External grants and publication: Sources, outlets, and implications. *PS: Political Science and Politics, 35*(4), 743–750.

Chen, S. H., Huang, M. H., & Chen, D. Z. (2013). Driving factors of external funding and funding effects on academic innovation performance in university–industry–government linkages. *Scientometrics, 94*(3), 1077–1098.

Chudnovsky, D., López, A., Rossi, M. A., & Ubfal, D. (2008). Money for science? The impact of research grants on academic output. *Fiscal Studies, 29*(1), 75–87.

Chung, K. C., & Shauver, M. J. (2008). Fundamental principles of writing a successful grant proposal. *The Journal of Hand Surgery, 33*(4), 566–572.

Clark, R. C., & Carter, K. F. (2019). Successful grant applications: Follow the 4 F's. *Nursing, 49*(2), 55–58.

Clarke, P., Herbert, D., Graves, N., & Barnett, A. G. (2016). A randomized trial of fellowships for early career researchers finds a high reliability in funding decisions. *Journal of Clinical Epidemiology, 69*, 147–151.

Crockett, S. D., Dellon, E. S., Bright, S. D., & Shaheen, N. J. (2009). A 25-year analysis of the American college of gastroenterology research grant program: Factors associated with publication and advancement in academics. *The American Journal of Gastroenterology, 104*(5), 1097–1105.

Cuhel-Schuckers, A., Martin-Tetreault, C., & Withers, C. (2016). The grants office and the RA generalist: Parallel life-cycles and development at small PUIs. *Journal of Research Administration, 47*(2), 80–93.

Davis, J. M., Soltis, P. S., Adams, D. C., Larkin, S. L., & Gilbert, R. A. (2020). Seed funds leverage external awards for research in natural resources and agricultural systems. *Forests, 11*(1), 76.

De Jongh, T. E., Harnmeijer, J. H., Atun, R., Korenromp, E. L., Zhao, J., Puvimanasinghe, J., & Baltussen, R. (2014). Health impact of external funding for HIV, tuberculosis and malaria: Systematic review. *Health Policy and Planning, 29*(5), 650–662.

Deatherage, J. F. (2019). Strategic planning for research grant applications. *Molecular Biology of the Cell, 30*(23), 2867–2869.

Defazio, D., Lockett, A., & Wright, M. (2009). Funding incentives, collaborative dynamics and scientific productivity: Evidence from the EU framework program. *Research Policy, 38*(2), 293–305.

Ding, H. (2008). The use of cognitive and social apprenticeship to teach a disciplinary genre: Initiation of graduate students into NIH grant writing. *Written communication, 25*(1), 3–52.

Dinov, I. D. (2019). Flipping the grant application review process. *Studies in Higher Education*, 1–9.

Appendix: The Science of Research Grants

Duchesne, A., Tannenbaum, C., & Einstein, G. (2017). Funding agency mechanisms to increase sex and gender analysis. *The Lancet*, *389*(10070), 699.

Easterly, D., & Pemberton, C. L. (2008). Understanding barriers and supports to proposal writing as perceived by female associate professors: Achieving promotion to professor. *Research Management Review*, *16*(1), 1–17.

Ecobici, N. (2011). Accounting of the external grants and its influence on the Romanian public institutions' surplus or deficit. *Annals-Economy Series*, *4*, 66–69.

Eloy, J. A., Svider, P. F., Kovalerchik, O., Baredes, S., Kalyoussef, E., & Chandrasekhar, S. S. (2013). Gender differences in successful NIH grant funding in otolaryngology. *Otolaryngology-Head and Neck Surgery*, *149*(1), 77–83.

Falk-Krzesinski, H. J., & Tobin, S. C. (2015). How do I review thee? Let me count the ways: A comparison of research grant proposal review criteria across US federal funding agencies. *The Journal of Research Administration*, *46*(2), 79–94.

Fogelholm, M., Leppinen, S., Auvinen, A., Raitanen, J., Nuutinen, A., & Väänänen, K. (2012). Panel discussion does not improve reliability of peer review for medical research grant proposals. *Journal of Clinical Epidemiology*, *65*(1), 47–52.

Fortin, J. M., & Currie, D. J. (2013). Big science vs. little science: How scientific impact scales with funding. *PLoS One*, *8*(6), e65263.

Fortunato, S., Bergstrom, C. T., Börner, K., Evans, J. A., Helbing, D., Milojević, S., ... & Vespignani, A. (2018). Science of science. *Science*, *359*(6379), eaao0185.

Freel, S. A., Smith, P. C., Burns, E. N., Downer, J. B., Brown, A. J., & Dewhirst, M. W. (2017). Multidisciplinary mentoring programs to enhance junior faculty research grant success. *Academic Medicine: Journal of the Association of American Medical Colleges*, *92*(10), 1410–1415.

Gallo, S. A., Carpenter, A. S., & Glisson, S. R. (2013). Teleconference versus face-to-face scientific peer review of grant application: Effects on review outcomes. *PLoS One*, *8*(8), e71693.

Gallo, S. A., Carpenter, A. S., Irwin, D., McPartland, C. D., Travis, J., Reynders, S., ... & Glisson, S. R. (2014). The validation of peer review through research impact measures and the implications for funding strategies. *PLoS One*, *9*(9), e106474.

Garrison, H. H., & Deschamps, A. M. (2014). NIH research funding and early career physician scientists: Continuing challenges in the 21st century. *The FASEB Journal*, *28*(3), 1049–1058.

Gaughan, M., & Bozeman, B. (2002). Using curriculum vitae to compare some impacts of NSF research grants with research center funding. *Research Evaluation*, *11*(1), 17–26.

Gerhardus, A., Becher, H., Groenewegen, P., Mansmann, U., Meyer, T., Pfaff, H., ... & Hummers-Pradier, E. (2016). Applying for, reviewing and funding public health research in Germany and beyond. *Health Research Policy and Systems*, *14*(1), 1–9.

Gholipour, A., Lee, E. Y., & Warfield, S. K. (2014). The anatomy and art of writing a successful grant application: A practical step-by-step approach. *Pediatric Radiology, 44*(12), 1512–1517.

Gillies, D. (2014). Selecting applications for funding: why random choice is better than peer review. *RT.A Journal on Research Policy and Evaluation, 2*(1), 1–14.

Ginther, D. K., Schaffer, W. T., Schnell, J., Masimore, B., Liu, F., Haak, L. L., & Kington, R. (2011). Race, ethnicity, and NIH research awards. *Science, 333*(6045), 1015–1019.

Goldfarb, B. (2008). The effect of government contracting on academic research: Does the source of funding affect scientific output? *Research Policy, 37*(1), 41–58.

Gopkinar-Shelton, E., & Asomani-Adem, A. A. (2020). Developing grant writing skills in the humanities and social sciences: A case for increasing program-level supports. *Journal of the Student Personnel Association at Indiana University*, 139–142.

Gordon, M. B., Osganian, S. K., Emans, S. J., & Lovejoy, F. H. (2009). Gender differences in research grant applications for pediatric residents. *Pediatrics, 124*(2), e355–e361.

Gordon, S. L. (1989). Ingredients of a successful grant application to the National Institutes of Health. *Journal of Orthopaedic Research, 7*(1), 138–141.

Gottlieb, M., Lee, S., Burkhardt, J., Carlson, J. N., King, A. M., Wong, A. H., & Santen, S. A. (2019). Show me the money: successfully obtaining grant funding in medical education. *Western Journal of Emergency Medicine, 20*(1), 71–77.

Grants.gov Program Management Office. (n.d.). *A short summary of federal grants*. Retrieved from www.grants.gov/web/grants/learn-grants/grants-101.html

Graves, N., Barnett, A. G., Clarke, P. (2011). Funding grant proposals for scientific research: Retrospective analysis of scores by members of grant review panel. *BMJ, 343*, d4797.

Green, L. W., & Mercer, S. L. (2001). Can public health researchers and agencies reconcile the push from funding bodies and the pull from communities? *American Journal of Public Health, 91*(12), 1926–1929.

Greipp, M. (1987). Grant application strategies for computers in nursing education. *Computers in Nursing, 5*(1), 20–23.

Grimpe, C. (2012). Extramural research grants and scientists' funding strategies: Beggars cannot be choosers? *Research Policy, 41*(8), 1448–1460.

Groves, P. S., Rawl, S. M., Wurzbach, M. E., Fahrenwald, N., Cohen, M. Z., McCarthy Beckett, D. O., ... & Conn, V. (2012). Secrets of successful short grant applications. *Western Journal of Nursing Research, 34*(1), 6–23.

Guillen-Grima, F., Annan, J. W., Álvarez, J. M. N., Gómez, J. M. S., & Ontoso, E. A. (2009). How to apply for research grants in allergology. *Allergologia et Immunopathologia, 37*(3), 146–154.

Halliday, M., & Matthiessen, C. M. I. M. (2014). *An introduction to functional grammar*. Routledge.

Hanney, S. R., Grant, J., Wooding, S., & Buxton, M. J. (2004). Proposed methods for reviewing the outcomes of health research: The impact of funding by the UK's Arthritis Research Campaign'. *Health Research Policy and Systems, 2*(1), 1–11.

Harper, L., Castagnetti, M., Herbst, K., Bagli, D., Kaefer, M., Beckers, G., ... Kalfa, N. (2018). How to apply for a research grant: 10 tips and tricks. *Journal of Pediatric Urology*, *14*(5), 453–454.

Harris, K. (1984). Factors associated with external funding in higher education: A review of research. *Journal of the Society of Research Administrators*, *15*(3), 39–47.

Head, M. G., et al. (2017). Global funding trends for malaria research in sub-Saharan Africa: a systematic analysis. *The Lancet Global Health* 5(8), e772–e781.

Herbert, D. L., Graves, N., Clarke, P., & Barnett, A. G. (2015). Using simplified peer review processes to fund research: A prospective study. *BMJ Open*, *5*, e008380.

Heutel, G. (2014). Crowding out and crowding in of private donations and government grants. *Public Finance Review*, *42*(2), 143–175.

Himanen, L., Auranen, O., Puuska, H. M., & Nieminen, M. (2009). Influence of research funding and science policy on university research performance: A comparison of five countries. *Science and Public Policy*, *36*(6), 419–430.

Hirsch, J. E. (2005). An index to quantify an individual's scientific research output. *Proceedings of the National Academy of Sciences of the United States of America*, *102*, 16569–16572.

Hojjat, H., Johnson, A. P., Svider, P. F., Hong, R. S., Zuliani, G., Folbe, A. J., & Shkoukani, M. A. (2015). Scholarly investigation into otitis media: Who is receiving funding support from the National Institutes of Health? *The Laryngoscope*, *125*(7), 1708–1714.

Holmes, B., Scarrow, G., & Schellenberg, M. (2012). Translating evidence into practice: The role of health research funders. *Implementation Science*, *7*(1), 39.

Horner, R. D. (2007). Demystifying the NIH grant application process: The rest of the story. *Journal of General Internal Medicine*, *22*, 1628–1629.

Hottenrott, H., & Lawson, C. (2014). Research grants, sources of ideas and the effects on academic research. *Economics of Innovation and New Technology*, *23*(2), 109–133.

Howie, J. (1978). How to do it. Apply for a research grant. *British Medical Journal*, *2*(6151), 1553–1554.

Hu, A. G. (2020). Public funding and the ascent of Chinese science: Evidence from the National Natural Science Foundation of China. *Research Policy*, *49*(5), 103983.

Huffman, W. E., & Evenson, R. E. (2006). Do formula or competitive grant funds have greater impacts on state agricultural productivity? *American Journal of Agricultural Economics*, *88*(4), 783–798.

Hug, S. E., & Aeschbach, M. (2020). Criteria for assessing grant applications: A systematic review. *Palgrave Communications*, *6*(1), 1–15.

Inouye, S. K., & Fiellin, D. A. (2005). An evidence-based guide to writing grant proposals for clinical research. *Annals of Internal Medicine*, *142*(4), 274–282.

Islam, M., Fremeth, A., & Marcus, A. (2018). Signaling by early stage startups: US government research grants and venture capital funding. *Journal of Business Venturing*, *33*(1), 35–51.

Jacob, B. A., & Lefgren, L. (2011). The impact of research grant funding on scientific productivity. *Journal of Public Economics*, *95*(9–10), 1168–1177.

Jayasinghe, U. W., Marsh, H. W., & Bond, N. (2001). Peer review in the funding of research in higher education: The Australian experience. *Educational Evaluation and Policy Analysis*, *23*(4), 343–364.

Jonisch, A. I., Kligerman, S., Nagy, E., Bhargavan, M., Forman, H. P., & Sunshine, J. (2006). What characterizes academic radiology departments that secure large amounts of external funding for research? *Academic Radiology*. *13*(12), 1513–1516.

Joshi, A. M., Inouye, T. M., & Robinson, J. A. (2018). How does agency workforce diversity influence Federal R&D funding of minority and women technology entrepreneurs? An analysis of the SBIR and STTR programs, 2001–2011. *Small Business Economics*, *50*(3), 499–519.

Kaplan, K. (2012). Funding: Got to get a grant. *Nature*, *482*(7385), 429–431.

Kaplan, R. M., Johnson, S. B., & Kobor, P. C. (2017). NIH behavioral and social sciences research support: 1980–2016. *American Psychologist*, *72*(8), 808–821.

Keskinen, S., & Silius, H. (2006). New trends in research funding – Threat or opportunity for interdisciplinary gender research? *Nordic Journal of Women's Studies*, *14*(2), 73–86.

Kintisch, E. (2005). Researcher faces prison for fraud in NIH grant applications and papers. *Science*, *307*(5717), 1851–1852.

Klein, J. T. (2008). Evaluation of interdisciplinary and transdisciplinary research: A literature review. *American Journal of Preventive Medicine*, *35*(2), S116–S123.

Kleinfelder, J., Price, J. H., & Dake, J. A. (2003). Grant writing: Practice and preparation of university health educators. *American Journal of Health Education*, *34*(1), 47–53.

König, B., Diehl, K., Tscherning, K., & Helming, K. (2013). A framework for structuring interdisciplinary research management. *Research Policy*, *42*(1), 261–272.

Kotchen, T. A., Lindquist, T., Malik, K., & Ehrenfeld, E. (2004). NIH peer review of grant applications for clinical research. *JAMA*, *291*(7), 836–843.

Kuhn, T. S. (2012). *The structure of scientific revolutions*. University of Chicago Press.

Kulage, K. M., Schnall, R., Hickey, K. T., Travers, J., Zezulinski, K., Torres, F., … & Larson, E. L. (2015). Time and costs of preparing and submitting an NIH grant application at a school of nursing. *Nursing Outlook*, *63*(6), 639–649.

Kundel, H. L., & Walsh, C. (1993). Preparing a research grant application budget. *Investigative Radiology*, *28*, S13–S16.

Kwekkeboom, K. L. (2014). Overview and tips for successful grant writing for infusion nurses. *Journal of Infusion Nursing*, *37*(5), 371–378.

Larivière, V., et al. (2010). Which Scientific Elites? On the Concentration of Research Funds, Publications and Citations. *Research Evaluation 19*(1), 45–53.

Laudel, G. (2005). Is external research funding a valid indicator for research performance? *Research Evaluation*, *14*(1), 27–34.

Laudel, G. (2006). The 'quality myth': Promoting and hindering conditions for acquiring research funds. *Higher Education*, *52*(3), 375–403.

Leak, R. K., O'Donnell, L. A., & Surratt, C. K. (2015). Teaching pharmacology graduate students how to write an NIH grant application. *American Journal of Pharmaceutical Education*, *79*(9), 138.

Leberman, S. I., Eames, B., & Barnett, S. (2016). Unless you are collaborating with a big name successful professor, you are unlikely to receive funding. *Gender and Education*, *28*(5), 644–661.

Lee, T. H., Ognibene, F. P., & Schwartz, J. S. (1991). Correlates of external research support among respondents to the 1990 American Federation for Clinical Research survey. *Clinical Research*, *39*(2), 135–144.

Lepori, B., Van den Besselaar, P., Dinges, M., Van der Meulen, B., Potì, B., Reale, E., ... & Theves, J. (2007). Indicators for comparative analysis of public project funding: concepts, implementation and evaluation. *Research Evaluation*, *16*(4), 243–255.

Ley, T. J., & Hamilton, B. H. (2008). The gender gap in NIH grant applications. *Science*, *322*(5907), 1472–1474.

Li, D., & Agha, L. (2015). Big names or big ideas: Do peer-review panels select the best science proposals? *Science*, *348*(6233), 434–438.

Liefner, I. (2003). Funding, resource allocation, and performance in higher education systems. *Higher education*, *46*(4), 469–489.

Lindgreen, A., Di Benedetto, C. A., Verdich, C., Vanhamme, J., Venkatraman, V., Pattinson, S., ... & Khan, Z. (2019). How to write really good research funding applications. *Industrial Marketing Management*, *77*, 232–239.

Lisanti, P., & Talotta, D. (2000). Tips for writing a NAON research grant proposal. *Orthopaedic Nursing*, *19*(2), 61–65.

Lisk, D. J. (1971). Why research grant applications are turned down. *BioScience*, *21*(20), 1025–1026.

Lowry, K., & Thomas-Anderson, T. (2017). How community colleges are closing the skills gap through CTE and STEM funding innovations. *New Directions for Community Colleges*, *2017*(178), 45–54.

Lusk, S. L. (2004). Developing an outstanding grant application. *Western Journal of Nursing Research*, *26*(3), 367–373.

Luukkonen, T. (2014). The European research council and the European research funding landscape. *Science and Public Policy*, *41*(1), 29–43.

Mackert, M., Donovan, E. E., & Bernhardt, J. M. (2017). Applied grant writing training for future health communication researchers: The health communication scholars program. *Health Communication*, *32*(2), 247–252.

McGroarty, E., Jimenez, T. R., Linley, J., Li, Y., Granberry-Russell, P., & Williams, K. P. (2014). External funding: Impact on promotion and retention of STEM assistant professors. *Journal of Academic and Business Ethics*, *8*, 1.

Merton, R. K. (1968). The Matthew effect in science: The reward and communication systems of science are considered. *Science*, *159*(3810), 56–63.

Moed, H. F. (2006). *Citation analysis in research evaluation* (Vol. 9). Springer Science & Business Media.

Moeller, R. M., & Christensen, D. M. (2009). System mapping: A genre field analysis of the National Science Foundation's grant proposal and funding process. *Technical Communication Quarterly*, *19*(1), 69–89.

Movsesian, M. A. (1990). Effect on physician-scientists of the low funding rate of NIH grant applications. *The New England Journal of Medicine, 322*, 1602–1604.

Munn, Z., Peters, M. D., Stern, C., Tufanaru, C., McArthur, A., & Aromataris, E. (2018). Systematic review or scoping review? Guidance for authors when choosing between a systematic or scoping review approach. *BMC Medical Research Methodology, 18*(1), 1–7.

Munro, S., Hendrix, C. C., Cowan, L. J., Battaglia, C., Wilder, V. D., Bormann, J. E., ... & Sullivan, S. C. (2019). Research productivity following nursing research initiative grants. *Nursing Outlook, 67*(1), 6–12.

Murray, D. L., Morris, D., Lavoie, C., Leavitt, P. R., MacIsaac, H., Masson, M. E., & Villard, M. A. (2016). Bias in research grant evaluation has dire consequences for small universities. *PLoS One, 11*(6), e0155876.

Murtinho, F., Eakin, H., López-Carr, D., & Hayes, T. M. (2013). Does external funding help adaptation? Evidence from community-based water management in the Colombian Andes. *Environmental Management, 52*(5), 1103–1114.

Muscio, A., Quaglione, D., & Vallanti, G. (2013). Does government funding complement or substitute private research funding to universities? *Research Policy, 42*(1), 63–75.

Mutz, R., Bornmann, L., & Daniel, H. D. (2012). Heterogeneity of inter-rater reliabilities of grant peer reviews and its determinants: A general estimating equations approach. *PLoS One, 7*(10), e48509.

Narahari, A. K., Mehaffey, J. H., Hawkins, R. B., Charles, E. J., Baderdinni, P. K., Chandrabhatla, A. S., ... & Ailawadi, G. (2018). Surgeon scientists are disproportionately affected by declining NIH funding rates. *Journal of the American College of Surgeons, 226*(4), 474–481.

Nelson, A. W., Lamb, A. D., & Gnanapragasam, V. J. (2016). Applying for research funding. Part 2 – Writing a grant application. *Journal of Clinical Urology, 9*(4), 230–233.

Nicholson, J. M., & Ioannidis, J. P. (2012). Conform and be funded. *Nature, 492*(7427), 34–36.

Norris, J. (2011). The crisis in extramural funding. *Academe, 97*(6), 28–31.

Novello, A. (1985). Evaluation of recent research grant applications to the National Institutes of Health in the area of pediatric nephrology. *Pediatric Research, 19*(11), 1139–1142.

Pagel, P. S., & Hudetz, J. A. (2011). An analysis of scholarly productivity in United States academic anaesthesiologists by citation bibliometrics. *Anaesthesia, 66*(10), 873–878.

Patil, S. G. (2019). How to plan and write a budget for research grant proposal? *Journal of Ayurveda and Integrative Medicine, 10*(2), 139–142.

Payne, A. A. (2003). The effects of congressional appropriation committee membership on the distribution of federal research funding to universities. *Economic Inquiry, 41*(2), 325–345.

Payne, A. A., & Siow, A. (2003). Does federal research funding increase university research output? *Advanced in Economic Analysis & Policy, 3*(1), 1.

Pellicano, E., Dinsmore, A., & Charman, T. (2014). What should autism research focus upon? Community views and priorities from the United Kingdom. *Autism, 18*(7), 756–770.

Penrod, J. (2003). Getting funded: Writing a successful qualitative small-project proposal. *Qualitative Health Research, 13*(6), 821–832.

Peters, M. D., Godfrey, C. M., Khalil, H., McInerney, P., Parker, D., & Soares, C. B. (2015). Guidance for conducting systematic scoping reviews. *JBI Evidence Implementation, 13*(3), 141–146.

Pier, E. L., Brauer, M., Filut, A., Kaatz, A., Raclaw, J., Nathan, M. J., … & Carnes, M. (2018). Low agreement among reviewers evaluating the same NIH grant applications. *Proceedings of the National Academy of Sciences, 115*(12), 2952–2957.

Pohlhaus, J. R., Jiang, H., Wagner, R. M., Schaffer, W. T., & Pinn, V. W. (2011). Sex differences in application, success, and funding rates for NIH extramural programs. *Academic Medicine, 86*(6), 759–767.

Porter, R. (2004). Off the launching pad: Stimulating proposal development by junior faculty. *Journal of Research Administration, 35*(1), 6–12.

Preuss, M. (2015). Assessing grant capacity and readiness: A systematic review of the periodical literature of research administration. *Research Management Review, 20*(2), 1–18.

Price, D. J. D. S. (1963). *Little science, big science*. Columbia University Press.

Rad, A. E., Brinjikji, W., Cloft, H. J., & Kallmes, D. F. (2010). The H-index in academic radiology. *Academic Radiology, 17*(7), 817–821.

Reiser, R. A., Moore, A. L., Bradley, T. W., Walker, R., & Zhao, W. (2015). Supporting faculty efforts to obtain research funding: Successful practices and lessons learned. *The Journal of Faculty Development, 29*(3), 43–50.

Rezaeian, M. (2015). How to construct a successful grant proposal. *World Family Medicine Journal: Incorporating the Middle East Journal of Family Medicine, 99*(1645), 1–2.

Rezek, I., McDonald, R. J., & Kallmes, D. F. (2011). Is the h-index predictive of greater NIH funding success among academic radiologists? *Academic Radiology, 18*(11), 1337–1340.

Roebber, P. J., & Schultz, D. M. (2011). Peer review, program officers and science funding. *PLoS One, 6*(4), e18680.

Rosenkrantz, A. B., & Jiang, A. (2016). Associations between NIH funding and advanced bibliometric indices among radiological investigators. *Academic radiology, 23*(6), 669–674.

Saraykar, S., Saleh, A., & Selek, S. (2017). The association between NIMH funding and h-index in psychiatry. *Academic Psychiatry, 41*(4), 455–459.

Saygitov, R. T. (2014). The impact of funding through the RF president's grants for young scientists (the field–medicine) on research productivity: A quasi-experimental study and a brief systematic review. *PLoS One, 9*(1), e86969.

Schembri-Wismayer, P., Cuschieri, S., & Grech, V. (2018). WASP (Write a Scientific Paper): Writing a research grant–1, applying for funding. *Early Human Development, 127*, 106–108.

Schumacher, D. (1994). Strategies for helping your faculty get more grants from companies. *Research Management Review*, *7*(1), 37–52.

Sehgal, A. R. (2018). Number of grant applications needed to fund research faculty: A probabilistic analysis. *Journal of General Internal Medicine*, *33*(8), 1232–1234.

Silvestre, J., Abbatematteo, J. M., Chang, B., Serletti, J. M., & Taylor, J. A. (2016). The impact of National Institutes of Health funding on scholarly productivity in academic plastic surgery. *Plastic and Reconstructive Surgery*, *137*(2), 690–695.

Simonton, D. K. (1994). *Greatness: Who makes history and why*. New York: Guilford Press.

Singh, J., Illes, J., Lazzeroni, L., & Hallmayer, J. (2009). Trends in US autism research funding. *Journal of Autism and Developmental Disorders*, *39*(5), 788–795.

Smith, J. L., Stoop, C., Young, M., Belou, R., & Held, S. (2017). Grant-writing bootcamp: An intervention to enhance the research capacity of academic women in STEM. *BioScience*, *67*(7), 638–645.

Smith, M. A., Kaufman, N. J., & Dearlove, A. J. (2013). External community review committee: A new strategy for engaging community stakeholders in research funding decisions. *Progress in Community Health Partnerships*, *7*(3), 301–312.

Sobkowicz, P. (2015). Innovation suppression and clique evolution in peer-review-based, competitive research funding systems: An agent-based model. *Journal of Artificial Societies and Social Simulation*, *18*(2), 13.

Solans-Domènech, M., Guillamón, I., Ribera, A., Ferreira-González, I., Carrion, C., Permanyer-Miralda, G., & Pons, J. (2017). Blinding applicants in a first-stage peer-review process of biomedical research grants: An observational study. *Research Evaluation*, *26*(3), 181–189.

Sonis, J. H., Triffleman, E., King, L., & King, D. (2009). How to write an NIH R13 conference grant application. *Academic Psychiatry*, *33*(3), 256–260.

Stavropoulou, C., et al. (2019). Most UK scientists who publish extremely highly-cited papers do not secure funding from major public and charity funders: A descriptive analysis. *PLoS One*, *14*(2). e0211460.

Sternberg, R., & Gordeeva, T. (1996). The Anatomy of Impact: What Makes an Article Influential? *Psychological Science*, *7*(2), 69–75.

Stone, D. (2009). How your grant proposal compares. *The Chronicle of Higher Education*, 1–4.

Svider, P. F., D'Aguillo, C. M., White, P. E., Pashkova, A. A., Bhagat, N., Langer, P. D., & Eloy, J. A. (2014). Gender differences in successful National Institutes of Health funding in ophthalmology. *Journal of Surgical Education*, *71*(5), 680–688.

Svider, P. F., Husain, Q., Folbe, A. J., Couldwell, W. T., Liu, J. K., & Eloy, J. A. (2014). Assessing National Institutes of Health funding and scholarly impact in neurological surgery. *Journal of Neurosurgery*, *120*(1), 191–196.

Svider, P. F., Lopez, S. A., Husain, Q., Bhagat, N., Eloy, J. A., & Langer, P. D. (2014). The association between scholarly impact and National Institutes of Health funding in ophthalmology. *Ophthalmology*, *121*(1), 423–428.

Svider, P. F., Mauro, K. M., Sanghvi, S., Setzen, M., Baredes, S., & Eloy, J. A. (2013). Is NIH funding predictive of greater research productivity and impact among academic otolaryngologists? *The Laryngoscope, 123*(1), 118–122.

Tamblyn, R., Girard, N., Qian, C. J., & Hanley, J. (2018). Assessment of potential bias in research grant peer review in Canada. *CMAJ, 190*(16), e489–e499.

Thyer, B. A. (2011). Harmful effects of federal research grants. *Social Work Research, 35*(1), 3–7.

Tress, B., Tress, G., & Fry, G. (2005). Integrative studies on rural landscapes: Policy expectations and research practice. *Landscape and Urban Planning, 70*(1–2), 177–191.

Tricco, A. C., Lillie, E., Zarin, W., O'Brien, K., Colquhoun, H., Kastner, M., ... & Kenny, M. (2016). A scoping review on the conduct and reporting of scoping reviews. *BMC Medical Research Methodology, 16*(1), 1–10.

Tung, V. W. S., & Law, R. (2017). Evaluating external research grant proposals in tourism and hospitality: Insights from senior researchers. *Tourism Recreation Research, 42*(4), 457–466.

Turaga, K. K., Green, D. E., Jayakrishnan, T. T., Hwang, M., & Gamblin, T. C. (2013). Attributes of a surgical chairperson associated with extramural funding of a department of surgery. *Journal of Surgical Research, 185*(2), 549–554.

Van Arensbergen, P., & Van Den Besselaar, P. (2012). The selection of scientific talent in the allocation of research grants. *Higher Education Policy, 25*(3), 381–405.

Van Bekkum, J. E., Fergie, G. M., & Hilton, S. (2016). Health and medical research funding agencies' promotion of public engagement within research: A qualitative interview study exploring the United Kingdom context. *Health Research Policy and Systems, 14*(1), 1–12.

van den Besselaar, P., & Sandström, U. (2015). Early career grants, performance, and careers: A study on predictive validity of grant decisions. *Journal of Informetrics, 9*(4), 826–838.

Van der Lee, R., & Ellemers, N. (2015). Gender contributes to personal research funding success in The Netherlands. *Proceedings of the National Academy of Sciences, 112*(40), 12349–12353.

van Leeuwen, T. N., & Moed, H. F. (2012). Funding decisions, peer review, and scientific excellence in physical sciences, chemistry, and geosciences. *Research Evaluation, 21*(3), 189–198.

Velarde, K. S. (2018). The way we ask for money... The emergence and institutionalization of grant writing practices in academia. *Minerva, 56*(1), 85–107.

Vernon, D., & Rainey, J. S. (2009). The school counselor as grant writer. *Journal of School Counseling, 7*(19), n19.

Villalba, J. A., & Young, J. S. (2012). Externally funded research in counselor education: An overview of the process. *Counselor Education and Supervision, 51*(2), 141–155.

Viner, N., Powell, P., & Green, R. (2004). Institutionalized biases in the award of research grants: A preliminary analysis revisiting the principle of accumulative advantage. *Research Policy, 33*(3), 443–454.

Vintzileos, W. S., Ananth, C. V., & Vintzileos, A. M. (2013). External funding of obstetrical publications: Citation significance and trends over 2 decades. *American Journal of Obstetrics and Gynecology, 209*(2), 150.e1–150.e6.

Wadman, M. (2011). NIH firm on grant application rules. *Nature, 471,* 558.

Walden, P. R., & Bryan, V. C. (2010). Tenured and non-tenured college of education faculty motivators and barriers in grant writing: A public university in the South. *Journal of Research Administration, 41*(3), 85–98.

Wang, J., & Shapira, P. (2011). Funding acknowledgement analysis: An enhanced tool to investigate research sponsorship impacts: The case of nanotechnology. *Scientometrics, 87*(3), 563–586.

Watson, J. (2006). External funding and firm growth: Comparing female-and male-controlled SMEs. *Venture Capital, 8*(1), 33–49.

Whitley, R., Gläser, J., & Laudel, G. (2018). The impact of changing funding and authority relationships on scientific innovations. *Minerva, 56*(1), 109–134.

Wichmann-Hansen, G., & Herrmann, K. J. (2017). Does external funding push doctoral supervisors to be more directive? A large-scale Danish study. *Higher Education, 74*(2), 357–376.

Wiebe, N. G., & Maticka-Tyndale, E. (2017). More and better grant proposals? The evaluation of a grant-writing group at a mid-sized Canadian university. *Journal of Research Administration, 48*(2), 67–92.

Winn, A. S., Nigrovic, L. E., Lovejoy, F. H., & Sandora, T. J. (2019). Impact of a resident research grant on scholarly output during pediatric residency. *Academic Pediatrics, 19*(4), 477–479.

Wisdom, J. P., Riley, H., & Myers, N. (2015). Recommendations for writing successful grant proposals: An information synthesis. *Academic Medicine, 90*(12), 1720–1725.

Witteman, H. O., Hendricks, M., Straus, S., & Tannenbaum, C. (2019). Are gender gaps due to evaluations of the applicant or the science? A natural experiment at a national funding agency. *The Lancet, 393*(10171), 531–540.

Woodward, D. K., & Clifton, G. D. (1994). Development of a successful research grant application. *American Journal of Health-System Pharmacy, 51*(6), 813–822.

Yan, Z. (2021). *Publishing Journal Articles.* New York: Cambridge University Press.

Young, K. D., & 2005–2006 and 2006–2007 Society for Academic Emergency Medicine Grants Committees. (2008). Productivity and career paths of previous recipients of Society for Academic Emergency Medicine research grant awards. *Academic Emergency Medicine, 15*(6), 560–566.

Zeng, A., Shen, Z., Zhou, J., Wu, J., Fan, Y., Wang, Y., & Stanley, H. E. (2017). The science of science: From the perspective of complex systems. *Physics Reports, 714,* 1–73.

Zhao, D. (2010). Characteristics and impact of grant-funded research: A case study of the library and information science field. *Scientometrics, 84*(2), 293–306.

Zhu, E. Y., Shemesh, S., & Moucha, C. S. (2017). The association between scholarly impact and national institutes of health funding in orthopaedic surgery. *Bulletin of the NYU Hospital for Joint Diseases, 75*(4), 257–263.

Index

accountability, 278
AI technology, 337
altmetrics, 321
the American Association for the Advancement of Science (AAAS), 48
the American Grant Writers' Association (AGWA), 42
award rates, 231, 245

basic dynamic model, 69
the Bayh-Dole Act of 1980, 311
bibliometrics, 321

career of grant professionals, 333
the Code of Federal Regulations (CFR), 284
competitive grants, 18
complex system, 29
Continuation Grants, 18

the displacement effect, 306
displacement hypothesis, 303
distribution of funding, 347
diversity, 5

early-established investigators (EEIs), 339
early-stage investigators (ESI), 339
economic impacts, 295
the economics of science, 22
elements, 5
the Engineering and Physical Sciences Research Council (EPSRC), 238
ERC, 17
excellent research centers on grantology, 335

feedback loops, 69
finance management, 269
Formula Grants, 18
funding rates, 231

grant administration, 269
grant agency, 69
grant amount, 19

grant cycles, 44, 64
grant decisions, 69, 231
grant developing, 69
grant ecosystem, 30
grant funding, 24
grant goals, 294
grant impacts, 69, 294
grant management, 268–9
plans, 292
grant managing, 69
the grant policy cycle, 71
grant professionals, 329
the Grant Professionals Association (GPA), 43
grant program, 9
grant project, 9
grant purpose, 19
grant rejection, 242, 262
grant resubmission, 242
cycle, 71
grant reviewing, 69
grant sizes, 349
grant system, 29
grant writing, 69
workshops, 341
grantee, 6
grant-level administrators, 279
grantology, 32
grantor, 6
grants, 5
gross expenditure on R&D (GERD, 32
growth of grant writers, 331

harmful effects, 319
h-index, 22
Horizon 2020, 242
Horizon Europe (2021–27), 243
human capital, 29

IES, 14
individual impacts, 295
informetrics, 321

405

innovation, 22
  ecosystem, 30
institutional impacts, 295
interdisciplinary research, 248
International Congress on Peer Review and Scientific Publication, 352
intuitive knowledge, 4, 328
investment, 25

Journal of the Grant Professionals Association, 43
journalists, 351
journalology, 32

Kahneman, Daniel, 6
Katalin Karikó, 298

lag effects, 313
later-career independent investigators, 339

management cycle, 231
the Matthew effect, 50
mismanagement, 278
the most desirable success rate, 247
MRC, 15

the National Bureau of Economic Research (NBER), 22
the National Grants Management Association (NGMA), 43
national impacts, 295
the new grant submission cycle, 71
new grant writers, 18, 39
new submission, 255
  cycle, 231
NIH, 12
NIH Grants Policy Statement (NIHGPS), 283
NIH Guide for Grants and Contracts, 283
Nobel Prizes, 298
No-Cost Extension (NCE), 272
non-scientific grants, 20
NSF, 11
NSFC, 16

Office of Sponsored Programs, 281

Pass-Through Grants, 18
personnel management, 269
policy-level administrators, 279
Portfolio Management Office, 281
portfolios, 31
post-award grant management, 269
pre-award management, 271
the private rate of return, 315
Proceedings of the National Academy of Sciences of the United States of America (PNAS), 53

program-level administrators, 279
Programme Management Office, 281
Project Management Office, 281
Proposal & Award Policies & Procedures Guide (PAPPG), 283
public and private funders, 20
the Public Health Service Act, 47

real success rate, 244
real-life cases, 6
registered reports, 61
replication, 61
reported success rate, 244
Research Administration Office, 281
research and development (R&D), 22
research management, 269
research misconduct, 273
resubmission, 255
  cycle, 231
  plan, 266
  rates, 231
  success rates, 231
resubmit a rejected proposal, 266
return, 31
the ripple effects, 304
risks, 31

science management, 269
the science of science, 44
science of science funding, 73
scientific grants, 20
scientific impacts, 295
scientific investments, 30
scientific knowledge, 5
scientometrics, 321
the social rate of return, 315
societal impacts, 295
the sociology of science, 50
the spillover effect, 306
submission rate, 231
success rates, 231
System 1, 6
System 2, 6
System 3, 6

tenure denial, 300
tenure failure, 299
tenure promotion, 300
three types of grant management, 282
threshold, 349
training impacts, 304
typology, 19

webometrics, 321
Weissman, Drew, 298

For EU product safety concerns, contact us at Calle de José Abascal, 56–1º,
28003 Madrid, Spain or eugpsr@cambridge.org.

www.ingramcontent.com/pod-product-compliance
Ingram Content Group UK Ltd.
Pitfield, Milton Keynes, MK11 3LW, UK
UKHW022240181025
464020UK00022B/1857